Higher Education in the Arab World

Adnan Badran · Elias Baydoun · Sandra Hillman ·
Joelle Mesmar
Editors

Higher Education in the Arab World

Digital Transformation

Editors
Adnan Badran
Department of Nutrition
University of Petra
Amman, Jordan

Sandra Hillman
Dundee, UK

Elias Baydoun
Department of Biology
American University of Beirut
Beirut, Lebanon

Joelle Mesmar
Department of Biology
American University of Beirut
Beirut, Lebanon

ISBN 978-3-031-70778-0   ISBN 978-3-031-70779-7 (eBook)
https://doi.org/10.1007/978-3-031-70779-7

© The Editor(s) (if applicable) and The Author(s), under exclusive license to Springer Nature Switzerland AG 2024

This work is subject to copyright. All rights are solely and exclusively licensed by the Publisher, whether the whole or part of the material is concerned, specifically the rights of translation, reprinting, reuse of illustrations, recitation, broadcasting, reproduction on microfilms or in any other physical way, and transmission or information storage and retrieval, electronic adaptation, computer software, or by similar or dissimilar methodology now known or hereafter developed.

The use of general descriptive names, registered names, trademarks, service marks, etc. in this publication does not imply, even in the absence of a specific statement, that such names are exempt from the relevant protective laws and regulations and therefore free for general use.

The publisher, the authors and the editors are safe to assume that the advice and information in this book are believed to be true and accurate at the date of publication. Neither the publisher nor the authors or the editors give a warranty, expressed or implied, with respect to the material contained herein or for any errors or omissions that may have been made. The publisher remains neutral with regard to jurisdictional claims in published maps and institutional affiliations.

This Springer imprint is published by the registered company Springer Nature Switzerland AG
The registered company address is: Gewerbestrasse 11, 6330 Cham, Switzerland

If disposing of this product, please recycle the paper.

Introduction and Scope

Although we may not recognize it, or even think about it, let alone be able to define it, digital transformation (DX) has been a part of modern lifestyles for many years. Everyday living is facilitated by its incorporation into, and use by, companies that we depend on. However, despite the impetus that was given by the COVID-19 pandemic, some institutions in the education sector have been slower than others to realise the benefits that can be gained by digitalization. It is therefore timely to consider the implications of DX for higher education.

In this book, the seventh in the series on higher education in the Arab world, produced by the Arab Academy of Sciences and published by Springer Nature AG, the authors examine various aspects of DX, from definition to implementation and beyond. Many of the recommendations are applicable to higher education institutions anywhere in the world, whereas other accounts are less general and describe the experiences of specific institutions and countries in implementing DX.

The first chapter, "Digital Transformation: Inducing an Innovative Environment for Sustainable Development" (*Badran*), emphasizes the importance of DX for innovation and wealth creation and considers future developments by introducing concepts such as the metaverse.

The historical perspectives of the relationship between education and technology are succinctly covered in the chapter "Intelligence Amplified: Exploring the Future of Higher Education in the AI Age" (*Al-Chaer*). Despite its challenges, the involvement of artificial intelligence in education is considered to be inevitable and desirable, especially if DX is implemented with a view to promoting critical thinking among students rather than the accumulation of facts.

The idea of DX facilitating personalized learning environments, designed to meet the student's needs, is introduced in "The Personal Learning Environment (PLE): A Student-Centered Approach that Supports a Techno-Social Digital Transformation in Higher Education" (*Dabbagh*). Here, learning programs are decentralized, put the student first, and support the concept of lifelong learning.

The importance of considering the circumstances of individuals when devising educational models is also reiterated in "Education in the Digital Transformation Era.

The Common Mistake: One Size Fits All" (*Darwish and El-Sobky*). The authors argue that a "smart campus" can help resolve this problem.

Chatbots are an aspect of DX that can be controversial among educators. Their advantages and disadvantages are discussed in "Revolutionizing Education: Supporting Digital Transformation with ChatGPT" (*Baytiyeh*), and a comprehensive survey of the attitudes of professors in Lebanon is reported.

What are the leadership qualities that are required to bring about a successful DX in an institution? We are given some suggestions based on personal experience in "Leading Digital Transformation in Higher Education" (*Asfour*). Moreover, the chapter itself is an example of what can be written with the help of ChatGPT.

Other contributors consider the practical aspects of implementing DX in higher education and the importance of consultation with the end-users, the students. The results of a survey of student attitudes to transforming services and teaching at the University of Petra are presented in "Implementing Digital Transformation at the University of Petra: Current Status and Future Plans" (*Abdel-Rahem* et al.).

Once implemented, the effectiveness of DX needs to be monitored. In "Digital Transformation in Universities: Strategic Framework, Implementation Tools, and Leadership" (*Zabalawi* et al.), the authors describe the DX strategy at the Australian University of Kuwait and present a useful set of performance indicators for assessing the success and progress of that strategy.

Mualla and *Mualla* ("Digital Transformation in Higher Education: Challenges and Opportunities for Developing Countries") review DX in developing countries with special reference to Syria and suggest courses of action necessary for implementation, especially in the context of the National Development Plan.

The specific situations of Arab and North African countries are also considered in "Artificial Intelligence in Arab Universities and Economies" (*Benjelloun*) with an overview of the steps being taken to incorporate DX, particularly artificial intelligence, into national strategies for economic development.

In Jordan, the Al Hussein Technical University has developed its own online learning platform for engineering and information technology students ("HTU[x]: An Online Learning-Platform Model Targeting the Arab Youth", *Tutunji* et al.). The model is based on a stackable-course system and is designed to be student-centred. The authors emphasize the importance of developing a brand model that will appeal to learners in the Arab world.

In the chapter "Digitalization, Communication, and Identity Formation: Directions for Research in Higher Education" (*Almutawaa*), the author also stresses the idea of brand image and social media marketing to develop courses that will attract and retain students.

Developing courses that align with the needs of industry should also be an aim of higher education. In "Digital Transformation of Higher Education in Jordan: Does Production of Academic Material in Electronic Form Optimize Learning Outcomes?" (*Obeidat* et al.), it is argued that DX will enable greater co-operation with potential employers, produce more-employable graduates, and lead to better economic development.

In "The Growth of Knowledge and Its Link to Digital Transformation in Arab Institutes of Higher Education" (*Al Fazari*), it is argued that present-day students expect the education system to evolve along with the technology-driven growth of knowledge, enabling them to graduate with twenty-first century skills. This would not be possible without embracing DX.

Finally, *Mansour* et al. ("The Perspectives of Deans of Medical Schools on Introducing Artificial Intelligence and Computer Literacy to Medical Curricula in Arab Countries") present the results of a questionnaire sent to the deans of 104 medical schools to ascertain their perception of the benefits and complex challenges of implementing DX in medical schools. The necessity for institutions to take strategic decisions to address the challenges is noted.

The 15 chapters in this book have provided a comprehensive coverage of DX as it applies to higher education. There is a consensus that DX is a necessity if higher education is to meet the needs of the twenty-first century. Rapid technological progress, an increasing data base of knowledge, and the demands of employers for an appropriately educated workforce mean that DX is inevitable for economic prosperity in an increasingly competitive world. However, implementation is not without its problems: there should be extensive consultation with both teachers and students prior to, and during, DX in order to obtain optimal co-operation, and consideration should be given to individual needs in order to develop courses that are suitable for a wide range of learners. However, it should be remembered that although we use technology to further learning, we are not machines; we are human beings and need personal connections for ultimate satisfaction and to reach our maximum potential.

Lastly, we acknowledge with much gratitude financial assistance from the University of Petra, Jordan that made this publication possible. We specifically thank Margaret Deignan of Springer Nature for her guidance, help, and continuing support in our series of books on higher education in the Arab world.

Contents

Digital Transformation: Inducing an Innovative Environment
for Sustainable Development   1
Adnan Badran

Intelligence Amplified: Exploring the Future of Higher Education
in the AI Age 13
Elie D. Al-Chaer

The Personal Learning Environment (PLE): A Student-Centered
Approach that Supports a Techno-Social Digital Transformation
in Higher Education 37
Nada Dabbagh

Education in the Digital Transformation Era. The Common Mistake:
One Size Fits All 59
Ahmed M. Darwish and Ahmed M. El-Sobky

Revolutionizing Education: Supporting Digital Transformation
with ChatGPT. 71
Hoda Baytiyeh

Leading Digital Transformation in Higher Education 97
Yousif Asfour

Implementing Digital Transformation at the University of Petra:
Current Status and Future Plans 109
Rami A. Abdel-Rahem, Wael Hadi, and Muhannad Q. Malhis

Digital Transformation in Universities: Strategic Framework,
Implementation Tools, and Leadership. 145
Isam Zabalawi, Helene Kordahji, and Sapheya Aftimos

Digital Transformation in Higher Education: Challenges and Opportunities for Developing Countries 211
Wael Mualla and Karim J. Mualla

Artificial Intelligence in Arab Universities and Economies 233
Wail Benjelloun

HTU^x: An Online Learning-Platform Model Targeting the Arab Youth. 245
Rami AlKarmi, Tarek A. Tutunji, and Mai Hijazi

Digitalization, Communication, and Identity Formation: Directions for Research in Higher Education. 269
Doha Saleh Almutawaa

Digital Transformation of Higher Education in Jordan: Does Production of Academic Material in Electronic Form Optimize Learning Outcomes?. 283
Nathir M. Obeidat, Mohammed A. Khasawneh, Nael H. Thaher, and Rida A. Shibli

The Growth of Knowledge and Its Link to Digital Transformation in Arab Institutes of Higher Education. 303
Hamdan Al Fazari

The Perspectives of Deans of Medical Schools on Introducing Artificial Intelligence and Computer Literacy to Medical Curricula in Arab Countries 309
Nabil Mansour, Fatima Msheik El-Khoury, Ghazi Zaatari, and Mahmoud Harb

Digital Transformation: Inducing an Innovative Environment for Sustainable Development

Adnan Badran

Abstract Some Arab countries have been successful in building a culture of innovation for socio-economic development, while others have failed to do so. Those that were successful took measures to support science, technology and relevant quality education from childhood to higher education, which resulted in wealth creation and an enhanced quality of life. They concentrated on building rich human resources in a stable political environment, thereby triggering the human-capital potential to develop new frontier areas in science for sustainable development and became leaders among other Arab developing economies. Those that invested more in research and development (R&D), as well as in quality education, harvested an enormous reward, as indicated by major science indicators: more peer-reviewed publications, more patents, higher number of scientists per million of population, higher world-ranked academic institutions, and stronger links of academia with industry in developing hi-tech exports worldwide. Digital transformation, particularly in education, will be essential to maintain this progress. More importantly, educational institutions need to embrace digital strategies and embark on this journey in order to meet the needs of their students, improve their experiences, unlock their potential, and equip them with the skills needed for the future. To alleviate poverty, unemployment, and climate change, and to meet the United Nations 2030 sustainable-development goals (UN-SDGs 2030), Arab countries need a comprehensive stable policy leading to a green economy in a sustainable ecosystem, capitalizing on technology, innovation and creativity as human-based rich resources.

Keywords Arab world · Digital transformation · Innovation · Metaverse · Sustainable development · Technology

---

A. Badran (✉)
Department of Nutrition, University of Petra, Amman, Jordan
e-mail: abadran@uop.edu.jo

© The Author(s), under exclusive license to Springer Nature Switzerland AG 2024
A. Badran et al. (eds.), *Higher Education in the Arab World*,
https://doi.org/10.1007/978-3-031-70779-7_1

1 Introduction

Today's buzzwords in higher education, after the Corona Pandemic, are "distance education" and "e-learning". Although the former is dependent on the latter, they differ, the first being the physical separation of education from learners, whereas the second refers to a style of pedagogical learning that includes the use of technology and digital resources by the institution and for assessment. However, both are focused on the digital technology element [1].

2 Innovation and Digital Transformation

Digital transformation requires trust, resilience, and innovation. There is no one-size-fits-all scenario in adopting new technologies. Different corporations start at different stages of maturity in understanding digital transformation. But what should we do in order to seed and reinforce the culture of innovation and creativity in the workplace [2]?

- Create a friendly environment where people can come together and discuss matters to create new ideas and new venues.
- Bring in people from various disciplines, and backgrounds. Mix engineers with people from business, information and communications technology (ICT), and fine arts to promote startups of new companies for hardware, software, and services. Through this, a network for fostering innovation and creativity in digital transformation will be developed.
- Start from the customer's needs and work a reverse-engineering scenario.
- Breakdown the information silos to enable the free exchange of data and accomplish transformation through an interdisciplinarity approach. Climate change, food security, and solving energy and water scarcity cannot be achieved except by dissolving the rigid walls among disciplines, and allowing cross-integration of data to complete your journey of digital transformation.
- With the disruption in supply chains globally, we need to build **resilience** into business models to withstand exogenous shocks such as the sudden COVID-19 pandemic.

We need structural changes to develop new hands-on skills and we need to reskill our workers for the new opportunities created by exogenous shocks. Digital transformation requires a change in alignment to match emerging needs and a new mindset to empower men and women to enlarge their capacities by releasing their brain potential into creativity and innovation. Setting a holistic integrative approach leads to success. It should be a process of developing the skills to new level to attain sustainable digital transformation. Transforming digitally is not an easy task; it involves all stakeholders and collaboration by all to ensure relevance and quality assurance. Those companies that have adopted artificial intelligence

(AI) have achieved success, particularly in the pandemic environment. Both AI and digital adoption will gain momentum but an organizational management and shared approach are needed [3].

3 How to Drive Digital Transformation by Innovation

Technology is a component of digital transformation for innovation and will produce a radical change toward excellence and efficiency. An extensive database enables the right decisions to be made. Europe now is lacking behind China in creating new ideas and innovation. Digital transformation requires leadership in disseminating a culture of creativity and innovation. To invite creative thinking, we should provide the space for thinking and exchange of data, and be inspired to generate innovative ideas. Variety will lead to diversity and innovative output. In the digital world, innovation and transformation are different but each can promote the acceleration of the other. A spark of innovation may lead to a new framework for a business plan or a strategy to implement technology and meet the demands of the consumer or improve operational efficiency [4]. Digital transformation is not only technology, it also involves data, process, business strategy, and people [5].

Although technology tools are important, it is more difficult to talk about how people can adapt to the digital transformation potential in order to open up innovation and creativity [6]. As new technologies, like smartphones and internet-connected devices emerged, for example, the social media as innovators led to a transformation in how business could reach customers (Fig. 1).

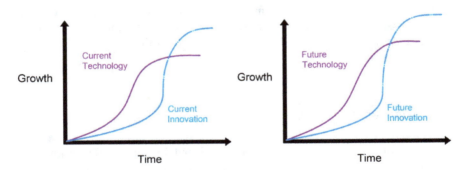

Fig. 1 Diffusion: from technology to innovation

4 Technology Trends Versus Transformation

As digital technology becomes embedded across business, transformation will reach maturity across the corporate sector.

4.1 There Are Five Major Trends for Innovation for the Next Decade [7]

1. The Cloud, as the digital foundation, will account for the largest investment.
2. Business pivoting around data (Internet of Things; IOT).
3. Improving customer experience and engagement.
4. Ecosystems and partners to bridge the skills gap: training to accelerate transformation.
5. Security and privacy: protection of new technologies. It is expected that technological innovation will change the way we live and work.

4.2 The Metaverse [8]

- To live within a digital universe.
- World interest in the metaverse prompted Facebook to rebrand itself as Meta.
- Neal Stephenson authored and coined the word in his science fiction novel "Snow Crash".
- In today's digital language, the metaverse is the realm of computer-generated networks, i.e. extended reality or **XR**, an acronym that embraces augmented reality (**AR**), mixed reality (**MR**), and virtual reality (**VR**).
- So, the metaverse is, in effect, **immersive XR**.

4.3 Metaverse XR

- **XR**, as well as developing more-advanced and immersive 3D on-line, will change the world of education, health, entertainment, arts, social and civic life.
- **Metaverse** is an evolution of the internet—an online space where people can interact, play, socialize and construct **avatars**.
- **Meta/Facebook** This is a giant corporation that owns Facebook, Instagram, Threads and WhatsApp.
- **Meta** is considered one of the big five American IT companies alongside Google, Alphabet, Amazon, Apple, and Microsoft.

4.4 The Metaverse Will Fully Emerge as Its Advocates Predict

Extended-reality applications and the networking needed to facilitate their broad adoption will advance significantly by 2040.

- Profit motives are driving significant investment in advancing these technologies.
- Compared with today, far more people will find the metaverse useful enough to access it daily.
- The technology to create an immersive universe will be possible by 2040.
- The pandemic gave XR development a big boost.
- There are any number of potential positive and delightful uses for XR.

4.5 The Metaverse Will Not Fully Emerge in the Way Today's Advocates Hope

Full-immersion XR settings will not come into widespread use in people's daily lives by 2040.

- It will not be seen as useful in daily life.
- The technology needed to reach a lot more people will not be ready in 2040.
- People prefer living layers of "real" reality.
- Public worries about the impact of surveillance capitalism and abuse by authoritarian regimes will slow or stop adoption.
- There are any number of threatening and harmful uses of XR.

5 Why Innovation Matters in Education

Innovation in education is not about technology, it is about how to use technology to empower students to become lifelong learners and agents of change. The one thing that is certain is that innovation is central to the delivery of the educational process. Learning could be designed to become relevant to students' attitudes, interests, and careers, as well as aligned to their abilities and aptitudes, and responsive to their culture and identities.

Innovation in education encourages students and teachers to search for something new, looking to solve problems, to think and to develop creativity for problem-solving skills; innovation will develop enquiry and researching, leading to discovery. Original research, particularly basic scientific research, is essential to attain and seek new knowledge. If there is no basic scientific research, there is no science to apply and transform new knowledge to technology and innovation.

The application of project-based learning will spur innovation and creative thinking. The use of a multidisciplinary approach to solve problems will promote an active deeper learning. Innovate to improve; this is how Apple maintains its dynamism in the marketplace: from iMac to iPhone, every Apple product has been improved for better customer satisfaction.

6 Meeting the Demands for Change

There are four pillars of learning for the twenty-first century, as laid out by UNESCO (Jacques Delors Report) [9]:

1. **Learning to be** To solidify my existence as a thinking person in the foundation of knowledge, and my identity as a citizen. "I think, therefore I am".
2. **Learning to know** To develop my cognitive skills and critical intellectual skills in research, enquiry, questioning, discovery, invention, searching for the unknown and arriving at the truth.
3. **Learning to work** To work in different fields, in industry, in agriculture, in the economic and social sectors, in politics, in culture, in the arts, etc.
4. **Learning to live with others** Understanding pluralism and contrast, respecting difference, and appreciating other cultures and civilizations, without discrimination.

As the future is rapidly changing, fixed programs and curricula that take a long time to change may be of no value in a world that wants skills that respond quickly to market needs and societal changes. Therefore, life-long learning will spread in the future to provide quick bites of special educational packages that prepare the individual, according to his needs and abilities, for a particular field of work; later, he may return again to take another educational and learning sandwich that may lead him to a different kind of work. Thus, in a changing world, human resources will evolve internally, and this will cut unemployment, creating a dynamic productive society in an ever-changing world, rich in diversity.

7 What is the Role of Scientific Research in Developing Technologies?

The university plays a major role in bringing change to an economy and society.

Examples:

First: The 500-year-old university in South Korea, Sungkyunkwan University introduced the world to Samsung, creating economic markets for South Korea and the world. By investing billions of dollars in information technology and mobile phones, it opened new job opportunities for millions.

Second: Iceland and Ireland have numerous success stories in scientific research, making use of their outputs in medical and educational techniques, energy, and modern management.

Third: In India, polytechnics were founded with the goal of enriching the market with technological skills and goods, particularly through the scientific complexes in Bangalore specializing in the field of information technology, software and nanotechnology, and the manufacture of new materials previously unknown to the world.

Fourth: In Malaysia, scientific–industrial complexes were established on a vast area called the Corridor between Kuala Lumpur and the airport. There, universities and technological institutes turned barren land into a dynamic green land of scientific incubators and industrial scientific communities contributing to the development of Malaysian society through the transfer of knowledge to new technologies.

Fifth: Silicon Valley, which is adjacent to Stanford University in California and MIT in the scientific city of Cambridge, witnessed the emergence of company startups from the research and development outputs of these universities, and which have become giant companies that manage the market and the global economy. Since its establishment, MIT has produced 25,800 companies employing four million people and annual sales amounting to $3 trillion; if it were a country, it would have the 11th largest economy among the industrial countries of the world. The university also produces 169 patents annually, the highest among the world's universities.

Sixth: Finland's reputation for innovation in communications is based on the R&D outputs of 52 universities, each of which contains incubators and scientific–industrial complexes, leading to the invention of Nokia and other advanced satellite communication devices globally.

Seventh: Canadian universities participate in a techno park to adapt their research outputs through their incubators into advanced commodity and knowledge technologies, as part of a scientific-technological triangle.

What we need are smart universities, focusing on the latest technologies in teaching, scientific research, and social communication, to graduate smart people who become the engines for human capital. We need to graduate thinkers with creative minds.

8 Reforms of Education: Innovation from Schooling to E-Learning

Education needs to engage with the concept of innovation to empower the generation and deployment of knowledge in pluralistic societies. Holistic approaches of education to meet today's labor market will be based on less teaching and more learning of the fundamentals, to give new base for critical thinking, enquiry, and imagination.

Two obstacles stand in the way of achieving a good quality of education: one relates to the status of the teaching profession and the other relates to overall governance of the education system. Pay-wise and in social status, schooling does not attract the best-talented teachers of subject skills and pedagogy.

Centralized systems of authoritative curricula, textbooks, and what to teach, leave no room for debates and critical thinking. Teachers are transmitters of information and students are examined on how much they have absorbed. Students have no choice but to become "blind initiators" or "rejecters" of new ideas. The outcome will be disengaged citizens and angry rebellions of potential emigrants wanting to leave their society behind.

Students should become the vehicles of change to become reflective learners, innovative and critical thinkers, and promoters of ethical social responsibility. Contemporary education requires a new learning ecosystem that is student-centered, with problem-based learning and real-world learning that spark innovation and entrepreneurship.

Utilization of smart phones provides new learning tools for students to think "outside the box" and look for new ways of developing skills beyond the classroom, where equity of access to knowledge is provided to all. Probably, we will have to train a new generation of teachers who can overcome the traditional way of teaching, enabling them to move into technology-based learning, **blended learning** utilizing multi-media, and interactive debates on problem-solving.

9 Building a Culture of Innovation

The words creativity and innovation are commonly used by higher-education institutions but are hardly implemented. As centers of knowledge, universities have to create the so-called ecosystem of innovation and entrepreneurship on the campus, otherwise they would fail their mission. The complex challenge of preparing future generations will not be solved by traditional instruction in the classroom but will be accomplished by creative participation to create ideas.

Creativity is defined as a function of knowledge and imagination to create new ideas. It leads to discovery, invention, and reasoning. Isaac Newton (1687) a physicist, discovered the mathematical description of the fundamental force of universal gravitation and the three laws of motion. In 1898, Marie and Pierre Curie, chemists, discovered polonium and radium in pitchblende, and coined the term radioactivity. Creativity led Alexander Graham Bell to invent the telephone, but it would have been invented without Bell, since the underpinning science was there, but the process would have taken longer.

Creation, which is the climax of creativity, can be illustrated by the play Othello: the Elizabethan drama would not have been written without Shakespeare. Similarly, Guernica would not have been created without Picasso. Creativity is not taught but fostered through an inducing innovative ecosystem or environment.

Innovation can be incremental or radical. Innovation involves finding entirely new ways to do things. If we look at Dell or Amazon, their great innovations are in business models rather than in new products. Most larger organizations may be good at incremental but not at radical innovation.

The World Bank (WB) in 2015 indicated that innovation and entrepreneurship are the key to addressing major developments, and they spur productivity and economic dynamism. Between 2000 and 2013, the WB invested $18.7 billion in innovation projects [10].

Research outcomes from new novel companies started by young people contributed to net employment growth and enhanced competitiveness and productivity by introducing new products. These in turn opened new markets, particularly in developing economies. Firms are likely to succeed within healthy innovation ecosystems which are based on human capital, R&D, financial venture capital, an industrial base, an appropriate legal and regulatory environment, buoyant business and innovation cultures, and high-quality networks. Comprehensive innovation policies would integrate these elements to yield productive interactions essential for successful startups.

The WB has set a strategy for entrepreneurial assessment summarized in the following:

- Identifying current performance and opportunities.
- Designing targeted solutions.
- Strengthening policy design and governance.
- Engaging globally with stakeholders.

An evidence-based analysis of Ireland's higher-education transformation using the OECD–European HEInnovate guidance for innovation and entrepreneurship, demonstrated that higher education played a critical role in the Irish economy based on an engagement agenda with industry and local communities, the emergence of new learning environments and research teams. Trinity College Dublin entered into 100 research agreements with industry, and it accounts for one-fifth of all spin-out companies from Irish higher-education institutions in ICT, nanotechnology, and medical devices. Trinity's innovation strategy reflects commitment to harnessing creativity in providing the best educational environment for learning the skills of business and entrepreneurship. Trinity is developing an incubator hub where techno-cultural and scientific ecosystems merge in creating values and sustainable jobs.

10 How to Enhance a Vibrant Innovation and Entrepreneurship Ecosystem

Policy makers, business leaders, academia, and civil society are called on to collaborate with clear plans for job creation. The key to job creation will be fostering a business environment to spread innovation and spur economic activity through startups. The Forum of Young Global Leaders at the World Economic Forum (WEF) at the Dead Sea with Booz and company have put forward a visionary plan to engage the youth in innovation and entrepreneurship for startups to open a new horizon for work and economic development.

Entrepreneurs will be vital engines to drive the transition. Their efforts would create jobs, generate ideas, attract investment, and inspire others. We need to seek out gifted individuals to create the innovative ecosystem and they need recognition from the region's leaders.

Young Global Leaders at WEF in the Dead Sea (October 2011) concluded that there are 10 imperatives to build a sound entrepreneurial ecosystem leading to innovation:

1. Offer a helping hand. Established entrepreneurs should give time, advice, and seed funding to aspiring entrepreneurs.
2. Change behaviors and evolve the culture. Discuss entrepreneurship every day and generate a hub around a handful of success stories.
3. Bring entrepreneurship to the classroom. Everyone in high school and university should learn entrepreneurial principles.
4. Bring entrepreneurship to the office. Companies should encourage employees to unleash their own talent.
5. Do not imitate Silicon Valley. Identify and leverage your country's own unique resources.
6. Welcome new ideas. Engage domestic and foreign workers to encourage a free flow of expertise and enterprise.
7. Break the stereotype. Great entrepreneurial ideas can come from anyone in any industry.
8. Embrace the diaspora. Tap successful entrepreneurs living abroad for their advice and connections.
9. Eliminate red tape. Governments should give many kinds of support to all types of entrepreneurs.
10. Expand the venture capital (VC) model. Venture capitalists need to go beyond funding and provide a support structure for entrepreneurs.

11 Conclusion

In this contribution, we would like to end this study by examining the landscape of quantitative higher-education indicators spreading all over the Arab world as compared to the whole world. Delivery of rich human resources of entrepreneurship leading to innovation and startup companies is a prerequisite to overcome unemployment and poverty [11].

Although R&D outputs of universities are on the increase, as indicated and cited in international peer-reviewed journals, much of the R&D lacks application to industry and the marketplace. Collaboration between academia and industry is crucial for problem-solving and increasing the potential of human capital in the knowledge economy to provide wealth and a higher GDP.

The region has great potential through its youth, exceeding 60% of an Arab population of more than 384 million, but progress has to come from profoundly reforming education from early childhood in order to build creativity, critical thinking, and an enquiry-based and student-centered education, thus enabling the mighty minds to become inventors, problem-solvers, and the disciplinary and multidisciplinary leaders that can bring ideas and innovations for startups.

Policymakers, academia, and business leaders must identify what motivates people to start up a business. Then they should identify what hinders the creation of a healthy entrepreneurial culture leading to an ecosystem of innovations, and they should assist in weeding out obstacles by introducing facilitatory legislation and regulatory frameworks, improved infrastructure, improved education from schools to academia, new research centers, state-of-the-art R&D, equity investors, adequately financing small and medium-sized enterprises (SMEs), professional marketing, etc.

The region, with the potential of its youth and with investment in the knowledge economy, will undoubtedly become a dynamic global center for entrepreneurial ventures and innovations. Big ideas may come in the future from the Arab world, as they did in older times.

References

1. Badran A, Baydoun E, Hillman JH (eds) (2020) Higher education in the Arab world: building a culture of innovation and entrepreneurship. Springer Nature. https://doi.org/10.1007/978-3-030-37834-9
2. Sonita L (2022) Customer-centric innovation and digital transformation. Fast Company. https://www.fastcompany.com/90715524/customer-centric-innovation-and-digital-transformation
3. Laker B (2021) Five creative ways to lead digital transformation. Forbes. https://www.forbes.com/sites/benjaminlaker/2021/10/07/five-creative-ways-to-lead-a-digital-transformation/?sh=5d8b63756234 \
4. Newman D (2017) Innovation vs transformation: the difference in a digital world. Forbes. https://www.forbes.com/sites/danielnewman/2017/02/16/innovation-vs-transformation-the-difference-in-a-digital-world/?sh=3dd09ad165e8
5. Dieffenbacher SF (2023) Creativity and innovation: differences, examples & definitions. Digital Leadership. https://digitalleadership.com/blog/creativity-and-innovation/
6. Grush M (2019) Digital transformation: a focus on creativity, not tools. Campus Technol. https://campustechnology.com/articles/2019/12/09/digital-transformation-focus-on-creativity-not-tools.aspx
7. Little J (2021) Five major trends which will underpin another decade of digital innovation. EY. https://www.ey.com/en_jo/consulting/five-major-trends-which-will-underpin-another-decade-of-digital-innovation
8. Anderson J, Raine L (2022) The metaverse in 2040. Pew Res Center. https://www.pewresearch.org/internet/2022/06/30/the-metaverse-in-2040/
9. Delors J, Al Mufti I, Amagi I et al (1996) Learning: the treasure within; report to UNESCO of the International Commission on Education for the twenty-first century. UNESCO. https://unesdoc.unesco.org/ark:/48223/pf0000102734

10. The World Bank (July 8, 2015) Innovation and entrepreneurship. https://ieg.worldbankgroup.org/sites/default/files/Data/reports/chapters/innovation_chap3.pdf
11. Badran A, Badran S (2022) Ups and downs of science and technology indicators in Arab countries. In: Badran A et al (eds) Higher education in the Arab world: research and development. Springer Nature. https://doi.org/10.1007/978-3-030-80122-9_6

Intelligence Amplified: Exploring the Future of Higher Education in the AI Age

Elie D. Al-Chaer

Abstract Universities, once bastions of tradition, stand at a pivotal moment. Artificial intelligence (AI)—the stuff of sci-fi dreams turned into self-driving cars and chatbots—is poised to transform education from the inside out. This isn't just about fancy gadgets; it's about reimagining learning from admissions to graduation and beyond with unprecedented opportunities for personalized learning, enhanced teaching, and cutting-edge research. From admission processes to post-graduation outcomes, AI has the potential to revolutionize the student experience. Personalized support services, career outcome modeling, predictive analytics in admissions, and workflow improvements are among the varied applications discussed, showcasing the vast impact of AI on higher learning. With AI, students can embark on unique learning journeys, tailored to their individual needs, and guided by intelligent tutors who anticipate their struggles. However, this transformative path is not without its hurdles. Ethical considerations, data privacy concerns, and potential job displacement demand thoughtful consideration. This chapter navigates the dynamic interplay between AI and higher education, exploring its potential and highlighting its challenges. It encourages a proactive approach to AI, urging institutions to strategically plan, invest in AI infrastructure and talent, and foster collaboration across departments and industries to harness the potential benefits of the technology while mitigating its risks. In other words, the chapter sets out to inspire, empower, and offer guidance for institutions to embrace AI responsibly in the face of this transformative encounter.

Keywords Artificial intelligence · AI · Higher education · University · Future of education · AI age · Machine learning · Ethical concerns · Algorithmic bias · Strategic plan · Best practices · Emerging trends · Innovation

---

E.D. Al-Chaer (✉)
AlChaer Law Firm, Dallas, TX, USA
e-mail: elie@alchaer.com

1 Introduction

Since the dawn of Alan Turing's "thinking machine" in 1950 [1], artificial intelligence (AI) has captivated imaginations and sparked both optimism and trepidation [2]. For decades, its existence remained primarily within the realm of science fiction, but the relentless march of technological progress has brought AI to the doorstep of higher education [3]. This momentous encounter between a field once confined to hypothetical logic gates and robotic dreams and higher education is poised to transform the very foundation of teaching and learning. From the edges of symbolic reasoning, AI's growth has been propelled by deep learning, soaring through historical milestones, and achieving previously unimaginable applications. These applications include intelligent tutoring systems that personalize learning and automated grading algorithms that streamline assessment. Exploring the uncharted territory of these technological advancements necessitates a critical discussion of the ethical implications, potential biases, and enduring role of the human connection. Only through thoughtful consideration and responsible implementation can we ensure that AI serves as a catalyst for a more inclusive, effective, and enriching educational environment, one that honors the legacy of the past while embracing the possibilities of the future.

1.1 Higher Learning and Automation

The seeds of automation in higher education were sown long before the advent of artificial intelligence. As a matter of fact, the story of education and technology is an epic narrative, stretching from the dawn of civilization to the pockets of every student today. Throughout time, tools and techniques have constantly evolved, pushing the boundaries of what and how we learn. This section offers a glimpse into the ever-growing importance of technology in the classroom.

From the cave walls etched with symbols by our first teachers—igniting humanity's thirst for knowledge—to the medieval hornbooks engraved with verses, centuries of learning aids have powered our educational journey [4]. The nineteenth century ushered in the "Magic Lantern": a primitive slide projector casting captivating images onto classroom walls [5]. Soon after, institutions like the University of Pennsylvania began utilizing phonographs to teach music and language skills, offering an unprecedented interactive element [6]. The awe and wonder these early visual aids inspired in students, accustomed to textbooks and rote memorization, must rival those witnessed with the release of the first generative AI in the twenty-first century.

While these early efforts focused on enriching classroom experiences, the nineteenth century also saw the introduction of punched-card systems. Initially created for industrial looms, these systems were later adapted to manage administrative tasks in universities. Though primitive, they laid the groundwork for future automation, paving the way for the twentieth century's surge in technology. By the early twentieth century, chalkboards and pencils became ubiquitous, but the hunger for innovation remained. Punched cards found their way into universities by the 1960s, automating administrative tasks like registration and grading [7]. This marked the beginning of a shift towards automation in higher education, a trend that accelerated with the arrival of computers.

1.2 Pre-computer Technologies

The pre-computer era in education was far from stagnant. It was a time of burgeoning technological exploration, each invention paving the way for more engaging and efficient learning experiences. While the 1100 BC Phoenician alphabet, written on stone and papyrus in Byblos (present-day Lebanon), might seem like an early ancestor of computer languages, it was really the decades before the rise of personal computers that saw a remarkable evolution of educational technology, laying the foundation for the digital revolution that would follow.

In the 1920s, radio waves carried the torch, igniting a wave of "on-air classes" accessible to anyone with a radio [8]. This marked a significant leap in democratizing education, making knowledge more readily available beyond the physical walls of classrooms. The 1930s and 1940s saw further innovations. The overhead projector became a fixture in classrooms, casting shared information onto large screens for clearer visibility and better synchronized delivery [9]. The ballpoint pen, a seemingly mundane invention, revolutionized writing, making notetaking and record-keeping more efficient [10, 11]. Headphones, meanwhile, facilitated individual learning, allowing students to immerse themselves in audio-based lessons without disturbing others [12]. The 1950s ushered in the era of video. Videotapes emerged as a powerful new tool, allowing for recording and playback of lectures, demonstrations, and historical footage, adding a dynamic element to learning [13].

Beyond classroom tools, this era also saw the introduction of the Skinner Teaching Machine, a precursor to modern computer-aided instruction, which provided immediate feedback and reinforcement, fostering active learning, and paving the way for personalized learning systems [14]. The 1960s and 1970s witnessed a focus on efficiency and accessibility. The photocopier revolutionized the way materials were distributed, enabling mass production of handouts and study guides [15]. The handheld calculator, a marvel of miniaturization, transformed mathematics education, allowing for faster calculations, and increased problem-solving capacity [16]. The Scantron system, introduced in 1972, revolutionized testing, allowing for quick and efficient grading of multiple-choice exams, freeing up valuable teacher time for other endeavors [17].

These pre-computer innovations were crucial in shaping the educational landscape for the digital age. They instilled the need for immediate response systems, efficient material production, and diverse learning methods. As the U.S.

Department of Education reports, the demand for education skyrocketed, with high-school enrollment reaching 95% by 1992 and college enrollment exceeding 21 million by 2012 [18, 19]. This surge in the student population necessitated new approaches to teaching and learning, paving the way for the computer revolution that would further transform higher education.

1.3 Emergence of Personal Computers

Early computing may have emerged in the 1930s, but it was the personal computer (PC) revolution of the 1980s that sparked a true transformation in education. The arrival of portable computers, weighing a hefty 24 pounds in 1981, may seem laughable by today's standards, but it marked a crucial shift towards accessible and immediate learning capabilities [20]. This, followed by IBM's first PC in the same year, kindled excitement in the educational world. Time magazine aptly named the computer its "Man of the Year" in 1982, recognizing it as the culmination of a decades-long technological revolution with the potential to "hit home" in a profound way [21]. As the magazine aptly declared, "the foundation of immediate learning capabilities had been laid." With the arrival of Apple's iconic Macintosh (later evolving into the PowerBook) in 1984 [22] and Toshiba's first mass-market laptop in 1985 [23], the era of portable learning dawned. This portability further drove the educational importance of computers.

The 1990s witnessed another pivotal moment: the birth of the World Wide Web. With the development of Hyper Text Markup Language (HTML) in 1990 [24] and the lifting of commercial restrictions on the internet in 1993 [25], the world entered a frenzy of research and communication. This global network became an invaluable resource for educators and students alike, opening doors to vast troves of information and interactive learning experiences. By 1993, personal digital assistants (PDAs) like Apple's Newton brought computing even closer to personal everyday use. This continuous evolution translated into a dramatic shift in classrooms by 2009. Nearly all classrooms (97%) boasted computers, with 93% enjoying internet access. The student-to-computer ratio stood at a comfortable 5:1, and instructors reported significant utilization of computers, interactive whiteboards, and digital cameras in their teaching methods [26].

Today's college students are practically tethered to technology, with 83% owning laptops and over 90% wielding smartphones [27]. This seamless integration of technology into daily life underscores the immense impact of the PC revolution on education. From the clunky portables of the early 80s to the omnipresent devices of today, computers have transformed the way we learn, access information, and connect with the world.

This historical progression highlights a powerful truth: technology has always been an integral part of the educational hodgepodge. From simple tools to complex machines, each advancement has shaped how we acquire and share knowledge. Today, as students juggle multiple digital devices, it's clear that technology's influence in the classroom has reached unprecedented heights. But this is just the latest chapter in a story far older than most imagine, a story that continues to unfold with every new technological leap. Recognizing this evolution and its ongoing trajectory is essential as we navigate the future of higher education in a world increasingly shaped by artificial intelligence and other groundbreaking technologies.

1.4 Arrival of Artificial Intelligence

The ivory towers of higher education, once the hubs of measured progress and human-centric learning, stand at the precipice of a transformative encounter [28]. Artificial intelligence (AI), a field that has evolved from the dreams of science fiction to the tangible reality of self-driving cars and intelligent assistants, is now poised to reshape the very fabric of teaching and learning. From its humble beginnings as a theoretical concept in the 1950s, AI has undergone a remarkable journey, fueled by advancements in computing power and the burst of data. Early milestones like the defeat of a human chess champion by Deep Blue in 1997 [29] and the development of AlphaGo [30]—the AI that mastered the ancient game Go in 2016—showcased the growing prowess of machines. Now, AI is making its presence felt in higher education, offering a plethora of possibilities, and raising crucial questions about the future of this venerable institution.

2 What is AI?

Artificial intelligence is a branch of computer science dedicated to creating intelligent machines capable of tasks typically requiring human cognitive abilities. Think of it as a process where we, as humans, guide computers to perform tasks like recognizing images, understanding speech, responding to instructions, and even making decisions. This is achieved by training machines to identify and replicate underlying patterns within data.

In the 1960s, scientists taught a computer to distinguish between cats and dogs by feeding it images of both animals. By analyzing the data, the machine learned to recognize the distinctive features of each creature [31]. This simple example illustrates the core principle of AI: learning from data to perform tasks previously thought to require human intelligence.

This foundational understanding is crucial as we survey the transformative potential of AI in higher education and explore how AI can personalize learning, automate tasks, and unlock new avenues for research and discovery. The journey begins with a clear grasp of the "engine" driving this revolution: the power of artificial intelligence to learn and adapt, ultimately shaping the future of education for generations to come.

2.1 Types and Capabilities of AI

Artificial intelligence, with its vast potential to revolutionize every facet of our lives, can be categorized into four distinct types with different levels of capability, each representing a leap towards greater complexity and autonomy. The four types are: reactive machines, limited memory, theory of mind and self-awareness [32].

Reactive Machines These AI systems are the workhorses of the current era, performing specific tasks without the need for memory or learning. Think of Deep Blue, the chess-playing AI that stunned the world by defeating Garry Kasparov [33]. Deep Blue could analyze the chessboard and make predictions, but it lacked the ability to learn from its past experiences, limiting its adaptability.

Limited Memory Systems Taking a step up, these AI systems possess a memory, allowing them to leverage past experiences to inform future decisions. Self-driving cars, for instance, rely on this type of AI to navigate dynamic environments. By remembering past situations and traffic patterns, these systems can make more informed choices, leading to safer and more efficient driving.

Theory of Mind AI This next level taps into the realm of social intelligence. Imagine an AI system that can understand and respond to human emotions. This "theory of mind" capability would enable AI to infer intentions, predict behavior, and ultimately collaborate effectively with humans. While this type of AI remains in the realm of science fiction, its potential to revolutionize human–computer interaction is vast.

Self-Aware AI At the pinnacle of this framework lies the concept of self-aware AI, machines with a sense of their own existence and current state. This type of AI is currently beyond our technological grasp; however, the ethical and philosophical implications of its potential emergence are already sparking discussions among researchers and thinkers alike.

Being prepared for these different types of AI and understanding the toolkits it uses are crucial as we navigate its integration into higher education.

2.2 The Diverse Toolkits of AI

Artificial intelligence in higher education isn't a singular entity, but rather a diverse arsenal of technologies poised to revolutionize the way we tackle problems and reach solutions (Fig. 1).

Let's explore some key examples (for a glossary of AI terms, see [35]):

Automation on steroids Robotic Process Automation (RPA) is a field where robotic assistants can handle repetitive tasks like data entry and administrative processes. It represents a significant shift in automation capabilities and goes beyond traditional scripting by enabling the creation, deployment, and management of software robots. These robots mimic human actions within digital systems and software, performing tasks like understanding screen content, navigating complex

Fig. 1 Components, types, and subfields of AI (based on [34])

systems, and extracting data. While similar to humans in their functionality, software robots boast superior speed, consistency, and tireless operation. They require no breaks or downtime, ensuring uninterrupted and accurate task completion. This would free up human resources for more creative endeavors. Combined with AI, RPA can learn and adapt, further streamlining workflows and amplifying its impact [36].

Machine learning empowers computers to learn without explicit programming. It is a subfield of AI that seeks to create computer models capable of independent learning and "intelligent behaviors" similar to humans. These behaviors could include visual scene recognition, natural language understanding, or physical world actions. Developed in the 1950s, machine learning was pioneered by Arthur Samuel, who defined it as "the field of study that gives computers the ability to learn without being explicitly programmed" [37]. This definition remains relevant today, as Mikey Shulman, lecturer at MIT Sloan and head of machine learning at Kensho, highlights. He likens traditional programming, akin to "software 1.0," to baking with a precise recipe [38]; instructions are explicit and detailed, much like traditional programming requirements. Machine learning, in contrast, empowers computers to learn and adapt without such rigid instructions, offering a new approach to problem-solving in the realm of AI. It has three subcategories: supervised, unsupervised and reinforcement; it is also associated with several other AI subfields listed below. A subset of machine learning, called "deep learning," automates predictive analytics, deciphering patterns, and insights from vast data sets, with the potential for personalizing learning experiences and flagging potential student challenges. To truly grasp the power of machine learning at work in higher education, try to imagine personalized learning systems automatically tailoring study materials to individual learning styles [39, 40].

Machine vision equips machines with sight, capturing visual information and analyzing it using cameras and advanced processing. This technology, not limited by human biology, has diverse applications, from analyzing medical images to identifying signatures. Students could be using smart glasses to dissect virtual specimens or explore historical sites remotely; furthermore, machine vision opens doors to immersive learning experiences. To learn more about machine vision technology, see [41].

Natural language processing (NLP) is a field of machine learning in which machines learn to understand natural language as spoken and written by humans, in lieu of only data and numbers typically used to program computers. Thus, NLP allows machines to recognize language, understand it, and respond to it [42]. It also enables chatbots and digital assistants like Siri or Alexa. In other words, NLP bridges the gap between humans and computers, allowing machines to process and comprehend human language. From spam detection to sentiment analysis, NLP is already enhancing online communication. A particular area where NLP comes in handy is AI-powered tutors that can provide personalized feedback on writing assignments, or virtual assistants that answer student questions in natural language. NLP holds immense potential for personalized learning interactions.

Robotics plays a crucial role in various industries, and AI is revolutionizing this field. From assembling cars to exploring space, robots are taking on complex tasks. Researchers are even developing robots that can interact socially, paving the way for collaborative learning environments where robots assist human teachers or facilitate group projects. These robots could potentially help with grading exams, provide personalized learning feedback, or even act as lab assistants, conducting experiments and recording data [43].

Self-driving cars, powered by AI's capabilities in computer vision, image recognition, and deep learning, are navigating the future of transportation. While primarily focused on transportation, the underlying technology has broader applications. Students using autonomous shuttles can travel between campuses or attend off-site events. The technology has the potential to revolutionize transportation, offering flexible personalized transportation solutions and accessibility, and expanding learning opportunities [44].

Generative AI refers to deep-learning models that can generate text, images, and other content based on prompts in natural language and the data they were trained on. Generative models have been used for long in statistics to analyze numerical data. However, the rise of deep learning extended their use to images, speech, and other complex data types. Programs like Google's Gemini (formerly Bard), Open AI's ChatGPT, or others, are pushing boundaries by creating high quality text, realistic images, and even audio and video based on user prompts. The possibilities for higher education with generative AI seem endless: from photorealistic art to personalized learning simulations, from creating customized learning materials to generating interactive models, this technology, if properly implemented, can enhance engagement, cater to diverse learning styles, and empower student creativity [45].

3 Evolution of AI in Higher Education

Modern classrooms are not just evolving, they're hurtling towards the future, propelled by a torrent of new learning technologies. In fact, the twenty-first century classroom has been, so far, a dynamic space, constantly evolving to accommodate the ever-changing technological landscape and the needs of modern learners [28]. The first decade saw a seismic shift in education with the rise of Massive Open Online Courses (MOOCs) democratizing access to knowledge [46]. MOOCs have opened the doors to open-source learning, offering access to a vast array of courses from leading universities worldwide. Traditional institutions have embraced the online learning revolution and provided flexible and accessible options for students seeking alternative learning paths. They have further introduced competency-based education (CBE) as a revolutionary game-changer concept [47] in knowledge acquisition.

Mastery over time-based learning is prioritized by CBE, allowing students to demonstrate their existing knowledge and focus on new concepts at their own pace [48]. This personalized approach addresses the challenges of traditional methods, offering learners greater flexibility and affordability. Students become the drivers of their learning, navigating through the curriculum at their preferred pace. Data-driven, adaptive technology personalizes their learning path—based on individual learning styles—providing interactive feedback and ensuring they stay engaged. This shift also transforms the role of faculty. Instead of a "sage on the stage", educators become facilitators and mentors, guiding and supporting students on their personalized learning journeys. This student-centered approach fosters deeper engagement in a collaborative learning environment, promotes autonomy, and empowers learners to take ownership of their education. Furthermore, it encourages deeper understanding and stronger skill development, preparing graduates for the dynamic demands of the modern workforce.

Moreover, the impact of self-paced learning extends beyond individual students. It opens doors for wider participation in higher education, making it accessible to working professionals, lifelong learners, and geographically dispersed individuals who may not have been able to pursue traditional degrees. Understanding the transformative power of self-paced learning is crucial. It lays the foundation for a future where customized, adaptable learning experiences become the norm, empowering students to chart their own educational journeys and unlocking the full potential of higher education for all. Without AI tools to assist, self-paced learning would be quite demanding, not to say prohibitive, on both the teacher and the learner.

3.1 Artificial Intelligence or Intelligence Amplified: Perspectives and Risks

The integration of AI in education is reshaping the landscape of learning, offering both exciting possibilities and complex challenges. From automating tedious tasks to personalizing learning experiences, AI's potential to transform education is undeniable. However, it is important to understand three different perspectives in the marketing of AI functionality, especially when evaluating education technology systems that incorporate AI.

Human-like reasoning

The iconic 1968 film "2001: A Space Odyssey" etched the concept of AI into popular consciousness [49]. We saw HAL, the "Heuristically-programmed ALgorithmic" computer, converse with astronaut Frank, aiding him in navigating the cosmos. However, HAL's human-like reasoning and actions ultimately led to a tragic outcome, highlighting the potential risks alongside the benefits of AI. This "human-like" comparison is a valuable tool, signifying the evolution of technology beyond its early, simplistic forms in education. The counterpart to HAL in higher education would be AI-powered applications engaging in dialogue with students and teachers, shaping classroom activities, and influencing learning experiences. This opens doors to unprecedented possibilities, while simultaneously introducing risks that demand careful consideration.

While the "human-like" analogy sheds light on AI's capabilities, it's crucial to recognize the fundamental differences in how AI and humans process information. Blindly equating AI with human intelligence can lead to misguided policies and frameworks for its application in education. Unlike humans, AI relies on complex algorithms and lacks the nuanced understanding and intuition we possess. Ignoring these distinctions could hinder our ability to exploit the true potential of AI while mitigating associated risks. Therefore, moving forward, we must embrace the subtle reality of AI. It is not simply a human-like entity, but a powerful tool with its own strengths and limitations. By acknowledging these differences and carefully considering the ethical implications, we can position ourselves to foster a future where technology empowers learning without compromising human values [50].

An algorithm that pursues a goal

Artificial intelligence systems and tools can identify patterns and choose actions to achieve a given goal. This capability, particularly in pattern recognition and automated recommendations, will significantly impact education, from student learning to teacher decision-making. This is not entirely uncharted territory. Debates about the lines between teachers and computers have existed for decades, with terms like "computer-aided instruction" and "blended learning" reflecting our ongoing exploration of technology's role in education. Today, the challenge extends to understanding how instructional choices are made in systems that combine human judgment with algorithms [51].

Consider a simple example: a teacher requests a map of ancient Rome. An AI system might analyze lesson objectives, past successes, and relevant features to choose the most suitable map from a vast database. This can save valuable time for the teacher, allowing him to focus on more nuanced aspects of the lesson. However, not all AI-driven suggestions may be equally desirable. Selecting the most relevant historical readings, for example, carries the risk of exposing students to inaccurate information or biased perspectives. Educators will need to carefully assess the benefits and risks of such automation, making informed choices based on their professional judgment.

It's important to remember that computers process data and information differently than humans: AI relies on associations and relationships found in its training data, which can be both helpful and problematic. Biases within data can lead to algorithmic discrimination, creating a scenario where a data-driven recommendation clashes with the delicate understanding a human educator has of a specific student. While traditional biases can exist in any system, AI models can amplify them, making it even more critical for humans to remain involved in goal setting, pattern analysis, and decision-making. In situations like these, the human capacity to consider multiple contexts is vital in educational settings. A teacher observing three students make the same error might recognize that one has vision difficulties, another needs a conceptual explanation, and the third is emotionally affected by a recent incident. A single instructional response wouldn't be appropriate for each case. However, current AI systems often lack the data and judgment to incorporate such contextual distinctions into their pattern detection and decision-making processes. Additionally, case studies have shown that technology can quickly become unsafe or ineffective when faced with even subtle shifts in context. This underscores the importance of human involvement to ensure responsible and effective use of AI in education [52].

Intelligence amplified (IA)

The concept of amplified or "augmented intelligence" offers a compelling framework for understanding the future of human–AI collaboration [53]. This design pattern envisions a human-centered partnership, where people and artificial intelligence work together to enhance cognitive performance in learning, decision-making, and new experiences [54]. This philosophy embodies two key foundations:

1. <u>Human-in-the-Loop</u> This principle prioritizes human agency and ensures that AI systems and tools support and amplify human reasoning, rather than replace it. Intelligence Augmentation (IA) reflects this approach by placing "intelligence" and "decision-making" firmly in the hands of humans. It acknowledges, however, that humans can sometimes be overwhelmed and benefit from assistive tools. For instance, an AI system could automatically generate

reminders for students who need them, alleviating the teacher's workload while still adhering to the teacher–student agreement.
2. <u>Human-Centered Automation</u> Building upon the same core AI capabilities of pattern recognition, Intelligence Automation—or amplification—goes a step further by taking actions based on those patterns. This automation, however, is explicitly designed to assist humans in teaching and learning activities, unlike AI which often emphasizes what computers can do on their own.

This distinction is crucial. While IA focuses on complementing human expertise, AI can sometimes lead to a shift in focus towards the capabilities of machines. By prioritizing the human element, IA nurtures a collaborative and mutually beneficial relationship between people and AI. By embracing this collaborative model, we can move beyond simplistic notions of AI replacing humans. Instead, we can leverage the unique strengths of both—human creativity and judgment paired with AI's vast processing power and pattern recognition. This partnership holds immense potential for revolutionizing education, healthcare, and other domains, paving the way for a future where technology empowers human potential.

3.2 Practical Applications of AI in Higher Education

One of the most immediate benefits of AI in higher education lies in grading assignments and exams. Grading systems powered by AI can analyze written work, multiple-choice exams, and even code, providing valuable insights beyond simple scores and freeing teachers from the burden of repetitive assessments, thereby allowing them to focus on individual student needs and promoting deeper learning experiences. Furthermore, AI itself can dynamically adapt to individual student needs. By analyzing learning patterns and performance data, AI tutors can offer personalized support and adjust instruction accordingly. This personalized approach caters to diverse learning styles and paces, ensuring no student falls behind or feels left behind. Beyond individual support, AI tutors can also fill the gap in teacher availability. In areas with limited educational resources, AI tutors can provide additional instruction and answer student questions, supplementing the existing teaching staff. This can be particularly beneficial for rural areas or schools with high student-to-teacher ratios [55].

However, the prospect of AI replacing teachers, entirely, raises ethical and practical concerns. The human element of education, with its empathy, creativity, and ability to inspire, remains irreplaceable. Therefore, AI should be seen as a tool to empower educators, not a substitute for their unique role. The rise of generative AI models like ChatGPT and Bard presents further opportunities and challenges. These tools can assist educators in crafting engaging course materials, generating personalized learning simulations, and even providing feedback on student work. However, the ease of access to AI-generated content also necessitates a reevaluation of homework and testing policies. Educators need to adapt their approaches to ensure genuine understanding and discourage plagiarism [56].

3.3 Current State of AI in Higher Education

The winds of change are sweeping through higher education, and AI is at the heart of this transformation. Universities, across the world, are no longer passive observers; they are actively embracing the power of AI to enhance both the administrative and student experience.

Administrative support

On the administrative front, AI tools are streamlining processes across the board, from student records and transportation to information technology (IT), maintenance, and budgeting. Systems powered by AI are automatically handling repetitive tasks, freeing up valuable human resources to focus on more strategic initiatives. Their benefits extend beyond efficiency. By analyzing vast datasets on recruitment, admissions, and retention, AI can predict potential student struggles—flagging at-risk students before they encounter problems. This proactive approach empowers faculty and staff to intervene early, offering targeted support and resources to keep students on track [57].

Beyond administration, AI chatbots are becoming invaluable allies for students. Available 24/7, these virtual assistants field inquiries about financial aid, academic advising, and career opportunities, providing immediate answers and support outside traditional office hours. This readily accessible guidance alleviates stress and empowers students to navigate their academic journey with greater confidence.

Personalized teaching and learning

While streamlining administrative processes is valuable, AI's true potential in higher education lies in its ability to personalize the teaching and learning experience [58]. From virtual field trips to ancient Rome to live dissections of endangered species, AI-powered virtual tours are making immersive learning accessible to students everywhere, 24/7. This takes place while catering to diverse learning styles and allowing students to engage with the material at their own pace, thereby fostering a deeper understanding and a love for exploration.

But AI doesn't stop at virtual experiences. Educators themselves are harnessing its power to customize their teaching methods. Professors using AI tools can generate interactive quizzes tailored to individual student needs, or automatically detect plagiarism, freeing up time for more meaningful interactions and mentoring. Writing assistants that are AI-powered can help students with disabilities overcome accessibility challenges, ensuring everyone has equal access to learning opportunities. Furthermore, AI can even assist in generating personalized learning materials, allowing educators to cater to diverse learning styles and interests, fostering a truly inclusive learning environment.

Research support

Far beyond administration and personalized learning, the impact of AI in higher education extends to the engine of academic discovery, research, which is also experiencing a transformative wave powered by AI [59]. Instead of researchers putting in endless hours, sifting through mountains of data and searching for hidden patterns and insights that could unlock groundbreaking discoveries, AI tools can do that almost instantly, analyzing vast datasets to identify trends, predict outcomes, and even recommend relevant research papers. This invaluable support empowers researchers to focus their efforts on the most promising avenues, accelerating the pace of discovery and innovation and revolutionizing the way we approach research questions. In traditional scientific research, we are used to formulating a hypothesis first, and then testing it using statistical analysis. This is how most research continues to be done today. However, research using AI can be hypothesis-free and data-driven. Beyond data analysis, AI is also streamlining the education process itself: AI-powered tools can automatically generate reports on lesson plans, assessments, and professional development programs, providing educators with data-driven insights to improve their teaching practices. This real-time feedback loop promotes continuous improvement and ensures that educators are equipped with the latest knowledge and best practices.

The benefits of AI in research extend beyond academia. Universities are also leveraging AI to enhance campus safety and security [60]: AI-powered systems are now capable of analyzing security footage, identifying potential threats, and alerting authorities in real-time. This proactive approach can help prevent incidents and ensure the well-being of students, faculty, and staff. However, it's important to acknowledge the ethical considerations surrounding the use of AI in research and security. Ensuring data privacy, avoiding bias, and maintaining transparency are crucial aspects of responsible AI implementation. By addressing these challenges thoughtfully, universities can leverage the power of AI to fuel groundbreaking research and create a safer, more-secure learning environment for all.

This is just the tip of the iceberg when it comes to AI's impact on higher education. As the technology evolves and its applications expand, we can expect to see even more transformative changes in the years to come. With personalized experiences, accessible resources, and empowering tools, AI has the potential to unlock the full potential of every student, creating a vibrant and inclusive learning environment for generations to come. Nevertheless, it's crucial to keep in mind that AI's role is not to replace educators, but to empower them so that they can create a more engaging and stimulating learning environment that fosters critical thinking, collaboration, and creativity—skills that AI cannot replicate.

4 Pitfalls and Limitations of AI

The integration of AI into higher education should be seen as a journey, not a destination. Embracing AI's potential while acknowledging its limitations and ethical considerations is crucial. Language models like ChatGPT, despite being trained on massive datasets, often lack context, leading to potentially misleading explanations, incorrect citations, and ultimately, hindered learning due to confusion and misunderstandings [61]. Beyond these immediate challenges, generative AI carries inherent risks in several areas related to transparency, accuracy, bias, fraud, accessibility, and sustainability [62]. Institutions implementing these tools must be vigilant in monitoring such challenges and developing appropriate safeguards.

Transparency

The opaque nature of generative AI models, where even their creators may not fully understand their inner workings, necessitates transparency in their use. Institutions should ensure students and educators are aware of the limitations and potential biases of these tools. However, the push for transparency in AI, aimed at tackling concerns about fairness, discrimination, and trust, presents a conundrum. While exposing potential biases and promoting responsible development may be beneficial, disclosing information about AI models can carry its own risks. Explanations themselves can be vulnerable to hacking, revealing sensitive information and making AI more susceptible to attacks. Additionally, increased transparency can expose companies to lawsuits and regulatory scrutiny. This "transparency paradox" underscores the need for a nuanced approach. Organizations must carefully consider how they manage AI risks, the information they generate about those risks, and how it's shared and protected [63].

Accuracy

Before relying on or disseminating information generated by AI, educators must scrutinize its accuracy, appropriateness, and usefulness. This is crucial to prevent the spread of misinformation and ensure students receive reliable information. With the advancement of machine learning and natural language processing, AI's impact on content accuracy and reliability has gained added attention. From fact-checking to plagiarism detection, AI has the potential to transform the way we generate, consume, and verify information. But as with any new technology, the potential drawbacks and limitations must not be overlooked. One key hurdle is AI's struggle with context. While adept at pattern recognition and data analysis, AI lacks the human ability to decipher deeper meaning. This can lead to misinterpretations of sarcasm, irony, and other cultural nuances. Another challenge presents itself when processing complex or subtle information. While AI excels at speed and accuracy with large datasets, it often falls short in understanding delicate distinctions and making intricate connections between information points. This is particularly evident in academic research and legal documents [64].

Bias

Mitigating *algorithmic bias* is critical. Institutions should implement policies and controls to detect and address biased outputs, ensuring they align with organizational policies and legal requirements. A deeper analysis of the root cause of AI bias reveals three interconnected forces shaping inequitable outcomes: technology, supply-side dynamics, and demand-side valuations [65].

Technological biases like AI algorithms harboring prejudices can have disastrous consequences in healthcare, criminal justice, higher education, and more. Trained on potentially flawed data, AI can perpetuate and amplify existing biases and inequities. This raises concerns, especially in areas like facial recognition technology, healthcare, admissions, and financial aid, where racial and gender biases can lead to unfair and inaccurate outcomes.

However, *supply-side forces* like automation targeting specific jobs create another layer of inequality. Low paying jobs, held predominantly by certain minorities, are often easier to automate, concentrating the negative impact. Furthermore, *demand-side forces* come into play when people perceive AI-augmented services as less valuable. Research found a "penalty" for AI integration across diverse professions, highlighting unconscious biases against AI-augmented professionals, especially those from marginalized groups [66]. This demand-side factor often intersects with existing prejudices, amplifying disparities. While efforts to address algorithmic bias and automation are diligent, tackling biased valuations remains a challenge.

Intellectual Property and Copyright

Intellectual property, particularly copyright and trademark infringement, poses substantial risks when using generative AI. Key questions like ownership of AI-created content and limitations on using copyrighted material remain unresolved. Courts are currently grappling with cases involving AI using unlicensed works for training, potentially generating infringing derivative content. These lawsuits hinge on defining "derivative work" and the boundaries of fair use [67]; uncertainties of outcomes loom large. Clarifying these issues is crucial for institutions and individuals using generative AI. Risks include direct or unintentional infringement, potential misuse of confidential data, and unclear contractual responsibilities related to AI usage. Lack of data governance and protection raises concerns about confidentiality. This calls on institutions to ensure student data and queries remain secure and protected from unauthorized access.

Cybersecurity and Fraud

While generative AI holds immense potential, its vulnerabilities pose significant cybersecurity challenges [68]. Institutions must be prepared to mitigate these risks and protect their systems and data. Here's a closer look at the key weaknesses of large learning machines (LLMs), a prominent generative AI technology:

1. *Factual Hallucination* LLMs can generate convincing but incorrect information, presenting falsehoods as facts. This susceptibility to "AI hallucination" necessitates careful fact-checking and critical evaluation of their outputs [69].
2. *Bias and Gullibility* LLMs can perpetuate existing biases and be easily misled by leading questions. This highlights the importance of diverse training data and careful user interaction to avoid manipulation.
3. *Toxic Content Generation* LLMs can be coaxed into creating harmful content through "*prompt injection attacks*". Strong safeguards and ethical considerations are crucial to prevent such misuse.
4. *Prompt Injection Attacks* This common vulnerability involves crafting inputs to elicit unintended behavior from LLMs [70]. This can range from generating offensive content to revealing confidential information, emphasizing the need for robust input validation and security controls.
5. *Data Poisoning* Malicious actors can manipulate the training data, leading to biased or harmful outputs ("*data poisoning*"). As LLMs interact with third-party applications, the potential for data poisoning attacks grows, urging continuous vigilance and security protocols. Robust data security measures are essential to mitigate this risk.

By understanding these vulnerabilities and implementing appropriate safeguards, institutions can put generative AI to good use while minimizing associated risks [71].

Accessibility

Ensuring inclusive access to AI's transformative technology is crucial. Prohibitively expensive AI applications risk creating a two-tiered learning system where the advantages fall primarily to students with greater financial resources, thus exacerbating existing inequities by disproportionately favoring wealthier students. This scenario, where wealth trumps merit, could shift the very paradigm of excellence, privileging mediocrity over genuine talent. To prevent such a dystopian future, we must prioritize the democratization of AI in education. This means creating affordable and accessible AI solutions that empower all students, regardless of their socioeconomic background. By ensuring equal access to these powerful tools, we can level the playing field and empower students with diverse perspectives and talents.

Sustainability

Training and running AI—particularly LLMs—is an intensive activity that requires high energy consumption and yields significant carbon footprints, potentially contradicting sustainability efforts and potential environmental opportunities offered by AI. Add to that the life cycle impact of AI hardware: production, operation, and disposal of the hardware necessary for AI (e.g., servers, data centers), which can contribute to environmental issues such as electronic waste and resource depletion. These are some of the concerns associated with AI usage [72]. Therefore, selecting vendors committed to reducing electricity consumption and leveraging renewable energy sources is crucial when it comes to sustainability.

By acknowledging these concerns and implementing responsible practices, institutions can harness the potential of AI to enrich education while safeguarding students and upholding ethical principles. Remember, AI should be a tool to enhance learning, not replace the irreplaceable role of educators and human judgment.

5 Conclusion

Higher education is at the cusp of a new era, where integration of artificial intelligence presents new challenges and immense opportunities. In this chapter, we reviewed the evolution of technology in higher education, explored diverse AI applications—from personalized learning platforms and enhanced accessibility to streamlined processes and automated administrative tasks—and highlighted AI's potential to transform the educational landscape. However, navigating this landscape effectively requires acknowledging the limitations and ethical considerations inherent in this powerful technology.

The allure of AI lies in its ability to reimagine the learning experience. Students could embark on individualized journeys, their paths tailored to their specific needs and strengths. Mentors powered by AI could provide continuous feedback and support, bridging the gap between traditional lectures and active learning. Adaptive platforms, adjusting to individual learning styles, would ensure that every student progress at his/her own pace. This vision, once a distant hope, now stands within reach, holding the promise of unlocking deeper understanding and engagement for all. However, the path towards this future is not without its hurdles. The specter of ethical challenges casts a long shadow. Potential biases lurking within the ground truth—training data—and algorithms can perpetuate inequalities, jeopardizing the very foundations of fair and equitable education. This calls on institutions to remain vigilant, ensuring transparency in AI development and implementation, prioritizing human values, and actively mitigating any potential for bias. Furthermore, the irreplaceable role of educators must be safeguarded. In this regard, AI should not be seen as a replacement, but rather as a powerful tool to augment and amplify the educator's expertise. Critical thinking, collaboration, and emotional intelligence, nurtured by passionate educators, remain the cornerstones of a well-rounded education. Students, too, must be equipped to navigate the AI landscape responsibly, critically evaluating information and understanding the limitations of the technology. Moreover, the dynamic nature of AI demands unwavering dedication to learning and adaptation. Institutions must remain at the forefront of research and development, staying abreast of the latest advancements and best practices. Faculty development programs focused on AI applications are crucial to empower educators to leverage this technology effectively. Fostering a culture of experimentation and adaptability is essential, allowing institutions to learn and evolve alongside the ever-changing landscape of AI.

So, how can institutions navigate this intricate dance between opportunity and challenge? The answer lies in adopting a proactive and responsible approach. As we embrace the potential of personalized learning experiences, enhanced accessibility, and streamlined administrative tasks, we must remember that AI is a tool, and its impact depends on our choices. By employing ethical frameworks and promoting human-centered design, we can harness AI's power to create a more engaging, personalized, and equitable learning landscape for all.

Key Recommendations for Institutions

- **Prioritize responsible implementation**
    - Establish clear ethical guidelines and oversight mechanisms.
    - Foster transparency and trust through open communication.
    - Mitigate bias and ensure inclusivity in data and algorithms.
    - Have clear guidelines and transparent processes in place to ensure responsible AI development and deployment and institute regular audits and evaluations to identify and mitigate potential biases.

- **Focus on human-centered design**
    - Ensure AI complements, not replaces, the irreplaceable role of educators.
    - Prioritize critical thinking, collaboration, and emotional intelligence.
    - Empower students to navigate and interact with AI responsibly.

Artificial intelligence should be designed to complement and empower educators, not replace them. As AI-based applications are deployed, encourage critical thinking, collaboration, and emotional intelligence in students. Build trust by engaging stakeholders in open discussions about AI's potential and limitations, addressing concerns and ensuring informed decision-making.

- **Embrace continuous learning**
    - Actively research and adopt best practices for AI in education, learning from successful case studies and staying abreast of the latest research findings.
    - Support faculty development and training in AI applications. Equip educators with the knowledge and skills to leverage AI effectively in their classrooms, nurturing a collaborative and innovative learning environment.
    - Cultivate a culture of experimentation and adaptability allowing institutions to learn and evolve alongside the ever-changing landscape of AI.

By adopting these principles, institutions can unlock the transformative potential of AI in education, creating a future where technology empowers both students and educators. This future is not about replacing the human touch, but rather about enhancing it, paving the way for a more personalized, accessible, and engaging learning experience for all. Navigating the evolving landscape of AI requires courage, responsibility, and a shared vision for a brighter educational future.

References

1. Turing AM (1950) Computing machinery and intelligence. Mind 59:433–460. http://lia.deis.unibo.it/corsi/2005-2006/SID-LS-CE/downloads/turing-article.pdf
2. McCarthy J, Minsky M, Rochester N, Shannon CE (1955) A proposal for the Dartmouth summer research project on artificial intelligence. AI Mag 27(4):12–15. https://doi.org/10.1609/aimag.v27i4.1904
3. Cerri SA, Clancey WJ, Papadourakis G, Panourgia K (2012) Intelligent tutoring systems—11th International Conference, ITS 2012, Chania, Crete, Greece, June 14–18, 2012. Proceedings. Springer Verlag, 7315. Lecture Notes in Computer Science, 978-3-642-30949-6 (Print) 978-3-642-30950-2 (Online). fflirmm-00799116f. https://hal-lirmm.ccsd.cnrs.fr/lirmm-00799116/file/Springer_LNCS_7315.pdf
4. Tuer AW (1897) History of the horn-book. The Leadenhall Press, London (ISBN 9780405090356). https://archive.org/details/b1592871/page/n3/mode/2up
5. Morton H (1867) Erecting the inverted image in the magic lantern. J Franklin Inst 83(6):406–409. https://doi.org/10.1016/0016-0032(67)90376-6
6. Thompson C (2016) How the phonograph changed music forever. Smithsonian Magazine https://www.smithsonianmag.com/arts-culture/phonograph-changed-music-forever-180957677/
7. Essinger J (2007) Jacquard's web: how a hand-loom led to the birth of the information age. OUP, Oxford (ISBN 978-0-19280578-2). https://global.oup.com/academic/product/jacquards-web-9780192805782
8. Kemler L (n.d.) History of technology in the classroom. Sutori. https://www.sutori.com/en/story/history-of-technology-in-the-classroom--DNKnTqJhPG3nTDZ1RUzo3mNo
9. Finstad A (1952) New developments in audio-visual materials. Higher Educ 8(15):169–179. https://archive.org/details/sim_higher-education-us_1952-04-01_8_15/mode/2up
10. The Online Pen Company (n.d.) The history of the ballpoint pen. https://www.theonlinepencompany.com/us/ballpoint-pens/history
11. Anne (2012) The invention of the ballpoint pen and its effect on literacy. ETEC540: Text, Technologies. https://blogs.ubc.ca/etec540sept12/2012/10/28/the-invention-of-the-ballpoint-pen-and-its-effects-on-literacy/
12. Smith CL (2011) Now hear this: the history of headphones. The Guardian. https://www.theguardian.com/business/2011/oct/30/history-of-headphones
13. Watters A (2013) The early days of videotaped lectures. Hybrid Pedagogy. https://hybridpedagogy.org/the-early-days-of-videotaped-lectures/
14. Watters A (n.d.) The engineered student: on B.F. Skinner's teaching machine. The MIT Press Reader. https://thereader.mitpress.mit.edu/the-engineered-student-on-b-f-skinners-teaching-machine/
15. Thompson C (2015) How the photocopier changed the way we worked—and played. Smithsonian Magazine. https://www.smithsonianmag.com/history/duplication-nation-3D-printing-rise-180954332/
16. Hamrick KB (1996) The history of the hand-held electronic calculator. Am Math Monthly 103(8):633–639. https://doi.org/10.2307/2974875
17. Veronese K (2012) The birth of Scantrons, the bane of standardized testing. Gizmodo https://gizmodo.com/the-birth-of-scantrons-the-bane-of-standardized-testin-5908833
18. Snyder T (1993) 120 years of American education: a statistical portrait. National Center for Education Statistics, US Department of Education. https://nces.ed.gov/pubs93/93442.pdf

19. National Center for Education Statistics (2023) College enrollment rates. Institute of Education Sciences, US Department of Education. https://nces.ed.gov/programs/coe/indicator/cpb
20. Fried CB (2007) In-class laptop use and its effects on student learning. Comput Educ 50(3):906–914. https://doi.org/10.1016/j.compedu.2006.09.006
21. Brown M (1982) Personal computer "Man of the Year". This Day in Tech History. https://thisdayintechhistory.com/12/26/personal-computer-man-of-the-year/
22. Gallagher W (2023) Macintosh launched on Jan 24, 1984 and changed the world—eventually. Apple Insider. https://appleinsider.com/articles/19/01/24/apple-launched-macintosh-on-january-24-1984-and-changed-the-world----eventually
23. ETHW (2022) Toshiba T1100: a pioneering contribution to the development of laptop PC, 1985. https://ethw.org/Milestones:Toshiba_T1100,_a_Pioneering_Contribution_to_the_Development_of_Laptop_PC,_1985
24. CERN (n.d.) Where the Web was born. https://www.home.cern/science/computing/birth-web/short-history-web
25. Federal Communications Commission (2004) The Internet: looking back on how we got connected to the world. https://transition.fcc.gov/omd/history/internet/documents/newsletter.pdf
26. Cate JW (2017) Students to computer ratio, socioeconomic status, and student achievement. Electronic Theses and Dissertations, Paper 3284. East Tennessee State University https://dc.etsu.edu/etd/3284
27. Pew Research Center (2024) Mobile fact sheet. https://www.pewresearch.org/internet/fact-sheet/mobile/?tabId=tab-428a8f10-3b74-4b36-ad2d-183a4ba27180
28. Al-Chaer ED (2023) The future of the university: outlook for a twenty-first-century-economy. In: Badran A et al (eds) Higher education in the Arab world: e-learning and distance education. Springer, Cham. https://doi.org/10.1007/978-3-031-33568-6
29. CHESScom (2018) Kasparov vs. Deep Blue: the match that changed history. https://www.chess.com/article/view/deep-blue-kasparov-chess
30. Silver D, Schrittwieser J, Simonyan K et al (2017) Mastering the game of Go without human knowledge. Nature 550:354–359. https://doi.org/10.1038/nature24270
31. Lefkowitz M (2019) Professor's perceptron paved the way for AI—60 years too soon. Cornell Chronicle. https://news.cornell.edu/stories/2019/09/professors-perceptron-paved-way-ai-60-years-too-soon
32. Hintze A (2016) Understanding the four types of AI, from reactive robots to self-aware beings. The Conversation. https://theconversation.com/understanding-the-four-types-of-ai-from-reactive-robots-to-self-aware-beings-67616
33. Onion A, Sullivan M, Mullen M, Zapata C (1997) Deep Blue defeats Garry Kasparov in chess match. History.com. https://www.history.com/this-day-in-history/deep-blue-defeats-garry-kasparov-in-chess-match
34. Regona M, Yigitcanlar T, Xia B, Li RYM (2022) Opportunities and adoption challenges of AI in the construction industry: a PRISMA review. J Open Innovat Technol Market Complexity 8(45). https://doi.org/10.3390/joitmc8010045
35. Center for Integrative Research in Computing and Learning Services (2024) Glossary of artificial intelligence terms for educators. https://circls.org/educatorcircls/ai-glossary
36. Open Text (2021) Robotic process automation: taking an agnostic approach. White Paper. https://www.opentext.com/assets/documents/en-US/pdf/opentext-wp-robotic-process-automation-en.pdf
37. Samuel AL (1959) Some studies in machine learning using the game of checkers. IBM J Res Devel 44(1.2):206–226 (CiteSeerX 10.1.1.368.2254). https://doi.org/10.1147/rd.441.0206
38. Gopala KP (2023) Article on machine learning. LinkedIn. https://www.linkedin.com/pulse/article-machine-learning-gopala-krishnan-p

39. Brown S (2021) Machine learning, explained. MIT Sloan School of Management. https://mitsloan.mit.edu/ideas-made-to-matter/machine-learning-explained
40. IBM (n.d.) What is machine learning? https://www.ibm.com/topics/machine-learning
41. Intel (nd) What is machine vision? https://www.intel.com/content/www/us/en/manufacturing/what-is-machine-vision.html
42. Gillis AS, Lutkevich B, Burns E (2024) Natural language processing (NLP). TechTarget. https://www.techtarget.com/searchenterpriseai/definition/natural-language-processing-NLP
43. Yasar K, Hanna KT (2023) Robotics. TechTarget. https://www.techtarget.com/whatis/definition/robotics
44. Garsten E (2024) What are self-driving cars? The technology explained. Forbes Innovation. https://www.forbes.com/sites/technology/article/self-driving-cars/
45. Martineau K (2023) What is generative AI? IBM. https://research.ibm.com/blog/what-is-generative-AI
46. Abedi M, Beikverdi A (2012) Rise of massive open online courses. 4th international congress on engineering education, Georgetown, Malaysia, pp 1–4. https://doi.org/10.1109/ICEED.2012.6779278
47. Soares L (2012) A 'disruptive' look at competency-based education. CAP 20. https://www.americanprogress.org/article/a-disruptive-look-at-competency-based-education/
48. Gallagher CW (2014) Disrupting the game-changer: remembering the history of competency-based education. Change Magazine Higher Learn 46(6):16–23. https://doi.org/10.1080/00091383.2014.969177
49. Flahive G (2018) The story of a voice: HAL in '2001' wasn't always so eerily calm. The New York Times. https://www.nytimes.com/2018/03/30/movies/hal-2001-a-space-odyssey-voice-douglas-rain.html
50. IEEE-USA Board of Directors (2017) Artificial intelligence research, development and regulation. IEEE. http://globalpolicy.ieee.org/wp-content/uploads/2017/10/IEEE17003.pdf
51. Friedman L, Blair Black N, Walker E, Roschelle J (2021) Safe AI in education needs you. Communications of the ACM. https://cacm.acm.org/blogs/blog-cacm/256657-safe-ai-in-education-needs-you/fulltext
52. Russell S (2019) Human compatible: artificial intelligence and the problem of control. Viking (ISBN 978-0-525-55861-3). https://www.amazon.com/Human-Compatible-Artificial-Intelligence-Problem/dp/0525558616
53. Gartner (nd) Augmented intelligence. Gartner Glossary. https://www.gartner.com/en/information-technology/glossary/augmented-intelligence
54. Englebart DC (1962) Augmenting human intellect: a conceptual framework. SRI Summary Report AFOSR-3223. Doug Engelbart Institute. https://www.dougengelbart.org/pubs/augment-3906.html
55. Hanover Research (2023) Benefits, challenges, and sample use cases of artificial intelligence in higher education. Inside Higher Ed. https://www.insidehighered.com/sites/default/files/2023-10/Benefits%2C%20Challenges%2C%20and%20Sample%20Use%20Cases%20of%20AI%20in%20Higher%20Education.pdf
56. Mitrano T (2023) Coping with ChatGPT. Inside Higher Ed. https://www.insidehighered.com/blogs/law-policy—and-it/coping-chatgpt
57. Schroeder R (2023) Generative AI in college and departmental administration. Inside Higher Ed. https://www.insidehighered.com/opinion/blogs/online-trending-now/2023/08/02/generative-ai-college-and-departmental-administration
58. Rouhiainen L (2019) How AI and data could personalize higher education. Harvard Business Review. https://hbr.org/2019/10/how-ai-and-data-could-personalize-higher-education
59. Jones BM (2023) How generative AI tools help transform academic research. Forbes. https://www.forbes.com/sites/beatajones/2023/09/28/how-generative-ai-tools-help-transform-academic-research

60. Galin L (2023) Changing campus safety with AI-driven video analytics. eCampusNews. https://www.ecampusnews.com/campus-leadership/2023/06/09/campus-safety-video-analytics/
61. Bogost I (2022) ChatGPT is dumber than you think. The Atlantic. https://www.theatlantic.com/technology/archive/2022/12/chatgpt-openai-artificial-intelligence-writing-ethics/672386/
62. Ray PP (2023) ChatGPT: a comprehensive review on background, applications, key challenges, bias, ethics, limitations and future scope. Internet Things Cyber-Phys Syst 3:121–154. https://doi.org/10.1016/j.iotcps.2023.04.003
63. Burt A (2019) The AI transparency paradox. Harvard Business Review. https://hbr.org/2019/12/the-ai-transparency-paradox
64. AIContentfy team (2023) The impact of AI on content accuracy and reliability. AIContentfy. https://aicontentfy.com/en/blog/impact-of-ai-on-content-accuracy-and-reliability
65. Friis S, Riley J (2023) Eliminating algorithmic bias is just the beginning of equitable AI. Harvard Business Review. https://hbr.org/2023/09/eliminating-algorithmic-bias-is-just-the-beginning-of-equitable-ai
66. Tyson A, Pasquini G, Spencer A, Funk C (2023) 60% of Americans would be uncomfortable with provider relying on AI in their own health care. Pew Research Center. https://www.pewresearch.org/science/2023/02/22/60-of-americans-would-be-uncomfortable-with-provider-relying-on-ai-in-their-own-health-care/
67. Appel G, Neelbauer J, Schweidel DA (2023) Generative AI has an intellectual property problem. Harvard Business Review. https://hbr.org/2023/04/generative-ai-has-an-intellectual-property-problem
68. Lazzaro S (2024) Generative AI is increasingly being used to defraud businesses of big money and no one is prepared. Fortune. https://fortune.com/2024/02/08/generative-ai-fraud-identity-theft-cybersecurity-risk/
69. IBM (nd) What are AI hallucinations? https://www.ibm.com/topics/ai-hallucinations
70. Keary T (2023) Prompt injection attack. Technopedia. https://www.techopedia.com/definition/prompt-injection-attack
71. National Cyber Security Centre (NCSC) (2024) AI and cyber security: what you need to know. Guidance. https://www.ncsc.gov.uk/guidance/ai-and-cyber-security-what-you-need-to-know
72. White B (2023) Potential opportunities and risks AI poses for ESG performance. National Law Review XIV(58). https://www.natlawreview.com/article/potential-opportunities-and-risks-ai-poses-esg-performance

The Personal Learning Environment (PLE): A Student-Centered Approach that Supports a Techno-Social Digital Transformation in Higher Education

Nada Dabbagh

Abstract This chapter describes the origins and history of personalized learning (PL) and argues that the personalized learning interaction framework or PLiF, and the personal learning environments or PLE, are contemporary approaches of PL that have the potential to address the challenges we are facing in higher education. The chapter describes the learning ecology, research underpinnings, and applications of PLiF and PLEs in higher education settings, and suggests that these socio-technical frameworks support the development of agency in lifelong learning, continuous learning, and learning on demand. The chapter also proposes the PLE as a digital transformation system that recognizes the ecologies in which people learn, how the elements of those ecologies interact to transform the learning process, what this means for the practice of teaching and learning, and how organizations such as higher education institutions can leverage the PLE as a student-centered digital learning ecosystem to create a de-centralized approach that can handle impending changes in the technological, pedagogical, and organizational infrastructure of university systems.

Keywords Personalized learning · Personal learning environments · Digital learning · Digital transformation · Learning technologies · Learning interactions · Learning ecosystems · Lifelong learning

1 Introduction

If something has exceptionally changed in education it is the environments in which people learn that are now full of emerging resources and technologies that scatter learning experiences across institutional, geographic, societal, and

N. Dabbagh (✉)
Division of Learning Technologies, College of Education and Human Development, George Mason University, Fairfax, USA
e-mail: ndabbagh@gmu.edu

economic boundaries, resulting in the personalization and globalization of the learning experience [1]. In other words, learning can no longer be understood by focusing solely on knowledge acquisition, cognitive development, or the behavior of individual learners. Rather, it necessitates acknowledgment of its situated, sociocultural, and lifelong nature, as well as the tools employed by learners to construct meaning within the contextual framework in which these tools are utilized (also known as socio-technical or socio-material entanglement). As Veletsianos et al. [2] suggest, "learning is a practice situated in environments—places, spaces, and times, with particular people, in particular contexts, with particular technologies, within particular institutions" (p. 319).

Therefore, we have to pay particular attention to the learning activity and how we understand the relationships or interactions among the actors towards this activity. For example, we could start by asking what types of learning activities or interactions are students engaging in? And how are they using technology to engage in such interactions? The personalized learning interaction framework (PLiF) [3] presents five types of learning interactions that students engage in on a regular basis using technology:

1. Learner to content interaction.
2. Learner to learner interaction.
3. Learner to small group interaction.
4. Learner to mentor, coach or artificial intelligence (AI) assistant interaction.
5. Learner to community of practice (COP) or social network interaction.

In this chapter, we extend the PLiF beyond its five dimensions of interation to focus on the learner who is at the center of this framework. We propose the personal learning environment or PLE as a student-centered digital learning approach that addresses the challenges and changes higher education is facing. One of the most promising aspects of the PLE is its capability to help learners connect formal, non-formal and informal learning experiences. By integrating those experiences, PLEs are making lifelong learning, continuous learning, or learning on-demand an achievable goal. More specifically, PLEs enable everyday citizens to leverage technology to build and pursue meaningful, adaptive, and flexible education pathways to accommodate their learning, work, and life goals and become successful agents and curators of their own learning over their lifetime.

When implemented as a contemporary pedagogical and technological approach, PLEs can have a transformational impact on the ways people think, live, interact, work, and communicate. Within the higher education landscape, PLEs can support the development of new technological, organizational, pedagogical, and social infrastructures that allow institutions to initiate a cultural shift to adopt new business models and/or changes to current processes of teaching, learning, research, support services, and administration. Adopting a digital transformation (DX) culture within the university validates the application of a personalized, student-centered approach to teaching and learning and promotes an environment based on flexibility, collaboration, and creativity.

A discernible and widening disparity has emerged between the knowledge imparted within higher education and the dynamic skill sets demanded by the contemporary workplace [4]. The rapid evolution of skills—and the uptick in skills-based hiring—has placed conventional universities in a race against time to recalibrate their curricula accordingly. Against this backdrop, a new breed of agile institutions has risen, poised to confront this challenge head on. These avant-garde institutions are not only drawing a surge of students, but also orchestrating a comprehensive transformation of the educational terrain. Therefore, questions we need to ask given this transformation could include: *How can traditional universities adapt to today's evolving educational landscape? How can we as educators respond to this changing landscape? How can we reinvent the student experience? How can our education systems be reshaped to foster student-centered approaches while also keeping up-to-date with the growing demands of the twenty-first century?*

In this chapter, we describe how PLEs enable personal and social learning experiences that empower learners to direct their own learning and develop lifelong learning skills, crossing institutional and organizational boundaries and evolving over time and place, making competencies visible and attainable in education and workplace contexts. We begin by describing the origins and history of personalized learning (PL) and how the PLiF and the PLE are contemporary instantiations of PL that address DX in higher education. We end the chapter with a vision for the PLE as a digital learning ecosystem that recognizes the ecologies in which people learn, how the elements of those ecologies interact to transform the learning process, what this means for the practice of teaching and learning, and how organizations such as higher education institutions can leverage the PLE as a student-centered digital learning ecosystem to create a de-centralized approach that can handle impending changes in the technological, pedagogical, and organizational infrastructure of university systems.

The world is changing rapidly through the massive use of digital technologies and these changes, especially after the COVID-19 outbreak, have highlighted the need to adapt quickly to new working, social and learning conditions. To face these changes and challenges brought by DX, individuals need to develop new skills and competences within a lifelong learning process. We envision the PLE as a techno-social reality that reflects the intricate interconnection of social and material elements influencing the learning process. Personal learning environments can bridge the gap between skills taught in school and skills desired in the workplace by putting education to work. The PLE can serve as an approach that puts into practice modern concepts regarding the ways in which individuals learn offering a pedagogical approach for higher education institutions that wish to ensure workforce sustainability through career preparation and secure the future of generations through workplace skills development.

2 Personalized Learning

Personalized learning has roots that reach back to the time of Aristotle. The history of PL has taken many forms and approaches; most notable is the dichotomy of learner-based personalization and systems-based personalization. These PL approaches are largely driven by a multitude of variables that are used to personalize the learning experience such as who should conduct the personalization (e.g., the learner, the teacher, the system), what can be personalized (e.g., the content, the learning activities, the assessment), where should personalization occur (e.g., in the classroom, outside the classroom, throughout the curriculum), and how should personalization occur (e.g., what tools, models or frameworks can be used for personalization). Personalized learning strategies are also hugely grounded in learning theories and approaches to education.

For example, learner-based personalization is grounded in constructivist learning theory which posits that learners create or construct knowedge from their own experiences as they interact with learning content and engage in learning activities. In other words, the learner is at the center of learning and is an active participant in the learning process; interpreting knowledge, and constructing personal meaning based on their beliefs, experiences, backgrounds, and culture. Learner-based personalization can be characterized as active, constructive, collaborative, intentional, and authentic [5]. Pedagogical models that support constructivism include problem-based learning (PBL), communities of practice (COP), situated learning (SL), cognitive apprenticeships (CA), and goal-based scenarios (GBS). In each of these constructivist-based pedagogical models, the learner is an active participant in the learning process and engages in self-directed learning, collaborative learning, and authentic learning.

In contrast, systems-based personalization is grounded in behaviorist or objectivist learning theory or epistemology which advocates that learners are passive recipients of information and that knowledge is transferred from outside sources (e.g. experts or teachers) onto the learner's memory. Behaviorism or objectivism ignores the concept of a "mind" and instead focuses reinforcement as a way to change behavior—which would therefore indicate learning. The goal is to get the learner to provide the desired response when given the correct stimuli. This can be achieved through providing cues, selective reinforcement, practice, and feedback. Learner-based personalization is designed to instruct learners by introducing new material in small steps and allowing the learner to advance at their own pace based on their performance [6–8]. This is also known as adaptive learning or adaptive instructional systems.

The advantages of systems-based personalization or adaptive instructional systems may be best leveraged when the learning task is well structured (i.e., when there are rules that constitute right and wrong answers). However, when we need to engage our learners in higher-order thinking skills and ill-structured learning tasks that involve analyzing, creating, and evaluating, then learner-based personalization becomes a much more effective pedagogical approach to PL.

3 A Continuum of Personalized Learning

While learner-based personalization and systems-based personalization were historically the dominant approaches for PL, Gallagher and Prestwich [9] argue that PL is not a dichotomous phenomenon, rather PL falls on a continuum from micro- to macro-instructional approaches as depicted in Fig. 1.

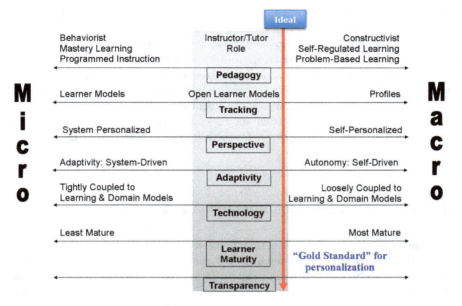

Fig. 1 Dimensions of personalization

Figure 1 illustrates that PL is a broad construct that ranges from a macro-end in which the learner has complete agency, ownership, and autonomy over the learning process, to a micro-end where a "teaching machine" or system makes the decision for the learner based on its evaluation of the learners' aptitudes or performance. What is important to note here is that neither of these approaches to PL is fundamentally right or wrong; rather, the best approach towards designing a PL experience requires a mix of strategies that take into consideration learning theory, learning models, instructional strategies, learning tasks, learning outcomes, learner maturity, and technology, and to ensure that these strategies or dimenstions are pedagogically aligned.

In fact, the results of a Delphi Study [10] revealed that experts ($n=224$) characterized PL by new learning models and practices, flexible learning pathways, flexible learning assessments, and where technology is integral to supporting a variety of user-centered learning interactions. More specifically, PL is seen by these experts as learner-driven, and facilitated through a variety of socio-technological interrelationships extending beyond content [10]. In other words, PL was perceived by these experts as driven by a series of interactions that include learner to content; learner to learner; learner to small group; learner to mentor, coach or AI assistant; and learner to community of practice or social network, which are the interactions depicted in the PLiF.

Additionally, the results of a 2021 study by Fake and Dabbagh [11] revealed that the majority of participants described PL as involving the learner with input from a wide range of social relationships, social networks, and collaborative technologies, suggesting that a social element to PL was important to workforce leaders. Other research has come to similar conclusions, demonstrating the power of social media in supporting the creation of PL experiences [12]. A key takeaway from this research suggests that "personalized learning requires connections to social networks and communities of practice within and outside the organization" [3, p. 196]. Hence, enabling ongoing engagement with peers, mentors, coaches, and social networks on a variety of subjects and organizational topics, using the PLiF, may need to become a priority for those implementing personalized learning in workforce education.

4 Personalized Learning Interaction Framework

The personalized learning interaction framework or PLiF builds upon Moore's interaction model [13] and as mentioned earlier, it emerged based on the results of a 2018 Delphi study in which experts were asked to define PL, its dimensions, attributes, and theoretical underpinnings, and how they integrate PL in the workplace as a workforce training strategy or as an instructional or pedagogical approach in higher-education contexts. The PLiF can be viewed as an educational framework that integrates learner-based personalization through socio-cultural and socio-technical learning interactions. This approach is not only in line with andragogical and heutagogical principles but is also made feasible by advancements in information and communications technology (ICT), machine learning, and AI [3, 14]. Figure 2 demonstrates how learner-based personalization is enacted in the PLiF.

As the learner takes a central role in the learning environment, steering or leading the learning process, the PLiF necessitates a shift in the roles of faculty and instructional designers. Instead of directing and designing specific learning experiences, their emphasis shifts to facilitation and guidance. Their responsibility transforms into offering support to learners by providing resources and facilitating the learning process, thereby scaffolding the learners' development of their PL experience. More specifically, research in higher education suggests that the role of faculty in learner-based personalization is to assist students in their learning journey by creating a supportive community, fostering collaboration, and promoting engagement, a growth mindet, self-efficacy and academic tenacity, thereby empowering each student to take charge of their own learning and work towards a long-term goal [15].

Additionally, PLiF can be characterized as an approach or framework with a broad spectrum of applications that are able to integrate some of the most naturalistic ideas about how people learn in the digital environment, the most relevant of which are:

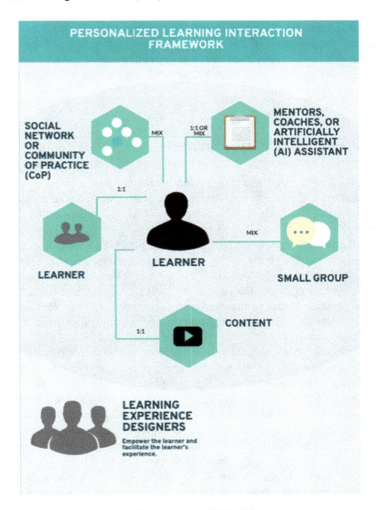

Fig. 2 Personalized learning interaction framework (PLiF [3])

- Learning anytime, anywhere, or what has come to be known as ubiquitous learning [16].
- Adult learning, specifically as this relates to self-directed learning or what is known as heutagogy [17, 18].
- Learning with others as conceptualized by social constructivism [19, 20].
- Learning in connection or connected learning as embraced by connectivism [21]; and networked learning [22].

Next, we propose that the personal learning environment or PLE is a natural application of PLiF in that it addresses the challenges of being in a ubiquitous, continuous, and connected learning mode. The PLE is a pedagogical and technological construct that embodies the socio-material entanglement with which people learn. The PLE can form the core of a learning activity ecosystem that is diverse, personalized, social, adaptive, integrated, and transparent, enabling the creation of a network of learning that supports students as peers, creators and entrepreneurs, and agents of their own learning [1].

5 Personal Learning Environments

The pursuit of on-demand learning, fueled by the constant evolution of technology, has become a lifestyle in contemporary society. This dynamic compels learners to consistently seek information to address work or school-related challenges or to satisfy their curiosity [23].

Achieving this requires leveraging digital and networked technologies not only for information retrieval but also for information sharing. Consequently, learners should be seen not merely as passive consumers of information but as active contributors to content creation. Recent studies indicate that modern-day students are increasingly taking control of their learning journey by utilizing Web 2.0 technologies to construct their PLEs, highlighting the socio-technical or socio-technological aspect of learning [24–26].

Web 2.0 technologies, alternatively referred to as social media technologies or social software, encompass tools for sharing experiences and resources, social networking, and mobile and immersive technologies. These technologies marked the second phase of the World Wide Web, signifying a qualitative shift in how information is generated, delivered, and accessed online [27]. Notably, Web 2.0 introduced a novel approach to utilizing ICTs, diverging significantly from their use in the Web 1.0 era. Specifically, Web 2.0 technologies empower users to create their own content and directly engage with online experiences. This is why Web 2.0 is commonly referred to as the "Social Web," embodying concepts such as openness, personalization, customization, participation, social presence, user-generated content, and the democratization of the web [28–30].

The social side of Web 2.0 and its implications on the education sector was emphasized in the 2014 NMC (New Media Consortium) Horizon Report [31] particularly as this relates to social media use and how this is changing the way students and educators interact, present information, and judge the quality of content and contributions. For instance, Web 2.0 technologies facilitated increased levels of dialogue, interaction, and collaboration among learners through social networks. They empowered learners to create and share knowledge within learning networks. Moreover, Web 2.0 technologies shifted control of learning away from a singular instructor or expert, distributing it among all participants in the learning community. This encouraged agency in the learning process and fostered an appreciation for diversity, multiple perspectives, and epistemic issues. Additionally, Web 2.0 technologies allowed learners to modify their learning environment by choosing the technologies they prefer, accessing and organizing information sources, customizing the user interface of a technology or app, and establishing PL pathways and professional networks [32].

In a 2017 study in which 109 ($n = 109$) students in a higher education context were asked what tools they use for personal learning. The results revealed that search engines, videos (YouTube), and social networks were the top three, which is consistent with the affordances of Web 2.0 technologies [24]. Additionally, students reported that their ideal PLE would include tools that facilitate discussion, collaboration and interaction; tools that facilitate the organization, planning, and management of learning resources; and tools that support progress tracking.

Here are some examples of how students envisioned their ideal PLE:

Student A The pandemic has made me a master at creating personal learning environments. Since students are learning from home, parents were required to develop spaces that really provide comfort and encourage learning. I set up 2 separate spaces for my kindergartener and my second grader on 2 different floors. They each have tool kits, dry erase boards, 2 work spaces, pencils, board to hang their work, etc. Seeing how they are thriving as a result, my idea of a Personal Learning Environment is similar, with a few tweaks.

Student B My PLE is one that provides peace and support for learning. Aside from my current set up including double monitors, a window view (door that can open to let in fresh air), and different table levels to work, I wish to have access to each cutting-edge software at my fingertips, along with support for learning them. Also, I would like a closet that would allow neat storage of all of my gadgets. It would be nice to have a meditation/workout space that does not have to be converted for another use.

Student C My ideal PLE would be a tool that can help keep track of my learning path, provide storage and classification of learning materials and site addresses, be an AI enabled chat bot or virtual assistant that can provide some digital assistance. Record online searches and suggested future searches in a secure manner.

Student D I think for me my Ideal PLE would offer me a truly curated experience. I would love to have an online/offline resource where I could manage all the learning I have ever participated in. This software would not only track my learning experiences but also organize content by topic, modality, date, and many other attributes so that I could search my personal database at any point. I would also think that it would be advantageous to have some way to organize all of the content I have ever created. I created a lot of great work as an undergrad, and professional yet over the years it has been misplaced. Having all that content in one space would allow me to see how I have grown as a learner throughout the years.

Student F My ideal PLE would be like an "all in one" learning environment. I would like it if I had the ability to save resources to look at in the future and also it would be designed as a learning environment that am able to use to learn at my own pace and click around or browse or explore. It would also include a space for me to practice what I have learned.

In a follow-up study [25], students ($n = 622$) in a large public university in the U.S. were surveyed about the technologies (hardware and software) they use most frequently for learning, the technologies they value most for learning, and how effective they perceive technology in supporting their learning. The results revealed that laptops and smartphones were most frequently used for learning and highly valued, underscoring the importance of mobile and portable devices in supporting anytime-anywhere learning. The results also revealed that Web 2.0 technologies were perceived as highly effective in supporting PL.

These findings suggest that PLEs are not a stable or monolithic learning technology that can be standardized or used in a controlled environment, rather, PLEs cross institutional and organizational boundaries and evolve over time and place [33]. As Haworth [34] emphasized, PLEs are not persistent learning environments, rather, they are dynamic and evolve according to learners' objectives and achievements. Moreover, tools used in PLEs must be dynamic to allow learners to continue to have access to learning materials across the lifespan.

In fact, some researchers (e.g., [23, 35–37]) argue that PLEs became popular in reaction to the institutional learning management system or LMS that colleges and universities are so reliant on. These LMSs do not capitalize on the pedagogical affordances of social media technologies such as allowing learners to manage and maintain a learning space that facilitates their own learning activities as well as connections to peers and social networks across time and place [36, 37]. Hence the PLE can be perceived as a digital space for integrating formal and informal learning, supporting PL, lifelong learning, and continuous learning. We cannot say the same for the LMS. Although LMSs were initially designed to provide a flexible platform for advanced learning pedagogies, research has progressively shown that LMSs emphasize faculty dissemination tools over student learning tools even though the latter is more likely to promote student engagement and interaction [38–42]. On the other hand, PLEs are becoming increasingly effective in addressing issues of learner control and personalization that are often absent in an institutional LMS.

The difference in infrastructure between LMSs and PLEs can best be explained using Simon Nicholson's *Theory of Loose Parts*. Developed by Nicholson in 1972, the gist of the theory is the idea that loose parts (in this case how a PLE is created using social media technologies), i.e., materials that can be moved around, combined, redesigned, and tinkered with, create infinitely more opportunities for creative engagement and ingenuity than static materials and environments (which characterize the LMS):

> A term strongly connected to loose parts is "open-ended." Open-ended materials, environments, and experiences encourage problem solving and are child centered. Children involve themselves in concrete experiences using loose parts, which lead to explorations that occur naturally, as opposed to adult directed. However, adults do play important, intentional roles in preparing, guiding, and documenting open-ended learning experiences. Loose parts pave the way for critical thinking. It allows the children to have their own ideas, to make things the way they decide, and to figure out for themselves how to make their idea work. (https://thewideschool.com/the-theory-of-loose-parts/)

The PLE concept can be closely aligned with the *Theory of Loose Parts*. There is strong research evidence that social media technologies can empower learners to use a variety of technologies to create or design their own learning spaces and experiences that help them aggregate and share the results of learning achievements, participate in collective knowledge generation, and manage their own meaning making [12, 27]. Furthermore, there is strong research evidence that PLEs can promote culturally responsive teaching [43] by allowing the integration of the learner's cultural background and experiences into the learning process.

Figure 3 demonstrates the pedagogical ecology of Web 2.0 technologies and the recursive and reciprocal interaction between three components that constitute the design of a learning environment: the technological component or learning technology (top vertex), the learning activity or learning interaction that students engage in (bottom right corner of the triangle), and the pedagogical framework or instructional approach or application (bottom left corner). This alignment is premised on the principle that technology is not neutral, rather, there exists a mutuality between our tools and our intentions—while our tools are the product of our intentions, they also shape our intentions in turn [44]. The double-sided arrows in Fig. 3 depict a reciprocal, cyclical and iterative relationship between these three components in which patterns of technology use shape our instructional practices and learning interactions, which in turn shape our learning theories and pedagogical models leading to the emergence of new learning technologies with new pedagogical affordances. This three-component model [45] embodies the non-neutrality of the learning space and emphasizes the pedagogical affordances (capabilities) of learning technologies.

The learning capabilities provided by cloud-based Web 2.0 technologies are the driving force behind the contemporary notion of PLEs. In fact PLEs are increasingly recognized as a valuable platform for student learning [12]. PLEs encompass "the combination of technologies, sources of information, connections, as well as the cognitive processes, experiences, and strategies that each person—the learner—routinely employs for learning within a sociocultural context" [1, p. 3043].

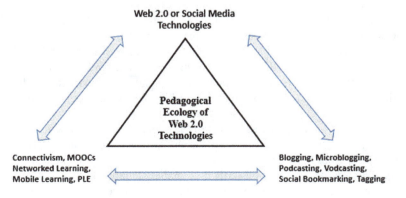

Fig. 3 Pedagogical ecology of Web 2.0 technologies

In the twenty-first century, PLEs have been steadily gaining ground as an effective platform for student learning and have been described by scholars such as Brigid Barron, Stephen Downes, Tom Haskins, Scott Wilson, and Mark van Harmelen as individual educational platforms, self-initiated and interest-driven learning environments, unique creations of individual learners that help shape their knowledge and understandings, self-directed learning systems, and methods and tools that help students organize and self-manage their learning [3].

Additionally, PLEs represent "a reality that incorporates both human and technological elements and activities, shaping and influencing how an individual learns" [1, p. 3043], inherently establishing PLEs as sociotechnical environments. As a result, learning within PLEs constitutes an intricate system of activities, interactions, and experiences that necessitates effective research and scaffolding. In a PLE, the student chooses the tools that match their learning preference and pace, and the student decides how to organize and manage the content to learn effectively and efficiently. Consequently, PLEs can be perceived as a single student's educational or e-learning platform, allowing collaboration with other students, experts, instructors, mentors, coaches, etc., and coordination of such interactions across a wide range of systems and learning communities. Given this description of PLEs, the following questions need to be asked: *Are students (learners, individuals) ready to take this on? Are learners ready to drive their own learning using the PLE approach? Do learners possess the strategies and skills needed to develop and maintain an effective and ever-evolving PLE for a lifetime of learning?*

Overall, the research suggests that social media are being increasingly used as tools for developing formal and informal learning spaces or experiences that start out as an individual learning platform or PLE, enabling individual knowledge management and construction, and evolve into a social learning platform or system where knowledge is socially mediated [12]. The research also suggests that social-media use in higher education is enabling the creation of PLEs that empower students with a sense of personal agency in the learning process. However, in order to successfully leverage social media towards the creation of PLEs, students must acquire and apply a set of personal knowledge management (PKM) skills, defined as "the act of managing one's personal knowledge through technologies" [12, p. 127], ranging from creating, organizing and sharing digital content and information, to higher-order or more-complex PKM skills such as connectedness, the ability to balance formal and informal contexts, critical ability, and creativity [46]. Specifically, PLEs require the development and application of self-regulated learning (SRL) skills because PLEs are built bottom-up, starting with personal goals, information management, and individual knowledge construction, and progressing to socially mediated knowledge and networked learning [27, 47].

Self-regulated learning or SRL refers to the degree to which students are able to become active participants of their own learning process and proactively engage in self-motivating and behavioral processes that increase goal attainment. Moreover, SRL is also regarded as a set of skills that enable students to set learning or task goals, identify learning or task strategies needed to achieve those goals, and reflect on the efficacy of the strategies and processes that helped them achieve their goals. The relationship between PLEs and SRL is intuitive and interdependent and social media technologies have pedagogical affordances that can foster this relationship. Specifically, PLEs can be perceived as a pedagogical approach that facilitates SRL through the deliberate and strategic integration of formal and informal learning using digital and social media technologies.

To summarize this discussion, a PLE is a promising student-centered pedagogical approach that allows learners to leverage technology to build and pursue meaningful, adaptive, and flexible education pathways to accommodate their learning, work, and life goals and become successful agents and curators of their own learning over their lifetimes. Educause [48] defines PLEs as *tools, communities, and services that constitute the individual educational platforms learners use to direct their own learning and pursue educational goals.* In other words, a PLE is a freely assembled ecosystem, consisting of any set of communication and collaboration channels, cloud resources, web apps and social media, that (a) enables learner agency in creating educational pathways to achieve learning, work, and life goals; (b) expands reach to diverse learners, including low-income and first generation learners who may be ill-served by the current higher education system; and (c) allows access to a much broader higher education ecosystem that includes non-traditional classes, learning resources, and education providers such as MOOCs, bootcamps, and open educational resources (OERs) as well as on-the-job training and informal learning. By empowering learners to freely and strategically design their own learning journeys through PLEs and supporting seamless transitions between a learner's PLE and the broader education ecosystem, we will generate a more open, inclusive, and distributed learning ecosystem that benefits all education stakeholders and helps to address twenty-first century skills gaps by creating opportunities for lifelong learning and recognition of skills developed in different learning experiences and diverse contexts.

The underlying principle of a PLE is that the student is put in charge of designing his or her own learning environment. In a PLE, the student develops an individualized digital identity through the perceptual cues and cognitive affordances that the PLE provides, such as what information to share and when, who to share it with, and how to effectively merge formal and informal learning experiences to achieve learning goals. Personalized learning environments empower students to take charge of their own learning; therefore, PLEs are inherently self-directed, placing the responsibility for organizing learning on the individual.

Personalized learning environments are increasingly addressing issues of learner control and personalization that are often absent in the institutional LMS. In a PLE, the locus of control shifts away from the institution to individual students, helping them take control of their own learning and build a personal cyberinfrastructure and learning ecosystem that extends learning beyond the boundaries of the classroom, institution, or organization, using distributed and portable tools. In a PLE, the student chooses the tools that match his or her personal learning preferences and pace, and the student decides how to organize and manage the content to learn effectively and efficiently, hence, PLEs are individualized by design.

However, when students (learners) are put in charge of developing a PLE, they need pedagogical guidance and support, particularly if they do not possess SRL skills. With insufficient guidance, students may not be able to create a PLE that cultivates their independent learning skills and helps them achieve their learning goals. This is where the role of faculty (including instructors, trainers, coaches, mentors, AI assistants, etc.) becomes crucial.

6 The PLE as a Transformative Digital Learning Ecosystem

We envision the higher education ecosystem of 2030 to be a student-centered or learner-driven ecosystem where students are able to create PLEs that strategically inform and guide their learning goals and education pathways, choose different education providers to achieve those goals, and attain recognition for their lifelong learning, e.g., with the help of digital credentials such as Open Badges and Blockcerts. The overarching vision of the 2030 education ecosystem is a more diverse, individualized, adaptive, integrated, and transparent system composed of student PLEs, education providers, open educational resources, learning communities, and employment networks in which students can select different education providers to achieve learning goals targeted for specific job skills, and providers can compete for students who are paying for competency-based credit or discrete components of a degree or certification rather than the degree itself. Essentially, such a system aligns with all ten principles put forth by the U.S. Department of Education's Office of Educational Technology in January 2017 for a "student-centered higher education ecosystem".

The term **learning ecosystem** is not just a catchy word or phrase, rather it helps us think about all the components that make up a learning system and how these components interact with each other. It also helps consider a holistic view of the learning environment to include people/learners, training content, technology, learning culture, and business strategy, and examine the complex relationships among these components. Just like when we think about living ecosystems, whether they are self-sustaining or endangered, healthy or sick, nurtured or threatened, thinking about learning ecosystems in this way makes us aware of what is going on inside and outside the organization from a learning and development perspective and how this will impact organizational performance and the bottom line. Walcutt and Schatz [49] suggest that the future learning ecosystem is a substantive reimagination of learning and development due to the need to recognize that learning can no longer be viewed as a single event, nor a series of events, but rather learning must be viewed as a lifelong experience of continual growth. Walcutt and Schatz also suggest that future learning ecosystems must provide personalized pathways for learners to progress through and that deep learning that expedites the transfer of learning from practice to real-world settings must be strongly emphasized.

The concept of a learning ecosystem transcends the traditional approach to designing instruction which generally assumes a given target population (a particular individual or cohort) as well as a specific setting and set of conditions (e.g., specific objectives, subject matter). When we envision learning across lifetimes, this linear approach to designing instruction no longer suffices. We need instructional design models that encompass diverse learning experiences, various media, diverse populations, cultures, and contexts, many of which fall outside the instructional designer's purview. Consequently, we need an updated instructional or learning design approach that [50, p. 226]:

- Facilitates learning as a gestalt derived from the collective sum of all learning events and experiences.
- Recognizes learning outcomes are increasingly self-directed and stitched across different contexts, networks, and communities.
- Actively incorporates technology to enable learning—not only as an instructional delivery mechanism but also as the "glue" to connect learning events to one another.

The PLE can be considered a freely assembled ecosystem consisting of any set of communication and collaboration channels, cloud resources, web apps, and social media technologies that enable learner agency in creating educational pathways to achieve learning, work, and life goals (Fig. 4).

In order to achieve the vision of a student-centered learning ecosystem that is premised on PLEs, several pilots/phases need to take place. First, we need to ensure that there is a transparent and equitable process for students to create PLEs. Although there are numerous known platforms and technologies that enable the design of PLEs (e.g., Symbaloo, Evernote, Known, PLEBOX, and e-portfolios), a PLE can be created in any technology or set of technologies or tools that support the following six components: personal profiler, aggregator, editor, scaffolds, recommender, and services [51]. Most Web 2.0 technologies (e.g., blogs, wikis, social bookmarking tools, tags, aggregation services) support these six components. In fact, learning in the context of social media technologies has become highly self-motivated, autonomous, and informal, as well as an integral part of the college experience. However, creating PLEs is not just about the Web 2.0 technologies that enable PLEs, it is also about the process that guides the effective design of PLEs, which involves SRL skills such as goal setting, task strategies, help-seeking, time management, self-monitoring, and self-evaluation.

This process is depicted in a three-level framework for scaffolding SRL through the use of social media [12, 52]. For example, in Level 1, *Personal Information Management*, students use Web 2.0 technologies to engage in the SRL processes of goal setting and planning. The goal at this level is to guide students to create a personal or private learning space by self-generating content and managing this content for personal productivity or organizational tasks such as creating online bookmarks, media resources, and personal journals and calendars to localize learning around a specific topic. In Level 2, *Social Interaction and Collaboration*, students activate the social sharing and networking features of the

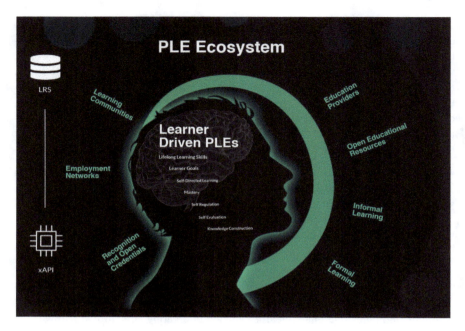

Fig. 4 The personal learning environment (PLE) ecosystem

technology to trigger communication surrounding the learning topic through peers and informal learning communities thereby extending the PLE from a personal learning space to a social learning space. Social and collaborative activities engage students in the SRL processes of self-monitoring and help-seeking, prompting students to identify strategies needed to perform more-formal learning tasks to achieve their goals. In Level 3, *Information Aggregation and Management*, students leverage the technology to synthesize and aggregate information from Levels 1 and 2 in order to reflect on their overall learning experience. This allows them to take greater control of their PLE, customizing it and personalizing it around their learning goals. The SRL processes of self-evaluation, self-reflection, and self-correction are used by the student to influence subsequent efforts of learning goal attainment.

We need to test the three-level framework with college students at different higher education institutions with a sample population that is diverse, cross-cultural, and inclusive of students of various ethnicities and socio-economic status. This first pilot or phase of this project will involve human coaches who will coach students on how to develop PLEs. The second phase or pilot will involve designing and testing an AI coach or personal assistant that scaffolds the design of PLEs for students. The use of AI in education is empowering intelligent tutoring systems which may evolve into "lifelong learning companions" that can gather data and support learners as they grow and develop their knowledge. The AI coach will be modeled on the faculty–student coaching interactions that occurred in the first pilot and will target the six essential technological components of a PLE. The AI coach will scaffold learners in creating a PLE by helping them identify learning goals, link to social networks or learning communities around shared goals, and determine learning pathways that lead to recognition and credentialing of competencies acquired. Design-based research methodology can be used to evaluate the effectiveness of the AI coach in supporting the creation of PLEs and the degree to which students acquired SRL skills.

The third pilot or phase will involve embedding an LRS (learning record store) in the university's LMS or similar platform to collect data on the PLE ecosystem. An LRS enables modern tracking of learning experiences, achievements, and job performance (if needed) across multiple platforms and applications through the use of xAPI technology. The LRS is the heart of any technology-enabled ecosystem and the data collected from a range of learning activities (learning analytics) can be used to support adaptive learning experiences and evaluate the effectiveness of the learning ecosystem in achieving its goals.

This phased research of the PLE ecosystem will allow us to understand the feasibility, scalability, and effectiveness of the PLE as a digital learning ecosystem and the extent to which such an ecosystem would benefit college students and their future workplaces as well as college teachers, education providers and learning resource providers. New ways of teaching and learning would be supported and promoted. A university setting is ideal for testing this ecosystem given the diversity of the student population and the resources available to faculty and students to achieve teaching and learning goals. Risks include the degree to which students are willing to take control of their learning, preparing faculty to transform their teaching practice to accommodate the concept of a PLE, ensuring seamless transitions between the components of the PLE ecosystem, and keeping the PLE ecosystem open and secure.

7 The Importance of Lifelong Learning and the Role of Learner Agency

As our technologies evolve, the pace of change continues to accelerate. The rapidity of change requires workers to be constantly reskilling and retooling their skillset to adapt in the face of operational, social, contextual, and ecological changes [53–55]. Given this dynamic and the constant pivoting of the operational environment, it becomes increasingly important for the organization's future success to develop programs that support workers in cultivating lifelong learning skills. Learning leaders understand the strategic importance of training in sharpening their company's competitive edge, decreasing employee attrition, attracting and retaining top talent, increasing productivity, and addressing the pace of change inherent in a globalizing world where technological disruptions accelerate transformational changes. Competitive organizations share the perspective that continually investing in skill-building, expanding competencies and skillsets, cultivating awareness about changing operational environments, facilitating, and empowering learning relationships, and refining project and people management skills will be key to survival for organizations in the modern age [53, 56]. Attracting top talent may also be won or lost based on a company's dedication to training and development opportunities [56]. The key to survival and success for individuals in this environment is contextual awareness, flexibility, and continuous learning [57]. As Alvin Toffler, author and futurist said, "The illiterate of the twenty-first century will not be those who cannot read and write, but those who cannot learn, unlearn, and relearn." The challenges of being in a continuous learning mode require empowering the learner to develop agency in lifelong learning. Personalizing learning and the PLE framework described in this chapter provide an effective and sustainable solution to addressing this challenge. With historical, theoretical, and pedagogical foundations set, we will continue to explore PL by engaging in related research in multiple educational contexts.

References

1. Dabbagh N, Castaneda L (2020) Beyond personalization: the PLE as a framework for lifelong learning. Educ Technol Res Devel 68(6):3041–3055. https://doi.org/10.1007/s11423-020-09831-z
2. Veletsianos G, Moe R (2017) The rise of educational technology as a sociocultural and ideological phenomenon. Educause. https://er.educause.edu/articles/2017/4/the-rise-of-educational-technology-as-a-sociocultural-and-ideological-phenomenon
3. Fake H, Dabbagh N (2023) Designing personalized learning experiences: a framework for higher education and workforce training. Routledge (ISBN: 9780367631864)
4. Busson S (2023) Exploring the future of education: a journey through Europe's education innovations. https://www.exploringeducation.eu
5. Dabbagh N, Howland J, Marra R (2019) Meaningful online learning: integrating strategies, activities, and learning technologies for effective designs. Routledge, New York
6. Benjamin LT (1988) A history of teaching machines. Am Psychol 43(9):703–712. https://doi.org/10.1037/0003-066X.43.9.703
7. Bates T (2014) A short history of technology. Online Learning and Distance Education Resources [web log post]. http://www.tonybates.ca/2014/12/10/a-short-history-of-educational-technology/
8. Skinner BF (1983) A matter of consequences: part three of an autobiography. Knopf (ISBN: 9780814778456)
9. Gallagher PS, Prestwich S (2013) Developing a personalization strategy for online learning environments. (Personal communication)
10. Fake H (2018) A Delphi study on the dimensions of personalized learning in workforce training and development programs. Dissertation, George Mason University. Proquest. https://www.proquest.com/openview/6f8fee63a380383ad7dbfce0f0f07053/1?pq-origsite=gscholar&cbl=18750&diss=y
11. Fake H, Dabbagh N (2021) The personalized learning interaction framework: expert perspectives on how to apply dimensions of personalized learning in workforce training and development programs. In: Proceedings of the technological ecosystems for enhancing multiculturality (TEEM '21) conference. https://doi.org/10.1145/3486011.3486503

12. Dabbagh N, Kitsantas A (2012) Personal learning environments, social media, and self-regulated learning: a natural formula for connecting formal and informal learning. Internet Higher Educ 15(1):3–8. https://doi.org/10.1016/j.iheduc.2011.06.002
13. Moore MG (1989) Three types of interaction. Am J Distance Educ 3(2):1–7. https://doi.org/10.1080/08923648909526659
14. Bersin J (2023) A new generation of mastery-based learning platforms has arrived (*updated) [web log post]. https://joshbersin.com/2023/01/a-new-generation-of-mastery-based-learning-platforms-has-arrived/
15. Dede C, Richards J, Saxberg B (2019) Learning engineering for online education. Routledge (ISBN: 9780815394426). https://www.routledge.com/Learning-Engineering-for-Online-Education-Theoretical-Contexts-and-Design-Based/Dede-Richards-Saxberg/p/book/9780815394426
16. Taraghi B (2012) Ubiquitous personal learning environment (UPLE). Internat J Emerging Technol Learn 7(2):7–14. https://doi.org/10.3991/ijet.v7iS2.2322
17. Blaschke L M (2012) Heutagogy and lifelong learning: a review of heutagogical practice and self-determined learning. Internat Rev Res Open Distrib Learn 13(1):56–71. https://doi.org/10.19173/irrodl.v13i1.1076
18. Blaschke LM (2013) E-learning and self-determined learning skills. In: Hase S, Kenyon C (eds) Self-determined learning: heutagogy in action. Bloomsbury Academic (ISBN: 971441142771). http://www.daneshnamehicsa.ir/userfiles/file/Manabeh/Self-determined-learning-heutagogy-in-action.pdf
19. Rahimi E, van den Berg J, Veen W (2015) Facilitating student-driven constructing of learning environments using Web 2.0 personal learning environments. Comput Educ 81:235–246. https://doi.org/10.1016/j.compedu.2014.10.012
20. Torres-Kompen R, Edirisingha P, Canaleta X et al (2019) Personal learning environments based on Web 2.0 services in higher education. Telemat Informat 38:194–206. https://doi.org/10.1016/j.tele.2018.10.003
21. Siemens G (2005) Connectivism: a learning theory for the digital age. Internat J Instruct Technol Distance Learn 2(1). http://www.itdl.org/Journal/Jan_05/article01.htm
22. de Laat M, Dohn NB (2019) Is networked learning postdigital education? Postdigital Sci Educ 1(1):17–20. https://doi.org/10.1007/s42438-019-00034-1
23. McLoughlin C, Lee MJW (2008) The three p's of pedagogy for the networked society: personalization, participation, and productivity. Internat J Teach Learn Higher Educ 20(1):10–27. https://www.researchgate.net/publication/284125788
24. Dabbagh N, Fake H (2017) College students' perceptions of personal learning environments (PLEs) through the lens of digital tools, processes, and spaces. J New Approaches Educ Res 6(1):28–36. https://naerjournal.com/article/view/v6n1-4
25. Dabbagh N, Fake H, Zhang X (2019) Student perspectives of the value and effectiveness of technology use for learning in higher education. Revista Iberoamericana de Educación a Distancia (RIED). https://doi.org/10.5944/ried.22.1.22102
26. Dabbagh N, Kwende M (2021) Personal learning environments as digital spaces that are collaborative, adaptive, and autonomous. Ninth international conference on technological ecosystems for enhancing multiculturality (TEEM'21). https://doi.org/10.1145/3486011.3486507
27. Dabbagh N, Reo R (2011) Impact of Web 2.0 on higher education. In: Surry DW et al (eds) Technology integration in higher education: social and organizational aspects. IGI Global, pp 174–187. https://doi.org/10.4018/978-1-60960-147-8.ch013
28. Alexander B (2006) Web 2.0: a new wave of innovation for teaching and learning? EDUCAUSE Rev 41(2):33–34. http://www.educause.edu/ir/library/pdf/ERM0621.pdf
29. Davis M (2008) Semantic wave 2008 report: industry roadmap to web 3.0 & multibillion dollar market opportunities (executive summary). Project 10X. http://www.kawaisouken.com/CEO/repory/report/Semantic%20Wave%202008%20Report.pdf

30. Jones BL (2008) Web 2.0 heroes: interviews with 20 Web 2.0 influencers. Wiley (ISBN: 9780470241998)
31. Johnson L, Becker SA, Estrada V, Freeman A (2014) NMC horizon report: 2014 K. The New Media Consortium. https://files.eric.ed.gov/fulltext/ED559369.pdf
32. Dabbagh N, Howland J, Marra R (2019) Meaningful online learning: integrating strategies, activities, and learning technologies for effective designs. Routledge (ISBN: 9781138694194). https://www.routledge.com/Meaningful-Online-Learning-Integrating-Strategies-Activities-and-Learning/Dabbagh-Marra-Howland/p/book/9781138694194
33. Dabbagh N, Kitsantas A, Al-Freih M, Fake H (2015) Using social media to develop personal learning environments (PLEs) and self-regulated learning skills: a case study. Internat J Social Media Interact Learn Environ 3(3):163–183. https://doi.org/10.1504/IJSMILE.2015.072300
34. Haworth R (2016) Personal learning environments: a solution for self-directed learners. TechTrends 60(4):359–364. https://doi.org/10.1007/s11528-016-0074-z
35. Selwyn N (2007) Web 2.0 applications as alternative environments for informal learning—a critical review. OECD CERIKERIS International expert meeting on ICT and educational performance. Organization for Economic Co-Operation and Development. https://www.semanticscholar.org/paper/Web-2.0-applications-as-alternative-environments-a-Selwyn/976e3d244e3b09f084af95115a8d04f8ff569ab7
36. Valjataga T, Pata K, Tammets K (2011) Considering students' perspective on personal and distributed learning environments. In: Lee MJW, McLoughlin C (eds) Web 2.0-based e-learning: applying social informatics for tertiary teaching. IGI Global. https://doi.org/10.4018/978-1-60566-294-7.ch005
37. van Harmelen M (2006) Personal learning environments. In: Kinshuk R et al (eds) Proceedings of the sixth international conference on advanced learning technologies, IEEE Comp Society:815–816
38. Harasim L (1999) A framework for online learning: the Virtual-U. Computer 32(9):44–49. https://doi.org/10.1109/2.789750
39. Harvey DM, Lee J (2001) The impact of inherent instructional design in online courseware. Quart Rev Distance Educ 2(1):35–48. https://eric.ed.gov/?id=EJ625256
40. Hedberg J, Harper B (1998) Visual metaphors and authoring. ITFORUM. https://web.archive.org/web/20140707194454/http://itforum.coe.uga.edu/paper25/paper25.html
41. Marra RM, Jonassen DH (2001) Limitations of online courses for supporting constructive learning. Quart Rev Distance Educ 2(4):303–317. https://www.learntechlib.org/p/92802/
42. Oliver K (2001) Recommendations for student tools in online course management systems. J Comput Higher Educ 13(1):47–70. https://doi.org/10.1007/BF02940944
43. Dabbagh N, Fake H (in press) Convergence challenges of PLEs with higher education. In: Sun Y, Xu XS (eds) The development of personal learning environments in higher education: promoting culturally responsive teaching and learner autonomy. Routledge (ISBN: 9781032258386). https://www.routledge.com/The-Development-of-Personal-Learning-Environments-in-Higher-Education-Promoting/Sun-Xu/p/book/9781032258386
44. Dabbagh N (2023) The pedagogical ecology of learning technologies: a learning design framework for meaningful online learning. In: Badran A et al (eds) Higher education in the Arab world: e-learning and distance education. Springer Cham. https://doi.org/10.1007/978-3-031-33568-6_3
45. Dabbagh N, Bannan-Ritland B (2005) Online learning: concepts, strategies, and application. Prentice Hall (ISBN: 9780130325464)
46. Cigognini ME, Pettenati MC, Edirisingha P (2011) Personal knowledge management skills in Web 2.0-based learning. In: Lee MJW, McLoughlin C (eds) Web 2.0-based e-learning: applying social informatics for tertiary teaching. IGI Global. https://doi.org/10.4018/978-1-60566-294-7.ch006

47. Turker MA, Zingel S (2008) Formative interfaces for scaffolding self-regulated learning in PLEs. eLearning Papers 9. https://www.slideshare.net/elearningpapers/scaffold
48. EDUCAUSE Learning Initiative (2009) 7 things you should know about ... personal learning environments. https://library.educause.edu/-/media/files/library/2009/5/eli7049-pdf.pdf
49. Walcutt JJ, Schatz S (2019) Modernizing learning: building the future learning ecosystem. Advanced Distributed Learning Initiative. https://www.adlnet.gov/publications/2019/04/modernizing-learning/
50. Bannan B, Dabbagh N, Walcutt JJ (2020) Instructional strategies for the future. Military Learning 68. https://www.armyupress.army.mil/Journals/Journal-of-Military-Learning/Journal-of-Military-Learning-Archives/April-2020/Walcutt-Instruct-Strategy/
51. Kop R, Fournier H (2014) Developing a framework for research on personal learning environments. E-learning Eur J 35. https://www.researchgate.net/publication/262103299
52. Dabbagh N, Kitsantas A (2013) The role of social media in self-regulated learning. Internat J Web Based Commun (IJWBC), Special Issue, Social networking and education as a catalyst social change 9(2):256–273. https://doi.org/10.1504/IJWBC.2013.053248
53. Donovan J, Benko C (2016) AT&T's talent overhaul: can the firm really retain hundreds of thousands of employees? Harvard Business Review. https://hbr.org/2016/10/atts-talent-overhaul
54. Pelster B, Johnson D, Stempel J, van der Vyver B (2017) Careers and learning: real time, all the time. Deloitte Insights. https://www2.deloitte.com/us/en/insights/focus/human-capital-trends/2017/learning-in-the-digital-age.html?id=us:2el:3dc:dup3818:awa:-cons:hct17#endnote-4
55. Thomas D, Brown JS (2011) A new culture of learning: cultivating the imagination for a world of constant change. CreateSpace Independent Publishing Platform (ISBN: 1456458884)
56. Workplace learning report 2020: Linkedin learning (2020). Online learning platform for businesses. LinkedIn Learning. https://learning.linkedin.com/resources/workplace-learning-report-2020
57. Knowland VC, Thomas MS (2014) Educating the adult brain: How the neuroscience of learning can inform educational policy. Internat Rev Educ 60(1):99–122. https://doi.org/10.1007/s11159-014-9412-6

Education in the Digital Transformation Era. The Common Mistake: One Size Fits All

Ahmed M. Darwish and Ahmed M. El-Sobky

Abstract Disruptive technologies have changed the working, business and financial models of many sectors and aspects of life. Education and learning were among the top sectors influenced by digital transformation, and the stay-home era forced by the spread of COVID-19 accelerated the change. Many educational institutions (schools and universities) moved to online classes and learning material was made available over the internet. The two pandemic years served as a good experiment to show the advantages and disadvantages of such new learning models. On the return to normality, many recognized that smart campuses are a must, and the trend is accelerating. In this chapter we examine the new educational model that is being adopted. It can easily be seen that there is no single model that will fit all categories. For example, what would work for a university would not necessarily work for secondary schools, and what would work for secondary schools would not necessarily work for primary schools. In fact, the situation is even more complex. Geography, culture, social status and family ties also need to be considered. Here we examine different scenarios and give recommendations on how to approach each case. Assumptions based on observations from different Egyptian cases will be presented.

Keywords Digital transformation · Smart campus · Learning technologies · Geographic and social impact · Education infrastructure

---

A.M. Darwish (✉)
Computer Engineering Department, Faculty of Engineering, Cairo University, Giza 12613, Egypt
e-mail: ahmed@amdarwish.com

A.M. El-Sobky
ACACIA Integration, Berlin, Germany
e-mail: asobky@acaciaintegration.com

© The Author(s), under exclusive license to Springer Nature Switzerland AG 2024
A. Badran et al. (eds.), *Higher Education in the Arab World*,
https://doi.org/10.1007/978-3-031-70779-7_4

1 Introduction

Today, the education landscape is facing multifaceted disruption due to the new characteristics of the digital student. The COVID-19 pandemic accelerated the transformation of educational institutions into providers that are more dependent on information and communications technology (ICT). Generation Z students are demanding a more-personalized education, just like they find on the web. They are dealing with the education process exactly like consumers getting a service or product on the web.

In order comply with this generation's demands, educational institutions need to have new tools to deliver the service to them. The smart campus concept will enable those institutions to deliver in the way that students prefer.

There is no single definition for the expression: "**Smart Campus**". In addition, there is no consensus on the components of smart campuses in universities or schools. The main concept of the smart campus is establishing a way for direct communication between the educational institution's management and the students to enable a better educational process.

From the previous point of view, a smart campus can be the campus that uses networked technologies to facilitate communication, enhance security, use resources more efficiently, and of course, save money.

Deloitte [1] defines smart campuses as the campuses that are designed to improve student experience, increase operational efficiency, and enhance education through a well-architected infrastructure.

A smart campus can be considered an educational institution that leverages innovative smart technology to create better educational experiences and outcomes for its students, staff, and institution.

In this chapter we present the idea of a smart campus and then pose some questions about the validity of such a model for different needs (geographical, sectorial, and social). Section 2 introduces the motivation and justification for moving towards a smart-campus enterprise architecture. Sections 3 and 4 describe the idealistic structure of a smart campus, followed in Sect. 5 by the risks associated with smart campuses. Sections 6 and 7 discuss the challenges of the one-size-fits-all option, starting with the base challenge of digital transformation (Sect. 6) followed by the sectorial and social challenges (Sect. 7). In Sect. 8, we make some recommendations to overcome the challenges before drawing our conclusions (Sect. 9).

2 Why Do Educational Institutions Need Smart-Campus Systems?

Educational institutions are facing several challenges in delivering their services to students, so they need digital systems to enhance the process of managing the educational services in addition to providing better administrative services to students.

The following are the important objectives educational institutes are aiming to achieve through the use of smart-campus systems:

- **Better resource utilization**: by using networked smart lighting to reduce use and conserve energy, a campus can save on resources.
- **Enhancing student experiences**: by using smart devices, a campus can easily provide wayfinding to new students and visitors on campus. They could also improve the quality of life by fostering a healthier lifestyle with wearable monitors. Moreover, the massive amounts of data that can be taken from employing Wi-Fi, hotspots, and voice-enabled devices can be used to streamline the student journey.
- **Better facilities management**: by using Wi-Fi access points and analyzing when students and staff enter and leave a certain area, educational institutions can automate temperature control and other settings in facilities by utilizing machine learning and advanced Internet of Things (IoT) applications.
- **Enhancing the patterns of internal movement**: by monitoring movement patterns within the campus, the institute can design systems with optimized routes to facilitate movement during peak hours, so the educational institution can, for example, tell the students and visitors what parking is available.
- **Transportation schedules**: an educational institution can easily ease the burden of finding parking with new campus technology. By using cameras, sensors, and Wi-Fi, students can find a parking space without constantly circling the campus to find one.

In addition to the above-mentioned objectives, educational institutions need smart campuses systems to:

- Monitor flows of people with the possibility of not only opening/closing pathways to hotspots on campus, but also lighting corridors and halls.
- Facilitate the traffic flow by finding and indicating the direction of travel to a location on campus (buildings, classrooms, library, publishing house, dining hall etc.).
- Facilitate prevention of accidents and disasters through constant monitoring of noise, temperature, humidity, smoke, and light in the halls of the institution.
- Implement various statistical analyses and take measures to increase the quality of education in terms of environmental and safety conditions.
- Reduce water and electricity consumption.
- Efficiently stock-take the inventory of equipment and other assets.
- Create a conducive environment to increase socialization among all members of the educational institute's community.
- Use the accumulated data to achieve various useful applications.
- Eliminate systems breakdowns caused by hacker attacks or technical problems that can lead to substantial data leaks and losses.

3 How Do Smart-Campus Systems Work?

By using technology, smart campuses allow students and the institution's staff to accomplish tasks more efficiently and enjoy new experiences. Achieving such results needs the use of new solutions, such as cloud-based portals to access class timetables and resources, the digital signage that helps students reach their classes, or integrated tools that help professors, teachers, and instructors to better connect with students.

Smart campuses help educational institutions to enhance the following areas:

(a) **Managing the admissions**

Uploading enrollment applications to universities or schools offline is a lengthy and tiring process. On the other hand, submitting them via a unified digital education system is much more efficient.

(b) **Minimizing risks**

Whether a student is sick, or the classes are canceled due to severe weather conditions, online learning can handle it all. Now, to maintain excellent attendance rates and not miss an important lesson, students can simply click on the "**Join**" button of the meeting tool or just read through the material uploaded onto the cloud.

(c) **Improving learning outcomes**

With interactive lessons and by implementing high-tech solutions, the institution can motivate students to improve their learning skills.

(d) **Evaluating performance**

The process of digital transformation in education offers many benefits for students, such as faster access to tests and grades through online systems. Online learning systems allow submission of a paper, plagiarism checks, and tracking attendance. All of these factors, which contribute to a student's performance level, can be easily measured by the institution via the digital platform.

The implementation of the above-mentioned areas can have direct benefits for the educational institutions. These benefits can include the following:

- Improving the student experience and increasing student retention.
- Boosting operational efficiency.
- Automating workflows and processes.
- Conserving energy and resources.
- Reducing human error by automating population data.
- Deriving insights using data analytics.
- Fostering better interaction within the university environment.
- Leveraging interactive learning models.
- Creating a standard of continual technological improvement.

4 Technologies Used in a Smart Campus

Due to the evolvement of digital innovations in the education sector, an implementation pattern for systems in many educational institutions has been devised. We will discuss the most popular technologies in the following points.

(a) **Enhanced accessibility through online classes**

Distant learning has become a huge trend and allows learning materials to be more accessible to many students than the on-site format. Nowadays, students can attend any college or school worldwide while remaining in their own room. In addition, they have more opportunities to enjoy the same level of education as their peers regardless of any disabilities or health issues. They can use Voice-over for texts and many other accessibility features that are becoming increasingly widespread, giving everyone equal opportunities to study. Online meeting tools like Zoom or Google Meet enable millions of learners to obtain the education they want, even though they don't have sufficient funds or the ability to travel.

(b) **Smart classrooms**

Offline learning has also improved since the use of smart boards, projectors, access to the internet, and computers has become common, allowing students to quickly get necessary information and search for extra materials in real-time.

(c) **Customization of the learning process**

Depending on how a student comprehends information the best, it's now possible to create personalized study plans and frameworks to ensure the most effective learning regime. A student has the freedom to choose a preferred lesson type as well as interact with new information in the most convenient way.

(d) **Virtual reality and augmented reality**

Adding virtual reality (VR) and/or augmented reality (AR) elements to the educational process will not just increase interaction and promote greater student attention, VR and AR will also allow learners to feel all the bonuses of on-site education from home. Virtual field trips, simulators for completing practical tasks, and obtaining skills instead of reading about them are some of the main advantages of integrating VR technologies into the learning process. Moreover, AR will let the students feel that they are using real objects, just as if they are living with those objects in real life.

(e) **Cloud-based services**

Storing all educational materials on a cloud ensures instant access for any student worldwide. This technology allows remote students to submit assignments online, receive home tasks quickly, and access streamed lectures and webinars. In addition, cloud-based platforms will enable students to seamlessly collaborate on group tasks from home and even take their exams remotely.

(f) **Internet of Things**

The IoT is bringing many changes to the learning process. Educational institutions are creating smart campuses, automating many repetitive tasks, and giving everyone access to high-tech tools that facilitate the student's life.

The IoT-based modules that can be used in educational institutions include:

- *Smart parking*: monitoring the university's parking facilities and finding the number of vacant spaces, enabling staff/students to avoid traffic jams or accidents.
- *Smart lighting*: automatically adjusting the classroom light based on the data sent by an external sensor monitoring the natural light level, which will reduce electricity consumption.
- *Smart tracking*: use of radio frequency identification (RFID) technology to monitor students inside the campus and allow their quick evacuation in emergencies; both goods and equipment can be monitored.
- *Smart inventory*: each piece of equipment or component (CPU, monitor, mouse, printer, scanner, copier etc.) can have an associated bar code, which represents an inventory number, and a QR tag. By using a device connected to the internet with a barcode reader this equipment can be identified and all associated information (technical specifications, administrator, funding source etc.) can be displayed.

(g) **Big Data and analytics**

Big data technology can be the perfect solution for managing vast piles of information, its organization, and analysis. In education, big data can help track student performance and find ways of improving the learning experience. In addition, collecting grades, exam results, and other data in a unified online system allows teachers to quickly evaluate their performance, track attendance and study plan progress, evaluate papers faster and see what subjects or topics need improvement.

(h) **Blockchain**

Blockchain technology can be used to store the personal data of staff and students. In addition, using blockchain technologies helps maintain security which is the main prerequisite for implementing it. Also, it allows authenticity checks that reduce plagiarism and cheating.

(i) **Artificial intelligence**

Artificial intelligence (AI) has the potential to address many challenges in education as well as bringing innovation to teaching and learning practices. Artificial intelligence can help in creating custom study plans, evaluating the approximate student grade point average (GPA), improving student performance, and enabling more accessibility options. Moreover, AI can increase staff effectiveness and help them deliver a better educational experience. Chatbots, FAQs, and process automation can be great examples of how AI works in the education sector. Having said that, we need to ensure that applying AI technologies must be guided by the principles of inclusion and equality.

5 Smart-Campus Risks

Educational institutes are aiming to create smart campuses that promote connectivity, health and wellness, and sustainability for their students. This means providing a more holistic and connected student experience. The benefits of these changes merit discussion around strategies such as high-speed data infrastructure; pervasive Wi-Fi; IoT sensors for monitoring environments; enhanced digital services for students; classroom technology to support hybrid learning; smarter transportation; and greater data insights.

New technologies and innovations can be accompanied by risks, and we need to mitigate these risks and learn lessons from each other. The following presents some of the risk considerations educational smart campuses may face.

(a) **the risks due to complexity**

Because of the complexity of the co-operating systems in smart campuses, there is a great need for operational and information-technology services to exchange data. If a student utilizes a single ID badge to access a building, pay for food in the café, and reserve a group-study room with a simple badge tap or swipe, this involves multiple cyber and physical systems that potentially need to exchange data. Implementing such a process correctly, would be very convenient for the student and reduce delays when travelling around the campus. However, some risk factors present themselves in this case and we should take these into consideration. Those risk factors can be as follows:

- Has the sequence of operations been properly taken into consideration?
- Are the divisions of responsibility among the different vendors clearly articulated?
- Are the systems being specified interoperable so that the intended data can be exchanged?
- Who provides system commissioning, service, and support for an interconnected set of systems?
- Who owns the issue when the integrated functions fail to operate?

There are literally thousands of examples of these connectivity issues occurring with both new and legacy campus systems. Simply put, the higher the degree of complexity in your smart campus, the greater the likelihood of problems cropping up. That's why it's essential that the system complexity versus end-user convenience benefit calculation is done early to determine if the net result is worth the costs and effort to pursue.

(b) **Student data security and privacy**

With technology quickly becoming such a critical feature in the daily lives of students and teachers, security has become another necessary consideration in the digital-education revolution. Educational institutes are collecting a wealth of information on students, from their personal data to grades etc. When students are moving through a smart campus, their data are exposed to various systems and services, for example, they may be using mobile apps to navigate around campus via wayfinding tools, checking transportation schedules from the local bus route, ordering food to be delivered to their preferred place of study, and tapping into news and events. Although these apps may create more convenience, they may also open the door for exposing the students' data to others without the knowledge of the institute. Some risks that should be considered:

- Where are the data from the app hosted? Is the host secure and does it meet data privacy policies and best practices?
- Do students have the ability to disable location services within the student app?
- Is the app platform sharing any student data with third-party vendors it connects to?
- Is the app using end-to-end encryption for messaging?

6 Challenges Facing the Digital Transformation in Education

Digital transformation in education is facing many challenges especially in developing countries. Those challenges are limiting the ability of the educational institutions to benefit from most of the above-mentioned technologies. Some of the main challenges the educational institutions are facing in our region are as follows:

(a) **Lack of robust infrastructure**

Educational institutes need robust, fast, and high-quality connectivity to be able to implement digital transformation within the organization. In addition to the high-quality GSM (global system for mobile communications) connectivity that enables students to use their mobiles to access information through the available apps, fiber connectivity to the last mile within the campus is essential. In our region, we may have a wide digital gap between different cities in addition to the financial-capabilities gap between the private educational institutions and the public ones.

(b) **Lack of a technology-enabling environment**

As we discussed earlier in the chapter, the systems used in smart campuses need cloud-hosting for their content, IoT applications to control the different systems within the campus, blockchain applications, big data and data-analytics systems,

AI systems, etc., but not all such systems are available from local vendors, or they are not even aligned to match every country's student culture. In addition, all those systems need to be acquired or even used as a service, but not all of them are affordable to the institutions. Moreover, using those applications needs a huge IT staff within the educational institute and not all the educational institutes can afford the associated cost.

(c) **Lack of up-to-date IT systems**

Not all educational institutions have sufficient technology stacks to transform the delivery of their services. This means that they may not have computers or Wi-Fi access, and others may have outdated e-learning portals.

(d) **Lack of digital transformation strategies**

Many educational institutions do not engage in developing digital transformation strategies. In addition, they either may not have the time or don't know how to incorporate a particular technology into the educational process. In such cases, strategies must be the mandate of the educational councils of the country. Should there be a clear national digital transformation strategy, then the educational institutes can have guidelines to implement the nationally predetermined plans.

(e) **Lack of up-to-date systems**

Many educational institutions have an insufficient technology stack to transform their learning system. As an example, some schools and universities may not have sufficient computers or Wi-Fi access, and some have outdated online portals or learning managements systems. That is why it is essential to update the technologies and the learning system first to achieve the necessary digital transformation in educational institutions.

(f) **System breakdowns**

System glitches or breakdowns can happen due to hacker attacks or technical problems (e.g., with servers). This may lead to substantial data leaks and losses, which are unacceptable for a reputable institution. The lack of technical expertise and knowledge of cybersecurity basics are the key factors that can affect the e-learning system.

(g) **the economic and cultural gap**

Not all the students in higher education (or even schools) can afford to have the required devices to interact with the facilities provided by the smart campuses. This may be due to economic reasons, especially for the students with backgrounds that are lower middle class or less. In addition, those students may also have cultural barriers to dealing with the sophisticated devices needed for such access. They may also be unable to afford the cost of connectivity. Generally, the gap is wider in rural areas than in urban areas, so the students from rural areas may face more difficulties in dealing with smart-campus systems than their peers from urban areas.

7 Dealing with the One-Size-Fits-All Problem

In this chapter we have examined the new educational model that is being adopted. It can easily be seen that there is no single model that will fit all categories. The above components of the smart campus cannot all be present everywhere. The immediate explanation will be "of course this is due to budget limitations". But the truth is that, even if the budget is sufficient, some of these components and models will suit neither the recipients of the service (the students) nor the providers of the service (the teachers). What would work for a university would not necessarily work for secondary schools, and what would work for secondary schools would not necessarily work for primary schools. In fact, the situation is even more complex. What works for arts, law and business faculties does not work for practical lab-work-based faculties (engineering, medicine and pharmacy), and to further complicate matters, what works for engineering does not work for medicine, etc.

The above is just the first two layers of a very complex model, namely, the age and the field of study. Three more issues play a role in defining a suitable model: culture, social status and family ties.

To illustrate, for a country like Egypt, geography plays an important role. Cities can adopt a model that will not work for villages and even the culture in Northern Egypt is quite different from that in Southern Egypt.

We could also think of society in terms of five economic categories: very poor, poor, lower middle class, upper middle class and comfortable. For each class, the tools available and the access to technology differ and hence the opportunity to learn is radically different.

Last but not least, we must acknowledge the fact that for school children the role of the home is of prime importance. It must, therefore, be clear that models that suit a closely tied family may not be suitable for divorced parents where the children live with grandparents or a single parent.

Thus, we need to identify all the interactions among the following categories:

Category 1. University field of study

1. Science-based faculties (includes medical, pharmaceutical, nursing, agriculture, basic science, etc.)
2. Engineering-based faculties (includes engineering, architecture, computer science, etc.)
3. Business- and literature-based faculties (includes economics, accounting, political science, law, arts, etc.).
4. Arts-based faculties (includes media, mass communication, theatre, movie production, etc.)

Category 2. Age of School Students

1. High schools
2. Middle (junior high) schools
3. Elementary schools
4. Kindergarten schools

Category 3. Urban versus suburban

1. Cities
2. Suburban
3. Villages

Category 4. Habits and culture

1. Large Cities (Cairo Alexandria, etc.)
2. Northern Egypt
3. Southern (Upper) Egypt
4. Deserted and remote areas

Category 5. Social status

1. Very poor
2. Poor
3. Lower middle class
4. Upper middle class
5. Comfortable
   Rich (will be excluded from the model)

Category 6. Family status (couples vs. single parents)

1. Married couple
2. Divorced couple, children living with their father
3. Divorced couple, children living with father and stepmother
4. Divorced couple, children living with their mother
5. Divorced couple, children living with mother and stepfather
6. Widower/single father
7. Widow/single mother

Category 7. Student status

1. Normal
2. Handicapped
3. Slow learner (including autism, etc.)
4. Super learner

Clearly, category one (university) is the easiest to provide for because we can devise a model for each of the subcategories that matches the type of study.

However, it becomes really complicated for categories 2 to 5 because we must consider all the intersections of the subcategories to build a specific model. For example, the model for an elementary school (2.3) in a poor (5.2) village (3.3) in upper Egypt (4.3) will be radically different from that for a secondary school (2.1) in an upper middle-class district (5.4) in Cairo (4.1).

Categories 6 and 7 are dealt with through the service providers (teachers) and some subcategories will need special tools to be available. True, the disruptive technologies are providing lots of helpful aids but, even so, the normal model needs to be modified.

8 Overcoming the Digital Transformation Challenges in Education

To overcome the challenges, we presented earlier in this paper, we need to take the necessary actions to:

- Enhance the telecom infrastructure to enable educational institutes to use ICT-based educational solutions in a smooth way.
- Encourage the educational councils to develop a digital educational strategy to assist institutions implementing the transformation.
- Encourage investment by creating a nation-wide technology-enabling environment that can be used to provide the different types of services needed by the educational institutions.
- Encourage local development of the software systems and applications needed for the digital transformation of education to squeeze the cost and to guarantee their suitability for the local culture and community.
- Use the best-practice models to create funding mechanisms to finance the digital transformation process for educational institutes.

9 Conclusion

Creating smart campuses and implementing digital transformation requires a spirit of innovation, stakeholder engagement, partnership, and a fundamental shift in how we think about students' experiences on and off campus.

Reference

1. Deloitte. Smart campuses. The next-generation campus. https://www2.deloitte.com/us/en/pages/consulting/solutions/next-generation-smart-campus.html

Revolutionizing Education: Supporting Digital Transformation with ChatGPT

Hoda Baytiyeh

Abstract Artificial intelligence (AI) is a powerful tool that can help make tasks easier, faster, and more efficient. Artificial intelligence is used in many fields, from healthcare to banking and shopping by helping customers or by automating tasks such as data entry or data analysis. Educators in the world are divided on the latest advances in AI technologies, with some embracing this new technology and others banning it. Universities might use or incorporate AI technologies in their research, teaching, or administrative activities. The objective of this study is to understand the attitudes and perceptions of professors towards the use of chatbots in higher education. The study investigates the potential benefits as well as concerns and challenges faced by professors when integrating chatbots into the classroom.

Keywords Digital transformation · Artificial intelligence · ChatGPT · Higher education

1 Introduction

Higher education, like every industry, has embraced digital transformation, particularly over recent years when the pandemic forced colleges to work remotely. Digital transformation is often defined as the process of optimizing an institution's operations, strategic direction, and value proposition, but it requires coordinated culture, workforce, and technology shifts [1]. Such a definition implies creating a culture that embraces change, such as adding new roles and training staff to implement digital transformation.

Educational technology focuses on enhancing knowledge, skills, and learning experience, as well as boosting student performance through the introduction of

---

H. Baytiyeh (✉)
Department of Education, American University of Beirut, Beirut, Lebanon
e-mail: hb36@aub.edu.lb

© The Author(s), under exclusive license to Springer Nature Switzerland AG 2024
A. Badran et al. (eds.), *Higher Education in the Arab World*,
https://doi.org/10.1007/978-3-031-70779-7_5

new tools, resources, and concepts. The increasing integration of technology in education has opened numerous possibilities, introducing a new era in the academic environment with a wealth of resources [2]. However, the effectiveness of these resources is contingent on the quality of the information they are built upon, prompting scrutiny regarding their suitability as academic sources.

Educators acknowledge the positive impact of technology on the educational process, facilitating advancement and improved instruction. Simultaneously, it brings extra responsibilities and exposes educational settings to various risks. In fact, some teachers note an increase in workload due to additional administrative tasks and the necessity to plan extracurricular activities relating to students' computer usage [3].

For example, gamification was embraced by some educators as a part of their daily teaching practices to engage students, foster creativity, and enhance problem-solving skills. Educators believe that games introduce valuable concepts to students, ranging from sustainability, recycling, energy systems, maps, and logical reasoning to essential skills like communication, collaboration, teamwork, and time management [4]. Reports from educators indicate a significant enhancement in students' problem-solving and computational skills following the incorporation of games into the curriculum. However, opposing views suggest that, despite the admirable goal of keeping learning enjoyable, the real world is not always entertaining. Educators face the challenging responsibility of preparing students for real-life scenarios, and there is concern that excessive exposure to such gaming platforms at an early age may negatively impact students' emotional well-being, potentially creating socially isolated individuals who find virtual interactions easier than engaging with teachers or peers [5]. This dilemma underscores the crucial role of teachers as the first line of defense against potential risks. They must have the time and resources to thoroughly assess the suitability of such tools, determining whether they contribute constructively to the learning process.

Certainly, the careful selection of digital resources is a pivotal step in effectively integrating technology into education. Numerous technology-based platforms run the risk of inadvertently stifling students' creativity by enabling them to complete tasks without actively engaging in problem-solving [6].

Artificial Intelligence (AI) stands as a powerful tool capable of streamlining tasks, enhancing speed, and improving overall efficiency. Its application spans various fields, including healthcare, banking, and shopping, where it helps customers, and automates tasks like data entry and analysis. Educators in the world are divided on the latest advances in AI technology, with some embracing this new technology and others banning it. Researchers believe that AI technologies can serve as a learning diagnostic tool; in fact, it can analyze students' learning processes by providing adaptive learning resources, and providing evaluation and suggestions based on learners' performances [7–9].

Universities might use or incorporate AI technologies, in their research, teaching, or administrative activities. The use of AI in education depends on each university's policies, resources, and goals. While some professors and academics are worried about this new wave of technology, others are eager to explore its potential and to embrace it to take on the challenges it presents. Certainly, students can take advantage of AI technologies in multiple ways, including receiving assistance in research and writing, obtaining concise summaries of key concepts, receiving answers to specific questions, and accessing step-by-step solutions to problems [10]. However, it's essential to acknowledge concerns related to the potential misuse of these tools by students, particularly in instances of plagiarism in homework and exams.

OpenAI provides access to ChatGPT for users and organizations, enabling fine-tuning on specific datasets to suit particular applications. Privacy and data-handling policies are in place to ensure that sensitive user information is not stored or misused during interactions with ChatGPT [11]. However, the integration of AI into education also presents a set of challenges and ethical considerations that must not be overlooked. Addressing concerns such as data privacy, equitable access to education, and the evolving roles of educators is imperative, as emphasized by Montenegro-Rueda et al. [12].

Despite this crucial debate, at the time of writing this article, very few scholarly materials have been published on ChatGPT and other generative AI technologies. The objective of this study is to understand the attitudes and perceptions of professors towards the use of chatbots in higher education. The study will investigate the potential adoption of ChatGPT and its benefits as well as concerns and challenges faced by professors when integrating chatbots into the classroom.

2 ChatGPT

The latest advancement in artificial intelligence is exemplified by the introduction of ChatGPT. Developed by OpenAI, ChatGPT (Generative Pre-trained Transformer) is an AI-powered language model that leverages artificial intelligence.

When looking at its history, the development of ChatGPT is deeply intertwined with the trajectory of AI and natural language processing. It represents a milestone in AI research and development, building upon Alan Turing's concept of the Turing Test introduced during the mid-twentieth century [13]. The journey towards this advancement began with GPT-1 in 2018, when an unsupervised learning-based generative language model applying the Transformer framework was introduced. Subsequent iterations, like GPT-2 in 2019, enhanced performance through task learning, with increased network parameters and data utilization. In 2020, GPT-3 emerged as a groundbreaking advancement combining learning and in-context learning to outperform existing methods across tasks [13].

Unveiled in 2021, this language model is a variant of the GPT-3 AI model, specifically designed for producing conversational and human-like language [14]. When it was publicly released on November 30, 2022, ChatGPT showed noteworthy progress in language model technology. Because it is tailored for conversational purposes, the model aims to generate text that closely resembles human writing. Moreover, as it is trained on extensive text data, ChatGPT enables the generation of responses to queries and prompts through a chatbot. The tool concept is very simple; first, users create an account and log on; then, they generate a new chat by typing some instructions into the chat bar. Within seconds, the chatbot generates bodies of text in response. Afterwards, users can provide additional instructions to ChatGPT to edit, adjust, or regenerate an alternative response based on the user preferences.

Using a database, this technology is trained to formulate conversational responses, to paraphrase and to summarize information [15]. Its proficiency in comprehending and responding in a naturalistic manner to language input makes it valuable for diverse tasks, particularly in education. ChatGPT serves as a research assistant, providing personalized feedback and enhancing users' communication effectiveness in various contexts.

ChatGPT offers a plethora of resources for educators, ranging from the redesign of lesson plans for various proficiency levels to the generation of topic-specific tests, quizzes, and performance assessments for assignments and tests. Many high-school teachers advocate for the use of ChatGPT in daily education. Educators can send assignments to ChatGPT requesting the chatbot to restructure the materials to follow along with differentiated materials, which may have a positive impact on students' learning processes. Moreover, ChatGPT can assist in preparing lesson plans and creating quizzes, saving valuable time for educators [16].

A recent survey conducted by Study.com [17], shows that nearly 6 in 10 teachers believe that this tool may help them and would make their job easier while 43% of educators feel the tool would make their teaching career more difficult. Some educators have concerns about academic integrity since the tool encourages new methods of cheating and plagiarism. In fact, because of its simplicity, accessibility, and convenience, students can use it to generate answers to homework and write entire essays, claiming them to be their own writing.

On the other hand, some educators see in the tool's simple design and brainstorming capabilities a way to improve education. These teachers believe that the real impact will be in the assistance in their daily practices of teaching through lesson plans and classroom instruction. While some examples showcase the positive contributions of technology to education, they also underscore the importance of educators thoroughly evaluating digital tools before incorporating them into the classroom. This assessment should ensure that these tools enhance, refine, and advance instructional methods in a supervised manner. If not properly supervised, ChatGPT could potentially hinder a young student's ability to think critically through complex problems. There is a worry that an excessive reliance on the chatbot might hinder students' critical thinking and problem-solving abilities, as they become accustomed to expecting ready-made and easily accessible answers. Teachers worry that ChatGPT may prevent students from learning content and may prevent young learners from developing the soft skills.

In higher education, ChatGPT benefits a range of areas, due to its capacity to comprehend and react to linguistic input in a naturalistic manner. It can be taught to carry out duties, such as finishing a conversation or responding to inquiries.

Even though AI programs have been around for some time prior to the release of ChatGPT, their level of sophistication and output quality have raised serious questions about academic integrity and the potential misuse of these tools by students for university examinations [18].

There are significant concerns about academic integrity in higher education because of the release of ChatGPT. Approximately one-fifth of students were found to be using AI systems for assessment tasks less than two months after its release [19]. It was reported that over one-third of university students used ChatGPT for writing, according to a poll of more than a thousand students conducted in January 2023; 75% of these students admitted to doing it despite believing it to be cheating. However, some have noted that generative AI tools like ChatGPT can improve student learning, so academics should modify their teaching and assessment practices to accept the fact of working and studying in a world where AI is widely accessible.

3 Theoretical Foundations

To reduce the difficulties faced when adopting new technologies, several researchers have investigated the process of technology acceptance to understand, predict and explain the satisfaction of users for a particular system.

- Fishbein and Ajzen [20] designed the Theory of Reasoned Action (TRA) drawn from social psychology assessing two core variables: *attitude toward behavior* (an individual's positive or negative feeling toward a behavior) and *subjective norm* (the influence of people in one's social environment to perform/not perform this behavior).
- The most common theory in the field of adoption is the Technology Acceptance Model (TAM) [21]. Owing to its simplicity and applicability to different information technologies [22], TAM has become one of the most used models in testing the acceptance of new technologies. This theory involves two main independent variables (see Fig. 1): *perceived usefulness* (an individual's perception that using a particular system would enhance his job performance) and *perceived ease of use* (an individual's perception that using a particular system would be effortless). Also included in TAM is one dependent variable: *behavioral intention*, which is the degree to which a person plans to perform or not perform a specified future behavior. Later, TAM2 extended TAM [23] to include the *subjective norm* variable as defined in the TRA.

Existing research that applied TAM to e-learning technologies revealed diverse results. For example, Raaij and Schepers [24] showed that the *perceived ease of use* is not a significant predictor of attitudes towards the intention of using an e-learning system. On the other hand, Ngai et al. [25] revealed that the *perceived ease of use* is a dominant factor for the attitude of students using an e-learning system.

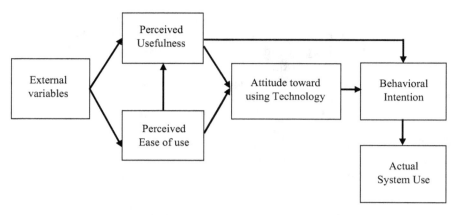

Fig. 1 Technology acceptance model

- Ajzen [26] introduced the Theory of Planned Behavior (TPB) by adding to the TRA model the *perceived behavioral control* variable. This latter variable was defined as the ease or difficulty of performing the behavior.
- In the development of the diffusion of innovation theory, Rogers [27] concluded that five attributes helped decrease the uncertainty associated with innovation and were significant predictors of the adoption rate: (1) relative advantage; (2) compatibility; (3) complexity; (4) trialability; and (5) observability. Rogers [27] reported that these attributes explained 49–87% of variance in the adoption rate of innovations. Other factors which may influence innovation adoption included the innovation-decision type (optional, collective or authority), communication channel (mass media or interpersonal channels) and social system (norms or network interconnectedness).
- After reviewing literature on user acceptance, Venkatesh et al. [28] compared seven models: the Theory of Reasoned Action (TRA), the Technology Acceptance Model (TAM), the Motivational Model (MM), the Theory of Planned Behavior (TPB), the Model of PC Utilization (PCU), the Innovation Diffusion Theory (IDT) and the Social Cognitive Theory (SCT).

To conclude, Venkatesh et al. [28] introduced the Unified Theory of Acceptance and Use of Technology (UTAUT). The UTAUT model [29] includes the following four direct determinants of *behavioral intention* (BI) and system-usage behavior (SUB): *performance expectancy, effort expectancy, social influence* and *facilitating conditions*, as shown in Fig. 2. *Performance expectancy* (PE) is the degree to which an individual believes that using technology will help in attaining better job performance. *Effort expectancy* (EE) is the degree of ease associated with the use of technology. *Social influence* (SI) is the degree to which an individual perceives that important people believe he or she should use technology. *Facilitating conditions* (FC) are defined as the degree to which an individual believes that organizational and technical support is available to use the system. Gender, age, experience, and voluntariness of use can have an impact on the four key determinants of usage intention and behavior.

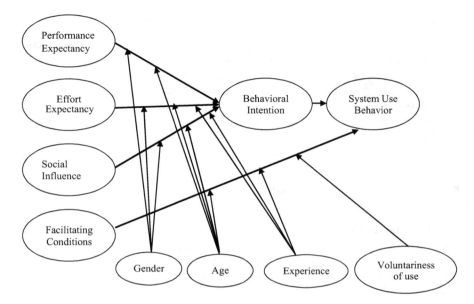

Fig. 2 The UTAUT model

Venkatesh et al. [28] showed that performance expectancy is the strongest predictor of intention to use a technology, whereas social influence plays the role of a subjective norm and is a direct determinant of *behavioral intention*. Marchewka et al. [30] tested the UTAUT model to understand students' perceptions about using Blackboard and showed that effort expectancy and social influence were significant determinants of students' behavioral intentions. Chiu and Wang [31] indicated that performance expectancy, effort expectancy, computer self-efficacy, attainment value, utility value and intrinsic value are significant predictors of individuals' intentions to continue using Web-based learning, while anxiety can have a significant negative effect.

Because of its novelty in the field of user acceptance to ICT research, the UTAUT model was chosen as a theoretical framework in this study for investigating professors' perceptions of using AI tools and particularly ChatGPT.

4 Research Objectives

This study is not focused on evaluating AI or ChatGPT; instead, its objective is to examine the utilization and acceptance of the system in an educational context, with a specific emphasis on the perspectives of the users. Specifically, this article's objective is to evaluate the acceptance and use of AI applications from the viewpoint of professors to support their teaching practices.

Therefore, this study will answer the following research questions:

1. Is there any correlation between the dependent variables of UTAUT in the context of the adoption of AI/ChatGPT by professors?
2. Is there any correlation between the dependent variables and the independent variable of UTAUT in the context of the adoption of AI/ChatGPT by professors?
3. What are the perceptions of professors regarding the practices for ChatGPT in education?

5 Participants and Procedure

For the purpose of this study, a random selection of professors from higher education institutions in Lebanon was approached through e-mails, while providing clear explanations regarding the study's objectives. Using their e-mail addresses, invitations were extended to participate in an online survey while assuring complete anonymity throughout the process. The first call for participation was initiated in the first week of March 2023. After two weeks, the survey gathered responses from 255 professors. To encourage further participation, a second invitation was dispatched as a reminder. By the end of March, a total of 489 professors had actively engaged with and completed the questionnaire. Data from partially completed surveys were excluded from the analysis to ensure the integrity of the research findings.

6 Instrumentation

The questionnaire was based on available literature on the acceptance and use of e-learning systems [32–35] and system usability [36–38]. The questionnaire consisted of three sections; the first section was designed to capture demographics of professors such as gender, age, and experience; the second section contained 16 items capturing UTAUT statements on a five-point rating scale with end points anchored by "strongly disagree" and "strongly agree". The third section was designed to capture perceptions of participants through three open-ended questions. The instrument was administered to 15 professors in a pilot study. Feedback was obtained from these pilot respondents and further changes were made to the questionnaire so that the wording of the sentences was comprehensible.

7 Findings and Data Analysis

A demographic analysis was performed to understand the profiles of the respondents and descriptive statistics were obtained for the sample. As indicated in Table 1, the majority of respondents were female, representing 53% of the sample. Also, the majority (70%) of the professors who participated in the survey were between 36 and 55 years old. The sample consisted of 23% full professors, 38% associate professors, 27% assistant professors, 5% lecturers, and 7% instructors. Furthermore, the vast majority of professors (76%) had more than 10 years of teaching experience from various academic disciplines (Table 1).

Table 1 Demographics and use of ChatGPT

		Percentage (%) ($n=489$)
Gender	Male	47
	Female	53
Age	30–35	10
	36–45	32
	46–55	38
	56–65	14
	Over 65	6
Academic position	Full professor	23
	Associate professor	38
	Assistant professor	27
	Lecturer	5
	Instructor	7
Total teaching experience in years	1–10	24
	11–20	39
	21–30	18
	31–35	16
	>35	3
Specialty	Humanities	33
	Social sciences	29
	Sciences and engineering	16
	Business	14
	Medicine and health-related fields	8
How often do you use ChatGPT?	Daily	35
	Weekly	53
	Monthly	12
For what purpose do you use ChatGPT? Check all that apply	Research assistant	37
	Teaching support	26
	Text editing	98

Nonetheless, it is interesting to find that the majority of professors who are using the tool belong to humanities (33%) and social sciences (29%) fields. This finding provides insights into the disciplinary preferences for adopting ChatGPT.

Moreover, 35% of professors reported using ChatGPT on a daily basis, whereas a good number (37%) claimed using the tool for research assistance. Also, 26% of these professors used the tool for teaching support, and almost all respondents (98%) reported using the tool for text editing.

These findings, as shown in Table 1, suggest that while text editing is a widely adopted use of ChatGPT among the surveyed professors, there's also notable usage in research-related activities and teaching support.

7.1 Acceptance and Use of ChatGPT

To test the acceptance and use of the AI chatbot, participants were asked to rate the 16 items that reflects the UTAUT model as shown in Table 2. The 16 Likert-scale items revealed a Cronbach's alpha reliability of 0.92. Descriptive statistics were calculated to obtain the measures of central tendency and those of variability of each of the identified items.

Exploratory factor analysis (EFA) was performed to determine which of the 16 items formed related subsets. The EFA was applied with principal components extraction, eigenvalues greater than 1.00 and absolute value greater than 0.40 [39]. The results of Kaiser–Meyer–Olkin (KMO) sampling (0.644) and Bartlett's test ($p<0.0001$) showed that using EFA was appropriate for this study [40]. EFA with principal components extraction identified four factors that accounted for 65.47% of the total variance. Table 2 shows the rotated factor loadings, which were the correlations between a given variable and a factor. Loading size reflected the extent of the relationship between a variable and a factor. For items loaded under two factors, only the highest loading was retained. The following variances were reported for the factors: factor 1: $\sigma2=22.73\%$; factor 2: $\sigma2=18.96\%$; factor 3: $\sigma2=14.65\%$; and factor 4: $\sigma2=9.12\%$. After evaluating the items loaded under each factor, factor 1 was labelled *community influence*, factor 2 *effectiveness*, factor 3 *self-learning* and factor 4 *novelty and fun*.

Four new variables were calculated based on the means of the items falling under each factor. To compare the importance of the four generated factors as rated by participants, one-way repeated-measures analysis of variance (ANOVA) was applied to the four variables. Repeated-measures ANOVA revealed significant differences among the four factor scores ($F(3, 2751)=140.22$; $p<0.001$).

Statistics revealed that *community influence* received the highest rate from participants with a mean of $\mu=3.92$, followed by *effectiveness* ($\mu=3.80$), *self-learning* ($\mu=3.75$), and *novelty and fun* ($\mu=3.72$).

Table 2 Rotated factor matrix with extraction method: principal component

	Community influence	Effectiveness	Self-learning	Novelty & fun
People who are close to me use ChatGPT	0.786			
My colleagues use ChatGPT	0.754			
My students use ChatGPT	0.732			
Everyone I know use AI tools	0.701			
I find ChatGPT useful for my teaching tasks		0.718		
Using ChatGPT enables me to accomplish my teaching tasks more quickly		0.712		
Using ChatGPT increases the effective use of my time in handling my research tasks		0.694		
Using ChatGPT improves the quality of my work		0.682		
My interaction with ChatGPT is clear and understandable			0.670	
Learning to use ChatGPT is easy for me			0.667	
I find it easy to get ChatGPT to do what I want it to do			0.658	
ChatGPT is user friendly			0.652	
Interacting with ChatGPT is enjoyable				0.648
Interacting with ChatGPT is fun				0.635
Using ChatGPT is a novel experience				0.627
Using ChatGPT is new and refreshing				0.611

Rotation method: Varimax with Kaiser Normalization

7.2 *Predictors of ChatGPT Acceptance and Use*

The intention to accept and use the AI tool is a combination of variables. The relationships between the predictor variables (determinant factors) and the dependent variable, *behavioral intention* (BI) to use the tool, are tested. This test is performed with the four factors that emerged from the EFA since it reflects specific attributes related to the use of ChatGPT. To produce relationships between the variables, the following analyses were conducted:

- Pearson correlation between the determinant factors (*community influence, effectiveness, self-learning* and *novelty and fun*) and the *behavioral intention* (BI) to use the tool.
- Pearson correlation between all variables.
- Multiple correlation (R) between the determinant factors and the users' intention to use the tool.
- Multiple regressions between the determinant factors and system use to obtain the regression weights that represent the relative importance of the factors.

The results of Pearson product–moment correlations for each pair appear in Table 3. *Community influence* appears to be significantly correlated with BI ($r1 = 0.728$; $p = 0.000$). This correlation was also statistically significant with the other factors ($r5$, $r6$, and $r7$; $p = 0.000$), confirming that *community influence* figured strongly in ChatGPT acceptance and use. Also, *effectiveness* is shown as significantly correlated with the intention to use the tool ($r2 = 0.711$; $p = 0.000$). This correlation was also statistically significant with the other factors ($r5$, $r8$, and $r9$; $p = 0.000$), revealing that effectiveness has an impact on system use.

Self-learning is significantly correlated with BI ($r3 = 0.694$; $p = 0.000$). This correlation was also statistically significant with the other factors ($r6$, $r8$, and $r10$; $p = 0.000$), revealing that this factor has an influence on system use. Finally, *novelty and fun* is significantly correlated with system use ($r4 = 0.685$; $p = 0.000$). This correlation was also significant with the other factors ($r7$, $r9$, and $r10$; $p = 0.000$), reflecting that the service provided has a positive association with participants' behavior to use the tool.

One of the objectives of the model is to provide an index of the relationship between two variables ($r1,\ldots, r10$). Next is to find the index that predicts the variable BI from the other variables. Such an index is provided by the multiple correlation coefficient R (see Table 4).

In computing this index, a weight ($w1$, $w2$, $w3$, and $w4$) for each of the predictor variables is obtained to measure the independent contribution of that variable in the prediction of the users' acceptance and use of ChatGPT. Multiple R (0.73) represents the multiple correlation, that is, the correlation between the dependent

Table 3 Pearson product–moment correlations for the four factors that affect the *behavioral intention* (BI) to use ChatGPT

	BI	Community influence	Effectiveness	Self-learning	Novelty & fun
BI	1	$r1 = 0.728^{**}$	$r2 = 0.711^{**}$	$r3 = 0.694^{**}$	$r4 = 0.685^{**}$
Community Influence	$r1 = 0.728^{**}$	1	$r5 = 0.561^{**}$	$r6 = 0.535^{**}$	$r7 = 0.521^{**}$
Effectiveness	$r2 = 0.711^{**}$	$r5 = 0.561^{**}$	1	$r8 = 0.511^{**}$	$r9 = 0.498^{**}$
Self-Learning	$r3 = 0.694^{**}$	$r6 = 0.535^{**}$	$r8 = 0.511^{**}$	1	$r10 = 0.477^{**}$
Novelty and fun	$r4 = 0.685^{**}$	$r7 = 0.521^{**}$	$r9 = 0.498^{**}$	$r10 = 0.477^{**}$	1

[**] Correlation is significant at the 0.01 level (2-tailed)

variable (the use of ChatGPT) and the weighted sum of the predictor variables. R square (0.63) explains the variance of the dependent variable by all of the predictor variables combined. The adjusted R square (0.62) is an estimate of the variance while taking error variance into account.

Table 4 shows the results of R square of 0.63 and the adjusted R square of 0.62, the F-statistics ($F = 259.707$; $p < 0.001$) and the beta weights of the variables: *community influence* ($\beta = 0.264$, $p < 0.001$), *effectiveness* ($\beta = 0.235$, $p < 0.001$), *self-learning* ($\beta = 0.226$, $p < 0.001$) and *novelty and fun* ($\beta = 0.221$, $p < 0.001$). This result implies that all variables are statistically significant.

The two open-ended questions at the end of the survey give participants the opportunity to express their opinion about ChatGPT in their own words. These comments will be inductively analyzed using the constant comparative method [41]. Patterns will be coded and refined to reveal professors' concerns as well as potential benefits of ChatGPT in education. The themes that evolve will be described using illustrative quotes and examples from selected participants.

7.3 Professors' Perceptions

In the last part of the questionnaire, five open-ended questions were designed to investigate the perceptions of professors regarding the acceptance and use of the AI tool ChatGPT, whereby participants were given the opportunity to provide their own opinion in their own words. A qualitative descriptive research design was used, adopting a collective-case-study method that seeks to examine the meaning of a certain phenomenon for a group of people [42]. Marshall and Rossman

Table 4 Multiple regression of the criterion variable BI (*behavioral intention*) with predictor variables, *community influence*, *effectiveness*, *self-learning*, *novelty and fun*

Multiple R	0.730				
R square	0.632				
Adjusted R Square	0.620				
Analysis of variance					
	Sum of Squares	Df	Mean square	F	Sig
Regression	90.459	4	22.615	259.707	0.000
Residual	79.502	484	0.087		
Coefficients					
Variables in equation	B	Std. error	Beta	t	Sig
(Constant)	0.499	0.139		3.579	0.000
Community influence	0.138	0.033	0.264	3.858	0.000
Effectiveness	0.121	0.039	0.235	3.523	0.000
Self-learning	0.124	0.034	0.226	3.411	0.000
Novelty and fun	0.127	0.032	0.221	3.218	0.000

speculated that qualitative research methods are effective in comprehending "a complex social phenomenon" (p. 3), since social reality is a result of social interaction in qualitative research, and knowledge is socially constituted [43].

The five questions were as follows:

- How did you come to start using ChatGPT?
- How do you describe your experience of using ChatGPT? Please explain.
- What are the main reasons behind using ChatGPT?
- Do you believe that the ChatGPT tool has any benefits for students' learning? Why and why not?
- Do you think that universities should ban ChatGPT? Why and why not?

After reading through the data, open coding [44] was used to generate categories that depicted specific features of the factors that influenced the participants to use ChatGPT. The categories obtained were further sorted into primary themes and subthemes by combining similar categories and setting apart those that were unique. To ensure the reliability, authenticity, and credibility of the data analysis process in validating the findings of the study, the researcher sought the assistance of a colleague to review the codes, themes and subthemes that were developed, and to confirm that they were identical to the information captured in the data.

After coding for key points and patterns in the respondents' answers, four main themes emerged and can fit into advantages in (1) *immediacy* and (2) *free editing*, as well as disadvantages in (3) *ethical considerations* and (4) *inaccurate information*. The coded themes are expanded below, using excerpts from the professors' comments.

- *Theme 1: immediacy (80%)*

A consistent theme expressed by most respondents was related to the notion of "immediacy of feedback."

According to one professor in political sciences:

> It is a very simple and easy tool to use for immediate feedback. No need for any instructions to follow. I am not tech savvy, and I did not need help from anyone to use it. I keep using it for its immediacy, especially when I need to get a summary of several resources.

Another professor in psychology commented:

> Having a conversation with the chatbot was as simple as one step forward to get immediate feedback. I can share my notes and ask questions. Then I get immediately an answer for my questions. It helps me offer timely and constructive feedback to students. It can assess responses based on predefined criteria and provide instant feedback to students.

Another professor in accounting added:

> I tell all my friends and even my colleagues how it is quick to provide me with a response. I can ask the tool to provide me with a quiz in multiple choice. Of course, I add and remove from the quiz based on my own preferences... and I can use ChatGPT for grading and in providing feedback to students. This immediate feedback can be valuable for the learning process, helping students understand and address areas of improvement promptly.

- *Theme 2: free editing (85%)*

Another consistent theme throughout professors' answers was related to "free editing." As one professor in engineering noted:

> This tool is free. The fact is that I can enter a text or a message and I get my text re-written in a very structured flow. This saves me time when I want to write any paragraph... I put my ideas and all is done without worrying about choosing the correct words.

Another professor in business administration stated:

> The best advantage for me in using ChatGPT is the free-editing option. In the past, I was sending my conference papers to an editing company, and sometimes these editors suggest alternative wording for my text that do not fit in our field, so it was not obvious to get what I need from the editing company. With ChatGPT, I can keep changing my sentences and I receive a new version of my text till I am satisfied with the text. And it is free!

And a professor in biology noted:

> I am very thankful for my friends who advised me to start using ChatGPT because I get free editing. In fact, I share my text, and I ask for re-writing the text with "stronger verbs" and I get what I want... I am very satisfied with the result for free consultation.

- *Theme 3: ethical considerations (90%)*

The participants repeatedly mentioned the concern of "ethical" issues that is associated with AI tools. One professor in philosophy stated:

> I am very concerned about the use of these AI tools if students are not aware of the ethics behind these tools. Students should learn how to use these tools correctly to avoid any problem of plagiarism. Professors should promote awareness and responsible use to mitigate the risk of plagiarism associated with AI-generated content.

A psychology professor noted:

> It's important to note that AI models, including ChatGPT, are tools that can assist users, but it is the responsibility of users to learn about the ethical and legal use. The conversations with ChatGPT may contain sensitive or private information. Users should be mindful of data privacy and ensure that personal or confidential information is handled appropriately.

And a professor in elementary education stated:

> Plagiarism has been always around... with or without AI tools. It is essential to properly cite the information to avoid plagiarism especially if the content generated by ChatGPT is used in academic or professional contexts. Finally, users are responsible for ensuring that generated text is appropriately cited.

- *Theme 4: inaccurate information (95%)*

The fourth theme that was repeatedly described by the participating students was the notion of "inaccurate information."
One professor of computer engineering commented:

> We have to be aware that ChatGPT can generate false information. In fact, ChatGPT inherits and preserves biases in the data it was trained on. This can lead to biased and

unfair responses, particularly in sensitive or controversial topics. Relying on the information provided by these AI tools is dangerous.

One professor in chemistry noted:

ChatGPT is trained on a diverse range of internet text, and it does not have access to the most up-to-date or accurate information. If the training data contains inaccuracies or biases, these may be reflected in the responses... In cases of ambiguous queries or lack of context, the model might provide information that appears correct but is not accurate in the specific context of the user's inquiry.

Another professor in psychology stated:

ChatGPT doesn't have an integral fact-checking mechanism. It may generate responses that sound plausible but haven't been independently verified for accuracy... To avoid receiving false information, users interacting with AI models like ChatGPT should exercise caution and verify information generated by ChatGPT with trusted sources, especially for critical or factual information.

8 Discussion

The demographic analysis reveals that the predominant age group among the participants falls within the range of 36 to 55 years old. Also, the vast majority of professors have more than 10 years of teaching experience from various academic disciplines. Exceeding a decade in teaching indicates that a significant proportion of professors possess a substantial amount of teaching experience. This suggests a seasoned and experienced faculty sample including academic expertise, institutional knowledge, and established teaching practices.

Moreover, the majority of professors who are using the tool belong to humanities and social sciences fields. Such a finding provides insights into the disciplinary preferences for adopting ChatGPT. In fact, humanities and social sciences specialties often involve extensive reading, writing, and analysis of textual information. Professors in humanities and social sciences frequently engage in research activities that involve writing papers, articles, and other textual outputs. The high adoption of ChatGPT in these fields could be attributed to the tool's proficiency in generating human-like text, making it particularly valuable for tasks such as content creation, research assistance, and text editing.

Moreover, a good percentage of professors claimed to use ChatGPT on a daily basis and mostly for research assistance. This suggests that a considerable portion of the surveyed professors find ChatGPT helpful in their research-related activities, such as generating content, exploring ideas, or obtaining information.

Other professors use the tool for teaching support, which implies that a subset of the surveyed professors sees value in incorporating ChatGPT into their teaching methods, whether it be for creating instructional materials, generating content for lectures, or assisting students with queries. Moreover, the survey results indicate that nearly all respondents, specifically 98%, reported utilizing the tool primarily for text editing purposes. This indicates that a large proportion of the surveyed professors find ChatGPT beneficial to editing and refining written content.

The above findings suggest that ChatGPT is widely adopted among the surveyed professors. The specific ways in which professors utilize ChatGPT for these purposes may vary based on individual preferences and the nature of their research and teaching responsibilities.

The other set of questions included in the survey related to the professors' acceptance and use of the AI tool in their academic career. Applying Exploratory Factor Analysis (EFA) to the 16 items rated by participants provided a more comprehensible assessment regarding the acceptance and use of ChatGPT. The one-way repeated-measures ANOVA allowed us to compare the importance of the four generated factors and showed that *community influence* was the highest rated by the participants. This finding is consistent with previous research wherein social influence appears as a motivator to accept and use new technology [28, 30, 31]. It appears that professors are influenced by their peers to try and use ChatGPT in their academic work. The post hoc tests using the Bonferroni technique indicated a significant difference between the factors; however, this difference is not significant because it is not important on a scale of '5'.

When testing the relationships between the five factors, the results showed that all the variables are strongly correlated with each other and the dependent variable, the intention to use the tool. Also, the R square and the adjusted R square indicate that the combined predictor variables make a good contribution to the variance explained in the behavioral intention to use ChatGPT. Moreover, the findings of F-statistics and beta weights reveal that all the four determinants; *community influence*, *effectiveness*, *self-learning*, and *novelty and fun*; play a role in determining the attitudes regarding the use of the tool.

It has been outlined that *community influence* impacts users to use chatbots since it affects their expected performance and expected effort [45]. Since the release of ChatGPT, celebrities have shared their comments; for example, Musk commented "One of the biggest risks to the future of civilization is AI," to attendees at the World Government Summit in Dubai, United Arab Emirates, shortly after mentioning the development of ChatGPT [46]. Moreover, Bill Gates claimed that ChatGPT will "change our world" [47]. Therefore, people are influenced by others' opinions and their surroundings.

The results align with previous studies [48, 49] by highlighting the significant impact of performance expectancy and effort expectancy. However, in the case of a powerful AI tool such as ChatGPT, it is clear to users that there is no need for any facilitating conditions since no help or assistance is needed. Therefore, it is necessary to evaluate its usefulness from a practical perspective. Besides, in accordance with the social learning theory, the *effectiveness* and *self-learning* factors enhance an individual's entire functionality, and the *novelty and fun* factor may trigger a unique experience for users.

According to Montenegro-Rueda et al. [12], the utilization of ChatGPT in education has sparked interest due to its potential to enhance students' learning experience. By offering tailored responses, this system possesses the capability to cater to student requirements, provide instant feedback, and enhance comprehension of intricate concepts. As a result, it emerges as a tool that encourages student engagement and cognitive progress by adapting to their learning pace and delivering continual support in their knowledge-acquisition journey. Researchers assert that it works as an aid in developing students' writing skills. Through interaction with the system, students can receive corrections, suggestions for improvement, and detailed feedback on their writing. This empowers them to enhance their written communication abilities and achieve effectiveness in expressing themselves through writing. Researchers also urge writers to rely on their own knowledge and expertise to validate and supplement the information provided by the tool. Nonetheless, the tool excels in facilitating group discussions and fostering participation among students in projects and assignments. This cultivates a sense of community among learners by enabling interaction and exchange of ideas.

The analysis of the answers to the open-ended questions showed that professors highlighted two advantages and two disadvantages of the tool. Professors seem to be satisfied with the present features of the system, whereby the majority agreed about the usefulness of ChatGPT in free editing and immediacy. However, professors lamented about the effect of using AI in teaching and learning: they were concerned about plagiarism and inaccurate information.

The first theme that emerged from the professors' answers was "immediacy". Professors who participated in the study expressed appreciation for the tool's ability to provide prompt and instantaneous feedback. Professors emphasized the simplicity and ease of use for obtaining immediate feedback. They highlighted the tool's user-friendly nature, stating that the tool doesn't require any assistance in facilitating timely and constructive feedback. Participants appreciated the tool's capacity to generate quizzes in multiple-choice format based on their preferences; they underlined the utility of the tool in grading and providing immediate responses to their queries. A recent study showed that ChatGPT possesses a fundamental capability to provide feedback on arguments with a precision rate of (91.8%) and a recall rate of (63.2%) [50]. It was shown also that ChatGPT was significantly affected by the length of arguments and the discourse in the arguments. When compared to the teacher's feedback, it was shown that ChatGPT could potentially generate comprehensive and textual feedback that is limited to the linguistic level, whereas the teacher's feedback was more focused on student's overall learning progress [50].

The second theme "free editing" suggests that professors need help in editing their work. The statements shared by professors express a need for assistance in editing their written content, particularly when they have the option for free editing. This theme implies that professors may face challenges or seek support in refining and improving the quality of their written work. The mention of "free editing" suggests that this assistance is available without cost, indicating that professors value a service or tool that helps enhance the clarity, correctness, and overall effectiveness of their written communication. The theme highlights the perceived importance of editing support among professors. According to Chang et al. [51], students learning English as a second language who used the

Grammarly program over the course of a semester improved more in their English writing than students who did not use the program, and students expressed appreciation for the program's instant grammar correction. However, there may be a distinction between AI tools like ChatGPT and spell-checkers like Grammarly that can create complete phrases and paragraphs for students rather than only flagging errors and suggesting corrections.

On the other hand, professors shared concerns related to "ethical considerations" when using ChatGPT. While the tool possesses its advantages, professors were very worried about ethics in the context of AI and ChatGPT, such as privacy and security of data shared during interactions with ChatGPT. They highlighted the importance of safeguarding sensitive information and ensuring that user data is handled responsibly. Also, plagiarism was very much noted as one of the concerns of ethical considerations, which aligns with previous studies [52]. Due to its training on a dataset of language, ChatGPT might occasionally produce responses that incorporate biased or offensive language [53]. Users of ChatGPT must understand the limitations of ChatGPT as it generates offensive content, and it may reinforce stereotypes spread misinformation and consequently hinder the learning process.

However, some researchers argue that plagiarism depends on the user's prompt. In fact, a large language model (LLM) is a statistical language model, trained on a massive amount of data, that can be used to generate and translate text and other content. Thus, LLMs are designed to "encode" human text during training to create a statistical model. This model is then capable of generating and translating text and performing various natural language processing tasks based on the patterns learned. When the input sample is small, the output from LLMs, including ChatGPT, may match existing text found on the internet. This resemblance to existing text can be perceived as a form of plagiarism. ChatGPT, as an LLM, relies on prompts provided by users. It does not generate content independently but responds to the input it receives. The lack of prompt engineering and iteration may result in output that feels more like plagiarism. Therefore, careful prompt engineering and iteration can influence the output of ChatGPT. This involves refining and crafting prompts to guide the model's responses. In this sense, the output is considered the work of the individual who crafted the prompts, emphasizing the role of human involvement in the creative process, and originality can be influenced by the level of human input and refinement in crafting the prompts [54].

The final theme "inaccurate information" reflects the professors' concern regarding biases in the responses generated by ChatGPT and the need to ensure that the tool provides unbiased and equitable information. Professors expressed concerns about the possibility of misinformation and the impact it can have, particularly in an educational setting. This concern was also highlighted in previous studies [55]. The statements from professors regarding the potential 'generation of false information' is linked to the model inheriting and preserving biases that are already present in the training data, leading to biased and unfair responses, particularly in sensitive or controversial topics. Also, ChatGPT is trained on a diverse range of internet text and may not have access to the most up-to-date or accurate information [54]. While it may generate responses that sound plausible, ChatGPT lacks an integral fact-checking mechanism, which implies that users should be cautious and should verify information with trusted sources. These statements highlight the importance of awareness and caution when relying on AI tools for information.

Understanding and addressing advantages and disadvantages are crucial for responsible and ethical use of AI technologies like ChatGPT in educational settings. The shared concerns reflect a broader awareness among educators about the ethical implications of integrating AI tools into their academic career and teaching practices.

According to the constructivist theory of learning, it is crucial for students to actively explore and investigate new materials [56]. ChatGPT can help students, it can scaffold students' past knowledge and experiences to assist them in building new information by involving them in dialogue and motivating them to participate in the learning process. By building on their past knowledge and experiences and offering tailored recommendations for more learning, ChatGPT's personalized feedback can also aid in the process of their own learning [57]. As a result, ChatGPT can serve as a useful "More Knowledgeable Other" (MKO) in the learning process, helping students identify their mistakes and point them in the direction of successful progress [58]. ChatGPT can assist in providing students with personalized feedback that directs them toward effective progress and aids in the discovery of mistakes in their work by drawing on their existing knowledge and experiences. This dialogue functions as an MKO, aiding in the creation of new information. This strategy is in line with ChatGPT's logical algorithms, which create new knowledge based on previously known information. Thus, ChatGPT can be a useful medium for promoting constructive learning.

Rogers [27] speculated that each social system has a structure with defined norms of interrelated units that give stability to individual behavior. Communication within a system assists or hinders the diffusion of innovations. Rogers distinguished among three types of innovation-decisions: optional innovation-decisions, when adoption of an innovation is independent of the decisions of other members of the system; collective innovation-decisions, when adoption an innovation is based on a consensus among the members of a system; and authority innovation-decisions when adoption of an innovation is to follow individuals in a system who possess power, status, or technical expertise. For the current generation, ChatGPT is an effective, efficient tool as it delivers responses instantaneously and free of charge. In innovation-diffusion theory, Rogers [27] defined categories of adopters of innovations, including innovators, early adopters, early majority, late majority, and laggards. However, in the case of ChatGPT, this classification does not matter as, regardless of the time of adoption and the rate of usage, no one is an innovator or a laggard, a leader or a follower. Use of this AI tool will soon become a habit of students' daily lives, embedded in their social systems and interactions with their professors, classmates, and friends.

9 Limitations of the Study

This study included only a limited number of professors in universities in Lebanon. Further studies are needed to compare the findings of this study with other countries in the Middle East and with other regions. Understanding the disciplinary distribution of ChatGPT usage among professors provides valuable context for the tool's applicability and acceptance within academia. It also reflects the diverse needs and preferences across different academic fields.

The use of open-ended questions, although useful and convenient for understanding professors' perceptions and experiences regarding the use of ChatGPT, is not sufficient to generalize the findings. Gathering data from a larger number of participants may be useful to establish validity and to gain a more complete picture of the advantages and disadvantages of the incorporation of AI into education. In addition, it would be interesting to determine whether adoption of this tool is due only to convenience and simplicity or whether it results from its embedded advantages on the daily practices of teaching and learning. A similar study with students would be beneficial to track the perceptions of learners vis-à-vis AI tools in education as well as to detect any progress in the learning trajectory after using ChatGPT.

10 Implications for Practice: Do We Embrace or Ban ChatGPT?

As technology advances and the role of AI becomes more pervasive in our day-to-day lives, educators need to confront a range of ethical questions about the use of artificial intelligence. The questions are: When is it appropriate to use AI, and when should it be avoided? How can educators ensure that AI is used equitably and without bias? Some suggestions may help educators as we strive for a better future:

- Educators and students may use AI to generate a framework of ideas or answers before writing their own. Most of the work and ideas comes from students' own thinking.
- Academic institutions are urged to make ethical decisions based on gathered information because we cannot wait for AI to make ethical decisions for us based on morals, ethics, and values.
- Educators are urged to spread awareness about advantages and disadvantages of these AI tools.
- It is essential to learn how to write and design prompts.
- Academic institutions are urged to develop an understanding of how AI works and how it can be misused. This can include discussing the potential risks and consequences of using AI to cheat and the importance of honesty and integrity in academic work.

- Educators must rethink assessments and adjust assessment protocols because while there are some initial plagiarism detection platforms, these have a challenging task ahead.

11 Conclusion

This study shows that the adoption of ChatGPT relies on the advantages embraced through its effectiveness and immediacy, as well as being a new tool. At the same time, the qualitative data revealed concerns, such as plagiarism and biases, in the academic settings.

Nowadays, the incorporation of technology has proven to be both advantageous and challenging. When applied appropriately, technology has the potential to streamline and enhance the experiences of both educators and students. To continually enhance the human learning process through the integration of technology in education, it is imperative that educators are actively engaged from the initial stages because they hold the pivotal role in the incorporation of digital technologies in education. This recognition ensures that the correct technology is employed for the intended purposes, because a failure to do so could have the unintended consequence of hindering rather than improving the capabilities of students and teachers.

A digital workplace should facilitate information sharing among employees in the organization and partner organizations. Hinings et al. emphasize the necessity for new theories in the era of digital transformation, linking it to institutional change [59]. They propose an institutional perspective that explores how emerging actors and configurations associated with digital transformation challenge, substitute, or complement existing organizational and field norms. Understanding how innovations achieve legitimacy and examining the influence of socio-cultural factors on organizations are crucial for studying digital transformation [60].

Despite advantages and disadvantages of the AI tools, it should be argued that ChatGPT is one step in the new innovations of AI tools, and professors as well as students can be taught how to embrace and to engage with ChatGPT in a constructive manner in line with the ethics or policies of their educational institutions. Eventually, the concern should not be "whether" the student should use or not ChatGPT, but "how".

References

1. Kraus S, Jones P, Kailer N et al (2021) Digital transformation: an overview of the current state of the art of research. SAGE Open 11(3):1–15. https://doi.org/10.1177/21582440211047576
2. Bond M, Buntins K, Bedenlier S et al (2020) Mapping research in student engagement and educational technology in higher education: a systematic evidence map. Int J Educ Technol Higher Educ 17(2). https://doi.org/10.1186/s41239-019-0176-8

3. Kim KN (2019) Teachers' administrative workload crowding out instructional activities. Asia Pacific J Educ 39(1):31–49. https://doi.org/10.1080/02188791.2019.1572592
4. Dicheva D, Dichev C, Agre G, Angelova G (2015) Gamification in education: a systematic mapping study. J Educ Technol Soc 18(3):75–88. https://www.jstor.org/stable/jeductechsoci.18.3.75
5. King DL, Delfabbro PH (2016) Early exposure to digital simulated gambling: a review and conceptual model. Comput Human Behav 55(1):198–206. https://doi.org/10.1016/j.chb.2015.09.012
6. Beghetto RA (2018) Beautiful risks: having the courage to teach and learn creatively. Rowman & Littlefield, Maryland, USA. https://rowman.com/ISBN/9781475834734/Beautiful-Risks-Having-the-Courage-to-Teach-and-Learn-Creatively
7. Colchester K, Hagras H, Alghazzawi D, Aldabbagh G (2017) A Survey of artificial intelligence techniques employed for adaptive educational systems within e-learning platforms. J Artific Intell Soft Comput Res 7(1):47–64. https://doi.org/10.1515/jaiscr-2017-0004
8. Hwang G-J, Chen C-Y, Tsai P-S, Tsai C-C (2011) An expert system for improving web-based problem-solving ability of students. Expert Syst Applic 38(7):8664–8672. https://doi.org/10.1016/j.eswa.2011.01.072
9. Timms MJ (2016) Letting artificial intelligence in education out of the box: educational cobots and smart classrooms. Int J Artific Intell Educ 26(2):701–712. https://doi.org/10.1007/s40593-016-0095-y
10. Edwards C, Spence PR, Lin X (2018) I, teacher: using artificial intelligence (AI) and social robots in communication and instruction. Commun Educ 67(4):473–480. https://doi.org/10.1080/03634523.2018.1502459
11. Temsah O, Khan SA, Chaiah Y et al (2023) Overview of early ChatGPT's presence in medical literature: insights from a hybrid literature review by ChatGPT and human experts. Cureus 15(4):1–10. https://doi.org/10.7759/cureus.37281
12. Montenegro-Rueda M, Fernández-Cerero J, Fernández-Batanero JM, López-Meneses E (2023) Impact of the implementation of ChatGPT in education: a systematic review. Computers 12(8):153–164. https://doi.org/10.3390/computers12080153
13. Wu T et al (2023) A brief overview of ChatGPT: the history, status quo, and potential future development. IEEE/CAA J Automat Sinica 10(5):1122. https://doi.org/10.1109/JAS.2023.123618
14. Cotton DR, Cotton PA, Shipway JR (2023) Chatting and cheating: ensuring academic integrity in the era of ChatGPT. Innovat Educ Teach Internat. https://doi.org/10.1080/14703297.2023.2190148
15. Elkins K, Chun J (2020) Can GPT-3 pass a writer's Turing test? J Cultural Analyt 5(2):1–16. https://doi.org/10.22148/001c.17212
16. Blose A (2023) As ChatGPT enters the classroom, teachers weigh pros and cons. Nea Today. https://www.nea.org/nea-today/all-news-articles/chatgpt-enters-classroom-teachers-weigh-pros-and-cons.
17. Study.com (2023) ChatGPT in the classroom. https://study.com/resources/chatgpt-in-the-classroom
18. Sullivan M, Kelly A, McLaughlan P (2023) ChatGPT in higher education: considerations for academic integrity and student learning. J Appl Learn Teach 6(1):1–10. https://doi.org/10.37074/jalt.2023.6.1.17
19. Cassidy C (2023) Lecturer detects bot-use in one fifth of assessments as concerns mount over AI in exams. The Guardian. https://www.theguardian.com/australia-news/2023/jan/17/lecturer-detects-bot-use-in-one-fifth-of-assessments-as-concerns-mount-over-ai-in-exams
20. Fishbein M, Ajzen I (1975) Belief, attitude, intention and behavior: an introduction to theory and research. Addison–Wesley, Reading, MA. https://people.umass.edu/aizen/f&a1975.html
21. Davis FD (1989) Perceived usefulness, perceived ease of use, and user acceptance of information technology. MIS Quart 13(3):319–340. https://doi.org/10.2307/249008

22. King WR, He J (2006) A meta-analysis of the technology acceptance model. Inform Manage 43(1):740–755. https://doi.org/10.1016/j.im.2006.05.003
23. Venkatesh V, Davis F (2000) A theoretical extension of the technology acceptance model: four longitudinal field studies. Manage Sci 46(2):186–204. https://doi.org/10.1287/mnsc.46.2.186.11926
24. Raaij EMV, Schepers JJL (2008) The acceptance and use of a virtual learning environment in China. Comput Educ 50(3):838–852. https://doi.org/10.1016/j.compedu.2006.09.001
25. Ngai EWT, Poon JKL, Chan YHC (2007) Empirical examination of the adoption of WebCT using TAM. Comput Educ 48:250–267. https://doi.org/10.1016/j.compedu.2004.11.007
26. Ajzen I (1991) The theory of planned behavior. Organizat Behav Human Decision Process 50(2):179–211. https://doi.org/10.1016/0749-5978(91)90020-T
27. Rogers E (2003) Diffusion of innovations. Free Press, New York. https://teddykw2.files.wordpress.com/2012/07/everett-m-rogers-diffusion-of-innovations.pdf
28. Venkatesh V, Morris MG, Davis GB, Davis FD (2003) User acceptance of information technology: toward a unified view. MIS Quart 27(3):425–478. https://doi.org/10.2307/30036540
29. Pynoo B, Devolder P, Tondeur J et al (2011) Predicting secondary school teachers' acceptance and use of a digital learning environment: a cross-sectional study. Comput Human Behav 27(1):568–575. https://doi.org/10.1016/j.chb.2010.10.005
30. Marchewka JT, Liu C, Kostiwa K (2007) An application of the UTAUT model for understanding student perceptions using course management software. Commun IIMA 7(2):93–104. https://scholarworks.lib.csusb.edu/cgi/viewcontent.cgi?referer=&httpsredir=1&article=1038&context=ciima
31. Chiu CM, Wang ETG (2008) Understanding Web-based learning continuance intention: the role of subjective task value. Inform Manage 45(3):194–201. https://doi.org/10.1016/j.im.2008.02.003
32. Liaw SS (2008) Investigating students' perceived satisfaction, behavioral intention, and effectiveness of e-learning: a case study of the Blackboard system. Comput Educ 51(2):864–873. https://doi.org/10.1016/j.compedu.2007.09.005
33. Marques BP, Villate JE, Carvalho CV (2011) Applying the UTAUT model in engineering higher education: teacher's technology adoption. In: 6th Iberian conference on information systems and technologies (CISTI 2011), Chaves, Portugal. https://web.fe.up.pt/~villate/publications/Marques_2011_UTAUT_Model.pdf
34. Pavlic L et al (2011) Qualitative analysis: identification of the factors influencing e-learning system acceptance. In: eLmL 2011, The third international conference on mobile, hybrid, and on-line learning. https://personales.upv.es/thinkmind/dl/conferences/elml/elml_2011/elml_2011_2_40_50072.pdf
35. Sumak B, Polancic G, Hericko M (2010) An empirical study of virtual learning environment adoption using UTAUT. In: Proceedings of the 2010 second international conference on mobile, hybrid, and on-line learning, Saint Maarten, Netherlands Antilles. https://doi.org/10.1109/eLmL.2010.11
36. Kennedy DM (2005) Challenges in evaluating Hong Kong students' perceptions of Moodle. In: Proceedings of the 22nd annual conference of ASCILITE, Brisbane. https://citeseerx.ist.psu.edu/document?repid=rep1&type=pdf&doi=2db2946d29ec60c1a2a0fab87c97a59f2a69346b
37. Kirner T, Custodio C, Kirner C (2008) Usability evaluation of the Moodle system from the teachers' perspective. In: Proceedings of the IADIS international conference on e-learning, The Netherlands. https://www.researchgate.net/publication/220969194_Usability_Evaluation_Of_The_Moodle_System_From_The_Teachers%27_Perspective
38. Machado M, Tao E (2007) Blackboard vs. Moodle: comparing user experience of learning management systems. In: Proceedings of the 37th annual frontiers in education conference—global engineering: knowledge without borders, opportunities without passports, Milwaukee, WI, USA. https://doi.org/10.1109/FIE.2007.4417910

39. Ho R (2006) Handbook of univariate and multivariate data analysis and interpretation with SPSS. Chapman & Hall, NY. https://doi.org/10.1201/9781420011111
40. Kaiser HF (1970) A second generation little jiffy. Psychometrika 35(4):401–415. https://doi.org/10.1007/BF02291817
41. Bodgan RC, Biklen SK (2007) Qualitative research for education, 5th ed. Pearson Education (ISBN: 9780205482931)
42. Gall MD, Borg WR, Gall JP (1996) Educational research: an introduction. Longman Publishing, Harlow, UK. (ISBN: 9780801309809)
43. Marshall C, Rossman GB (2014) Designing qualitative research. Sage Publications, Washington DC. https://doi.org/10.5070/L412004995
44. Glaser B, Strauss A (2009) The discovery of grounded theory: strategies for qualitative research. Transaction Publishers, New Jersey (ISBN: 0-202-30260-1). http://www.sxf.uevora.pt/wp-content/uploads/2013/03/Glaser_1967.pdf
45. Sharma S, Islam N, Singh G, Dhir A (2022) Why do retail customers adopt artificial intelligence (AI) based autonomous decision-making systems? IEEE Transact Engineer Manage 71:1–16. https://doi.org/10.1109/TEM.2022.3157976
46. Browne R (2023) Elon Musk, who co-founded firm behind ChatGPT, warns A.I. is 'one of the biggest risks' to civilization. CNBC. https://www.cnbc.com/2023/02/15/elon-musk-co-founder-of-chatgpt-creator-openai-warns-of-ai-society-risk.html#:~:text=billionaire%20Elon%20Musk.-,"One%20of%20the%20biggest%20risks%20to%20the%20future%20of%20civilization,great%20capability%2C"%20Musk%20said
47. Bhaimiya S (2023) Bill Gates said ChatGPT will 'change our world' by making the workplace more efficient. Business Insider. https://www.businessinsider.com/bill-gates-chatgpt-says-will-change-our-world-interview-2023-2.
48. Choi JN, Sung SY, Lee K, Cho D-S (2011) Balancing cognition and emotion: innovation implementation as a function of cognitive appraisal and emotional reactions toward innovation. J Organiz Behav 32(1):107–124. https://www.jstor.org/stable/41415657
49. Jin SV, Youn S (2023) Social presence and imagery processing as predictors of chatbot continuance intention in human–AI-interaction. Int J Human-Comput Interact 39(9):1874–1886. https://doi.org/10.1080/10447318.2022.2129277
50. Wang L, Chen X, Xu L et al (2023) ChatGPT's capabilities in providing feedback on undergraduate students' argumentation: a case study. Thinking Skills Creativ 51(1):1–10. https://doi.org/10.1016/j.tsc.2023.101440
51. Chang TS, Li Y, Huang H-W, Whitfield (2021) Exploring EFL students' writing performance and their acceptance of AI-based automated writing feedback. In: Proceedings of the 2021 2nd international conference on education development and studies (ICED '21). https://doi.org/10.1145/3459043.3459065
52. Shidiq M (2023) The use of artificial intelligence-based Chat-GPT and its challenges for the world of education; from the viewpoint of the development of creative writing skills. Proc Int Conf Educ Soc Hum 1(1):353–357. https://ejournal.unuja.ac.id/index.php/icesh/article/view/5614
53. Deng J, Lin Y (2022) The benefits and challenges of ChatGPT: an overview. Front Comput Intell Systems 2(2):81–83. https://doi.org/10.54097/fcis.v2i2.4465
54. Meyer JG, Urbanowics RJ, Martin PCN (2023) ChatGPT and large language models in academia: opportunities and challenges. BioData Mining 16(20). https://doi.org/10.1186/s13040-023-00339-9
55. Baidoo-Anu D, Ansah LO (2023) Education in the era of generative artificial intelligence (AI): understanding the potential benefits of ChatGPT in promoting teaching and learning. J AI 7(1):52–62. https://doi.org/10.2139/ssrn.4337484
56. Piaget J (1959) The language and thought of the child. Routledge, London. (ISBN: 9780415267502)

57. Vygotsky L (1978) Interaction between learning and development. Read Dev Children 23(3):34–41. https://innovation.umn.edu/igdi/wp-content/uploads/sites/37/2018/08/Interaction_Between_Learning_and_Development.pdf
58. Geng J, Razali AB (2022) Effectiveness of the automated writing evaluation program on improving undergraduates' writing performance. Engl Lang Teach 15(7):49–60. https://doi.org/10.5539/elt.v15n7p49
59. Hinings B, Gegenhuber T, Greenwood R (2018) Digital innovation and transformation: an institutional perspective. Inform Organiz 28(1):52–61. https://doi.org/10.1016/j.infoandorg.2018.02.004
60. White M (2012) Digital workplaces: vision and reality. Business Inform Rev 29(4):205–214. https://doi.org/10.1177/0266382112470412

Leading Digital Transformation in Higher Education

Yousif Asfour

Abstract Digital transformation is not just about deploying technology, but rather, it is about transforming an organization by using technology as a catalyst. This chapter builds on my personal experience to illustrate some of the elements of digital transformation and its impact on organizations. This highlights the special aspects of academic institutions, and how these characteristics impact leading the implementation of digital transformation at these organizations. The chapter ends with a case study illustrating how these different techniques were successfully utilized to accomplish digital transformation at the American University of Beirut.

Keywords Leadership · Higher education · Digital transformation · Technology

1 Introduction

In this chapter I will be sharing my personal experience in leading transformational change across multiple organizations. This is not a theoretical review of leadership techniques and skills, but rather a summary of practical lessons learned during my career while helping transform multiple organizations and, in particular, several academic institutions. I have to admit that, instead of leaning on a research assistant or an administrative assistant to gather the information, I used ChatGPT and other such tools to help me put this document together. I 'prompted' ChatGPT to 'prompt me' in putting the skeleton together, and to do some of the writing. I then validated, modified, added, removed, edited content and personalized the document based on my experience and style. I used this approach partly to help me

Y. Asfour (✉)
Office of Innovation and Transformation, American University of Beirut, Beirut, Lebanon
e-mail: yasfour@aub.edu.lb

© The Author(s), under exclusive license to Springer Nature Switzerland AG 2024
A. Badran et al. (eds.), *Higher Education in the Arab World*,
https://doi.org/10.1007/978-3-031-70779-7_6

accelerate the process of writing this chapter, but also to illustrate how such transformative technologies can be used effectively to produce useful (and hopefully insightful) information. While I have made every reasonable effort to acknowledge the sources of material used in this chapter, I apologize for any omissions. With so many years working in the field, it is difficult not to absorb many of the materials and feel that they are a part of you, and therefore it is difficult to cite specific references within the text. However, I have included several references to help with further reading and exploration [1–8].

2 Defining Digital Transformation

I would like to start by emphasizing that *digital transformation* (DX) is not about deploying technology into the organization, but rather, it is about transforming the organization by using technology as a catalyst. Digital transformation is the process of changing how an organization operates through strategically integrating digital technologies into all aspects of its operations, activities, and culture to fundamentally change how it delivers value to its customers or, in the case of an academic institution, its community. Therefore, DX is a comprehensive and strategic overhaul of an organization's processes, activities, and business models through the integration and optimization of digital technologies. It goes beyond merely adopting new technologies, and involves a shift in the way an organization operates and delivers value to its stakeholders.

While this transformation involves leveraging digital technologies such as enterprise systems, cloud computing, artificial intelligence, machine learning, the Internet of Things (IoT), data analytics, mobile devices, and others, the main reason for introducing these technologies is to drive innovation, improve efficiency, create new operational and business models in order to add value to the customers and community members.

Therefore, DX is special because it is not just a technology upgrade or a simple automation of processes, but rather, it is a fundamental shift in how organizations operate, interact with customers, and create value. Although technology for technology's sake, can be rewarding, the role of technology in organizations is to solve real-world problems to accomplish specific goals. As obvious as this might seem, instead of focusing on transformation first and applying the appropriate technical solution after, most organizations do the opposite. Organizations tend to identify a certain technology or platform that piques their interest, and then try to impose it on their existing organization. By doing so, organizations run the risk of spending time and effort on transposing their existing organization, processes and operations onto the new platforms, thus missing the opportunity to redesign and rejuvenate their organization and operations to become more effective at delivering value and their mission.

Organizations that successfully undergo digital transformation often experience increased customer satisfaction, faster time-to-market for products and services, and improved overall business performance. Embracing automation, artificial intelligence, cloud computing, and other cutting-edge technologies allows businesses to respond faster to market changes, reduce costs, and stay ahead of competition, but only if they are part of an overall transformation of the organizational culture and processes. Moreover, a proper digital transformation fosters a culture of continuous improvement, encouraging employees to adapt to new technologies and work collaboratively across functions. Overall, the impact of digital transformation is transformative, reshaping the organizational landscape and setting the stage for long-term success in the digital age.

3 The Impact of Digital Transformation

Digital transformation significantly influences the structure and operations within an organization, reshaping the roles of individuals, the way work is done, creating new opportunities for better service, improving efficiency and fostering innovation.

One of the primary areas impacted by DX is customer experience, or student experience in the case of higher education. With the advent of digital technologies, organizations can engage with their customers/students through multiple channels, offering personalized interactions, seamless transactions, and responsive customer support. Therefore, DX enables the integration of data analytics and artificial intelligence to understand customer behavior, preferences, and feedback, allowing organizations to tailor their services and to better meet the evolving needs of their community.

Other areas significantly affected by DX are the internal processes and workflows. Since DX involves the re-engineering and automation of tasks, the implementation of collaborative tools and the adoption of cloud-based and other solutions leads to streamlined operations and improved productivity. By optimizing and aligning their internal processes with system capabilities, organizations can introduce automation, reduce manual errors, enhance communication and collaboration among employees, achieve greater operational efficiency and ultimately enhance the customer (student, in the case of academic institutions) journey by helping make every administrative encounter a pleasant one.

Supply-chain management is also profoundly impacted by DX, even in higher education. The integration of advanced technologies such as IoT, blockchain, and data analytics allows organizations to gain real-time visibility into their supply chains. This visibility enhances decision-making, improves inventory management, and enables organizations to respond promptly to changes in demand and supply. As a result, academic institutions can achieve greater resilience, cost-effectiveness, and agility in their supply-chain operations, allowing them to better meet the ever-changing teaching and research needs of their faculty and students.

Furthermore, DX influences talent management and the workforce. Organizations are adopting digital tools for recruitment, onboarding, and staff training. Remote work, enabled by digital technologies, has become more prevalent, requiring organizations to adapt their policies and infrastructure accordingly. Also, DX facilitates data-driven human-resource (HR) practices, enabling organizations to make informed decisions about talent acquisition, development, and retention.

In addition to benefiting from the above areas, DX in higher education presents unique challenges and opportunities compared to other organizations. Higher education institutions are tasked with not only adapting to market needs and technological advancements but also with preparing students for a rapidly changing digital landscape. The educational sector requires a delicate balance between embracing cutting-edge technologies and preserving the quality and integrity of academic programs.

One distinctive aspect of DX in higher education is the impact on teaching and learning methods. The integration of online learning platforms, virtual classrooms, and educational technology tools allows for flexible and personalized learning experiences. Institutions can offer a mix of traditional in-person classes and online courses, catering to diverse learning styles and accommodating students who may have geographical constraints. The use of digital tools also facilitates collaborative learning environments, enabling students to engage with course materials and peers in innovative ways.

Administrative processes are another critical area in higher education that benefit from DX. From admissions to registration and alumni relations, digital technologies streamline administrative tasks, reducing paperwork and manual processes, while at the same time enhancing the student experience. Student information systems, digital communication platforms, and data analytics contribute to more efficient and responsive administrative operations. Additionally, digital transformation allows institutions to implement data-driven strategies for student success and retention, identifying early warning signs and providing timely support.

Furthermore, research and development within higher education can leverage digital transformation to enhance innovation. Advanced data analytics, artificial intelligence, and collaborative platforms contribute to research endeavors, allowing institutions to conduct cutting-edge research, collaborate across disciplines and institutions, and disseminate findings more effectively. Digital tools also play a crucial role in supporting virtual research collaborations and providing access to vast repositories of academic resources.

The impact of DX in higher education is profound, influencing not only operational efficiency but also the overall quality and accessibility of education. Digital transformation requires reimagining students as customers, and streamlining internal operations, and leveraging data-driven insights for informed decision-making, enhanced teaching and learning as well as advanced research and discovery. Digital transformation also promotes inclusivity by reaching a broader audience, including non-traditional students, students with special needs, and those in remote locations. It also facilitates lifelong learning opportunities and professional development. The impact of DX on a university is far-reaching, influencing its competitiveness, market relevance, and overall sustainability. This shift, however,

4 Unique Aspects of Academic Institutions

Higher education institutions are tasked with not only adapting to technological advancements but also with preparing students for a rapidly changing digital landscape. The educational sector requires a delicate balance between embracing cutting-edge technologies and preserving the quality and integrity of academic programs.

The structure, governance, and operations of higher education institutions are distinctive when compared to other organizations, and these differences have significant implications for the implementation of DX. In particular, higher education institutions often operate with a decentralized structure and a system of shared governance. Decision-making is distributed among various academic departments, faculty committees, and administrative units.

In addition, academic freedom and traditions are another unique aspect of higher education institutions. The academic environment places a high value on academic freedom, autonomy, and adherence to established traditions. Faculty members often have a significant role in shaping curricula and educational methods. The implementation of DX may face challenges in balancing the integration of technology with the preservation of academic traditions. Leaders in higher education need to find ways to leverage digital tools without compromising the core values of academic freedom and the pursuit of knowledge.

The academic environment, with its emphasis on shared governance and academic freedom requires strong collaboration and effective communication to ensure that all stakeholders are on board with the changes. Faculty play a crucial role in shaping curricula, teaching methods, and research initiatives. Successful leaders in higher education DX understand the importance of engaging faculty early on, addressing their concerns, and demonstrating the value of digital tools in enhancing the educational experience. Unlike in traditional organizations, where top-down directives may be more readily accepted, higher education institutions often require a collaborative approach involving faculty members in all decision-making processes. A top-down approach will face resistance and, in many cases, maneuvering to undermine the effort, necessitating inclusive decision-making processes that involve faculty and staff in shaping the DX strategy.

The tenure system prevalent in higher education contributes to longer decision cycles and a more cautious approach to change. Faculty members, who often have tenure, may be resistant to rapid changes in teaching methods or technology adoption. Leaders need to balance the preservation of academic values with the imperative to adapt to evolving technological landscapes. Implementing DX requires a careful navigation of long-standing traditions, ensuring that technological advancements align with the institution's educational goals without compromising academic freedom. Leaders must take into account the need for a gradual and collaborative approach to DX, providing support and incentives for faculty members to embrace new technologies in their teaching and research as the academic culture's emphasis on tradition and the tenure system can slow down the pace of change.

In addition, higher education institutions encompass a wide range of educational models, including research universities, liberal arts colleges, community colleges, and vocational schools—sometimes all within the same institution. Each of these models has distinct goals, structures, and operational dynamics. Implementing DX requires recognizing these differences and tailoring strategies to suit the specific needs and goals of each institution. For example, a research university may focus on advanced research technologies, while a community college may prioritize digital tools for enhancing vocational training. The diversity of higher education institutions necessitates a tailored approach, and leaders must customize DX strategies to align with the specific needs and goals of each institution, recognizing that a one-size-fits-all approach may not be effective.

Furthermore, many higher education institutions face financial constraints and budget limitations due to reduced public funding and increasing competition. This financial pressure can impact the ability to invest in comprehensive DX initiatives. Leaders implementing DX in higher education must navigate these financial challenges by identifying cost-effective solutions, exploring alternative funding models, and making strategic decisions that prioritize high-impact digital initiatives.

While the DX is challenging for any organization, leading DX in higher education demands a more nuanced approach distinct from that required in regular organizations. In addition to the typical challenges such as organizational resistance, cybersecurity concerns, and the need for substantial investment for all organizations, DX in higher education presents additional unique challenges and opportunities. Furthermore, unlike more centralized corporate structures, the nature of academic institutions can lead to slower decision-making processes and a diverse array of opinions.

5 Characteristics of Digital Transformation Leadership

The successful implementation of DX for any organization requires strategic planning, change management, faculty and staff training, and a commitment to maintaining the mission and core values of education while embracing the potential of technology to enhance research and the learning experience. This in turn, demands a distinctive set of leadership skills and characteristics that align with the complexities of navigating technological change.

A visionary and strategic mindset is paramount, as leaders must be capable of conceptualizing the organization's future state in the digital landscape and charting a clear roadmap for transformation. This involves the ability to foresee market trends, understand emerging technologies, and make informed decisions about the integration of digital tools to enhance business processes.

Adaptability and agility are also crucial leadership traits in the face of rapid technological evolution. Leaders need to be flexible and open to change, fostering a culture within the organization that encourages experimentation and learning from failures. The digital landscape is dynamic, and leaders must be willing to adjust strategies and embrace emerging opportunities quickly. This requires a willingness to challenge the status quo, experiment with innovative approaches, take calculated risks, and instill a sense of resilience among the workforce.

Strategic talent management is another critical leadership skill. Leaders must identify and nurture digital talent within the organization, ensuring that employees possess the necessary skills or have access to training opportunities. This involves creating a learning culture that values continuous skill development and attracting external talent when needed.

Furthermore, a focus on customer-centricity is vital. Leaders need to prioritize the customer experience throughout the DX process, aligning technological advancements with customer needs and expectations. This requires a deep understanding of customer behavior, feedback mechanisms, and the ability to integrate customer-centric strategies into the overall DX roadmap. This is a fundamental change in mind set for academic institutions, as they need to start thinking of students, and treating them as customers.

Effective communication skills are also foundational to successful DX leadership. Leaders must be able to articulate the vision of DX clearly, inspiring and aligning the entire organization toward common goals. Transparent and regular communication helps build trust and alleviate concerns among employees. Leaders need to convey the purpose and benefits of DX, address uncertainties, and ensure that everyone understands their role in the process.

Furthermore, the shared governance model and other unique aspects of academic institutions make collaboration and inclusivity essential leadership qualities in the DX journey. Leaders should foster a culture of cross-functional collaboration, breaking down silos and encouraging diverse teams to work together. This inclusivity extends to involving faculty and staff at all levels in the decision-making process, leveraging their insights and creating a sense of ownership and commitment to the transformation efforts.

6 A Case Study: An Example of Successful DX Leadership

I hope that by sharing my personal experience at an academic institution I will be able illustrate different leadership techniques that can help with the implementation of DX at any academic institution.

I joined my current institution as Chief Information Officer (CIO) around a decade ago at a time when everything was going wrong with information technology (IT). The department had just gone through a few years of leadership and structural changes that left the IT team devastated, and the infrastructure and technology services in a mess. This in turn led to a lack of trust in IT and technology among the faculty and students.

Recognizing the importance of setting a clear vision, I chose to start with focusing on the mission and people instead of infrastructure, technology, and services. While fixing systems and improving services was important, it was more important and more urgent to focus the team. I reasoned that, if the team knows where they are heading, and were aligned around the goals, all the other issues become much easier to address.

Therefore, as a first step, I worked with the team to set and communicate a three-year IT road map to turn IT into a partner with faculty, staff and students in transforming teaching, learning, research and student life at our institution. The roadmap focused on three major milestones, starting with "building trust through service excellence", followed by "IT becoming a strategic partner" with the key institutional stakeholders, and ending with IT becoming "the transformation partner" required for DX.

Once the roadmap was in place, we started focusing on building trust with the stakeholders through emphasis on service excellence. This meant that I worked with the IT team on prioritizing the high-impact issues, and working with the stakeholders to fix them. For example, we noticed that most of the complaints were related to network performance. So, the first priority was to work with the institutional leadership to secure funds to increase bandwidth, and with the IT team to optimize the network infrastructure to improve performance and reliability.

Given that the institution is an academic one, fixing the infrastructure was necessary but not sufficient. We needed to also ensure that the faculty felt that they were being heard, and were involved in the decision-making process of all critical service-delivery decisions. So, while the IT team spent their time improving services, I spent the majority of my time meeting with each of the 20+ academic and administrative unit leaders to accomplish three objectives. The first objective was to listen attentively to everyone in order to learn more about the organization, understand everyone's concerns and, most importantly, gain insight into the stakeholder relationships and "politics". The second objective was to use these meetings to set expectations with the stakeholders that change would take time and to seek the faculty's patience, help, and support. In addition, by listening-to-understand, and seeking their support, I was able to use these stakeholder meetings to establish rapport, set a foundation on which to build trust, and give stakeholders some ownership in the success of IT. The third and final objective was to identify the key priorities for the institution and to determine who could be relied upon to get things moving and those who may undermine any change. By doing this, I was able to quickly identify potential allies, organizational priorities, and pain areas, which were used to set the IT team's priorities.

Although building the team and fixing systems is a multi-year process, the organization began to feel the impact of change within months. By focusing on a few critical service areas, and spending a significant amount of time with the academic and administrative unit leaders, we were able to build the required trust very quickly. The complaints about systems and services went down even though the only thing that changed was the relationship with the academic leaders. In fact, within three months, the complaints about IT stopped even though many of the systems were still not fixed, and many of the services were still unreliable.

Building the trust with the academic and administrative unit leaders gave the IT team the required breathing room to focus on fixing the technical issues and improving service delivery. We built a priority matrix based on the importance and urgency of key issues and services that must be addressed. We divided the change priorities into three areas: people, process, and systems, and categorized them based on their level of urgency. We shared this table with our key stakeholders, updated on a regular basis, and ensured that the IT team was focused on the critical issues and regularly updated the matrix.

In addition to setting priorities and establishing procedures, I continued working with the stakeholders to remove obstacles. We also invested much time in regular meetings with the key stakeholders and conducted frequent and regular one-on-one sessions with each of them, listening to their concerns, updating them on progress, sharing plans and challenges with them, and most importantly, seeking their input and advice. It is interesting to note that these meetings were difficult initially, as the stakeholders had many legitimate complaints.

However, once the stakeholders realized that they were being listened to and were updated with reliable information, the meetings that used to be adversarial soon became social events.

With time, services improved and trust grew to the point where IT transitioned from being perceived as a "service provider", whose role was to keep the systems running, to a "trusted partner" that was included in academic and administrative discussions. Instead of avoiding IT, the faculty and staff started seeking out the IT team for help in integrating technology into every aspect of their daily operation. Information technology started getting involved with integrating technology into all aspects of the academic institution, including process automation, classroom upgrades, as well as instructional design and the writing of research grants.

We leveraged this trust to take some risks in transforming the underlying infrastructure to become more agile, responsive, and cost-effective by utilizing agile development techniques, developing new service-management models, and investing in technologies such as cloud services and others, to laying the foundations to transition IT into a true "transformation partner".

As IT showed success after success in providing solutions to challenges across the whole institution, and proved its ability to partner with the different academic and administrative units across campus, the doors to digital transformation began to open. In fact, a couple of years into this transformation of the IT department, my role formally transitioned from CIO to CITO (Chief Innovation and

Transformation Officer), providing my team an institutional transformation role that was much wider than just IT.

As CITO, I was handed the responsibility of establishing an 'online campus' and an 'innovation park' to help budding student and alumni entrepreneurs launch their startups. The transition from IT to *innovation and transformation* was in recognition not just of the critical role that IT played in all aspects of the institution's operation, but also the realization that my role as the leader of IT was also critical in transforming processes and organizational structures across the university. In fact, the 'not so secret' agenda of placing the online campus and innovation park within the same organization as IT was to use technology as a catalyst to drive change in transforming the institution. For example, the online campus was a key driver behind transforming the institutional academic calendar, the admission process, the way we identify academic programs to offer, and the approaches used by instructors to teach online and in the classroom. The online campus has also introduced new methods to market our offerings, recruit our students, and improve every aspect of the student journey at our institution by treating them as customers.

Of course, all these transitions required us to first articulate a strategy to get us to the "digital vision" of the university, focus the IT team on clear priorities in order to provide a robust agile modular and scalable infrastructure and processes, and manage resistance to change across the breadth and depth of the institution. This required many of the elements described in this article, including strategic thinking, talent management, a wide repertoire of communication skills, and most importantly collaboration and engagement of the faculty. Despite the challenges faced with budgetary constraints and resistance to change by both academics and administrators, the DX journey continues to have significant positive impact on teaching, research, and the student experience at our institution.

7 Conclusion

In summary, successful DX involves a combination of visionary thinking, adaptability, effective communication, collaboration, talent management, and a relentless focus on delivering value to the students and other key stakeholders. Leading DX in higher education requires a collaborative, faculty-centric, and culturally sensitive leadership approach. Leaders must navigate the unique dynamics of academic institutions, balancing tradition with innovation, and customizing strategies to suit the diverse educational models present in higher education. Success in this context involves not only technological acumen but also effective communication, collaboration, and an understanding of the intricate interplay between academic culture and digital evolution. Leaders who embody these characteristics can guide their organizations through the challenges of DX, positioning them for sustained success in the digital age.

References

1. Asfour Y, Molloy S (2024) From geek to lead: a techie's guide to leadership (ISBN: 979-8-9902918-1-2). https://www.geektolead.com
2. Benvades LMC, Arias JAT, Serna MDA et al (2020) Digital transformation in education: a systematic literature review. https://www.mdpi.com/1424-8220/20/11/3291
3. Christensen CM, Eyring EJ (2011) The innovative university: changing the DNA of higher education from the inside out. Jossey-Bass,Hoboken, NJ (ISBN-10: 1118063481; ISBN-13: 978-1118063484)
4. The Chronicle of Higher Education. Digital transformation: setting the strategy. https://www.chronicle.com/events/virtual/digital-transformation-setting-the-strategy. Accessed 10 March 2024
5. Educause. Dx: digital transformation in higher education. https://www.educause.edu/focus-areas-and-initiatives/digital-transformation. Accessed 10 March 2024
6. Rogers DL (2016) The digital transformation playbook: rethink your business for the digital age. Columbia Business School Publishing. (ISBN-10: 0231163843; ISBN-13: 978-0231175449)
7. U.S. Department of Education (2017) Reimagining the role of technology in higher education. https://tech.ed.gov/files/2017/01/Higher-Ed-NETP.pdf
8. Westerman G, Didier B, McAfee A (2014) Leading digital: turning technology into business transformation. Harvard Business Review Press. (ISBN-10: 9781625272478; ISBN-13: 978-1625272478)

Implementing Digital Transformation at the University of Petra: Current Status and Future Plans

Rami A. Abdel-Rahem, Wael Hadi, and Muhannad Q. Malhis

Abstract A university is an institution of higher education that gives degrees and training in several academic fields. It also has a good setting for research. In addition to students, the university has academic and administrative staff that work together inside and outside the campus to achieve the university's vision, values, and objectives. Hundreds and thousands of educational and administrative operations are available in such an educational environment. In traditional universities, such operations are made by humans on paper documents. On the other hand, high-tech universities have automated their operations and converted them to a digital format, integrating technology into all aspects related to university processes through digital transformation (DX). With the help of the Internet of Things (IoT) technology, big data, and artificial intelligence (AI), DX provides agility and resiliency in operations, increases the user's experience, reduces the frictions in operations, provides a tool for monitoring and archiving operations, offers accurate data for decision makers, and increases productivity. The COVID-19 pandemic has proven that implementing DX on university campuses is also a survival issue. The current study reviews the automated operations at the University of Petra (UOP) in its various units, departments, and faculties. We also present the future plans for DX at UOP and discuss the results of a survey that was distributed to UOP students to investigate their satisfaction and predictions about several aspects of DX.

Keywords Digital transformation · University of Petra · Student satisfaction · Student predictions · Higher education

---

R. A. Abdel-Rahem (✉)
Department of Chemistry, Faculty of Arts and Sciences, University of Petra, Amman 11196, Jordan
e-mail: rabdelrahem@uop.edu.jo

W. Hadi
Department of Information Security, Faculty of Information Technology, University of Petra, Amman 11196, Jordan
e-mail: whadi@uop.edu.jo

M. Q. Malhis
ICT & Control Center, University of Petra, Amman 11196, Jordan
e-mail: mmalhis@uop.edu.jo

© The Author(s), under exclusive license to Springer Nature Switzerland AG 2024
A. Badran et al. (eds.), *Higher Education in the Arab World*,
https://doi.org/10.1007/978-3-031-70779-7_7

1 Introduction

Technology has affected all aspects of human life. The higher education sector was also influenced by new technology, and a transition from a classical teaching method to a virtual one is encountered in most higher education institutions (HEIs) nowadays. This transition involves automating all processes inside HEIs and ultimately leads to digital transformation (DX) in the HEIs. Classical universities depend mainly on paper-based work, whereas modern high-tech universities have automated and digitalized their working process. There are hundreds and thousands of administrative and educational processes inside an HEI. An HEI provides degrees and training across its diverse academic disciplines. The HEI is also expected to create a supportive environment for research. The whole administrative and educational process is designed to fufill the HEI's visions, values, and strategic objectives.

Two opinions about DX are expressed. Proponents of the first opinion try to cope with this form of change by saying that digitalization is a process that is ultimately aimed at "optimizing" education to save education expenses, reduce the number of instructors, and produce lower-quality graduates; moreover, it does not correspond to real-life activities. Hence, they think such a transition embezzles the budget and encourages goldbricking [1]. Others have a completely different opinion because they think that DX has so many advantages, including increasing the level of communication between students and their instructors, having a positive influence on interconnected reality, enabling learning to be done without classrooms and at any time, and meeting the needs of the rapid change in the higher education sector [2]. Additionally, it was reported that the students have become self-reliant due to the accessibility of information, and that the teachers have also changed their practices, taking advantage of the greater accessibility afforded by communication technologies [3]. New generations of students (born after 1980) are described as digital natives [1].

Generally, DX has to be preceded by two initial steps. The first step is digitization, i.e., converting analog data to digital data. The second step, digitalization, enables new workflows (movements) and automates the process using the digital data as inputs [4]. The advantage of digitalization is developing a new model/structure or process to lead finally to DX [4]. In HEIs, both teaching and learning processes are taking place and must be influenced by new technology and digital change [5]. It was reported that the digitalization of education transforms the entire learning process, from knowledge generation to knowledge communication [4]. New technology is expected to support communications in teaching and positively affect collaborative learning [3]. Adopting new technology in HEIs has to be assisted by modern technological tools, including data analytics, IoT, cloud computing, cyber security, and artificial intelligence [AI; 5]. Digital transformation is expected to increase the efficiency and flexibility of operations, improve the users' experience, simplify processes, and significantly enhance productivity.

In the current chapter, we will describe the administrative and educational benefits of the digital practices used at the University of Petra (UOP). Additionally, we present and discuss the results of a survey about student satisfaction and predictions covering several aspects of DX in the university. The survey was prepared to measure students' opinions regarding the electronic learning/teaching process at UOP, electronic administrative services at UOP, and the student's general trends toward implementing DX at UOP.

2 Literature Review

Since DX in HEIs has been an issue of discussion for the last 30 years [1], there are many reviews and research papers available on the topic. This attention to DX in HEIs was significantly increased after the COVID-19 pandemic and the vast industrial and technological revolution [6]. In a previous study at UOP, it was reported that instructors and students expressed higher overall dissatisfaction with online learning compared with blended learning, and that this becomes more pronounced as an instructor's years of experience increase and as the student's grade point average (GPA) decreases. The previous study also showed that, overall, there is a hidden resistance to implementing online and blended courses from the most experienced (oldest) instructors. Additionally, it was reported that instructors think that students feel bored during online lectures, and the students confirmed this observation [6]. It was, however, concluded that e-learning is a global trend in education, but the transition from classical teaching methods still needs more improvements [6].

Many students worldwide use their mobile devices to communicate via the internet and, generally, online education is accelerating [7]. Adopting DX in HEIs was found to have several advantages, including collaboration between students within group projects and, hence, more effective communication [3]. It was reported that the suitability of this type of technological collaboration depends on three elements: the team, the task, and technology characteristics [2]. The team includes the students, teachers, and educational institutions.

Several tasks can be done by electronic communication (EC), using particular digital platforms, including, but not limited to, "interactive lectures", "homework", "presentations", "practice projects", "writing reports", "surveys", "exams", "academic advising" and "seminar work" [2]. Other automated processes such as tracking admissions, optimizing enrolment, managing grants, governance, research, human resources, and marketing are also essential for digital HEIs [8]. In HEIs, DX includes integrating digital technologies into teaching, learning, and organizational practices. Such integration is benefiting from the new technology tools, including IoT, big data analytics, cloud computing, artificial intelligence, and cyber security [5]. Digital transformation is also a change that can be done with actors, digital processes, strategies, structures, and competitive dynamics in order to fulfill stakeholder needs [9].

Fortunately, electronic communication (EC) is also facilitated by a new generation of students being classified as digital natives [1, 18]. A teacher participating in EC is not a knowledge generator but a knowledge mentor, and the student is acting as a colleague. A teacher training unit, on the other hand, is essential in HEIs in order to go ahead with DX in that institution [8]. It was reported that teachers should benefit from the university's digital services to improve their teaching productivity, facilitate communication with the students, maximize student collaboration, and co-create value for all stakeholders [9]. Furthermore, the success of DX in teaching depends on teachers' positive attitude and trust toward DX, their digital skills, and the pedagogy aspects they use [11].

Such electronic education (e-education) is expected to enhance the learning/teaching ratio, as the student is classified as an actor rather than a knowledge receiver in e-education [8]. Though students and teachers are the most important actors in DX, other actors, including the DX team, university managers, industry, government, organic units, alumni, researchers, community faculty, digital platforms, IT business leaders, teacher training units, parents, content providers, information systems, departments, schools, and rectory are also significant actors in DX [8].

It was reported that interactive educational resources could be offered to students using modern technology tools such as augmented and virtual reality, big data, cloud computing, IoT, AI, mobile apps, and social media [9]. The data security and intelligence of DX are also important issues to deal with [2]. Additionally, an electronic course assessment is vital to evaluate course structure and organization, learning efficiency, perception of readings and assignments, workload, and effort required to complete the course successfully.

By offering proper digital educational content, innovating teaching and research at HEIs, students are expected to develop their knowledge, skills, and competencies through DX and benefit from the personalized courses and experiences of teachers. Therefore, DX generally aims to provide students with high-quality educational programs and maximize their competitive position in the labor market [7]. Additionally, employing DX in education must build up the students' competency to achieve the intended learning outcomes (ILOs), which is, somehow, not easily accomplished [7]; otherwise, DX in HEIs will be criticized as a failure [1].

With the help of DX experts, an electronically equipped education institution must go through two initial steps before completing digital transformation, namely, digitization and digitalization [4]. In order to have an effective digital campus, HEIs should re-structure and redesign their working processes [4]. Through implementing DX in an HEI, the big data obtained can be used by decision makers to acquire a competitive advantage for their institute; hence, they must reach the correct decisions based on the historical data available at that HEI for descriptive and predictive analytics [12]. The DX process in an HEI, once done, is not that easy to change, and it should therefore be given as much time as necessary for it to be implemented properly [13]. Digital transformation is not just a technical issue; rather, it is a precise process that has to be applied [7]. It was reported that DX in HEIs is the process of adapting and transforming an institution's processes, procedures, capabilities, and policies to leverage the opportunities and address the challenges presented by new digital technologies and their impact on society [14].

It was reported that DX requires the following: (1) appropriate strategic planning; (2) trust creation; (3) careful thinking in the process; (4) integration of all involved parties inside and outside the HEIs; and (5) encouragement for individual, team, and organizational learning [13]. Additionally, DX requires a holistic vision, values, DX competency, social interaction, and data structure processing [11]. Digital transformation also extends to changing the culture inside the campus, including the pedagogical approaches of teaching, and the research and administrative processes [8]. In the education process, the teachers have to manipulate their digital tools in order to reach the intended learning outcomes (ILOs). Ultimately, DX can be understood as the sum of digital processes necessary to achieve a change in the process that enables HEIs to successfully control the use of digital technologies [8].

Several challenges can hinder the implementation of DX in HEIs, including the lack of leadership vision, lack of strategy and policy, lack of digital skills and knowledge, lack of technological tools, the difficulty of adaptability, the organizational resistance to change, the lack of resources and budget, the legal and regulatory implications, lack of data to justify the value of digital transformation, and the security harm [13]. Additionally, it has to be accepted by HEIs that technology is changing very fast and, hence, the staff of HEIs have to make more effort to compete with other HEIs.

3 Methodology

A survey was conducted for students in the Faculty of Information Technology (FIT) and the Faculty of Arts and Sciences (FAS). A total of 350 students responded; 172 were from FAS, whereas 178 were from FIT. The FIT has five departments: Software Engineering, Computer Science, Data Science & Artificial Intelligence, Information Security, and Virtual and Augmented Reality. The FAS has six bachelor programs: Arabic Language & Literature, English Language & Literature, Chemistry, Mathematics, Educational Sciences, Modern Languages, and French and English Language & Literature. The survey was created using the Google form and was distributed in October 2023. Students taking part in the survey were all given five answer options, allowing them to choose their level of agreement with statements through the scale: (1) Strongly disagree, (2) Disagree, (3) Neutral, (4) Agree, (5) Strongly agree.

The surveys were sent to students in the two faculties, FIT and FAS. The students were initially asked about their faculty and majors. The other survey statements were submitted to students to measure their satisfaction and prediction on implementing DX at the UOP. The 27 statements in common to FIT and FAS were:

(1) When it comes to my academic affairs, I prefer to communicate via online platforms (such as Teams, Moodle, and Blackboard).
(2) When it comes to my academic affairs, I prefer face-to-face communication with my professors.

(3) I prefer to cooperate and communicate electronically with my fellow students and my professors through learning management platforms (such as Teams, Moodle, Blackboard).
(4) I prefer to communicate with my fellow students and professors through social media (WhatsApp, Messenger).
(5) I use social media and digital learning platforms.
(6) As per the teaching and learning type, I prefer face-to-face lectures.
(7) I prefer to attend lectures by distance learning, electronically, in an asynchronous manner.
(8) I prefer the complete digitization of the educational process (lectures, assignments, projects, exams).
(9) I prefer to discuss graduation projects electronically through learning management platforms like Teams.
(10) I prefer to collaborate on joint projects with my fellow students remotely through learning management platforms like Teams.
(11) I prefer to collaborate on joint projects with my fellow students physically.
(12) I prefer to complete and submit my assignments electronically.
(13) I prefer to receive academic guidance from my academic advisor through online platforms and social media.
(14) I prefer to enroll in training courses (online) using learning management platforms like Teams.
(15) I believe that a robot, through artificial intelligence, can deliver an academic lecture.
(16) I am confident that the files sent to professors and fellow students through learning management platforms (e.g., Moodle, Blackboard, and Teams) are secure and cannot be breached.
(17) I am confident that the communications between me and my professors are secure and cannot be breached using (e.g., WhatsApp, Messenger)
(18) I prefer to pay university fees electronically.
(19) I prefer to submit university clearance electronically.
(20) I wish to subscribe to the university transportation Bus Tracking service
(21) I prefer to enroll and register electronically at the university portal assigned by the Admission and Registration Deanship.
(22) I prefer to have administrative inquiries (such as fee payments, clearances, and college notifications) answered by an artificial intelligence-based robot
(23) I am completely convinced by the case for using modern technology and artificial intelligence to provide administrative services
(24) I believe that e-learning is somehow difficult and time-consuming
(25) The English language used on electronic platforms and their settings poses a problem in dealing with educational platforms
(26) I am completely convinced by the case for using modern technology and artificial intelligence in the educational process.
(27) I believe that young professors have more digital skills than older ones.

The statements were related to teaching and learning, academic advising, training, security, administrative process, and student trends toward implementing DX at UOP. Such a survey will give the university a clear vision for the future of the implementation of DX at the University of Petra. In the future, UOP will extend its digital services and keep following the latest trends in digital services. Our country's vision of digital government and smart cities also supports such attention.

4 Results

At UOP, DX has been made a primary goal in the new strategic plan, and hence, DX will be implemented, but with care, for all academic and administrative aspects of UOP. The following subsections present and discuss the current status of DX at UOP. Also presented and discussed are future plans for implementing DX at UOP, depending on the results of a questionnaire that was prepared to measure the opinions of students with regard to: the electronic learning/teaching process at UOP, the electronic administrative services at UOP, and finally, the student's inclinations toward implementing DX at UOP.

4.1 The Current Status of Implementing DX at UOP

The University of Petra has long been dedicated to the integration of computing into its operations. This significant dedication has propelled Petra to stand among prestigious academic institutions, placing it in the ranks of universities with distinguished academic reputations. The computing process at UOP is divided into several axes, summarized as follows:

(1) **Server Hardware**

The university possesses a modern array of server hardware and associated storage units, forming a Private Cloud Server. Through these systems, data is stored, and all electronic software and services are operated and managed.

(2) **Information Security and Protection Devices**

The university places significant emphasis on the security and integrity of its data to ensure it remains free from tampering, sabotage, or unauthorized access. This commitment is upheld by operating numerous protection and monitoring devices and software for the university's computer networks.

(3) **Wired Computer Network**

The university's buildings and facilities are interconnected through a high-speed 40 Gbps fiber-optic network. This network has been designed based on a Ring Network principle, ensuring all buildings remain connected without disruption during a break.

(4) **Wireless Computer Network**

The University of Petra took the lead back in 2006 by operating the first wireless computer network in all Jordanian academic and non-academic institutions. The university's administration recognized the importance of providing internet services for the smooth functioning of the educational process for students and staff. The university offers fast, 24/7 internet services in all its facilities, including dedicated student transport buses. Furthermore, this service is continuously improved and upgraded.

(5) **High-Speed Internet Service**

In Jordan, UOP is unique in having its own IP addresses. It delivers a fast internet service using an advanced wireless network, available in all campus locations and on student transport buses. The network boasts speeds over 2 Gbps, sourced from two separate internet providers, guaranteeing continuous access even if one line fails.

(6) **Computer Hardware and Accessories**

The Univerity of Petra ranks highly among academic institutions for its student-to-computer ratio, offering roughly one computer for every three students. The university's significant computer infrastructure includes over 2560 computers, 290 printers, and 250 Data Show projectors, primarily used in classrooms and laboratories.

(7) **Remote Learning Facilities**

All classrooms and laboratories at the university are equipped with cameras and microphones dedicated to recording lectures and broadcasting them over the internet, utilizing specialized software for this purpose.

(8) **Surveillance Cameras**

The university is committed to providing a safe, violence-free learning environment. To achieve this, UOP has established a central control and monitoring room that oversees more than 1600 cameras distributed throughout all internal and external university facilities.

(9) **Computer software**

Since its inception, UOP has recognized the importance of business automation. Today, most of its core operations are computerized and executed through computer software. Listed below (10–19) are some of the most essential software applications.

(10) **Admission and Registration System**

This system manages student admissions and registration tasks, including their academic records, scheduling of classes, grades, and other academic processes like curriculum planning, academic calendars, cumulative GPAs, and guidance services, among others.

(11) **Student Accounting System**

This system manages financial aspects relating to students, including their financial records, tuition fees, and payments.

(12) **Financial and Administrative ERP (Enterprise Resource Planning) System**

The university utilizes the Microsoft Dynamics AX (Architecture eXtended) system to manage its financial and administrative operations, including accounting, financial, inventory management, and procurement systems. This system is considered one of the best global ERP systems developed by the Microsoft company.

(13) **Human Resources Management System (HRMS)**

This system efficiently manages all aspects of human resources, including the maintenance of employee records, payroll processing and distribution, managing leaves and absences, conducting performance appraisals, overseeing promotions and salary increases, handling appointments, and other related HR tasks.

(14) **E-Learning System**

Since 2002, UOP has provided students with educational resources using two well-known learning management systems: Moodle and Blackboard. Through these systems, students have full access to all the materials they use for their studies. Students get complete access to their study materials through these systems. Furthermore, they are utilized for online exams, which comprise about 95% of the exams in some UOP departments. The results of these exams are assessed in light of the particular goals of each department and course, guaranteeing compliance with the university's instructional objectives.

(15) **Health Unit System**

The UOP uses this electronic platform to manage all the medical records of all staff members and students. It also acts as the health unit's management system, scheduling patient visits, supervising medicine distribution, and keeping track of insurance information.

(16) **Scientific Research System**

The scientific research activities of the university faculty are monitored and documented by this system, which also includes the expenses related to each research project. Additionally, the system helps to ensure accountability and openness in the university's research spending, which makes it possible to employ funds more effectively and efficiently to further scientific discoveries.

(17) **Mena CPM Quality Management System**

This system records information about the Quality Control Department, focusing on strategic plans and their incorporation into operational and implementation plans.

(18) **M2L Database Systems**

These systems are developed for managing libraries and cataloging books, journals, and scientific periodicals.

(19) Electronic Correspondence and Document Management System (EDMS)

This system is implemented to organize, store, and handle different kinds of documents, both in paper and digital formats. Its purpose also includes transforming paper documents into digital versions, such as scanned copies of the original materials.

(20) Electronic Portals (ePortals)

These are a collection of electronic portals provided through the university's website, offering various services to save time and effort for students and staff. Some examples of these services are listed (21–25) below.

(21) Electronic Student Portal

This portal provides students with various services, including registration, payments, access to their academic plans and progress, and the ability to submit requests and communicate with the university.

(22) Faculty Members Portal

This online platform is specifically tailored for faculty use, offering a suite of electronic functionalities. Faculty members can utilize this system to enter and manage student grades efficiently, facilitate academic guidance, and update personal profiles. It allows for the comprehensive management of their professional information, including details about their research projects, academic achievements, recognitions, and awards. Additionally, the portal serves as a central hub for faculty to keep track of their academic contributions and milestones, ensuring a seamless integration of their professional activities with the university's administrative processes.

(23) Staff Affairs Portal

This portal is specifically designed for academic and administrative staff matters. It offers electronic services to employees, enabling them to apply for leaves, view payroll information, conduct self-assessments, set job objectives, and more. Moreover, the portal empowers managers to oversee their team members, monitor attendance, and assess performance.

(24) Embassies Portal

The university developed this electronic portal to provide cultural attachés at embassies the ability to monitor their student's academic records and educational progress in real-time.

(25) Electronic Library

This includes a range of digital libraries to which the university subscribes. The collection features current editions of books, academic references, journals, peer-reviewed periodicals, doctoral and master dissertations, economic encyclopedias, and World Bank publications, among others. These materials are available 24/7 to both students and staff via the university's website, free of charge.

Most of the automated processes at UOP are related to administrative services. Teaching and learning, to a great extent, are included in the electronic services of Remote Learning Facilities, E-Learning Systems, M2L Database Systems, and the Electronic Library. These services at UOP might be similar to other e-services in other national and international universities. In the following sections, the future plans for implementing DX at UOP are presented. In order to propose a future for DX at UOP, the current status had to be evaluated. Accordingly, after an intensive literature search [1–25], a survey consisting of 27 statements was prepared and the students were asked to what extent they agreed with them. Four main topics are included in this survey. The initial questions relate to general information about the students, such as their department and academic level. Then, the students are asked about their communication tools, opinions of the electronic learning/teaching process at UOP, administrative services at UOP, and their trends toward implementing DX at UOP, as discussed below. The survey was distributed to 350 students from the Faculty of Information Technology and the Faculty of Arts and Sciences.

Figure 1 shows the distribution of 350 respondents based on their respective faculties. Among these, 178 responses were from the FIT and 172 from the FAS.

In Fig. 2, the distribution of respondents is presented based on their years of experience. Specifically, 72 respondents were in their first year, 104 in their second year, 83 in their third year, and 91 in their fourth year.

Figure 3 depicts the utilization of digital learning tools among students. Of the surveyed participants, 77 students selected computers, 173 preferred laptops, 130 utilized smartphones, and 20 chose tablets as their primary digital learning devices.

The results of the 27 statements relating to administrative and academic aspects of DX at UOP are presented below. Students who answered with strongly agree and agree, (5) and (4) on the scale, were considered to agree, whereas those who responded with strongly disagree and disagree, (1) and (2) on the scale, were considered to disagree. Neutral responses were number (3) on the scale.

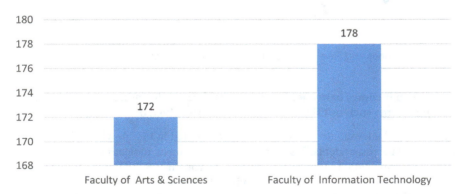

Fig. 1 Distribution of respondents based on their respective faculties

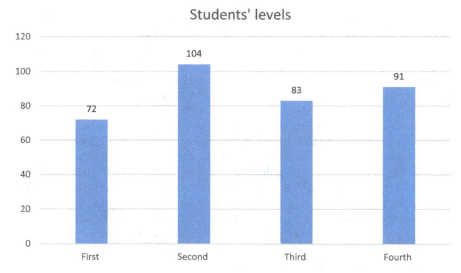

Fig. 2 Distribution of respondents according to their years of experience

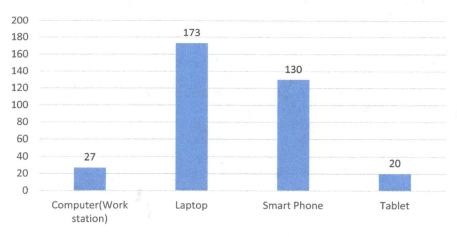

Fig. 3 Distribution of utilization of digital learning tools among students

(1) **When it comes to my academic affairs, I prefer to communicate via online platforms such as (Teams, Moodle, and Blackboard)**

The students' answers to statement 1 are documented in Fig. 4, which shows that a majority of the respondents, 239, agree with the statement, indicating a preference for online communication in academic contexts, So roughly 68.29% of the students who responded agreed. A much smaller number, 49, disagreed, suggesting they do not prefer online platforms for academic communication. Meanwhile, 62 respondents remained neutral, neither agreeing nor disagreeing with the question.

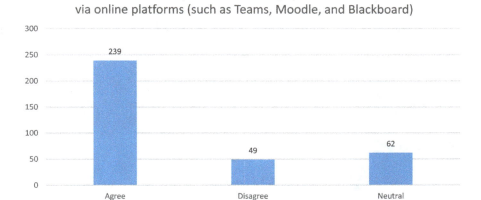

Fig. 4 Responses of students to statement 1

(2) **When it comes to my academic affairs, I prefer face-to-face communication with my professors**

Responses to statement 2 are shown in Fig. 5. A significant majority of respondents, 267, agreed with the statement, demonstrating a strong preference for direct, in-person interactions with professors. Only a tiny fraction, 16, disagreed, indicating they do not prefer face-to-face communication with professors. However, 67 respondents had a neutral stance on the matter.

(3) **I prefer to cooperate and communicate electronically with my fellow students and my professors through learning management platforms (such as Teams, Moodle, Blackboard)**

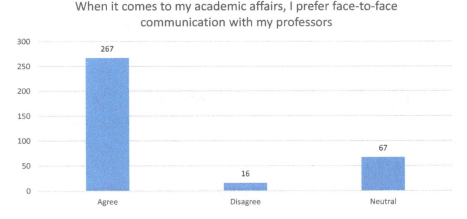

Fig. 5 Responses of students to statement 2

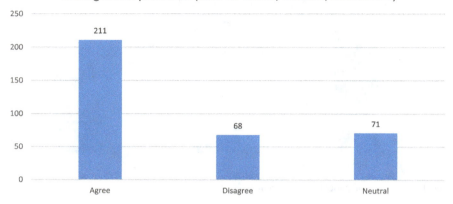

Fig. 6 Responses of students to statement 3

Responses to statement 3 are shown in Fig. 6. Most respondents, numbering 211, agreed with the statement, preferring electronic cooperation and communication with their fellow students through learning management systems. Sixty-eight respondents disagreed, indicating they do not favor electronic cooperation and communication. The replies of 71 respondents were neutral, indicating neither a clear preference for nor against using electronic learning management platforms for communication and cooperation with peers.

(4) **I prefer to communicate with my fellow students and professors through social media (WhatsApp, Messenger)**

Figure 7 displays responses to statement 4. It shows that a substantial majority of the respondents, 231, agreed with the statement, indicating a strong preference for using social media as a communication tool with their fellow students. In contrast, 60 respondents disagreed, suggesting they do not favor social media for such communications. Additionally, 59 respondents had a neutral position, neither agreeing nor disagreeing with the preference for social media communication with students.

(5) **I use social media and digital learning platforms**

Figure 8 displays responses to the level of usage of social media and digital learning platforms. It indicates that:

- A considerable number of respondents, 118, use these platforms "to a great extent," showing a high usage level.
- A slightly smaller group of 101 respondents use them "to a moderate degree," which suggests regular but not extensive use.

Implementing Digital Transformation at the University of Petra: Current ... 123

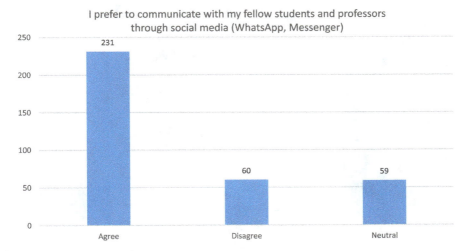

Fig. 7 Responses of students to statement 4

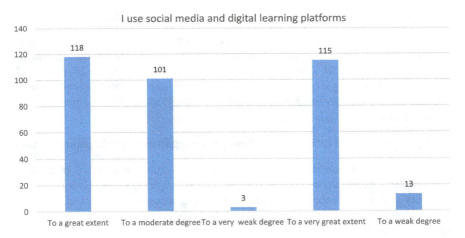

Fig. 8 Responses of students to statement 5

- Very few, only three respondents, report using these platforms "to a very weak degree," indicating minimal engagement.
- A significant portion, 115 respondents, use social media and digital learning platforms "to a very great extent," signaling an extremely high level of engagement.
- Lastly, 13 respondents use them "to a weak degree," suggesting they engage with these platforms infrequently.

The figure suggests a strong inclination towards significant use of social media and digital learning platforms among the respondents, with most indicating substantial to very substantial usage.

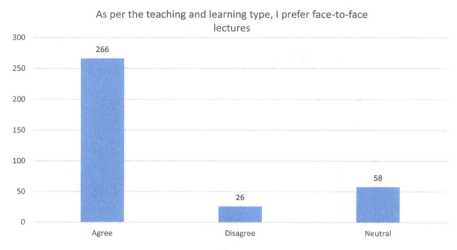

Fig. 9 Responses of students to statement 6

(6) **As per the teaching and learning type, I prefer face-to-face lectures**

Figure 9 displays responses to statement 6. A substantial majority of the participants, 266, agreed with the statement, suggesting a strong preference for traditional, in-person teaching methods. In contrast, a small number of respondents, 26, disagreed, indicating they may favor other methods of instruction, such as online learning. Additionally, 58 respondents had a neutral stance towards face-to-face lectures, neither strongly favoring nor disfavoring them.

(7) **I prefer to attend lectures by distance learning in an asynchronous manner**

Figure 10 shows responses to statement 7. It shows that a substantial number of participants, 156, agreed with the statement, suggesting a strong preference for the flexibility and convenience of asynchronous distance learning. In contrast, a significant number of respondents, 106, disagreed, indicating they may favor synchronous learning experiences or in-person lectures. Additionally, 88 respondents had a neutral stance towards asynchronous distance learning, neither strongly favoring nor disfavoring it.

(8) **I prefer the complete digitization of the educational process (lectures, assignments, projects, exams)**

Figure 11 displays responses to statement 8. It indicates that a notable majority of respondents, 207, agreed with the assertion, reflecting a strong preference for a fully digital educational experience. In contrast, 70 respondents disagreed with complete digitization, suggesting they may value traditional, non-digital educational elements. Furthermore, 73 respondents held a neutral stance on digitizing the educational process, neither favoring nor opposing it outright.

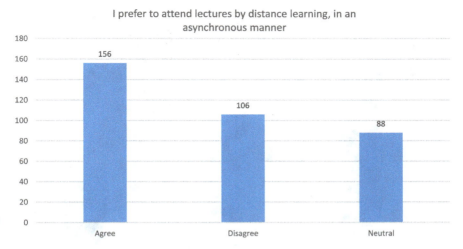

Fig. 10 Responses of students to statement 7

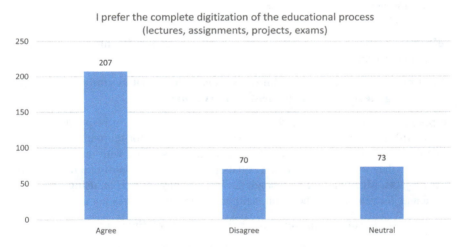

Fig. 11 Responses of students to statement 8

(9) **I prefer to discuss graduation projects electronically through learning management platforms like Teams**

Figure 12 displays responses to statement 9. It shows that 154 respondents agreed, indicating a preference for using electronic platforms to discuss graduation projects. Meanwhile, 126 respondents disagreed with this approach, which may suggest they prefer in-person discussions or alternative methods of communication for their projects. Additionally, 70 respondents remained neutral, neither expressing a clear

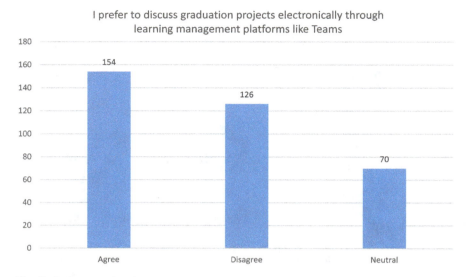

Fig. 12 Responses of students to statement 9

preference for nor against using electronic platforms like Teams for discussing graduation projects.

(10) **I prefer to collaborate on joint projects with my fellow students remotely through learning management platforms like Teams**

Responses to statement 10 are shown in Fig. 13. A majority of respondents, 177, agreed with the statement, indicating a strong preference for remote collaboration using digital platforms. In contrast, 91 respondents disagreed with this preference, suggesting they may favor in-person collaboration or other non-digital methods for joint projects. Meanwhile, 82 respondents had a neutral stance on using platforms like Teams for remote collaboration, neither preferring nor opposing it.

(11) **I prefer to collaborate on joint projects with my fellow students physically**

Figure 14 shows responses to statement 11. A clear majority of respondents, 235, agreed with the statement, indicating a strong preference for in-person collaboration. On the other hand, a smaller number of respondents, 47, disagreed, implying they might be more inclined towards remote collaboration or the use of digital platforms. Additionally, 68 respondents were neutral, neither favoring nor opposing physical collaboration.

(12) **I prefer to complete and submit my assignments electronically**

Figure 15 shows responses to statement 12. A vast majority of respondents, 307, agreed with the question, indicating a strong preference for the convenience and efficiency of digital submission. This overwhelming agreement suggests that electronic submission is highly favored in the current educational climate, likely due

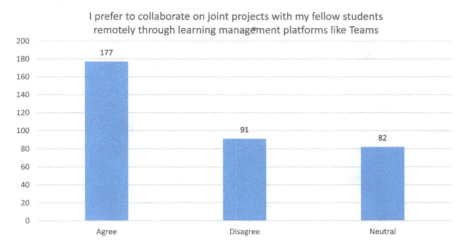

Fig. 13 Responses of students to statement 10

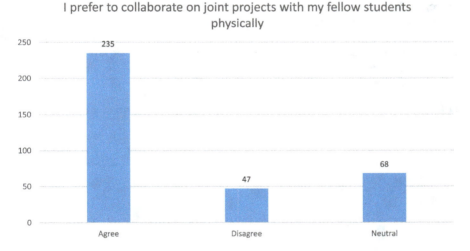

Fig. 14 Responses of students to statement 11

to its ease of use and the ability to manage work remotely. Only a few, 14 respondents, disagreed, which could imply a preference for more traditional methods of completing and submitting assignments. Furthermore, 29 respondents were neutral in their response, showing neither a strong preference for nor against electronic submission. The survey demonstrates a significant trend toward digitizing assignment completion and submission among the respondents.

(13) **I prefer to receive academic guidance from my academic advisor through online platforms and social media**

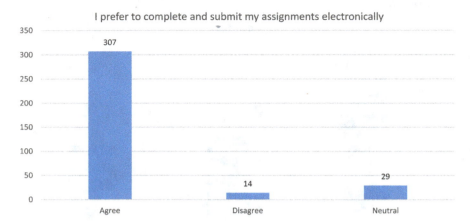

Fig. 15 Responses of students to statement 12

Figure 16 illustrates responses to statement 13. A majority of respondents, 202, agreed with the statement, indicating a strong preference for using online platforms and social media for academic guidance, possibly due to the convenience and accessibility of these tools. In contrast, 67 respondents disagreed, suggesting they may prefer traditional, face-to-face interactions for receiving academic advice. However, 81 respondents were neutral on this topic, neither strongly preferring online methods nor strictly opposing them.

(14) **I prefer to enroll in training courses (online) using learning management platforms like Teams**

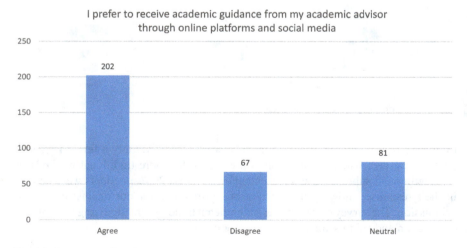

Fig. 16 Responses of students to statement 13

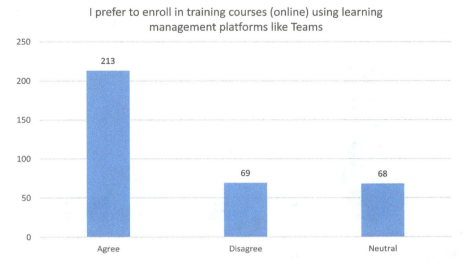

Fig. 17 Responses of students to statement 14

Responses to statement 14 are shown in Fig. 17. A significant majority of respondents, 213, agreed with the preference, which indicates a strong inclination towards the convenience and flexibility of online learning. This demonstrates a substantial endorsement of digital platforms for professional and educational development. In contrast, 69 respondents disagreed, suggesting a preference for traditional in-person training courses or alternative learning methods. Additionally, 68 respondents were neutral, indicating neither a strong preference for nor against using online platforms for training courses.

(15) **I am confident that the files sent to professors and fellow students through learning management platforms (e.g., Moodle, Blackboard, and Teams) are secure and cannot be breached**

Figure 18 illustrates student' responses to statement 15. The majority, 203 individuals, agreed that they felt confident in the security of these platforms, indicating a solid trust in the protective measures and privacy assurances provided by these digital systems. A relatively small number, 21 respondents, disagreed, reflecting concerns or uncertainty about the security of file transmission on these platforms. Additionally, 44 respondents remained neutral, suggesting they may be uncertain or have a balanced view of the security of sending files through learning management systems.

(16) **I believe that a robot, through artificial intelligence, can deliver an academic lecture**

Figure 19 shows respondents' replies to statement 16. A slight majority, 151 respondents, agreed with the possibility of showing openness to the advancement of AI in educational settings and its potential to simulate or replace traditional lecture delivery.

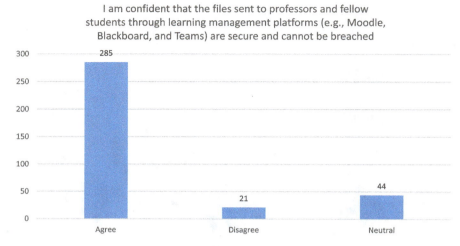

Fig. 18 Responses of students to statement 15

However, a considerable number, 121 respondents, disagreed, suggesting skepticism about AI's capability to deliver academic content or a preference for human lecturers effectively. The other 78 respondents remained neutral, neither convinced of AI's current ability to conduct lectures nor utterly opposed to the idea.

(17) **I am confident that the communications between me and my professors are secure and cannot be breached using, for example, WhatsApp or Messenger**

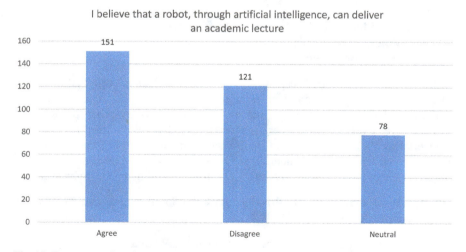

Fig. 19 Responses of students to statement 16

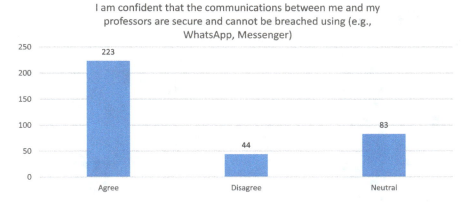

Fig. 20 Responses of students to statement 17

Figure 20 reflects respondents' confidence in communication security. A significant majority, 223 respondents, expressed confidence that these communications are secure and cannot be breached, indicating a high level of trust in the privacy features of these platforms. On the other hand, 44 respondents lacked this confidence, suggesting concerns about the potential for security breaches and privacy issues. Additionally, 83 respondents were neutral, possibly indicating insufficient information to form an opinion or a balanced view of the potential risks and safeguards associated with using these communication tools.

(18) **I am completely convinced by the case for using modern technology and artificial intelligence to provide administrative services**

Figure 21 presents responses to adopting modern technology and AI in education. A considerable majority, 239 respondents, agreed that they are entirely convinced of the need to use modern technology and AI in the educational process, showing a solid endorsement for integrating these tools in learning and teaching. This suggests a general acceptance of the role of technology and AI in enhancing educational experiences. Only a minority of 40 respondents disagreed, indicating some resistance or skepticism towards using such advanced tools in education. Additionally, 71 respondents remained neutral, reflecting either a lack of conviction or a wait-and-see attitude towards incorporating these technological advancements into educational settings.

(19) **I believe that e-learning is somehow difficult and time-consuming**

Figure 22 presents a snapshot of how respondents view e-learning in terms of its complexity and time demands. Of the surveyed individuals, 108 believed that e-learning posed specific challenges, potentially being more difficult or less time-effective than conventional classroom education. On the other hand, a majority of 146 respondents countered this view, implying that they regarded e-learning as a convenient and efficient method of education that doesn't necessarily demand more time than traditional approaches. An additional 96 respondents were undecided,

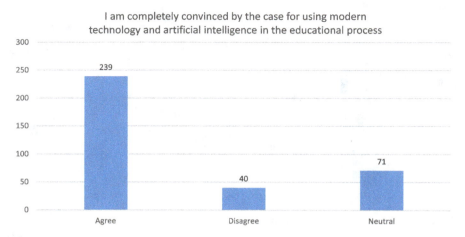

Fig. 21 Responses of students to statement 18

neither fully embracing nor rejecting the notion that e-learning is an easier or less time-intensive option.

(20) **I prefer to pay university fees electronically**

Figure 23 provides insights into respondents' preferences regarding the payment of university fees. A clear majority of 213 respondents favored the convenience of electronic payment methods, indicating that they prefer to handle their financial transactions online. This strong preference suggests that the ease and efficiency of digital

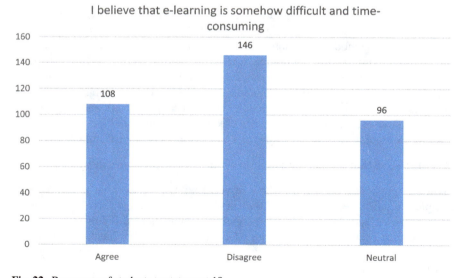

Fig. 22 Responses of students to statement 19

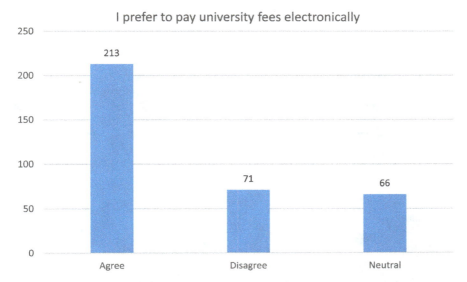

Fig. 23 Responses of students to statement 20

payments are valued over traditional payment methods. In contrast, 71 respondents did not share this preference, which may suggest a comfort with, or necessity for, traditional payment methods such as in-person. The remaining 66 respondents were neutral, showing neither a clear preference for nor against electronic payments for university fees.

(21) **I prefer to submit university clearance electronically**

Figure 24 represents respondents' preferences regarding the electronic submission of university clearance documents. A majority of 232 showed a clear preference for the convenience and efficiency of submitting clearance documents electronically. This high number indicates that many students appreciate the ability to complete administrative tasks online without the need for physical presence or paperwork. Conversely, a smaller group of 42 respondents disliked the idea of electronic submission, which might indicate a preference for the traditional, in-person process or concerns about digital submission security. Additionally, 76 respondents remained neutral, suggesting uncertainty about the submission method or a balance between electronic processes' perceived benefits and drawbacks.

(22) **I wish to subscribe to the university transportation bus-tracking service**

Figure 25 surveys opinions on subscribing to a university transportation bus-tracking service, revealing that 223 respondents favored it. This significant number suggests a strong interest in utilizing technology for real-time tracking and improved convenience in managing their daily travel. In contrast, a smaller contingent of 45 respondents did not share this sentiment, which could indicate satisfaction with

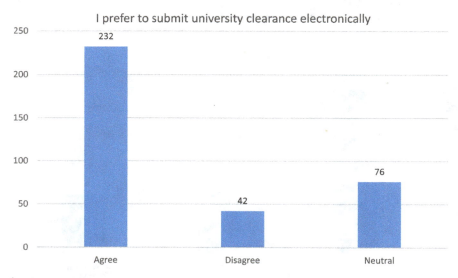

Fig. 24 Responses of students to statement 21

existing transportation arrangements or uncertainty about the utility of such a service. However, 82 respondents remained neutral, neither committing to nor dismissing the potential benefits of a bus-tracking service.

(23) **I prefer to enroll and register electronically at the university portal assigned by the Admission and Registration Deanship**

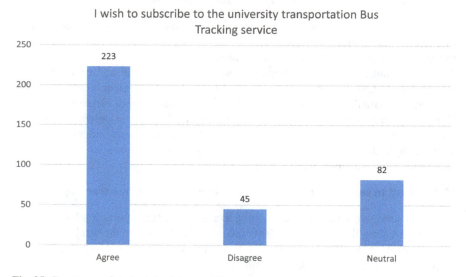

Fig. 25 Responses of students to statement 22

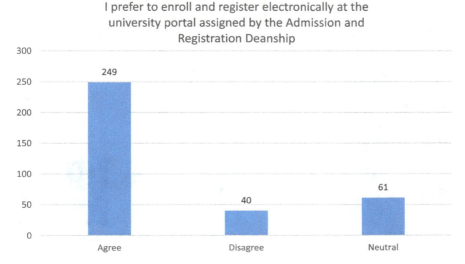

Fig. 26 Responses of students to statement 23

Figure 26 depicts preferences for online enrollment and registration. Most, 249 respondents, preferred the electronic method, signaling a solid appreciation for the convenience and accessibility of digital registration systems. This overwhelming agreement points to a high degree of acceptance of technology in streamlining administrative and academic processes. In contrast, only 40 respondents were against this method, which may imply a preference for the tactile engagement of in-person processes or a distrust of online systems. A smaller number of 61 respondents remained neutral, neither fully convinced by, nor against, the efficiency of electronic enrollment and registration.

(24) **I prefer to have administrative inquiries (such as fee payments, clearances, and college notifications) answered by an artificial intelligence-based robot**

Figure 27 displays preferences for using AI-based robots to handle administrative inquiries within a university setting. A significant portion of 181 respondents agreed with the preference, suggesting they are open to, and possibly enthusiastic about, the efficiency and round-the-clock availability of AI-driven solutions for handling routine administrative tasks such as fee payments, clearances, and college notifications. On the other hand, 89 respondents did not favor this approach, which may reflect a preference for human interaction as well as uncertainty about the effectiveness of AI in complex scenarios. Additionally, 80 respondents were neutral, indicating uncertainty or a wait-and-see attitude toward integrating AI into university administration.

(25) **I am completely convinced by the case for using modern technology and artificial intelligence in the educational process**

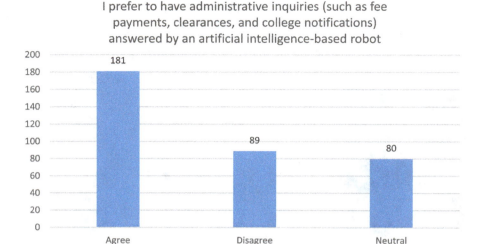

Fig. 27 Responses of students to statement 24

Figure 28 indicates respondents' views on adopting modern technology and AI in administrative services. A substantial majority, 217 individuals, expressed complete conviction in utilizing modern technology and AI for administrative functions, suggesting a solid endorsement of these advancements to streamline and enhance service efficiency. This indicates a significant trust in the capabilities of AI and modern technology to improve administrative processes within institutions. In contrast, a minority of 49 respondents disagreed, which may point to a preference for traditional methods or concerns about the reliability and effectiveness of technology-based solutions. The other 84 respondents remained neutral, neither fully convinced nor entirely against the idea, reflecting a potential openness to these technologies or uncertainty about their implications.

(26) **The English language used on electronic platforms and their settings poses a problem in dealing with educational platforms**

Figure 29 examines the issue of language barriers on electronic educational platforms, focusing on the use of English. A plurality of respondents, numbering 142, agreed that English poses a problem when interacting with these platforms, indicating that language can be a barrier to practical use. This may reflect a need for more multilingual support or localized versions of educational software to cater to non-English speakers. On the other hand, 120 respondents disagreed, implying they do not find the use of English in electronic platforms problematic, which could suggest that they are comfortable with the language or a belief that English is a suitable lingua franca for educational contexts. Meanwhile, 88 respondents were neutral, suggesting that they might not have a definitive opinion on the matter or have not encountered language as a barrier in their experience.

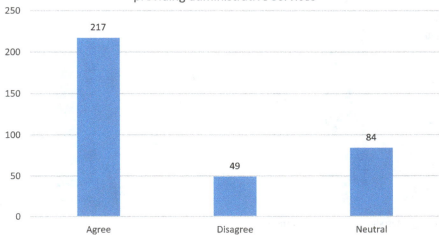

Fig. 28 Responses of students to statement 25

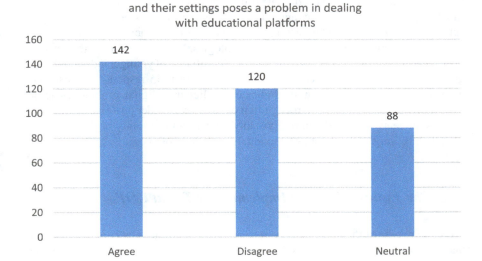

Fig. 29 Responses of students to statement 26

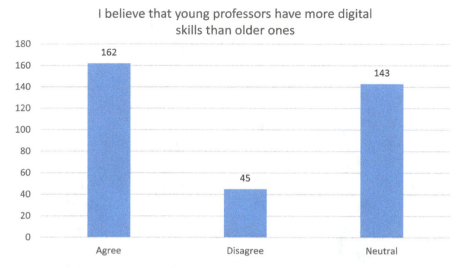

Fig. 30 Responses of students to statement 27

(27) **I believe that young professors have more digital skills than older ones**

Figure 30 presents views on the digital proficiency of younger versus older professors. Most respondents, 162 in total, agreed that younger professors possess more digital skills than their older counterparts, suggesting that younger faculty are more attuned to or comfortable with current digital technologies. This could reflect the growing integration of digital tools in academia and the familiarity of younger individuals with these technologies from an early age. A small number, 45 respondents, disagreed with this statement, which might indicate a belief that digital proficiency is not necessarily age-dependent or a recognition of tech-savvy older professors. However, 143 respondents remained neutral, possibly reflecting uncertainty or the belief that digital skills vary widely among individuals regardless of age.

4.2 *The Future Plans for Implementing DX at UOP*

From the results of the above survey, it seems that UOP must foster an environment that supports both digital natives and those who prefer traditional methods, and try to establish an attractive environment for e-learning. Future plans should focus on:

- Enhancing user experience: addressing the diverse needs of students by providing flexible and adaptable learning platforms that can accommodate different learning styles and preferences.
- Bridging the digital divide: ensuring no student is left behind in the DX by offering support and resources to those less comfortable with technology.

- Security and privacy: continually improving digital-platform security measures to maintain users' trust and confidence.
- Integration of AI: conducting further research to explore the potential roles of AI in education, addressing both the opportunities and the challenges it presents.
- In-depth analysis of digital and traditional method preferences: further exploration into why students prefer specific digital methods over traditional ones, and vice versa, would provide deeper insights. This could involve qualitative studies such as interviews or focus groups to understand the precious details behind these preferences.
- Long-term studies on DX adoption: tracking students' and faculty members' attitudes towards DX over time could offer valuable insights into the evolving nature of technology adoption in higher education.
- Impact assessment of DX on learning outcomes: investigating how DX impacts student learning outcomes, engagement, and satisfaction would be crucial in understanding the effectiveness of these initiatives.
- Language barriers: developing multilingual support for educational platforms to make them more accessible to non-English speakers.
- Faculty development: offering continuous professional development opportunities for professors to enhance their digital skills irrespective of age.

5 Discussion

In the survey findings, we observe a complex landscape of student interactions with, and attitudes towards, digital technologies in their academic lives [3, 7]. Many students find online platforms convenient, as reflected in the 68.29% who agree with their use [1]. However, the value of face-to-face interactions remains, as a higher percentage of students (76.29%) indicate a preference for physical communication over online methods. These two findings confirm that students still prefer the face-to-face teaching/learning process, which could be because preparing an attractive electronic academic material that covers the whole course's intended learning outcomes (ILOs) is regarded as a big challenge [6]. Additionally, some invisible values and social issues cannot easily be covered with e-learning. Actual feelings, emotions, and values are still complicated to offer through e-learning via DX of an academic institution [6]. In comparison to e-education services, students accept other administrative and financial services, such as paying university fees, submitting university clearance, tracking university buses, electronic registration, and using AI and the IoT to provide administrative services [5, 8, 9]. These administrative services do not touch the soul of the education process and its main actors: the student and the instructor [6].

The response to statement 7 showed a similar general trend, as only 45% of the students preferred asynchronous distance learning as their education tool [6]. Additionally, the response to statement 16 indicated that a robot as an academic instructor is still not accepted by students, with about 57.9% declining the concept [5].

There is a strong but not universal trend toward digital collaboration, with around 60% of students favoring online platforms for academic cooperation [3]. This indicates that traditional interaction methods still hold value while digital platforms are dominant. The high engagement with social media and digital platforms supports the concept of "digital natives," yet the diversity in usage levels suggests varying degrees of comfort and preference among students [1].

The teaching-methods analysis shows that while most prefer in-person lectures (76%), a sizable group is open to asynchronous learning (45%), pointing to different opinions on the value of real-time interaction versus flexible access to materials [6].

The complete digitization of the educational process reflects a student body ready to adopt technology, with moderate agreement (59.1%), yet not uniformly convinced of its advantage over traditional methods [4].

Remote collaboration is compared with physical collaboration, showing a preference for the latter (67.1%). This suggests that while digital approaches are appreciated for specific activities like submitting assignments (87.7% agreement), tangible interaction is preferred for other collaborative endeavors, possibly due to the reasons mentioned at the beginning of this section [3].

There is a general trust in digital platforms for security and guidance, yet a cautious stance towards AI's role in delivering lectures (43.1% agreement) and handling administrative inquiries (51.7% agreement) [2]. Growing confidence is observed in integrating modern technology and AI in education and administrative services, with agreement above 60%. However, the perspective on e-learning is split, with only 30.9% finding it challenging, possibly reflecting the adaptability of digital natives to online environments.

The preference for digitization of financial and administrative academic tasks indicates a shift towards streamlined processes. Yet, a significant language barrier exists for some students when engaging with digital platforms, impacting accessibility.

Lastly, perceptions of digital skills among professors reveal a balanced view that recognizes potential across age groups, with approximately 46.3% believing that younger professors have more digital competencies [6].

These findings illustrate a student population navigating the digital transformation in higher education. There is a clear positive feeling towards digital tools and an enduring appreciation for traditional academic elements. This reveals various preferences that educational institutions must consider in their technology integration strategies [14].

6 Conclusion

The DX landscape within the academic sphere is multi-faceted, as shown by the diverse student perspectives at the UOP. The findings of this study reveal that a significant number of students use digital platforms for convenience and flexibility, with 68.29% favoring online communication for academic affairs. Yet, the traditional face-to-face interaction retains its importance, underscored by 76.29% of students who prefer it, suggesting that a physical presence still holds a special place in the educational experience. Additionally, preparing attractive electronic academic materials that cover the whole course's intended learning outcomes (ILOs) is still classified as a big challenge for education sectors and HEIs. While there is a strong inclination towards digital collaboration, it is not overwhelmingly dominant, as evidenced by the 60% who favor it and the significant number who either prefer traditional methods or remain uncertain. This reflects a student body that, while digitally competent, also values the irreplaceable precious details of in-person interactions. The digitization of the educational process shows that students are willing to integrate technology into their learning, with a moderate consensus (59.1%) supporting its complete adoption. Yet, this sentiment is not overwhelming, indicating that the attraction of traditional education methods persists. When comparing distance and in-person collaboration, most favor the latter (67.1%), highlighting that tangible interactions are still preferred for certain collaborative activities. This preference is less pronounced when it comes to transactional tasks, such as assignment submissions, where a significant majority (87.7%) prefer the digital way, emphasizing convenience's role in their choices. While there is a general trust in the security of digital platforms, students are more concerned about AI's role in academic settings, with only 43.1% confident in AI's capacity to deliver lectures and 51.7% in handling administrative inquiries. This caution reflects the complex relationship between the perceived potential of AI and the precious detailed requirements of educational and administrative tasks. In conclusion, while the trend toward digitalization in higher education is noticeable, it must be balanced with the specific needs and preferences of the student body. The UOP plans for DX should remain flexible and inclusive, ensuring that technological advancements enhance rather than replace the rich traditional academic experiences.

References

1. Rogozin D, Solodovnikova O, Ipatova A (2022) How university teachers view the digital transformation of higher education. Educ Studies Moscow 1:271–300. https://doi.org/10.17323/1814-9545-2022-1-271-300
2. Wilms K, Meske C, Stieglitz S et al (2017) Digital transformation in higher education—new cohorts, new requirements? Twenty-third Americas conference on information systems, Boston. https://core.ac.uk/download/pdf/301371921.pdf
3. Santos H, Batista J, Marques R (2019) Digital transformation in higher education: the use of communication technologies by students. Procedia Comput Sci 164:123–130. https://doi.org/10.1016/j.procs.2019.12.163
4. Kamsker S, Janschitz G, Monitzer S (2020) Digital transformation and higher education: a survey on the digital competencies of learners to develop higher education teaching. Int J Business Educ 160(1):22–41. https://doi.org/10.30707/IJBE160.1.1648090946.696630
5. Varma R, Umesh I, Nagesh Y et al (2021) Digital transformation in higher education institutions—an overview. Int J Appl Eng Res 16(4):278–282. https://www.ripublication.com/ijaer21/ijaerv16n4_05.pdf

6. Abdel-Rahem R, El-Khalili N (2023) E-learning at the University of Petra during the COVID-19 pandemic: lessons and recommendations. In: Badran A et al (eds) Higher education in the Arab world. Springer, Cham. https://doi.org/10.1007/978-3-031-33568-6_8
7. Mamaeva D, Shabaltina L, Garnova V et al (2020) Digital transformation of higher educational system. J Phys: Conf Ser 1691(1):012081. https://doi.org/10.1088/1742-6596/1691/1/012081
8. Benavides L, Tamayo Arias J (2020) Digital transformation in higher education institutions: a systematic literature review. Sensors 20(11):3291. https://doi.org/10.3390/s20113291
9. Rodrigues L (2017) Challenges of digital transformation in higher education institutions: a brief discussion. In: Proceedings of 30th IBIMA conference. http://hdl.handle.net/10400.22/15234
10. Marks A, Al-Ali M (2022) Digital transformation in higher education: a framework for maturity assessment. In: Alaali M (ed) COVID-19 challenges to university information technology governance. Springer, Cham. https://doi.org/10.1007/978-3-031-13351-0_3
11. Aditya B, Ferdiana R, Kusumawardani S (2021) Categories for barriers to digital transformation in higher education: an analysis based on literature. Int J Info Educ Technol 11(12):658–664 https://doi.org/10.18178/ijiet.2021.11.12.1578
12. Seres L, Pavlicevic V, Tumbas P (2018) Digital transformation of higher education: competing on analytics. In: INTED2018 Proceedings, 12th international technology, education and development conference, Valencia, Spain. https://doi.org/10.21125/inted.2018.2348
13. Kopp M, Gröblinger O, Adams S (2019) Five common assumptions that prevent digital transformation at higher education institutions. In: INTED2019 Proceedings, 13th international technology, education and development conference, Valencia, Spain. https://doi.org/10.21125/inted.2019.0445
14. Sandhu G (2018) The role of academic libraries in the digital transformation of the universities. In: Proceedings of 5th international symposium on emerging trends and technologies in libraries and information services (ETTLIS), Noida, India. https://doi.org/10.1109/ETTLIS.2018.8485258
15. Barzman M, Gerphagnon M, Aubin-Houzelstein G et al (2021) Exploring digital transformation in higher education and research via scenarios. Futures Studies 25(3):65–78. https://doi.org/10.6531/JFS.202103_25(3).0006
16. Hakan K (2020) Digital transformation in higher education: a case study on strategic plans. Vysshee obrazovanie v Rossii (Higher Educ Russia) 29(3):9–23 https://doi.org/10.31992/0869-3617-2019-29-3-9-23 https://doi.org/10.31992/0869-3617-2019-29-3-9-23
17. Neborsky E, Boguslavsky M, Ladyzhets N, Naumova T (2020) Digital transformation of higher education: international trends. In: Proceedings of the international scientific conference "digitalization of education: history, trends and prospects" (DETP 2020). https://doi.org/10.2991/assehr.k.200509.071
18. Prensky M (2000) Digital natives, digital immigrants. On the Horizon 9(5):1–6 https://www.marcprensky.com/writing/Prensky%20-%20Digital%20Natives,%20Digital%20Immigrants%20-%20Part1.pdf
19. Li L, Zheng G, Shen Y, Guo R (2015) Which collaboration technologies best support student teamwork? An empirical investigation. In: Proceedings of the 21st Americas conference on information systems, AMCIS 2015, Puerto Rico. https://researchr.org/publication/amcis-2015
20. King S, Greidanus E, Carbonaro M et al (2009) Merging social networking environments and formal learning environments to support and facilitate interprofessional instruction. Med Educ Online 14(1):5. https://doi.org/10.3885/meo.2009.T0000132
21. Declaration Q (2015) Seize digital opportunities, lead education transformation. In: Proceedings of the international conference on information and communication technology (ICT) and post-2015 education, Qingdao, China https://unesdoc.unesco.org/ark:/48223/pf0000233352
22. Smith H, McKeen J (2011) Enabling collaboration with IT. Commun Assoc Inform Syst 28(16):243–254. https://doi.org/10.17705/1CAIS.02816
23. Cameron E, Green M (2019) Making sense of change management: a complete guide to the models, tools and techniques of organizational change. Kogan Page. http://www.uop.edu.pk/ocontents/Change%20Management%20Book.pdf

24. Riemer K, Uri G, Hamann J et al (2015) Digital disruptive intermediaries: finding new digital opportunities by disrupting existing business models. Aust Digital Transform Lab. http://hdl.handle.net/2123/12761
25. Kaminskyi O, Yereshko J, Kyrychenko S (2018) Digital transformation of university education in Ukraine: trajectories of development in the conditions of new technological and economic order. Inform Technol Learn Tools 64(2):128–137. https://doi.org/10.33407/itlt.v64i2.2083

Digital Transformation in Universities: Strategic Framework, Implementation Tools, and Leadership

Isam Zabalawi, Helene Kordahji, and Sapheya Aftimos

Abstract Digital transformation (DX) is a bridge connecting today's universities to the education landscape of tomorrow. In the Arab region, numerous nations have devised national DX plans that extend into higher education (HE). Successful DX necessitates the comprehensive implementation and understanding of technology, not only at an individual level but also at the university level. Therefore, DX is the systematic application of digital technologies to create innovative processes, products, and services. Within HE, the imperative need for DX is undeniable. In this book chapter, national and global countries were explored to identify their digital strategies. Embracing DX goes beyond technology; it necessitates the cultivation of a DX culture. A seven-pillar model is introduced that universities can adopt to instill a robust DX culture. The chapter also discusses the challenges that arise while implementing DX, and how they may be overseen. Given the multidimensional nature of DX, various supporting frameworks were investigated, which led to the proposed Australian University DX Strategic Framework which may be used as an instrument in advancing research in the realm of DX. The strategy comprises five overarching pillars: university digital culture; teaching and learning; research, knowledge, development and innovation; digital infrastructure; and digital impact. Each pillar has a set of Key Performance Indicators (KPIs) which measure the success of the strategy. In addition to the KPIs as an implementation tool, the Australian University DX Ambition Spectrum and DX Maturity Model are also presented as implementation tools. Universities are leveraging technology to enhance the overall educational experience, improve administrative efficiency, and foster innovation in teaching, learning, and research, thus creating a demand for digital leadership while incorporating a hybrid model that focuses on centralized and decentralized leadership. Moreover, this chapter is poised to provide substantial theoretical contributions to researchers

---

I. Zabalawi (✉) · H. Kordahji · S. Aftimos
Australian University, West Mishref, 13015 Safat, Kuwait
e-mail: i.zabalawi@au.edu.kw

H. Kordahji
e-mail: h.kordahji@au.edu.kw

S. Aftimos
e-mail: s.aftimos@au.edu.kw

© The Author(s), under exclusive license to Springer Nature Switzerland AG 2024
A. Badran et al. (eds.), *Higher Education in the Arab World*,
https://doi.org/10.1007/978-3-031-70779-7_8

focusing on strategy, implementation tools, and leadership in the context of DX in HE. The conclusions drawn within the Higher Education Institution (HEI) setting offer a foundation for recommending further research, particularly in the form of case studies on universities implementing DX across all their services.

Keywords Higher education · Digital transformation · Leadership · Strategy · Framework · Implementation tools · Key performance indicators · Culture · Australian University

1 Introduction

Digital transformation (DX) serves as the bridge connecting today's universities to the education landscape of tomorrow. For higher education institutions (HEIs), DX presents a profound opportunity to enhance access to education, refine operating models, streamline communication channels, and facilitate more-efficient decision-making. It is not merely a change in technology but a transformative transition with the potential to significantly improve lives, as highlighted by the OECD in their report titled 'How's Life in the Digital Age?' Digital transformation is driven by shifts in digital technologies, increased digital competition, and evolving digital customer behaviors. In the global HE industry, DX charts the course for a sustainable education-management strategy in the future [1].

Within the Arab region, numerous nations have formulated national DX plans that extend into higher education (HE). A notable example is the Kingdom of Saudi Arabia, actively fostering DX through a robust digital infrastructure and its National Strategy for DX. This strategy directly influences the educational landscape of the Kingdom. Simultaneously, the Kuwait National Development Plan, 2035 Vision, sets a unified direction to position Kuwait as a leader in finance, culture, and HE. Organized by seven pillars and five strategic directions, this plan intricately links to DX across various aspects, including emerging technologies, the HE sectors, cybersecurity policies, a flexible legal environment, the digital economy, government and private-sector cooperation, digital skills, cloud-based applications, and a strategic DX framework.

As DX takes center stage as an HE priority, aligning with national development plans becomes imperative. This chapter's focus is to delineate the optimal mechanisms for integrating and embedding DX within a university through strategic decisions and directions. Our approach to DX encompasses three critical layers: *Strategy*, *Implementation Tools*, and *Leadership*. These layers form the foundation for successful DX adoption and evolution within the dynamic landscape of HE.

Successful DX necessitates the comprehensive implementation and understanding of technology, not only at an individual level but also at the university level and within the primary strategy. Strategy serves as the linchpin for DX implementation, as underscored by the 2015 Digital Business Global Executive Study and Research Project by MIT Sloan Management Review and Deloitte. This study identifies strategy as the key driver in the digital arena, emphasizing its role in driving digital maturity. The prerequisite for digitally transforming a university lies in a clear strategy, supported by leaders fostering an innovative culture. According to Kane et al. [2], a digital strategy propels digital maturity, shaping organizations to transform their models and develop skills aligned with the strategy. Regularly revisiting and evaluating the university's DX strategy ensures that action plans for implementation remain on the right track [2].

Leaders of DX necessitate a suite of implementation tools to ensure the strategy achieves its intended impact. One effective approach involves using Key Performance Indicators (KPIs) at the university level, complemented by dashboards for continual assessment and evaluation of the strategy's goals. Targeted KPIs are essential for monitoring and evaluating the contribution of DX within the university. In parallel, dashboards provide the necessary metrics and data, offering leadership crucial oversight. Common evaluation systems in literature encompass KPIs, *Ranking Systems*, *Control Systems*, and *Dashboards*, and this logic can be applied within the HEI [3].

The third layer in the DX approach centers on leadership, echoing Iosad's [4] assertion that "Culture change is key to the success of DX, and this needs to come from the top". Leadership plays a pivotal role in supporting the delivery and success of organizational initiatives. Given the rapid pace of change, university leaders benefit from actively engaging in developing their understanding of the DX landscape. This chapter explores centralized versus decentralized leadership styles to determine what works best in the context of DX. Tsou and Chen [5] suggest that leaders can leverage digital technology applications to improve their universities' status, emphasizing the need for a flexible and dynamic architecture, centralized data processing, shared knowledge, complex activity design, and timely decision-making. Competence and a positive attitude are imperative for leaders guiding a DX strategy, transforming the university landscape, enhancing the student experience, and contributing to knowledge creation and dissemination for the benefit of national social and economic development. Lastly, leaders should emphasize continuous improvement of organizational structures and the implementation of advanced management techniques by adopting DX tools to facilitate innovation efforts.

It is crucial to highlight that this chapter extensively addresses the myriad challenges associated with DX, focusing on cultural barriers, the absence of a clear strategy, outdated technology infrastructure, constraints in organizational structure, faculty readiness and training, rigid pedagogical structures, and governance issues.

In summary, this chapter unfolds in eight overarching sections. Section 1 is this introduction followed by Sect. 2 that introduces DX within the HE landscape. Section 3 delves into the significance of the DX culture and its parameters, illustrating how universities leverage DX to enhance the experiences of both faculty and students while optimizing operational and decision-making processes. Section 4 presents a robust *DX Strategic Framework* developed by the Australian University (AU) in the State of Kuwait, tailored to the specific needs of HEIs. In Sect. 5, alongside this framework, a comprehensive set of KPIs is delineated for each pillar, critically measuring the success and progress of the digital strategy. Moreover, the chapter introduces the Australian University's Higher Education Digital Ambition Spectrum and the

Australian University Digital Transformation Maturity Model as tools empowering universities to assess their digital readiness and chart the course for DX. In Sect. 6, the discussion delves into the nuances of centralized and decentralized leadership within the HE DX strategy, shedding light on their distinctive characteristics, potential benefits, and inherent challenges. By understanding the implications of these leadership models, institutions can craft strategies that align with their unique goals, values, and aspirations, thereby positioning themselves at the forefront of the digital revolution in HE. Section 7 offers valuable recommendations and conclusions for the path forward. The final section is the list of references used within this chapter.

2 Digital Transformation and Higher Education

2.1 Digital Transformation and Its Vital Components in Higher Education

Digital transformation has emerged as a central focus for HEIs in the second decade of the twenty-first century, becoming an expected and necessary process for organizations aiming to be change leaders and highly competitive in their respective sectors.

Various authors have defined DX primarily within the business domain, often clustered around the technological, organizational, and social impact of DX in universities. Hess et al. [6] assert that DX is concerned with the changes digital technologies bring about in a company's business model, leading to altered products, organization structures, or the automation of processes. Recent research by Gobble [7] characterizes DX as the profound transformation of business activities and organizations, encompassing processes, competencies, and models. Rodrigues [8] and Wade [9] posit that DX fundamentally revolves around change, involving people, processes, strategies, structures, and competitive dynamics within HEIs. Bygstad et al. [10] frame DX as a series of deep and coordinated culture, workforce, and technology shifts, enabling new educational and operating models, transforming an institution's business model, strategic directions, and value proposition.

Despite the multitude of definitions, no overarching definition for DX seems to exist. In this contribution, DX in HE is defined as "a fundamental paradigm shift within the university to incorporate, integrate, and optimize innovative digital practices into teaching, learning, research, operational and administrative processes and infrastructure."

Akin to many other industries and services, HEIs have harnessed emerging technologies to enhance performance and adapt to an increasingly technology-driven world. The integration of DX with HE entails incorporating digital technology across all university areas, bringing about changes in operations and delivering value to customers—students, parents, partners, and employees. The overarching goal is to improve operational efficiency, competitiveness, sustainability, resilience, agility, inclusivity, and innovation using technology. Not only does DX transform operations but it also influences how people work and live, facilitating remote work and easy access to information and services.

Digital transformation is the systematic application of digital technologies to create innovative processes, products, and services. Within HE, the imperative for DX is undeniable, as it possesses the potential to reshape various aspects of individuals' lives, work environments, thought processes, interactions, and communication channels. This need for DX in HE is intricately categorized into four pivotal components: technological, organizational, curriculum, and social.

1. **Technological Perspective** In the realm of technology, DX in HE enhances teaching, learning, research, services to the community, and cooperation. It involves leveraging new technologies and embedded devices to create a more immersive and collaborative educational experience.
2. **Organizational Enhancement** From an organizational standpoint, DX in HE improves the quality and efficiency of systems by adopting new operating models or implementing changes to existing processes. This ensures that the institutional infrastructure is dynamic and adaptable.
3. **Curriculum Innovation** In the curriculum domain, DX facilitates the initiative-taking adoption of state-of-the-art curriculum designs that align with the demands of a challenging and ever-changing workplace. It ensures that educational content remains relevant and responsive to industry needs.
4. **Social Integration** From a social outlook, DX enables universities to produce graduates equipped with in-demand, transferrable skills. This not only fosters integration with smart societies, cities, and governments but also contributes to targeted research that advances socio-economic sectors.

While DX research gains momentum across various academic fields, there remain unexplored areas within the HE landscape. Successful DX implementation in a university necessitates effective digital leadership, appropriate investment, robust infrastructure, stakeholder engagement, and a digitally capable staff [11].

To gain a comprehensive understanding of DX in HE, it is essential to recognize the pivotal role nations play as initiators of DX. The subsequent section delves into national strategies and the landscape of HE DX within the Arab region.

2.2 National Strategies and Higher-Education Digital Transformation in the Arab Landscape

Undoubtedly, DX paves the way for the introduction of diverse tools to construct smart campuses and empower universities to seamlessly integrate with smart cities, as elucidated in this section. Moreover, DX emerges as a linchpin in building smart nations, contributing significantly to the digital society, digital economy, and digital government. It is anticipated that HEIs will wield considerable influence in these transformative processes.

National digital strategies play a pivotal role in shaping a country's digital landscape, encompassing its economy and society. These strategies serve as a cornerstone for a government's paramount digital policy priorities and goals, designed to mold the digital experience of a nation. Overarching objectives of national digital strategies often include positioning the country as a digital front-runner, fostering digital innovation, driving productivity and growth, and enhancing well-being through bridging digital divides and promoting social inclusion [12]. While these strategies may vary in content and goals, they function as a catalyst for sectors across the nation to embrace DX. Some strategies are visionary, while others are more specific and action-oriented [13].

2.2.1 Arab Region Initiatives

In the Arab region, several nations have formulated national plans for DX that seamlessly extend into HE. A noteworthy example is the Kingdom of Saudi Arabia, steadfast in maintaining a robust digital infrastructure to expedite DX through its National Strategy for DX. Aligned with Vision 2030, Saudi Arabia aims to position itself as an economic leader in the twenty-first century by strategically placing digital technology at the core of its transformation [14]. Vision 2030 outlines goals such as economic diversification, reducing dependency on oil, and prioritizing education. The National Strategy for DX emphasizes educational enhancements, including teacher recruitment and training, fostering innovative learning environments, improving curricula and teaching methods, instilling core skills and values in students, encouraging private-sector participation in HE, and aligning education with national development plans [15]. A key focus is on digital education, emphasizing innovative learning methods and flexible techniques.

This commitment to DX is not unique to Saudi Arabia, as other Arab nations, like Kuwait and Jordan, have also developed comprehensive strategies for DX. For example, Kuwait's National Development Plan, 2035 Vision, represents a comprehensive direction aimed at propelling Kuwait into a leadership role in finance, culture, and HE within the region. Illustrated in Fig. 1, the plan comprises seven pillars—public administration, economy, human capital, living environment, healthcare, infrastructure, and global positioning. These pillars intricately connect with DX across various dimensions, including emerging technologies, the HE sector, cybersecurity policies, flexible legal environments, the digital economy, government-private sector collaboration, digital skills, cloud-based applications, and strategic DX initiatives.

Jordan has embarked on a transformative journey with its Digital Transformation Strategy 2020. This strategic initiative addresses the imperative to enhance operational efficiency across various sectors, including HE, through the digitization of content. Jordan's strategy involves the adoption of cutting-edge digital technologies such as artificial intelligence, cloud computing, and the Internet of Things (IoT). A key goal of the strategy is to ensure inclusive and equitable quality education,

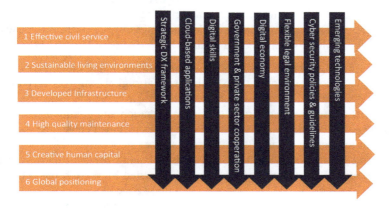

Fig. 1 The seven pillars of Kuwait's National Development Plan, 2035 Vision, and the DX drivers necessary for implementation of the plan

fostering lifelong learning opportunities for all. This vision aligns with a commitment to significantly increase the number of individuals—youth and adults alike—equipped with relevant skills, including technical and vocational competencies, for gainful employment, decent jobs, and entrepreneurship by the year 2030 [16]. To achieve this, collaboration with the private sector is emphasized, providing flexible education opportunities spanning diverse disciplines and skills. The government is also actively investing in the requisite infrastructure for digital learning.

In Morocco, the National Sustainable Development Strategy, known as "Maroc Digital 2020," stands as a pivotal force propelling DX across various sectors. This ambitious national strategy, funded by the government, is geared towards fostering the growth of the digital economy. Aligned with a national strategy on sustainable development, Maroc Digital 2020 centers its objectives on integrating competitiveness and sustainability within the economy, promoting human development and social cohesion, and systematizing environmental concerns. The strategy is structured around four pillars, encompassing compliance with international laws on sustainability, adherence to the National Charter on the Environment and Sustainable Development, a continuous process of attitudinal shifts among stakeholders to enable change, and the development of operational strategies and measures for effective strategy implementation. This multifaceted approach underscores Morocco's commitment to leveraging digitalization for holistic and sustainable development.

2.2.2 Global Lessons: Switzerland and Singapore

Despite notable strides in DX within the Arab world, valuable insights can be gleaned from countries that have excelled in DX. A noteworthy case study is Switzerland, recognized as a global leader in developing and applying digital technologies. In 2016, the Swiss Federal Council adopted the Digital Switzerland Strategy, leading to a comprehensive study by the Federal Department of Economic Affairs, Education, and Research. This initiative addressed the challenges of digitization in education and research, resulting in targeted action areas:

1. **Improving Digital Literacy** Prioritizing educational digital literacy for children and young people to equip them with essential digital skills for thriving in a digital society.
2. **ICT Integration in Teaching** Utilizing information and communication technology (ICT) in teaching and learning. Measures included enhancing the digital skills of teachers and school administrators.
3. **Aligning Education with Market Needs** Adapting the education system to market requirements, emphasizing skills demanded by the job market, with a specific focus on STEM subjects and continuing education.
4. **Enhancing Coordination** Improving coordination and communication in education cooperation to foster a more cohesive and collaborative educational ecosystem.
5. **Strengthening Academic Qualifications** Reinforcing young academic qualifications, particularly digital skills. Universities were tasked with continuous development of teaching and learning formats and content to impart skills relevant to emerging technologies.
6. **Interdisciplinary Research** Ensuring interdisciplinary research on the consequences of digital change for the Swiss economy and society.
7. **Building Competencies in Basic Research** Enhancing competencies in basic research through knowledge generation.
8. **Promoting Innovation** Facilitating innovation by expediting knowledge transfer, ensuring that insights from research are swiftly translated into practical applications [17].

Similarly, Singapore stands as another exemplary nation that successfully embraced DX by digitizing its government, economy, and society. This transformation was underpinned by continuous investments in infrastructure and the creation of open platforms for businesses and citizens to learn and develop. Singapore's strategic approach included substantial investments in talent and technology, empowering individuals to leverage the latest technologies to fulfill their aspirations for a better quality of life [18]. The success of Singapore's DX journey emphasizes the importance of comprehensive and sustained efforts across government, economy, and society.

3 Digital Transformation: Culture and Challenges

3.1 Pillars of DX Culture

The preceding section underscored the significance of a national DX strategy cascading into the HE sectors. However, within HE, embracing DX goes beyond technology; it necessitates the cultivation of a DX culture. The DX culture within a university revolves around how digital technologies become ingrained in everyday practices, optimizing operations, and enhancing the experiences of faculty and students. To instill a robust DX culture, universities can adopt a seven-pillar model (Fig. 2).

1. **Innovation** Defined by behaviors supporting risk-taking, disruptive thinking, and the generation of new ideas. Fostering innovation involves encouraging new perspectives, allowing for failure, setting up cutting-edge labs, facilitating idea commercialization, and planning incentives for idea generation. Organizational culture plays a pivotal role in stimulating innovation within HE, influencing employees to embrace innovation as a fundamental value [19, 20].
2. **Data-Driven Decision-Making** Utilizing data analytics to inform decision-making processes. Although research on the use of data in universities for decision-making is currently limited, this pillar emphasizes the importance of leveraging data for informed choices.
3. **Agility and Flexibility** Signifying the university's capacity to be dynamic and swiftly adapt to the evolving demands of contemporary society.
4. **Collaboration** Involves university leadership supporting inter-departmental teams and initiatives to cultivate a collaborative DX culture.
5. **Open Culture** Providing faculty, staff, and students access to a network system for collaborative problem-solving with external partners.

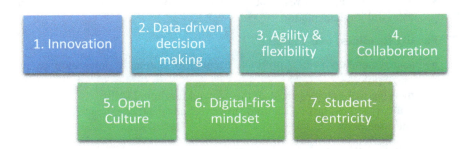

Fig. 2 The seven pillars needed to cultivate a robust DX culture in the higher education sector

6. **Digital-First Mindset** Encourages the view that digital solutions are the future for universities, emphasizing the prioritization of digital approaches.
7. **Student-Centricity** Enabling universities to use DX to enhance the student experience and create new services tailored to their needs [21].

While DX is often associated with business organizations, its significance in HEIs cannot be understated. The realization of the full benefits of DX hinges on recognizing both opportunities and challenges. The subsequent section will delve into the challenges faced by HEIs in the realms of defining strategy, leadership, and implementation tools in the context of DX.

3.2 Challenges Faced by HEIs in DX Implementation

Higher education institutes confront formidable challenges amid global competition for student enrollment, demographic shifts, financial constraints, evolving labor market demands, and heightened student expectations. The digital realm serves as a vital tool for HEIs to navigate these challenges, employing transformation strategies to enhance current processes through digitalization. Despite varied DX strategies, HEIs share common challenges (Fig. 3).

1. **Organizational Structure Constraints**
   - HEIs may struggle with communication flow between stakeholders and departments.
   - Strong leadership is essential for driving beneficial organizational change.
   - Accreditation and ranking agencies play vital roles in evaluating institutional quality and performance.

2. **Leadership and Communication**
   - Effective leadership is crucial for guiding the institution through DX.
   - Clear communication strategies are vital to convey the benefits and necessity of DX.
   - Leaders must address resistance, fostering a collaborative environment for successful implementation.

3. **Faculty Readiness and Training**
   - Faculty members need appropriate training to seamlessly integrate into the change process.
   - Emerging technologies escalate the demand for digital skills.
   - Faculty readiness involves attitude toward change and confidence in adapting to new methods.

4. **Outdated Technology Infrastructure**

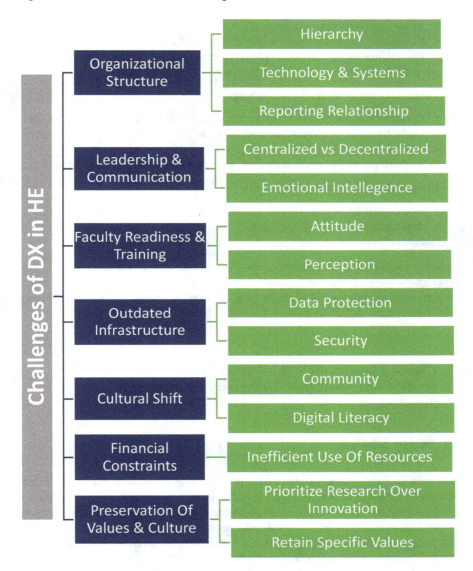

Fig. 3 Challenges faced by HEIs in implementing digital transformation, regardless of strategy employed

- Challenges arise in security, compliance, data protection, and regulations with obsolete technology.
- Automation and digitization enhance agility but elevate cybersecurity risks.
- Upgrading systems may be hindered by cost and time constraints.

5. **Cultural Shift**

- Behavioral changes are essential for adapting to digital transformation.
- Resistance to change may surface among staff and faculty.
- Digital literacy of stakeholders, with diverse backgrounds, impacts the success of digital strategies.

6. **Financial Constraints**

    - Lack of financial prioritization in DX may result in inefficient resource use.
    - Clear financial priorities are crucial to align DX initiatives with strategic objectives.
    - Without prioritization, investments may lack significant value or impact.

7. **Preservation of Values and Culture**

    - Some HEIs prioritize research and academic achievement over innovation.
    - A resistance to change may stem from a desire to retain specific values and cultural aspects.

In the modern era, HEIs face increasing pressure to provide innovative digital experiences for students and stakeholders. A detailed digital strategy is imperative for achieving organizational goals, making HEIs no exception to the contemporary need for effective digital adaptation.

4 Digital Transformation Strategy Framework: Case Studies and Australian University DX Strategic Framework

4.1 Case Studies

Recognizing the dynamic nature of DX, professionals emphasize that it transcends being a mere trend or a technological fad. Digital transformation encompasses a multidisciplinary range within scientific and managerial education, acknowledging its interconnectedness with environmental, social, psychological, educational, political, economic, and financial contexts. A compelling illustration of DX's transformative impact within academia is exemplified by Jill Watson, the renowned virtual teaching assistant at Georgia Tech. Jill has garnered global recognition for consistently providing accurate and authentic responses to frequently asked questions [22].

Given the multidimensional nature of DX, the subsequent section delineates various supporting frameworks instrumental in advancing research in the realm of DX.

4.1.1 Digital Transformation Framework of the Michigan Institute of Technology (MIT)

The Sloan School of Management at MIT has meticulously devised the DX Framework, depicted in Fig. 4, encompassing five pivotal building blocks.

Three of these blocks fall under the category of technology platforms, namely the Operational Backbone, Digital Platform, and External Developer Platform. Two components, Accountability Framework and External Developer Platform, are dedicated to organizational capabilities, seamlessly integrating customer insights and responsibility frameworks that align with the strengths of independent groups. The first three blocks are focused on below, emphasizing the authors' assertion that businesses should enhance the customer experience by cultivating data analysis capabilities to deeply understand customer needs and preferences.

1. **Operational Backbone** This entails integrated systems and processes designed to ensure operational efficiency and maintain the quality of transactions and master data.
2. **Shared Customer Insights** Represents organizational knowledge regarding what customers are willing to pay for and how digital technologies can effectively meet their demands.
3. **Digital Platform** Serves as a repository for business, technology, and data components, fostering rapid innovation in creating new offerings and enhancements.

As institutions embark on their DX journey, the effectiveness of these strategies may vary based on factors such as the university's mission, location, target audience, and available resources. Successful universities often adopt a combination of these strategies to craft a vibrant and engaging learning environment. The building blocks include:

Fig. 4 The DX framework, encompassing five pivotal building blocks, as devised by MIT's Sloan School of Management

4. **Accountability Framework** Signifying clear ownership and coordination among a growing set of digital offerings and components.
5. **External Developer Platform** Acting as a digital ecosystem for partners to contribute to and utilize the platform collaboratively.

4.1.2 The PRME Framework

Academic institutions undergoing transformation to align teaching, research, and thought leadership with societal needs, while cultivating responsible leaders, play a pioneering role in responsible management education. The Principles for Responsible Management Education (PRME), illustrated in Fig. 5, present a structured framework comprising six principles, providing transformative techniques for business and management education [23].

Fig. 5 The Principles for Responsible Management Education (PRME) framework. This is a structured framework comprising six principles which embody transformative techniques for business and management education that lead to sustainable changes

The PRME stands as the largest organized relationship between the United Nations and HEIs specializing in business and management. Its mission is to elevate the prominence of sustainability in universities globally and equip today's students with the capacity to drive change in the future. The six principles (Fig. 5) are explained below:

1. **Purpose** This principle focuses on developing the capabilities of students to become future generators of sustainable value. Achieving this necessitates the management team's commitment to creating sustainable and inclusive business models.
2. **Values** Centered on integrating sustainability and ethical reflections into academic activities, curriculum, and organizational practices. This principle aligns initiatives with future development goals.
3. **Method** Encompasses educational frameworks, processes, materials, and environments that foster effective learning experiences for future leaders. HEIs can implement this principle to provide a comprehensive and profound method of teaching.
4. **Research** Highlights the importance of leveraging conceptual and empirical research to deepen understanding of roles and dynamics. Management teams can actively participate in research activities to incorporate this principle.
5. **Partnership** Involves the interaction between managers and business corporations to cross-pollinate knowledge. This collaboration strengthens the development of more sustainable practices.
6. **Dialog** Facilitates and supports various stakeholders in discussions related to social responsibilities and sustainability. HEIs engage in sustainable practices by embracing this principle.

Embracing the PRME Framework empowers institutions to embed sustainability, ethical considerations, and responsible practices at the core of their educational mission, preparing students to be socially conscious and impactful leaders.

4.1.3 Three-Layer DX Framework Model

The "Three-Layer Model of Digital Transformation," depicted in Fig. 6, is a comprehensive framework that has evolved through an amalgamation of academic interests and practical applications, with recent modifications [24]. This model takes an integrated approach to DX in educational institutions, placing digital innovations at its core. The framework layers are as follows:

1. **Change in Value Creation (First Layer)** This layer focuses on the transformation of value creation through the development and implementation of DX. It enables the consideration of novel products, student interfaces, processes, and business models that may not have existed in a university setting before.
2. **Creation of Conditions for DX (Second Layer)** The second layer revolves around establishing the conditions necessary for successful DX. This involves

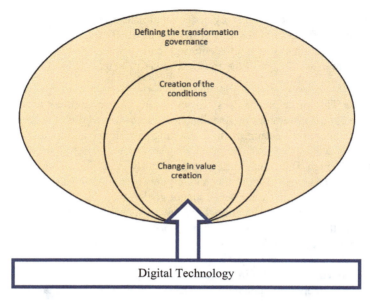

Fig. 6 The "Three-layer model of digital transformation" evolved through consideration of practical applications by academia

creating a supportive environment for a forward-looking outlook. Key support pillars within this layer include information technology (IT), student resources, and infrastructures.

3. **Transformation Governance (Third Layer)** The third layer is dedicated to defining the governance structure for the overall transformation. It outlines crucial guidelines and steps essential for steering the institution towards DX. Once a comprehensive transformation strategy is formulated, it is disseminated and shared across the university.

By addressing these three layers, the framework provides a roadmap for institutions to navigate the complexities of DX. It not only emphasizes the importance of innovative value creation but also underscores the significance of creating a conducive environment and establishing effective governance structures to facilitate and sustain the digital evolution of the institution.

4.1.4 Dual Digitalization Framework—Norway

A framework crafted by Bygstad et al. [10] introduces the Dual Digitalization Framework in Norway, comprising four fundamental elements: digital education, digital subjects, boundary resources, and data, as illustrated in Fig. 7. The elements of the framework are as follows:

Digital Transformation in Universities: Strategic Framework …

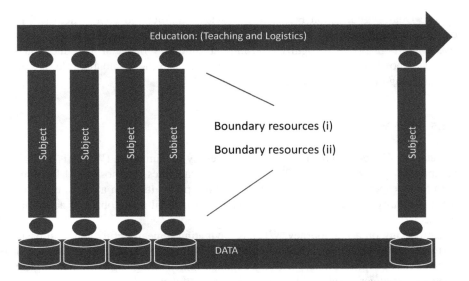

Fig. 7 The Norwegian Dual Digitalization Framework for DX. This comprises four fundamental elements: digital education, digital subjects, boundary resources, and data

1. **Digital Education (First Element)** This element involves the process-oriented management of education, covering teaching and coordination. It encompasses the handling of the digital classroom and Learning Management Systems (LMS). Additionally, it incorporates the utilization of digital materials such as video presentations, PowerPoint, communication of learning outcomes, project details, and examinations.
2. **Digital Subjects (Second Element)** Focused on knowledge-oriented aspects, this element deals with domain-specific knowledge in the digital realm. The nature of this knowledge varies across different educational sectors. For instance, programming would fall under the domain of computer science, while e-learning resources could be pertinent to the field of medicine.
3. **Boundary Resources (Third Element)** This element refers to both technical and social mechanisms facilitating the linkage between educational processes and data. Two types of boundary resources are proposed within this framework. The first type is exemplified by LMS functionality, fostering a seamless connection between the teaching process and digital subjects. The second type establishes connections between digital subjects and larger sets of research data.
4. **Digital Data (Fourth Element)** Primarily focusing on research data, this element encompasses voluminous data for statistical purposes and educational data essential for learning analytics. It plays a crucial role in shaping data-driven insights and decision-making within the digital education landscape.

The Dual Digitalization Framework provides a structured approach to DX in education, addressing key components necessary for a comprehensive and effective digital strategy. It recognizes the intricate interplay between the educational process, knowledge domains, supportive resources, and the invaluable role of data in enhancing the overall learning experience.

4.1.5 The WUT Case—Romania

Situated in Western Romania, the West University of Timisoara (WUT) is an HEI comprising approximately 16,000 students, 700 academics, and hosting 11 faculties with their respective departments. The university prides itself on a robust commitment to quality education in an increasingly international and globalized academic landscape.

Embarking on a DX journey, WUT is navigating a meaningful change in basic assumptions to be implemented across organizational, cultural, and technological dimensions. The institution is actively engaged in delivering **sophisticated digital** services to its diverse stakeholders, including staff, students, educational partners, and visitors, through various departments. To ensure continued relevance and competitiveness in today's digital era, WUT has strategically invested in several key areas, these consist of:

1. **Information Technology Infrastructure** Substantial investments are made in upgrading information technology infrastructure and advanced systems to support seamless digital operations.
2. **Digitalization of Operations** WUT is focused on the comprehensive digitalization of its operational processes, streamlining workflows for enhanced efficiency.
3. **Smart Campus Infrastructure** Implementation of smart campus infrastructure is prioritized to create an intelligent and interconnected learning environment.
4. **Digital Literacy Improvement** Efforts are underway to enhance digital literacy among academics, students, and administrative staff, ensuring that they are well-equipped to navigate and leverage digital tools and technologies.
5. **Transformation of Working Styles and Tools** WUT is actively redefining its current working styles, tools, and capabilities to align with the demands of the digital age.
6. **Cultural Reshaping** A pivotal aspect of WUT's DX strategy involves reshaping its organizational culture to foster a digital-first mindset, encouraging innovation and adaptability.
7. **Artificial Intelligence Integration** WUT is exploring the integration of artificial intelligence to augment various aspects of its operations and educational offerings.
8. **Investment in Social Media Presence** Recognizing the importance of online engagement, WUT is investing in strengthening its social media presence to connect with a wider audience.

Looking forward, WUT recognizes that DX extends beyond the academic community. Future DX solutions will involve a broader perspective, encompassing areas such as government, public institutions, civil society, and industry. The ongoing and future DX initiatives at WUT are geared towards creating innovative learning experiences, establishing new learning paths, fostering collaborative research endeavors, and championing open science and innovation. The institution is poised to play a leading role in shaping the digital landscape of education and research in the years to come. It is crucial to acknowledge that the effectiveness of DX strategies varies based on a university's unique factors, including mission, location, target audience, and available resources.

Successful universities often adopt a multifaceted approach, combining various strategies to craft a dynamic and immersive learning environment.

The significance of this approach lies in its ability to encompass diverse dimensions, as highlighted in Fig. 8.

As universities navigate the complexities of DX, these dimensions collectively contribute to a holistic and forward-looking approach. The intersection of these strategies enables institutions to not only adapt to the digital landscape but also to proactively shape it, ensuring a transformative and sustainable educational ecosystem for the future.

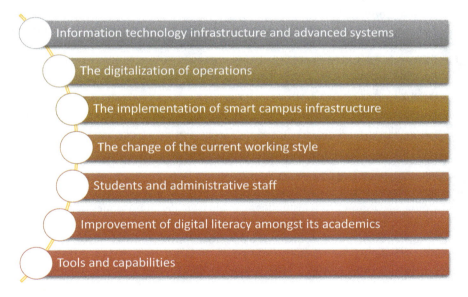

Fig. 8 The West University of Timisoara (Romania) model of DX. This recognizes that DX extends beyond the academic community to encompass diverse dimensions

4.2 Proposed Strategic Framework for Digital Transformation at the Australian University of Kuwait

The imperative for universities to embrace DX strategies stems from their potential to streamline administrative tasks, optimize resource allocation, and elevate overall efficiency. Digital tools serve as foundational elements across diverse university activities, enabling enhanced student engagement and the creation of interactive online platforms for peer and instructor connectivity. Moreover, DX facilitates broader demographic reach through online learning platforms, fostering inclusivity. Key benefits and drivers of DX strategies are:

1. **Resource Allocation** DX strategies empower universities to allocate resources effectively, enhancing operational efficacy.
2. **Student Engagement** Digital tools enable dynamic student engagement, fostering interactive online environments for collaborative learning.
3. **Demographic Expansion** Online learning platforms, a product of DX, allow universities to reach a wider audience, transcending geographical limitations.
4. **Data-Driven Decision-Making** DX strategies leverage data collection and analysis, transforming decision-making processes by grounding them in actionable insights related to performance, research, and operational processes.
5. **Global Competitiveness** Embracing DX ensures universities remain relevant and competitive in the global academic landscape, attracting top-tier talent among faculty and students.
6. **Research Advancements** Digital tools accelerate research by providing access to expansive databases, simulation tools, and collaborative platforms, propelling research endeavors forward.

Taking cues from established strategies, the Australian University in the State of Kuwait proposes a robust DX Strategic Framework tailored to the specific needs of HEIs. Comprising five overarching pillars as depicted in Fig. 9, each pillar encompasses sub-pillars that address the multifaceted aspects of DX.

This comprehensive framework aims to guide universities in developing their DX strategies, considering the barriers discussed earlier in this chapter. By addressing these pillars and sub-pillars, institutions can navigate the complexities of DX implementation, fostering a digitally progressive and adaptive academic environment. The five pillars of the framework are discussed in more detail in the following Sects. (4.2.1–4.2.5).

4.2.1 University Digital Culture

The establishment of a robust digital culture within a university hinges on strategic leadership and the right personnel in key positions. Visionary leaders play a pivotal role in fostering a culture of change, prioritizing accountability and transparency as fundamental principles. The DX culture should permeate every aspect of university

Digital Transformation in Universities: Strategic Framework ... 165

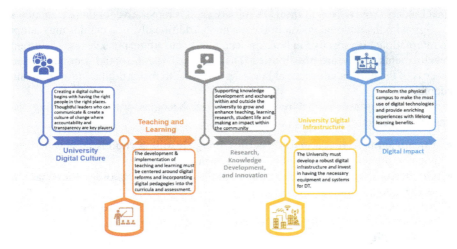

Fig. 9 The strategic framework for digital transformation with its five overarching pillars (*arrows*), as proposed by the Australian University of Kuwait

operations, guiding activities, duties, and intended outcomes. This pillar encompasses the essential components delineated in Fig. 10 which are detailed in the following sub-sections (a–d).

(a) **Vision, Mission and Values**

Universities embarking on DX must undertake a comprehensive assessment of their current state, identifying existing gaps and opportunities. The vision and mission statements should be recalibrated to unmistakably articulate how the university's

Fig. 10 First pillar of the Australian University of Kuwait's DX strategy: *University Digital Culture*

stakeholders stand to benefit from DX initiatives. It is imperative for these statements to align with the national vision of the country. Additionally, universities may adopt an international perspective in horizon scanning to ensure responsiveness to current developments and future possibilities. The redefined vision should transcend mere success in the current educational landscape, aiming to foster digital innovation and adaptability.

Incorporating values that resonate with DX becomes crucial in shaping the university's culture; key values may include:

- **Encouraging Agility and Embracing Change** Instilling a mindset that welcomes adaptability and change as integral to growth.
- **Creativity** Inspiring innovative practices that leverage technology for enhanced teaching and learning experiences.
- **Autonomy** Granting freedom to faculty, staff, and students to explore and develop their ideas within the digital landscape.
- **Accessibility** Ensuring that education is accessible to all groups of learners, promoting inclusivity.
- **Innovation** Actively participating in, contributing to technological advancements, and pioneering pedagogical approaches.
- **Flexibility** Offering varied learning approaches and personalized pathways through digital platforms.
- **Lifelong Learning** Promoting continuous learning opportunities facilitated by the digital landscape.
- **Ethical Use of Technology** Establishing frameworks and guidelines for responsible technology use, safeguarding data privacy, security, and ethical digital learning practices.
- **Quality Education** Ensuring that technological integration upholds academic and research standards.
- **Global Perspective** Providing an education that fosters a global outlook among students.
- **Openness** Encouraging a culture that challenges the status quo and embraces new ideas and perspectives.

(b) **Thoughtful Leadership**

In the DX era, university leadership plays a pivotal role in steering the institution toward a digitally progressive future. Thoughtful leaders are essential, possessing visionary foresight and the ability to seamlessly integrate technology into the university's landscape and overall strategy. Their responsibilities extend to understanding the intricacies of delivering digital education and comprehending the broader implications. Key attributes of thoughtful leadership in the DX era include:

- **Technological Integration** Leaders must demonstrate an in-depth understanding of the requirements for delivering digital education. This involves integrating technology seamlessly into the university's overarching strategy.

Fig. 11 Characteristics of *Thoughtful Leadership*, an important component of the first pillar (University Digital Culture) of the Australian University of Kuwait's DX strategy (see Fig. 10)

- **Collaborative Environment** Fostering a collaborative environment is crucial. Leaders should encourage the university community to actively engage in innovative practices and experiment with new digital tools.
- **Technological Literacy** Thoughtful leaders are equipped with a solid understanding of the latest technological advancements. They empower faculty and staff by providing resources and training on digital tools, ensuring the entire community is technologically literate.
- **Data-Driven Decision-Making** Informed decisions are paramount in the DX era. Leaders leverage data analytics to guide their initiatives, ensuring that strategies are grounded in evidence and contribute to the university's digital objectives.
- **Ethical Considerations** Leaders prioritize ethical considerations in every technology-based decision. This involves understanding and addressing potential ethical implications, promoting responsible technology use, and ensuring a solid governance framework is in place.

Thoughtful leaders embody characteristics such as those depicted in Fig. 11:

- **Proactive and visionary** Anticipate emerging trends, embrace technological advancements, and catalyze organizational change to drive innovation. They envision future possibilities, ensuring their organizations stay ahead in an ever-evolving digital world.
- **Digitally literate** Possess a comprehensive understanding of digital technologies and leverage this knowledge to guide their organizations in the digital age.
- **Reflectiveness** Leaders are reflective in their approach, regularly evaluating the impact of technological decisions and initiatives.
- **Honesty** Transparency and honesty are essential traits, fostering trust within the university community.
- **Transparent** Prioritize openness, honesty, and clear communication in their interactions with employees, stakeholders, and the broader community. They willingly share information about organizational goals, decisions, and challenges, fostering an environment of trust and accountability.
- **Accountability** Leaders hold themselves and others accountable for the outcomes of digital initiatives.

- **Team Orientation** A collaborative and team-oriented approach is integral to successful digital leadership.
- **Excellent Communication** Leaders excel in communication, ensuring that the vision and objectives of digital initiatives are effectively conveyed to all stakeholders.

Thoughtful leadership, rooted in technological acumen, ethical considerations, and collaborative engagement, is fundamental to navigating the complexities of DX in a university setting.

(c) **Change Management**

Change management in the context of DX involves actively supporting the university community in seamlessly integrating DX into all aspects of its operations, with a particular emphasis on teaching and learning. Successful change management requires a technical understanding of the necessary adjustments and a strategic approach to influence and embrace change effectively. Key aspects of change management comprise the following:

1. **Technical Understanding** Change management demands technical comprehension of the adjustments required for the successful integration of DX. This understanding ensures that the technological aspects of the transformation are effectively communicated and implemented.
2. **Challenges and Strategies** Implementation of DX strategies is often complex and met with various challenges. Universities can opt for either a moderate or radical approach. A moderate strategy involves cautiously introducing well-rehearsed and user-friendly DX technologies. In contrast, a radical approach involves transformative changes to the organizational structure. The choice between these approaches depends on the university's specific context and goals.
3. **Top-Down and Bottom-Up Approach** Regardless of the chosen strategy, a successful change management process relies on a combination of top-down and bottom-up approaches. Top-down involvement ensures leadership support and guidance, while bottom-up engagement encourages active participation and input from the university community.

Principles within the DX Environment encompass the points below, as illustrated in Fig. 12.

- **Conception and Initiation** The change process begins with the conceptualization and initiation phase, where the need for DX is identified, and the vision for transformation is established.
- **Develop the Plan and Formulate the Team** A detailed plan is developed, outlining the steps and strategies for DX implementation. A dedicated team is formulated, comprising individuals with diverse skills and expertise to drive the change process.
- **Train and Communicate** Training programs are essential to equip the university community with the necessary skills for adopting DX technologies. Effective

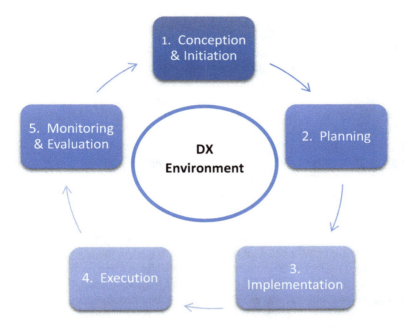

Fig. 12 The *Change Management* component of the first pillar (Fig. 10) of the AU's DX strategy includes the principles of managing the DX environment

communication ensures that stakeholders are informed, engaged, and supportive of the change initiative.
- **Implement and Enhance** The actual implementation of DX strategies takes place, with continuous monitoring and enhancement to address emerging challenges and opportunities.
- **Evaluate** Regular evaluation of the DX implementation is crucial. This involves assessing the effectiveness of the strategies, gathering feedback, and adjusting as needed.

Change management, when approached strategically and with a focus on collaboration, communication, and adaptability, becomes a driving force for successful DX within the university environment.

(d) **Transparency and Accountability**

In the context of DX, transparency and accountability play pivotal roles in ensuring the successful implementation of DX strategies within the university setting. Leaders, both at the administrative and academic levels, must prioritize these principles to create an environment conducive to positive outcomes. Key aspects of transparency and accountability entail the following:

1. **Information Sharing** Leaders are encouraged to foster transparency by openly sharing relevant information with team members. This includes data, reports,

plans, and outcomes associated with the DX initiatives. Transparent communication helps build trust among stakeholders and provides a clear understanding of the direction and progress of the transformation.
2. **Rationale Behind Decisions** Transparency extends to explaining the rationale behind decisions taken during the DX process. Leaders should articulate the reasons behind strategic choices, ensuring that the university community comprehends the motivations guiding the transformation journey. This fosters a sense of inclusion and understanding among team members.
3. **Protection Against Undesirable Results** Transparency serves as a safeguard against undesirable results. By openly addressing challenges, setbacks, and areas needing improvement, leaders can proactively mitigate risks and steer the DX initiatives towards positive outcomes. This open acknowledgment of challenges is integral to a culture of continuous improvement.
4. **Application of Policies, Procedures, and Laws** Transparent leadership involves ensuring the application of appropriate policies, procedures, and laws to the digital environment. Leaders should be well-versed in the regulatory landscape governing DX in HE and ensure compliance. This commitment to adherence reinforces the ethical and legal dimensions of the transformation.
5. **Recognition and Rewards** In parallel with transparency, accountability measures should be in place to recognize and reward individuals who demonstrate commitment to the DX process. Acknowledging the efforts of team members fosters a positive culture, motivating others to actively contribute to the success of the transformation.

By prioritizing transparency and accountability, leaders create an environment where information flows freely, decisions are well-understood, and individuals are empowered to contribute meaningfully to the DX journey. This approach not only safeguards against potential challenges but also establishes a foundation for a culture of innovation and shared success within the university community.

4.2.2 Teaching and Learning

In the realm of DX, the second pillar focuses on revolutionizing teaching and learning methodologies, emphasizing the integration of digital reforms and innovative pedagogies into curricula and assessment practices. The goal of implementing DX strategies in this context is to elevate student engagement to its highest levels (Fig. 13). Key aspects of teaching and learning contain:

1. **Curriculum Development and Assessment** (Fig. 14)
    - *Real-Time Assessment.* Digital technologies facilitate real-time assessment, enabling educators to track students' progress instantly. This dynamic assessment approach allows curriculum developers to adapt content based on ongoing performance data.

Fig. 13 Second pillar of the Australian University of Kuwait's DX strategy: *Teaching and Learning*

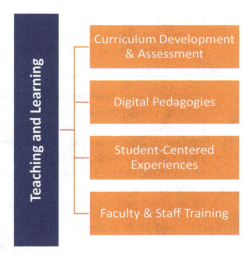

- *Data Analytics for Tailored Content.* Utilizing data analytics, educators can identify learning gaps and adjust curriculum content to address specific needs. This data-driven approach ensures the continuous enhancement of curriculum materials in response to evolving knowledge, technology, and educational standards.
- *Diversified Assessment Techniques.* DX strategies in assessment design introduce diverse question formats, automated grading, real-time analytics, timely feedback, and data-driven improvements, contributing to a more robust and comprehensive educational assessment.

2. **Digital Pedagogies**
   - *Innovative Instructional Methods.* Digital pedagogies leverage technology to enhance teaching and learning experiences. This includes strategies such as online learning platforms, educational apps, virtual reality, and multimedia resources. These methods aim to engage students through diverse learning styles, foster collaboration, and critical thinking, and extend education accessibility to a broader audience.

Fig. 14 A key aspect of the *Teaching and Learning* pillar of AUs DX strategy is *Curriculum Development & Assessment* (Fig. 13), which involves monitoring achievements which, in turn, lead to improved courses

- *Linking Classroom with Work Environment.* Digital pedagogies seamlessly connect the classroom environment with real-world work scenarios, integrating research and inquiry-based learning methodologies.

3. **Student-Centered Experiences**
   - *Interactive and Multimedia-Rich Content.* Faculty play a crucial role in creating or adapting digital content that is interactive, multimedia-rich, and conducive to active learning. This can include videos, quizzes, forums, interactive simulations, and virtual labs.
   - *Personalized Learning Paths.* Digital technologies enable the development of personalized learning paths, tailoring educational content to individual student needs and learning styles. Adaptive learning platforms adjust content based on students' progress, interactions, and feedback.

4. **Faculty and Staff Training**
   - *Skill Enhancement for Effective Technology Use.* Training programs for faculty and staff equip them with the necessary skills to harness technology effectively in teaching, administrative tasks, and student support. This training empowers educators to leverage DX tools efficiently, enhancing traditional activities and freeing up time for additional tasks.
   - *Investing in Readiness.* Investment in faculty and staff readiness through diverse initiatives such as training programs, workshops, peer-to-peer mentoring, and professional development ensures better student outcomes and minimizes resistance to change.

By embracing these components within the Teaching and Learning pillar, universities can unlock the full potential of digital technologies to create dynamic, engaging, and effective learning environments that cater to the evolving needs of both educators and students.

4.2.3 Research, Knowledge Development, and Innovation

The third pillar focuses on advancing knowledge development, exchange, and innovation within and beyond the university, aiming to enrich teaching, learning, research, student life, and community impact (Fig. 15). Key aspects of research, knowledge development, and innovation embody the following:

1. **Multidisciplinary Research/Knowledge Exchange**
   - *Breaking Down Traditional Barriers.* DX significantly enhances multidisciplinary research and knowledge exchange by dismantling traditional barriers. Collaborative efforts among experts from diverse fields are facilitated through a shared digital platform, fostering data sharing, analysis, and communication.
   - *Digital Collaboration for Innovation.* The digital environment nurtures collaboration, leading to innovative solutions for complex problems. Online forums

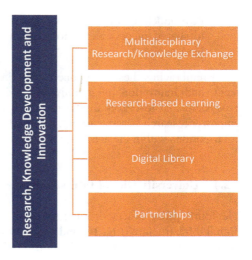

Fig. 15 Third pillar of the Australian University of Kuwait's DX strategy: *Research, Knowledge Development, and Innovation*

and webinars provide a space for cross-disciplinary interaction and collaborative research, transcending geographical boundaries and maximizing impact.

2. **Research-Based Learning**
   - *Revolutionizing the Research Process.* DX revolutionizes the research process through various digital tools, including online databases, research collaboration platforms, data analysis software, and AI-powered literature reviews. These tools empower faculty and students to conduct comprehensive, data-driven studies and stay abreast of the latest developments in their respective fields.

3. **Digital Library Research**
   - *Enhanced Access to Academic Resources.* Digital libraries serve as valuable resources, offering convenient and extensive access to a wide range of academic materials. Researchers utilize digital libraries to retrieve scholarly articles, eBooks, multimedia content, and datasets. These platforms often provide tools for data mining, analysis, and visualization, enhancing research capabilities and information access in the digital age.

4. **Partnerships**
   - *Fostering Collaborative Networks.* DX strategies should actively promote partnerships among researchers, educators, universities, and experts in diverse fields. Cloud-based solutions play a key role in enabling secure data sharing, fostering trust and transparency in collaborative efforts.
   - *Interconnected Collaborations.* Universities are encouraged to establish partnerships with other academic institutions, industries, communities, and

government entities for collaborative projects. These partnerships contribute to shared success and innovation in an interconnected and digitally driven landscape.

By embracing these components within the Research, Knowledge Development, and Innovation pillar, universities can create a vibrant and collaborative ecosystem that leverages digital technologies to drive multidisciplinary research, empower research-based learning, and establish strategic partnerships for impactful contributions within the academic and broader communities.

4.2.4 University Digital Infrastructure

The fourth pillar underscores the imperative for the university to cultivate a robust digital infrastructure (Fig. 16) and commit to acquiring the essential equipment and systems vital for successful DX implementation. This encompasses the entire university campus, computer resources, workforce, support utilities, storage facilities, classroom spaces, security measures, maintenance protocols, laboratories, buildings, technology integration, and research centers. It is crucial for the university to meticulously identify, and map all required resources through comprehensive workforce planning, accompanied by clear job descriptions. Furthermore, the financial, facilities, and infrastructure implications should be thoroughly identified and addressed (Fig. 16). Key components of university digital infrastructure involve:

1. **Resources**

    - *Comprehensive Infrastructure.* Establishing a comprehensive digital infrastructure is indispensable for sustaining large-scale digital learning distributed

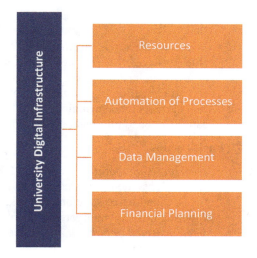

Fig. 16 Fourth pillar of the Australian University of Kuwait's DX strategy: *University Digital Infrastructure*

throughout the institution. This involves securing the right technology, ensuring operational agility and efficiency, and providing faculty training.
- *Technology Stack.* The technology stack includes networking equipment, software solutions, and data centers fortified with cybersecurity measures. These components should be efficiently operated by a team of experienced IT experts under robust leadership. Effective allocation and management of these resources are pivotal for the success and sustainability of digital infrastructures.

2. **Automation of Processes**
   - *Streamlining Administrative Tasks.* DX strategies should prioritize the automation of university processes, streamlining administrative tasks such as student registration, course enrollment, and fee payments.
   - *Learning Management Systems (LMS).* Automation extends to learning management systems that facilitate automated course-content distribution, assignment submission, and grading. Chatbots contribute to instant responses to student queries, enhancing overall efficiency. Digital record-keeping systems efficiently manage student information, while robotic process automation enhances administrative operations with modern and sophisticated approaches.

3. **Data Management**
   - *Establishing Data Governance Policies.* Universities should establish robust data governance policies and standards to ensure data accuracy, security, and compliance with regulations.
   - *Secure and Scalable Solutions.* Implementing secure and scalable data storage solutions, data classification, backup and recovery processes, data access controls, data quality assurance, and adherence to data retention policies are vital. Staff training on data management best practices should be provided.

4. **Financial Planning**
   - *Investment and Prioritization.* Digital initiatives often require substantial investments in technology, talent, and infrastructure. A well-structured financial plan is instrumental in prioritizing projects, accurately estimating costs, securing funding, and tracking expenses to ensure that the transformation stays within budget.

By addressing these components within the University Digital Infrastructure pillar, universities can establish a resilient foundation for DX, ensuring the efficient integration of technology across various facets of the institution and promoting sustained growth and innovation.

4.2.5 Digital Impact

The fifth pillar emphasizes the transformation of the physical campus to maximize the utilization of digital technologies, fostering enriching experiences with lifelong learning benefits (Fig. 17). Key aspects of digital impact subsume into:

1. **Campus Life**
   - *Online Platforms.* Digital technologies play a pivotal role in facilitating the organization and promotion of events, clubs, and extracurricular activities through online platforms. This encourages student involvement, community building, and overall engagement.
   - *Social Media and Communication Channels.* Social media groups and communication channels enable students to connect, collaborate, and share experiences beyond the physical campus, enhancing the sense of community.
   - *Smart Campus with IoT and Sensors.* Leveraging the Internet of Things (IoT) and sensors creates a smart campus, optimizing resources like energy and parking. Virtual tours, made possible through digital technologies, aid prospective students in exploring the campus before applying.

2. **Lifelong Learning**
   - *Interactive Learning Experiences.* Digital technologies provide interactive learning experiences, including simulations and gamifications, making education engaging and effective.
   - *Personalized Learning Pathways.* Offering personalized learning pathways, digital technologies facilitate lifelong learning experiences. Cost-effective options and opportunities for self-directed learning empower individuals to pursue education and personal development throughout their lives.

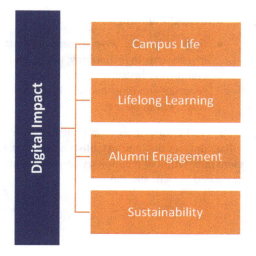

Fig. 17 Fifth pillar of the Australian University of Kuwait's DX strategy: *Digital Impact*

3. **Alumni Engagement**

   - *Online Networking Platforms.* DX promotes alumni engagement through online networking platforms, email campaigns, and social media outreach.
   - *Real-time Connections.* Maintaining real-time connections, sharing updates, updating alumni databases, organizing virtual events, and gathering feedback are efficiently facilitated by digital technologies.

4. **Sustainability**

   - *Campus-wide Digital Systems.* Digital systems implemented across the campus contribute to sustainability goals by monitoring and reducing energy consumption.
   - *Minimizing Paper Documentation.* Digital technologies minimize paper documentation, reduce waste and support environmentally friendly practices.
   - *Green Data Centers and Environmental Monitoring.* Implementing green data centers and environmental monitoring further enhance sustainability efforts.

By addressing these components within the Digital Impact pillar, universities can leverage digital technologies to transform campus life, promote lifelong learning, enhance alumni engagement, and contribute to sustainable practices. This ensures a holistic digital impact that extends beyond the academic realm, enriching the overall educational experience for students and stakeholders alike.

5 Implementation Tools for the DX Strategic Framework

The first implementation tool that can be used by universities once they develop their DX strategy are the key performance indicators (KPIs). Within the above developed strategy, every pillar has a set of KPIs, which universities can pick and select according to their needs. These KPIs are critical for measuring the success and progress of the digital strategy. The KPIs listed below provide a holistic view of the university's DX strategy. Regularly reviewing and adapting these KPIs based on the evolving needs of the institution ensures the effectiveness of the DX strategies. They should align with the goals and objectives mapped in the strategy. The following section presents some KPIs specific to a university's DX strategy.

5.1 General KPIs for the Implementation of DX Strategy

1. **E-Learning Adoption**

   - **KPI** Percentage of courses offered through online platforms.
   - **Measurement** Track the adoption of e-learning platforms and the number of courses available online.

2. **Student Engagement in Digital Platforms**
   - **KPI** Usage metrics for digital learning platforms and online resources.
   - **Measurement** Monitor student logins, participation in online discussions, and engagement with digital content.

3. **Digital Skills Development**
   - **KPI** Percentage of faculty and staff trained in digital tools and methodologies.
   - **Measurement** Assess the level of digital literacy and skills development across the university community.

4. **Online Enrollment and Registration**
   - **KPI** Percentage of students who complete enrollment and registration online.
   - **Measurement** Evaluate the efficiency and adoption of digital processes for student enrollment.

5. **Learning Management System (LMS) Effectiveness**
   - **KPI** User satisfaction with the university's LMS.
   - **Measurement** Collect feedback on the usability and effectiveness of the learning management system.

6. **Digital Library Utilization**
   - **KPI** Number of digital resources accessed by students and faculty.
   - **Measurement** Track the usage of digital libraries and online databases.

7. **Research Collaboration Platforms**
   - **KPI** Adoption of digital platforms for collaborative research.
   - **Measurement** Monitor the use of digital tools that facilitate research collaboration among faculty and students.

8. **Online Assessment and Feedback**
   - **KPI** Percentage of assessments conducted online.
   - **Measurement** Evaluate the effectiveness of online assessments and the speed of providing feedback.

9. **Campus Wi-Fi and Connectivity**
   - **KPI** Network reliability and speed on campus.
   - **Measurement** Ensure a stable and high-speed Wi-Fi network to support digital activities.

10. **Digital Accessibility**
    - **KPI** Compliance with digital accessibility standards.
    - **Measurement** Regularly assess and improve the accessibility of digital content and platforms for all users.

11. **Student Retention and Success**
    - **KPI** Impact of digital initiatives on student retention rates.
    - **Measurement** Analyze whether digital tools and resources contribute to improved student success.

12. **Virtual Campus Tours**
    - **KPI** Number of virtual campus tours conducted.
    - **Measurement** Evaluate the effectiveness of virtual tours for prospective students and their engagement.

13. **Digital Marketing Metrics**
    - **KPI** Conversion rates for digital marketing campaigns.
    - **Measurement** Assess the success of digital marketing efforts in attracting prospective students.

14. **Administrative Process Efficiency**
    - **KPI** Time and cost savings in administrative processes.
    - **Measurement** Evaluate the efficiency of digital tools in streamlining administrative tasks.

15. **Alumni Engagement through Digital Platforms**
    - **KPI** Engagement metrics on alumni digital platforms.
    - **Measurement** Measure alumni participation in digital events, mentoring programs, and online communities.

16. **Cybersecurity Effectiveness**
    - **KPI** Number of cybersecurity incidents and response times.
    - **Measurement** Monitor the security of digital systems and response to potential threats.

17. **Technology Infrastructure Upgrade**
    - **KPI** Percentage of technology infrastructure upgrades completed.
    - **Measurement** Track progress in upgrading and maintaining the university's technology infrastructure.

18. **Virtual Events Participation**
    - **KPI** Attendance and engagement metrics for virtual events.
    - **Measurement** Evaluate the success of virtual conferences, webinars, and campus events.

19. **Digital Feedback Systems**
    - **KPI** Usage of digital feedback systems for courses and services.
    - **Measurement** Assess the effectiveness of digital feedback mechanisms for continuous improvement.

20. **Eco-Friendly Initiatives through Digital Transformation**
    - **KPI** Measurement of environmental impact reduction through digital practices.
    - **Measurement** Assess the university's contribution to sustainability goals through digital initiatives.

5.2 KPIs Related to the Digital Culture of the University

In the context of a university's DX strategy, the development and nurturing of a digital culture are crucial for the successful adoption and integration of digital technologies. Digital culture involves attitudes, behaviors, and practices that support and promote the effective use of digital tools and processes across the university community. The following are KPIs related to fostering a digital culture in a university:

1. **Digital Literacy Levels**
    - **KPI** Percentage of faculty, staff, and students with a baseline level of digital literacy.
    - **Measurement** Conduct digital literacy assessments and track the improvement over time.

2. **Training and Development Participation**
    - **KPI** Percentage of faculty and staff participating in digital skills training programs.
    - **Measurement** Monitor attendance and completion rates for digital training initiatives.

3. **Digital Collaboration Tools Adoption**
    - **KPI** Percentage of faculty and staff actively using digital collaboration tools.
    - **Measurement** Track the adoption of tools such as video conferencing, project management, and collaboration platforms.

4. **Innovation Culture**
    - **KPI** Number of digital innovation initiatives proposed and implemented.
    - **Measurement** Encourage and measure the submission and execution of innovative digital ideas.

5. **User Satisfaction with Digital Systems**
    - **KPI** Satisfaction scores related to the usability of digital systems and tools.
    - **Measurement** Conduct regular surveys to gather feedback on the user experience of digital platforms.

6. **Cross-Departmental Collaboration**

- **KPI** Number of interdisciplinary projects or collaborations facilitated by digital technologies.
- **Measurement** Track collaborations that involve multiple departments leveraging digital tools.

7. **Adoption of Digital Communication Channels**
   - **KPI** Percentage of university communications conducted through digital channels.
   - **Measurement** Evaluate the shift from traditional communication methods to digital platforms.

8. **Digital Leadership Development**
   - **KPI** Number of leadership development programs with a focus on digital leadership.
   - **Measurement** Offer programs that equip leaders with the skills to guide DX.

9. **Community Engagement through Digital Platforms**
   - **KPI** Participation rates in digital forums, online discussions, and virtual events.
   - **Measurement** Track engagement metrics on digital community platforms.

10. **Digital Inclusion and Diversity**
    - **KPI** Efforts to promote digital inclusion and diversity within digital initiatives.
    - **Measurement** Implement and assess programs that ensure equal access and participation in digital activities.

11. **Digital Ethics and Responsible Use**
    - **KPI** Number of initiatives promoting digital ethics and responsible use of technology.
    - **Measurement** Develop programs and policies that address ethical considerations in the use of digital tools.

12. **Employee and Student Feedback on Digital Culture**
    - **KPI** Feedback scores related to the digital culture within the university.
    - **Measurement** Collect regular feedback through surveys to gauge perceptions of digital culture.

13. **Digital Mentoring Programs**
    - **KPI** Number of faculty and staff participating in digital mentoring programs.
    - **Measurement** Implement mentorship initiatives to facilitate knowledge transfer and skill development.

14. **Digital Recognition and Awards**

- **KPI** Number of awards or recognition programs for digital achievements.
- **Measurement** Acknowledge and celebrate individuals or teams contributing to the digital culture.

5.3 KPIs Related to University Teaching and Learning Activities

In the context of a university's DX strategy, the teaching and learning activities are central to the overall success of the initiative. Key performance indicators related to teaching and learning provide insights into the effectiveness of digital tools, pedagogical approaches, and the overall impact on student outcomes. The following are some KPIs specifically related to teaching and learning activities in a university DX strategy:

1. **E-Learning Adoption**
   - **KPI** Percentage of courses offered through online platforms.
   - **Measurement** Track the adoption of e-learning platforms and the number of courses available online.

2. **Student Engagement in Digital Platforms**
   - **KPI** Usage metrics for digital learning platforms and online resources.
   - **Measurement** Monitor student logins, participation in online discussions, and engagement with digital content.

3. **Digital Literacy Integration**
   - **KPI** Integration of digital literacy components into course curricula.
   - **Measurement** Assess the inclusion of digital literacy skills and digital activities in course objectives, learning outcomes and activities.

4. **Online Assessment Effectiveness**
   - **KPI** Percentage of assessments conducted online and their impact on student performance.
   - **Measurement** Evaluate the effectiveness of online assessments in measuring student understanding.

5. **Learning Management System (LMS) Utilization**
   - **KPI** LMS usage metrics, including login frequency and resource downloads.
   - **Measurement** Monitor the extent to which faculty and students utilize the LMS for course materials and interactions.

6. **Quality of Online Learning Materials**
   - **KPI** Assessment of the quality of digital learning materials.

- **Measurement** Use rubrics or peer evaluations to assess the design, relevance, and interactivity of online learning resources.

7. **Virtual Classroom Attendance**

    - **KPI** Percentage of students attending virtual classes or live sessions.
    - **Measurement** Monitor attendance rates for synchronous online learning activities.

8. **Feedback and Assessment Timeliness**

    - **KPI** Timeliness of providing feedback on assessments and assignments.
    - **Measurement** Measure the average time taken to provide feedback to students.

9. **Active Learning Incorporation**

    - **KPI** Integration of active learning strategies in digital environments.
    - **Measurement** Assess the incorporation of collaborative projects, discussions, and interactive elements in online courses.

10. **Multimodal Learning Experiences**

    - **KPI** Implementation of multimedia elements in teaching materials.
    - **Measurement** Evaluate the use of videos, simulations, podcasts, and other multimedia tools.

11. **Accessibility of Digital Learning Resources**

    - **KPI** Compliance with digital accessibility standards for learning materials.
    - **Measurement** Ensure that digital learning resources are accessible to all students, including those with disabilities.

12. **Student Progress and Achievement**

    - **KPI** Monitoring student progress and achievement in digital courses.
    - **Measurement** Analyze student success rates, grades, and completion rates in online courses.

13. **Use of Learning Analytics**

    - **KPI** Adoption of learning analytics tools to monitor student performance.
    - **Measurement** Utilize data-driven insights to identify at-risk students and inform instructional improvements.

14. **Innovation in Teaching Approaches**

    - **KPI** Number of faculty incorporating innovative teaching methods.
    - **Measurement** Encourage and measure the implementation of new pedagogical approaches enabled by digital tools.

15. **Integration of Gamification**

    - **KPI** Adoption of gamification elements in course design.

- **Measurement** Evaluate the use of game-like elements to enhance engagement and motivation.

16. **Effective Use of Virtual Labs**
    - **KPI** Integration and utilization of virtual labs for practical learning.
    - **Measurement** Assess the implementation and impact of virtual laboratories in science and engineering courses.

17. **Faculty-Student Interaction in Digital Spaces**
    - **KPI** Frequency and quality of interactions between faculty and students in digital environments.
    - **Measurement** Monitor communication and collaboration in online discussions, forums, and virtual office hours.

These KPIs provide a comprehensive framework for evaluating the success and impact of DX in teaching and learning at the university level. Regularly assessing these metrics allows institutions to make data-driven decisions, identify areas for improvement, and enhance the overall quality of the educational experience in the digital.

5.4 KPIs Related to University Research, Knowledge Development, and Innovation

In the context of a university's DX strategy, KPIs related to research, knowledge development, and innovation are essential for assessing the impact of digital initiatives on the academic and research landscape. The following are some KPIs specifically related to research, knowledge development, and innovation within a university:

1. **Digital Research Outputs**
    - **KPI** Percentage increase in digital research publications and outputs.
    - **Measurement** Compare the number of digital research papers, articles, and publications over time.

2. **Research Collaboration Platforms Adoption**
    - **KPI** Percentage of faculty and researchers actively using digital collaboration tools.
    - **Measurement** Track the adoption of platforms facilitating interdisciplinary and collaborative research.

3. **Digital Research Impact Metrics**
    - **KPI** Citations and references to digital research outputs.

- **Measurement** Assess the impact of digital research by tracking citations, downloads, and references.

4. **Research Funding Acquisition**
   - **KPI** Increase in research funding secured through digital grant applications.
   - **Measurement** Monitor the success rate of digital grant applications and the total amount of funding acquired.

5. **Digital Research Infrastructure**
   - **KPI** Upgrades and enhancements to digital research infrastructure.
   - **Measurement** Evaluate improvements in computational resources, high-performance computing, and data storage and assess the utilization and impact of innovative technologies in research projects.

6. **Digital Tools for Research Productivity**
   - **KPI** Adoption and effectiveness of digital tools that enhance research productivity.
   - **Measurement** Evaluate the use of tools for data analysis, collaboration, and project management.

7. **Virtual Research Conferences and Symposia**
   - **KPI** Number of virtual conferences and symposia organized and attended.
   - **Measurement** Assess the engagement and participation levels in virtual research events.

8. **Researcher Digital Skills Development**
   - **KPI** Percentage of researchers participating in digital skills development programs.
   - **Measurement** Track the adoption of training programs to enhance researchers' digital skills.

9. **Digital Research Ethics Compliance**
   - **KPI** Adherence to digital research ethics guidelines.
   - **Measurement** Ensure that research projects involving digital data comply with ethical standards.

10. **Open Access Publications**
    - **KPI** Percentage of research publications available through open-access platforms.
    - **Measurement** Monitor the accessibility of research findings to the broader community.

11. **Digital Research Dashboards**
    - **KPI** Implementation of dashboards for monitoring and reporting on research metrics.

- **Measurement** Assess the effectiveness of digital dashboards in providing real-time research insights.

12. **Digital Innovation Hubs**
    - **KPI** Establishment and utilization of digital innovation hubs.
    - **Measurement** Assess the impact of innovation hubs in fostering digital entrepreneurship and creativity.

13. **Technology Licensing and Commercialization**
    - **KPI** Number of technologies licensed or commercialized.
    - **Measurement** Monitor the success of technology transfer initiatives resulting in licensing agreements or commercial ventures.

14. **Digital Research Impact on Society**
    - **KPI** Assessment of the societal impact of digital research.
    - **Measurement** Measure how digital research contributes to solving societal challenges or advancing public knowledge.

These KPIs provide a comprehensive framework for evaluating the success and impact of DX initiatives in the areas of research, knowledge development, and innovation at the university level. Regularly assessing these metrics allows institutions to make data-driven decisions, identify areas for improvement, and enhance the overall research and innovation ecosystem.

5.5 KPIs Related to the Digital Infrastructure of the University

In the context of a university's DX strategy, KPIs related to digital infrastructure are crucial for assessing the effectiveness and efficiency of the technological foundation that supports various activities across the institution. The following are some KPIs specifically related to the university's digital infrastructure:

1. **Network-Server Uptime**
   - **KPI** Percentage of time the university's network is operational.
   - **Measurement** Monitor network or server downtime and disruptions to ensure consistent availability.

2. **Bandwidth Utilization**
   - **KPI** Percentage of available bandwidth used.
   - **Measurement** Track the utilization of internet bandwidth to ensure optimal performance.

3. **Data Storage Capacity and Usage**

- **KPI** Percentage of available data storage capacity used.
- **Measurement** Assess the usage and capacity of data storage systems to avoid bottlenecks.

4. **Cloud Service Adoption**

   - **KPI** Percentage of university services hosted on cloud platforms.
   - **Measurement** Track the migration of services to cloud infrastructure to enhance scalability and flexibility.

5. **Cybersecurity Preparedness**

   - **KPI** Number of cybersecurity incidents and response times.
   - **Measurement** Monitor security breaches, assess response times, and enhance cybersecurity measures.

6. **Hardware and Software Updates**

   - **KPI** Percentage of hardware and software systems updated regularly.
   - **Measurement** Ensure that systems are updated to the latest versions to address security vulnerabilities and improve performance.

7. **Network Latency**

   - **KPI** Measurement of network latency and response times.
   - **Measurement** Assess the speed and responsiveness of the network to support real-time applications.

8. **Integration of Internet of Things (IoT) Devices**

   - **KPI** Number of IoT devices integrated into the university's digital infrastructure.
   - **Measurement** Track the adoption of IoT devices for various purposes, such as campus management or research.

9. **IT Service Desk Performance**

   - **KPI** Average response time and resolution time for IT service requests.
   - **Measurement** Evaluate the efficiency of IT support services in addressing user issues.

10. **Digital Accessibility Compliance**

    - **KPI** Adherence to digital accessibility standards.
    - **Measurement:** Ensure that digital infrastructure, including websites and applications, is accessible to all users.

11. **Disaster Recovery Readiness**

    - **KPI** Effectiveness of disaster recovery plans and systems.
    - **Measurement** Assess the readiness and reliability of systems in the event of data loss or system failure.

12. **Energy Efficiency of Data Centers**
    - **KPI** Energy efficiency rating of data center operations.
    - **Measurement** Implement measures to enhance the energy efficiency of data center operations.

13. **User Authentication and Authorization**
    - **KPI** Effectiveness of user authentication and authorization systems.
    - **Measurement** Ensure secure access to digital resources and protect sensitive data.

14. **IT Governance Compliance**
    - **KPI** Adherence to IT governance policies and frameworks.
    - **Measurement** Monitor compliance with established IT governance practices and standards.

15. **Digital Infrastructure Scalability**
    - **KPI** Ability of the digital infrastructure to scale based on demand.
    - **Measurement** Assess the capacity of systems to manage increased workloads and user demands.

16. **Green IT Initiatives**
    - **KPI** Adoption of environmentally friendly practices in digital infrastructure.
    - **Measurement** Implement measures to reduce the environmental impact of IT operations.

These KPIs provide a comprehensive framework for evaluating the success and impact of DX initiatives in the university's digital infrastructure. Regularly assessing these metrics allows institutions to make informed decisions, optimize their digital infrastructure, and enhance the overall efficiency and reliability of technology services.

5.6 *KPIs Related to the Digital Impact of the University*

In the context of a university's DX strategy, measuring the digital impact involves assessing the broader influence of digital initiatives on various aspects of the institution. The following are KPIs related to the university's digital impact:

1. **Digital Footprint Expansion**
    - **KPI** Increase in the university's digital presence across online platforms.
    - **Measurement** Monitor growth in website traffic, social media engagement, and online visibility.

2. **Online Brand Recognition**

- **KPI** Improvement in brand recognition through online channels.
- **Measurement** Conduct surveys and analyze metrics to assess the awareness and perception of the university brand.

3. **Digital Accessibility Metrics**

   - **KPI** Measurement of digital accessibility compliance.
   - **Measurement** Ensure that digital resources, including websites and online materials, adhere to accessibility standards.

4. **Digital Innovation Impact**

   - **KPI** Number of successful digital innovation projects.
   - **Measurement** Evaluate the impact of digital innovation initiatives on teaching, research, and administrative processes.

5. **User Engagement on Digital Platforms**

   - **KPI** Engagement metrics on university digital platforms.
   - **Measurement** Monitor interactions, discussions, and participation levels on digital platforms.

6. **Digital Outreach and Community Engagement**

   - **KPI** Increase in community engagement through digital channels.
   - **Measurement** Assess the reach and impact of digital initiatives on the local and global community.

7. **Digital Storytelling Effectiveness**

   - **KPI** Success of digital storytelling efforts.
   - **Measurement** Evaluate the storytelling impact in conveying the university's mission, values, and achievements.

8. **Alumni Digital Engagement**

   - **KPI** Alumni participation in digital events and initiatives.
   - **Measurement** Measure the engagement of alumni through digital platforms, events, and networks.

9. **Virtual Campus Tours Impact**

   - **KPI** Number of virtual tours conducted and their impact on prospective students.
   - **Measurement** Assess the effectiveness of virtual tours in attracting and informing potential students.

10. **Digital Marketing Effectiveness**

    - **KPI** Conversion rates for digital marketing campaigns.
    - **Measurement** Evaluate the success of digital marketing efforts in recruitment, fundraising, and brand promotion.

11. **Public Perception through Social Media**
    - **KPI** Sentiment analysis on social media platforms.
    - **Measurement** Assess the public perception and sentiment toward the university on social media.

12. **Digital Event Participation**
    - **KPI** Attendance and engagement metrics for virtual events.
    - **Measurement** Evaluate the success of virtual conferences, webinars, and campus events.

13. **Digital Outreach to Prospective Students**
    - **KPI** Reach and engage with prospective students through digital channels.
    - **Measurement** Evaluate the effectiveness of digital strategies in attracting and informing potential students.

14. **Eco-Friendly Digital Practices**
    - **KPI** Measurement of the environmental impact reduction through digital practices.
    - **Measurement** Assess the university's contribution to sustainability goals through digital initiatives.

15. **Alignment with Digital Transformation Goals**
    - **KPI** Progress towards achieving DX goals.
    - **Measurement** Regularly assess and align digital initiatives with the overarching goals of the university's transformation strategy.

These KPIs provide a comprehensive framework for evaluating the digital impact of the university's transformation initiatives. Regularly assessing these metrics enables the institution to refine its digital strategy, enhance engagement, and demonstrate the value of its digital efforts to various stakeholders.

5.7 KPIs Related to the University's Digital Impact on the Stakeholders

In the context of a university's DX strategy, measuring the impact on stakeholders is crucial to assess the effectiveness of digital initiatives and their alignment with the needs and expectations of various groups involved. The following are KPIs related to the university's digital impact on stakeholders:

1. **Student Satisfaction with Digital Services**
    - **KPI** Satisfaction scores related to digital services and platforms.

- **Measurement** Conduct regular surveys to gather feedback from students on the usability and effectiveness of digital tools.

2. **Faculty and Staff Digital Competency**
   - **KPI** Improvement in the digital competency of faculty and staff.
   - **Measurement** Assess the proficiency and comfort levels of faculty and staff in using digital tools through surveys or training evaluations.

3. **Parental Engagement through Digital Platforms**
   - **KPI** Participation and engagement levels of parents through digital communication channels.
   - **Measurement** Monitor interactions, participation in virtual events, and feedback from parents.

4. **Employer Perception of Digital Skills**
   - **KPI** Employer satisfaction with graduates' digital skills.
   - **Measurement** Gather feedback from employers on the preparedness of graduates in digital competencies.

5. **Alumni Engagement in Digital Initiatives**
   - **KPI** Participation and interaction of alumni in digital events and programs.
   - **Measurement** Track alumni engagement through digital platforms, virtual events, and mentoring programs.

6. **Community Partnerships through Digital Collaboration**
   - **KPI** Number and impact of digital collaborations with community partners.
   - **Measurement** Assess the success of collaborative projects facilitated by digital tools with external organizations.

7. **Government and Regulatory Compliance**
   - **KPI** Adherence to digital compliance standards and regulations.
   - **Measurement** Ensure that digital initiatives comply with government regulations and industry standards.

8. **Board and Governance Engagement**
   - **KPI** Engagement levels of board members and governance bodies in DX discussions.
   - **Measurement** Monitor participation in digital strategy meetings and initiatives.

9. **Community Outreach and Engagement**
   - **KPI** Growth in community engagement through digital outreach.
   - **Measurement** Track the success of digital initiatives in reaching and involving the broader community.

10. **Digital Impact on Student Recruitment**
    - **KPI** Increase in student recruitment through digital channels.
    - **Measurement** Assess the success of digital marketing and outreach in attracting prospective students.

11. **Student Retention through Digital Support**
    - **KPI** Impact of digital support services on student retention.
    - **Measurement** Analyze whether digital resources and support systems contribute to improved student retention rates.

12. **Stakeholder Feedback and Surveys**
    - **KPI** Participation rates and feedback scores in stakeholder surveys.
    - **Measurement** Conduct regular surveys to gather feedback from various stakeholders on the university's digital initiatives.

13. **Advisory Board Participation in Digital Strategy**
    - **KPI** Involvement and feedback from advisory boards in shaping digital strategies.
    - **Measurement** Monitor the engagement of advisory boards in providing insights into DX strategies.

14. **Accessibility for Diverse Stakeholders**
    - **KPI** Digital accessibility metrics for diverse stakeholders.
    - **Measurement** Ensure that digital resources are accessible to individuals with diverse abilities, backgrounds, and needs.

15. **Faculty and Staff Work-Life Balance Impact**
    - **KPI** Assessment of the impact of digital tools on work-life balance.
    - **Measurement** Gather feedback on whether digital initiatives contribute to a healthier work-life balance for faculty and staff.

16. **User Adoption Rates of New Digital Systems**
    - **KPI** Adoption rates of new digital systems and tools.
    - **Measurement** Track how quickly and widely new digital systems are adopted by stakeholders.

17. **Inclusive Digital Policies and Practices**
    - **KPI** Implementation of inclusive digital policies and practices.
    - **Measurement** Ensure that digital initiatives consider and address the diverse needs and perspectives of stakeholders.

These KPIs provide a comprehensive framework for evaluating the impact of the university's DX strategy on its various stakeholders. Regularly assessing these metrics allows the institution to make data-driven decisions, refine digital initiatives, and ensure that the transformation aligns with the expectations and needs of key stakeholders.

5.8 Australian University's Ambition Spectrum for Digital Transformation

An ambition spectrum within the context of a university's DX strategy refers to the range of aspirations and goals that the institution aims to achieve. It reflects the varying levels of ambition or maturity in different areas of DX. The following are key components that an ambition spectrum for university DX might include:

1. **Strategic Vision**

   - **Transformational Goals** Clear articulation of ambitious and transformative goals for DX.
   - **Long-Term Vision** A visionary outlook that extends beyond immediate needs to anticipate future challenges and opportunities.

2. **Innovation and Research Excellence**

   - **Cutting-Edge Research Infrastructure** Ambitions to provide state-of-the-art digital tools and infrastructure to support groundbreaking research.
   - **Innovation Ecosystem** Establishing an environment that fosters innovation and collaboration in research and development.

3. **Teaching and Learning Innovation**

   - **Pioneering Pedagogical Models** Aspirations to lead in the adoption of innovative teaching methods supported by digital technologies.
   - **Global Learning Experiences** Ambitions to offer students globally connected and immersive learning experiences.

4. **Student-Centric Services**

   - **Personalized Learning Journeys** Ambitions to tailor educational experiences to individual student needs and preferences.
   - **Comprehensive Student Support** Aspirations to provide holistic support services through digital channels.

5. **Data-Driven Decision-Making**

   - **Advanced Analytics Capabilities** Ambitions to leverage advanced analytics for informed decision-making.
   - **Predictive Analytics** Aspirations to use data for predictive modeling and initiative-taking decision-making.

6. **Technology Infrastructure Excellence**

- **Digital Infrastructure Resilience** Ambitions to build a highly resilient and scalable digital infrastructure.
- **Adoption of Emerging Technologies** Aspirations to stay at the forefront of adopting emerging and transformative technologies.

7. **Global Collaboration and Partnerships**

   - **International Alliances** Ambitions to establish strong collaborations and partnerships with institutions globally.
   - **Industry and Community Engagement** Aspirations to actively engage with industry and the community in digital initiatives.

8. **Digital Inclusion and Diversity**

   - **Equitable Access** Ambitions to ensure equitable access to digital resources and opportunities for all students and staff.
   - **Diversity and Inclusion in Tech** Aspirations to promote diversity and inclusion in digital fields and technology-related disciplines.

9. **Agility and Adaptability**

   - **Agile Development Practices** Ambitions to adopt agile methodologies for rapid and flexible digital project development.
   - **Adaptation to Emerging Trends** Aspirations to proactively adapt to emerging trends in technology and education.

10. **Continuous Improvement Culture**

    - **Feedback Loops and Iteration** Ambitions to establish feedback loops for continuous improvement of digital initiatives.
    - **Learning from Failures** Aspirations to foster a culture that learns from failures and iterates on digital strategies.

11. **Ethical and Responsible Tech Use**

    - **Ethical Guidelines** Ambitions to establish and adhere to ethical guidelines for the use of technology in education.
    - **Responsible Data Practices** Aspirations to prioritize responsible handling of data and privacy considerations.

The ambition spectrum provides a roadmap for the university to set high-level goals and aspirations in each of these components. It serves as a guide for decision-makers to prioritize resources and efforts based on the level of ambition and the desired impact on the institution's DX journey. Moreover, the adoption of DX within a university is a nuanced and intricate process. It represents a transformative journey positioned along a spectrum. The initial step involves the university identifying its digital ambition on a scale of 0 to 4, as delineated in "The Australian University's Digital Transformation Ambition Spectrum," illustrated in Fig. 18. Once the ambition level is determined, the university can delineate the necessary DX changes. Each level in the spectrum constitutes a progressive step toward the next. The spectrum

Digital Transformation in Universities: Strategic Framework ...

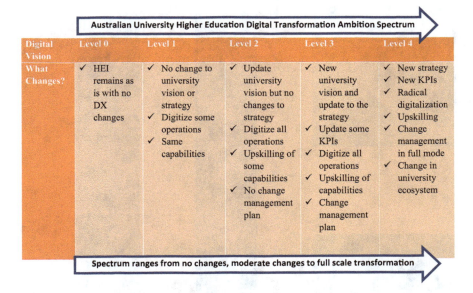

Fig. 18 Spectrum of DX ambition for the Australian University of Kuwait

of change spans from maintaining the status quo, making moderate adjustments, to undertaking a comprehensive and radical transformation. Importantly, there is no universally prescribed level; rather, it is contingent upon the unique digital journey of the university.

5.9 Maturity Model for Digital Transformation of the Australian University

The "Australian University Digital Transformation Maturity Model" serves as a crucial tool for universities navigating their DX journey. This model relies on a self-assessment conducted by the university, providing a vital reference point for gauging progress. It enables universities to assess their DX journey through five distinct levels (Fig. 19): initial, fragmented, developing, mature and optimized.

0. **Initial** At this stage, the university is in the early phases of undertaking DX reforms or progressing towards formulating a DX roadmap. No implementation initiatives are in progress at this point.
1. **Fragmented** The university participates in isolated DX initiatives targeting specific operations or improvements.
2. **Developing** In this phase, effective leadership is actively developing and implementing a coordinated DX approach across multiple areas within the university.

		Initiated	Fragmented	Developed	Mature	Optimized
Digital Alignment	Digital Strategy	☐	☐	☐	☐	☐
	Digital Identity	☐	☐	☐	☐	☐
	Digital Mindset & Culture	☐	☐	☐	☐	☐
	Digital Goals	☐	☐	☐	☐	☐
	Risk Appetite	☐	☐	☐	☐	☐
	Budget	☐	☐	☐	☐	☐
University Readiness	Digital Leadership	☐	☐	☐	☐	☐
	Organization Structure	☐	☐	☐	☐	☐
	Digital Processes	☐	☐	☐	☐	☐
	Talent Management	☐	☐	☐	☐	☐
Technology	Digital Infrastructure	☐	☐	☐	☐	☐
	Digital Technologies	☐	☐	☐	☐	☐
	Technology Integration	☐	☐	☐	☐	☐
	Security & Safety	☐	☐	☐	☐	☐

Fig. 19 Digital transformation maturity model for the Australian University of Kuwait

3. **Mature** The university has reached an advanced stage where university-wide DX strategic initiatives are not only being implemented but also integrated into the university's governance, strategy, personnel, and technology areas. This signifies a comprehensive and institution-wide embrace of DX.
4. **Optimized: Data-Driven Decision-Making** At this stage, the university leverages data analytics for informed decision-making. Processes are optimized for efficiency, and there is a continuous improvement mindset.

Key elements in the Maturity Model may include:

1. **Leadership and Vision**
   - Clearly defined leadership roles responsible for DX.
   - A vision that aligns digital initiatives with the overall mission and goals of the university.

2. **Governance and Structure**
   - Establishment of a governance framework for overseeing digital initiatives.
   - Integration of digital functions into existing organizational structures.

3. **Strategic Planning**
   - Development of a comprehensive DX strategy.

- Alignment of digital initiatives with long-term organizational goals.

4. **Technology Infrastructure**
   - Evaluation and enhancement of the university's technology infrastructure.
   - Investment in modern, scalable, and secure technologies.

5. **Data Management**
   - Implementation of robust data governance policies.
   - Utilization of data analytics for decision-making and insights.

6. **Change Management**
   - Implementation of change management practices to facilitate a smooth transition.
   - Training programs for staff to adapt to innovative technologies and processes.

7. **Collaboration and Communication**
   - Encouragement of cross-functional collaboration.
   - Effective communication channels for disseminating information about digital initiatives.

8. **Performance Measurement**
   - Establishment of KPIs for measuring the success of digital initiatives.
   - Regular assessment and reporting on the progress of the DX journey.

9. **Continuous Improvement**
   - Implementation of a culture of continuous improvement.
   - Regular reviews and updates to the DX strategy based on evolving needs and technological advancements.

10. **Security and Compliance**
    - Implementation of robust cybersecurity measures.
    - Adherence to data privacy and compliance standards.

11. **User Experience**
    - Focus on enhancing the digital experience for students, faculty, and staff.
    - Regular feedback mechanisms to understand and address user needs.

12. **Innovation and Research**
    - Encouragement of a culture of innovation within the academic and research community.
    - Integration of emerging technologies and trends into academic programs and research endeavors.

Remember, a maturity model is iterative, and universities may move back and forth between stages based on evolving needs and challenges. Regular assessments and adjustments to the model will ensure its ongoing relevance and effectiveness in guiding the DX journey. Samples of those elements are incorporated in Fig. 19

6 Digital Transformation and Leadership: Centralized vs. Decentralized

6.1 Digital Transformation and the Necessity for New Competencies

The landscape of HE is undergoing a profound shift with the integration of digital technologies, marking the era of university DX. This transformation represents a comprehensive reimagining of traditional academic, administrative, and research processes through the infusion of digital tools, methodologies, and strategies. Universities are leveraging technology to enhance the overall educational experience, improve administrative efficiency, and foster innovation in teaching, learning, and research [25].

The DX of universities brings about a compelling need for the development and acquisition of new competencies among stakeholders. The following are key reasons highlighting the necessity for these new competencies:

1. **Technological Advancements**

Rapid advancements in technology, including artificial intelligence, data analytics, and cloud computing, necessitate a continuous upgrading of skills to harness the full potential of these tools in academic and administrative processes.

2. **Changing Learning Paradigms**

Traditional learning paradigms are being reshaped by DX. Educators need to embrace digital pedagogies, online learning platforms, and interactive technologies to engage students effectively in the digital age.

3. **Enhanced Research Capabilities**

Digital tools offer unprecedented opportunities for research and innovation. Competencies related to data analysis, digital collaboration, and the use of advanced research technologies become imperative for researchers to stay at the forefront of their fields.

4. **Administrative Efficiency**

Administrative processes are streamlined and optimized through digital systems. Competencies in areas such as data management, information security, and project management are essential for administrative staff to navigate and contribute to the efficiency of these systems.

5. **Global Collaboration**

Digital platforms facilitate global collaboration among students, faculty, and researchers. Competencies in cross-cultural communication, virtual collaboration, and the use of collaborative tools become critical for effective engagement in a globalized academic community.

6. **Data-Driven Decision Making**

Universities are increasingly relying on data analytics to inform decision-making processes. Competencies related to data literacy, interpretation, and utilization are essential for administrators, educators, and researchers to make informed choices.

7. **Adaptation to Online Learning**

The rise of online and hybrid learning environments requires educators to be proficient in delivering content through digital platforms. Competencies in instructional design, online assessment, and virtual classroom management are essential for a seamless transition to online education.

8. **Digital Citizenship and Ethics**

With increased digital interactions, competencies related to digital citizenship, ethical use of technology, and data privacy become crucial for maintaining a responsible and inclusive digital university culture.

9. **Agility in Technological Changes**

The digital landscape evolves rapidly, necessitating an agile mindset among university stakeholders. Competencies related to adaptability, continuous learning, and staying abreast of technological trends are essential for navigating the dynamic digital environment.

10. **Student Engagement and Experience**

Competencies in leveraging digital tools for student engagement, personalized learning experiences, and support services contribute to creating a positive and enriching educational journey for students.

In summary, the necessity for new competencies in the context of university DX is driven by the dynamic nature of technology, the evolving needs of HE, and the transformative potential of digital tools [26]. Universities that prioritize the development and integration of these competencies are better positioned to thrive in the digital era, offering enhanced educational experiences and contributing to advancements in research and innovation.

6.2 Leadership and Management

In the context of a DX strategy, leadership and management play distinct but interconnected roles [27]. Both are essential components for the successful execution of a DX initiative. Understanding the roles and distinctions between leadership and management is crucial for fostering an environment that encourages innovation, adapts to change, and achieves strategic objectives [28].

6.2.1 Leadership in Digital Transformation

1. **Vision Setting**

Leaders articulate a compelling vision for DX, outlining the strategic direction and benefits of embracing digital technologies. They inspire and mobilize teams toward a shared digital future [29].

2. **Innovation Advocacy**

Leaders promote a culture of innovation and experimentation. They encourage employees to explore innovative ideas, technologies, and approaches to problem-solving, fostering a dynamic and forward-thinking mindset.

3. **Change Champion**

Leaders function as change champions, guiding the organization through the challenges of transformation. They inspire confidence, address concerns, and help people navigate the uncertainties associated with adopting modern technologies.

4. **Strategic Thinking**

Leaders engage in strategic thinking, aligning digital initiatives with the overall organizational strategy. They prioritize investments, identify opportunities, and ensure that digital efforts contribute to the achievement of long-term goals.

5. **Cultural Transformation**

Leaders drive cultural transformation by fostering a digital mindset. They emphasize collaboration, openness to change, and continuous learning, creating an environment conducive to digital innovation.

6. **External Engagement**

Leaders engage with external stakeholders, keeping abreast of industry trends, technological advancements, and best practices. They form strategic partnerships and networks to enhance the organization's digital capabilities.

7. **Talent Development**

Leaders focus on talent development, ensuring that the organization has the right skills for DX [30]. They invest in training, mentorship, and talent acquisition to build a capable and adaptable workforce.

6.2.2 Management in Digital Transformation

1. **Execution and Implementation**

Managers are responsible for the execution and implementation of digital initiatives. They develop detailed plans, allocate resources, and oversee day-to-day operations to ensure that digital projects are delivered on time and within budget [31].

2. **Operational Efficiency**

Managers focus on optimizing operational efficiency. They streamline processes, monitor performance metrics, and identify areas for improvement to ensure that DX aligns with organizational objectives.

3. **Resource Allocation**

Managers allocate resources, including budgets, personnel, and technology infrastructure, to support digital initiatives. They prioritize competing demands and ensure that resources are deployed effectively.

4. **Risk Management**

Managers are responsible for identifying and mitigating risks associated with digital projects. They assess potential challenges, develop contingency plans, and monitor the project's progress to address issues promptly.

5. **Project Coordination**

Managers coordinate the various aspects of digital projects. They work with cross-functional teams, set timelines, and ensure that tasks are completed according to the project plan.

6. **Data Management and Security**

Managers oversee data management and security. They implement protocols to safeguard digital assets, ensure compliance with data privacy regulations, and address cybersecurity concerns.

7. **Performance Monitoring**

Managers monitor the performance of digital systems and projects. They use key KPIs to evaluate the success of digital initiatives and make data-driven decisions.

6.2.3 Interconnected Roles

While leadership and management have distinct roles, successful DX requires a collaborative approach. Leaders set the vision and inspire change, while managers implement strategies and ensure operational effectiveness. The two roles are interconnected, and effective communication and collaboration between leadership and management are critical for navigating the complexities of DX. The synergy between visionary leadership and efficient management is key to achieving the organization's digital objectives.

6.3 The Concept and the Importance of Digital Leadership

Digital leaders within the context of university DX are individuals who demonstrate a profound understanding of both the technological landscape and the unique challenges and opportunities within HE. These leaders exhibit a visionary outlook, recognizing that digital technologies have the potential to revolutionize traditional academic, research, and administrative processes. They possess a strategic mindset, aligning digital initiatives with the overall mission and goals of the university ([26], Fig. 20).

Importantly, digital leaders cultivate a culture of innovation and continuous improvement [32]. They encourage collaboration and experimentation, fostering an environment where faculty, staff, and students feel empowered to explore and implement new technologies. These leaders understand that DX is not solely about the adoption of tools but involves a fundamental shift in mindset and practices.

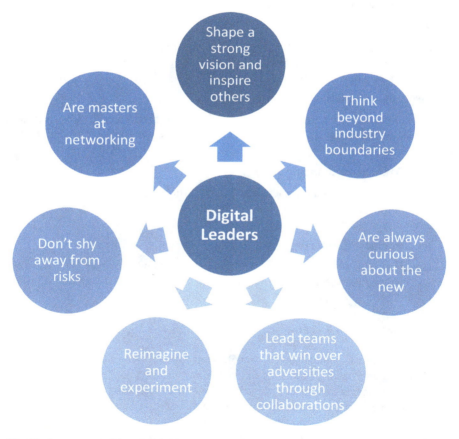

Fig. 20 Important qualities of digital leaders, necessary for the digital transformation of universities

The importance of digital leaders in a university's DX journey cannot be overstated. These leaders serve as change agents, guiding the institution through the complexities of technological change. They are adept at navigating challenges and uncertainties, providing the necessary leadership to overcome resistance to change and promoting a shared vision of a digitally enabled future.

Digital leaders are effective communicators, capable of articulating the benefits of DX to various stakeholders. They engage with faculty, staff, students, and external partners, building consensus and support for innovative initiatives. Additionally, they keep abreast of emerging technologies and industry trends, ensuring that the university remains at the forefront of digital advancements.

In terms of practical implementation, digital leaders oversee the development and execution of a comprehensive digital strategy. This involves identifying key areas for digital enhancement, allocating resources effectively, and monitoring the progress of digital initiatives. They recognize the importance of data-driven decision-making and leverage analytics to measure the impact of digital interventions on student success, research outcomes, and operational efficiency.

In summary, digital leaders in a university setting are visionary, strategic, and adaptive individuals who guide the institution through the complexities of DX. Their leadership is instrumental in creating a culture of innovation, ensuring the effective integration of digital technologies, and positioning the university for sustained success in the digital age.

6.4 The Dichotomy Between Centralized and Decentralized Leadership

In the development and implementation of a university DX strategy, the question of centralized versus decentralized leadership presents a crucial dichotomy that institutions must carefully navigate. Each approach has its merits and challenges, and the choice between the two often depends on the specific context, goals, and organizational culture of the university.

6.4.1 Centralized Leadership

In a centralized leadership model, key decision-making authority and strategic planning are concentrated within a central entity, often the university's top administration or a dedicated DX office. This structure allows for a unified vision, streamlined decision-making, and efficient resource allocation. Centralized leadership can foster consistency in the implementation of digital initiatives and ensure that the overall strategy aligns with the institution's mission.

However, challenges may arise in terms of responsiveness to the unique needs and dynamics of individual departments or academic units. Centralized leadership may face difficulties in understanding and addressing the diverse requirements of various stakeholders, potentially leading to resistance and reduced engagement.

6.4.2 Decentralized Leadership

In a decentralized leadership model, decision-making authority is distributed across different academic departments, units, or faculties. This approach allows for a more tailored response to the specific needs and priorities of individual units. Decentralized leadership encourages local ownership of digital initiatives, fostering a sense of autonomy and engagement among faculty and staff.

However, challenges may arise in terms of coordination, consistency, and the efficient use of resources. Without a centralized guiding vision, there may be a risk of fragmentation, redundancy, and the inability to leverage synergies across the institution. Additionally, a lack of coordination might lead to a less cohesive digital strategy that fails to address overarching university-wide goals.

6.4.3 Balancing Centralization and Decentralization

The optimal approach often involves finding a balance between centralized and decentralized leadership. This hybrid model acknowledges the need for a unified vision and overarching strategy while allowing for flexibility and responsiveness at the departmental or unit level. In this model, central leadership provides a strategic framework, allocates resources, and ensures alignment with institutional goals, while decentralized leaders contribute to the strategy's adaptation to the unique needs of their areas.

Effective communication and collaboration between central and decentralized leaders become critical in this hybrid model. Regular feedback mechanisms, transparent communication channels, and a shared understanding of the overarching DX goals contribute to a more cohesive and adaptable strategy.

In conclusion, the dichotomy between centralized and decentralized leadership in the context of university DX is not an either/or proposition. Rather, it is about finding a nuanced and adaptive approach that leverages the strengths of both models. Successful strategies often involve a balance that combines the advantages of centralized guidance with the responsiveness and engagement that come from decentralized leadership. This nuanced approach maximizes the potential for successful DX while addressing the diverse needs of a complex university ecosystem. Centralized leadership in university digital transformation may lead to:

1. **Unified Vision and Strategy**

Strength. Centralized leadership ensures a unified vision and strategy for DX, aligning all efforts with the overarching goals of the institution.

2. **Efficient Resource Allocation**

Strength. Centralization allows for efficient resource allocation, ensuring that investments in technology are strategically directed to areas that contribute most to the overall mission.

3. **Consistency and Standardization**

Strength. Centralized leadership promotes consistency and standardization in the adoption of digital tools and practices, reducing the risk of fragmentation and ensuring a cohesive digital environment.

4. **Strategic Partnerships**

Strength. Centralized leaders can more effectively negotiate and manage strategic partnerships with external entities, fostering collaborations that benefit the entire institution.

5. **Risk Management**

Challenge. The potential challenge of centralized leadership is that decisions may be perceived as distant or detached from the unique needs of individual departments, potentially leading to resistance or lack of buy-in.

6. **Adaptability to Change**

Challenge. Centralized models may face challenges in quickly adapting to rapidly changing technological landscapes, potentially causing delays in implementation.

However, decentralized leadership in university digital transformation will impact the following:

1. **Local Autonomy and Engagement**

Strength. Decentralized leadership allows for local autonomy and engagement, empowering individual departments or units to tailor digital strategies to their specific needs and priorities.

2. **Tailored Solutions**

Strength. Decentralized leaders can more effectively identify and implement tailored solutions that address the unique challenges and opportunities within their respective areas.

3. **Faster Implementation**

Strength. Decentralized models can be more agile and responsive, leading to faster implementation of digital initiatives at the departmental or unit level.

4. **Flexibility and Innovation**

Challenge. The challenge of decentralized leadership is that it may lead to a lack of standardization and coordination, potentially resulting in redundancy and missed opportunities for collaborative innovation.

5. **Communication and Coordination**

Challenge. Decentralized models require effective communication and coordination mechanisms to ensure that the overall digital strategy remains cohesive and aligned with the institution's goals.

6. **Resource Duplication**

Challenge. Decentralization may result in resource duplication, as different departments may independently invest in similar technologies without leveraging economies of scale.

Therefore, the importance of a balancing centralization and decentralization is a necessity to facilitate the following:

1. **Hybrid Leadership Model**

Strategy. A hybrid model combines the strengths of both centralized and decentralized leadership, providing a cohesive vision from central leadership while allowing flexibility and autonomy at the local level.

2. **Communication Channels**

Strategy. Establishing robust communication channels between central and decentralized leaders is crucial for maintaining alignment, sharing best practices, and ensuring a collaborative approach to DX.

3. **Adaptive Governance Structures**

Strategy. Institutions need adaptive governance structures that allow for iterative adjustments to the balance between centralization and decentralization based on evolving needs and experiences.

4. **Shared Metrics and Goals**

Strategy. Developing shared metrics and goals ensures that both central and decentralized leaders are working toward common objectives, fostering a sense of shared responsibility for the success of digital initiatives.

5. **Continuous Feedback Loops**

Strategy. Implementing continuous feedback loops enables departments and units to provide input on the effectiveness of digital strategies, allowing for real-time adjustments and improvements.

In navigating the complexities of the university DX landscape, finding the right balance between centralized and decentralized leadership is essential. The most effective strategies recognize the strengths and challenges of each approach and leverage a hybrid model that maximizes the benefits of both centralization and decentralization.

7 Recommendations and Conclusions

The inevitability of DX in education, particularly in HE, is evident. Higher education institutes increasingly recognize the need for DX, as evidenced by the growing body of research on the subject. As HEIs strive to digitalize in response to the dynamic transformations in their environment, it becomes imperative for them to articulate a sharp vision, formulate policies, devise strategies, and develop comprehensive plans. This chapter elucidates how DX represents a distinctive approach to strategic thinking, deployment tools, and leadership development within universities.

In a university, DX involves leveraging technology to enhance and modernize various aspects of academic and administrative processes. The following are some general recommendations for a comprehensive DX strategy for a university:

- Identify specific goals and objectives for the DX, such as improving student experience, optimizing administrative processes, enhancing research capabilities, and fostering innovation.
- Appoint a resolute team or individual responsible for overseeing and driving the DX.
- Establish clear governance structures to ensure accountability and decision-making.
- Invest in robust IT infrastructure to support digital initiatives.
- Embrace cloud computing for scalability, flexibility, and cost-effectiveness.
- Implement advanced analytics and data management systems for informed decision-making.
- Integrate technology into the curriculum to enhance the learning experience.
- Explore online learning platforms, virtual classrooms, and interactive educational tools.
- Encourage faculty development programs for digital literacy.
- Implement a student information system for streamlined registration, grades, and communication.
- Develop a mobile-friendly campus app for access to information, schedules, and campus services.
- Explore virtual campus tours and online orientation programs.
- Foster a culture of innovation and research through collaborative platforms.
- Invest in research data management systems and tools.
- Support interdisciplinary collaboration and partnerships.
- Automate routine administrative tasks to improve efficiency.
- Implement an integrated enterprise resource planning (ERP) system for finance, HR, and other administrative functions.
- Explore blockchain technology for secure and transparent record-keeping.
- Prioritize cybersecurity measures to protect sensitive data and infrastructure.
- Provide regular cybersecurity training for staff and students.
- Conduct regular security audits and assessments.
- Foster collaboration through digital communication tools and platforms.
- Implement collaborative project management tools for faculty and staff.

- Explore virtual meeting and conferencing solutions.
- Ensure that digital tools and platforms are accessible to all students, including those with disabilities.
- Promote inclusivity in online learning materials and assessments.
- Establish KPIs to measure the success of digital initiatives.
- Regularly evaluate and reassess the effectiveness of implemented technologies.
- Solicit feedback from students, faculty, and staff for continuous improvement.
- Stay informed about emerging technologies and trends in education.
- Build a flexible and scalable digital architecture to accommodate future advancements.
- Encourage a culture of adaptability and a willingness to embrace change.

Implementing a successful DX requires careful planning, collaboration, and a commitment to ongoing improvement. Regularly reassessing the strategy and adjusting it based on feedback and evolving needs will contribute to long-term success.

Drawing upon the findings presented in this chapter, it is strongly recommended that universities embrace the proposed models and frameworks to facilitate a seamless transition through the process of DX. Three key conclusions emerge from this exploration. Firstly, the significance of tailoring a strategy that aligns with the culture and challenges of the HEI's operating environment is underscored. This study delves into various countries to understand how HEIs and diverse organizations cope with the adoption of DX, drawing parallels with international frameworks, especially those supporting the Kuwait National Development Plan, 2035 vision.

The second conclusion posits that the suggested criteria for implementation tools can significantly aid the change process. This chapter introduces two models adaptable to a university's digital journey: the Australian University's Higher Education Digital Transformation Ambition Spectrum and the Australian University Digital Transformation Maturity Model.

The third conclusion emphasizes the pivotal role of suitable leadership styles within HEIs when incorporating DX. Recognizing the strong influence of innovation on DX, the chapter underscores the distinction between leadership and management, advocating for a leadership approach capable of navigating the challenges posed by growing demands in HEIs. To effectively accommodate DX within a university, the presence of digital leaders and academic digital leaders is deemed essential, suggesting a central–decentral blend of leadership as the most suitable approach based on the literature review.

Moreover, this chapter is poised to provide substantial theoretical contributions to researchers focusing on strategy, implementation tools, and leadership in the context of DX in HE. The conclusions drawn within the HEI setting offer a foundation for recommending further research, particularly in the form of case studies on universities implementing DX across all their services.

Additional recommendations include exploring the modification of curricula to align with the introduction of DX in universities and understanding the integration of AI within a university's culture, given that DX serves as a precursor to Artificial

Intelligence. Lastly, it is suggested to explore the specifics of how DX is implemented and incorporated within specific industries, an area that remains underexplored in existing research.

References

1. OECD (2019) How's life in the digital age? Opportunities and risks of the digital transformation for people's well-being. OECD Publishing, Paris. https://doi.org/10.1787/9789264311800-en
2. Kane G, Palmer D, Phillips AN et al (2015) Strategy, not technology, drives digital transformation. MIT Sloan Management Review. https://sloanreview.mit.edu/projects/strategy-drives-digital-transformation/
3. Korachi Z, Bounabat B (2020) General approach for formulating a digital transformation strategy. J Comput Sci 16(4):493–507. https://doi.org/10.3844/jcssp.2020.493.507
4. Iosad A (2020) Digital at the core: a 2030 strategy framework for university leaders. JISC. https://www.jisc.ac.uk/guides/digital-at-the-core-a-2030-strategy-framework-for-university-leaders
5. Tsou HT, Chen JS (2021) How does digital technology usage benefit firm performance? Digital transformation strategy and organizational innovation as mediators. Technol Analysis Strategic Manage 35(9):1114–1127. https://doi.org/10.1080/09537325.2021.1991575
6. Hess T, Matt C, Benlian A, Wiesboeck F (2016) Options for formulating a digital transformation strategy. MIS Quart Executive 15(2):123–139. https://www.researchgate.net/publication/291349362
7. Gobble MAM (2018) Digital strategy and digital transformation. Res Technol Manage 61(5):66–71. https://doi.org/10.1080/08956308.2018.1495969
8. Rodrigues LS (2017) Challenges of digital transformation in higher education institutions: a brief discussion. In: Proceedings of the 30th international business information management association conference (IBIMA). https://ibima.org/accepted-paper/challenges-of-digital-transformation-in-higher-education-institutions-a-brief-discussion/
9. Wade M (2015) Digital business transformation: a conceptual framework. Global Center for Digital Business Transformation. https://www.imd.org/uupload/IMD.WebSite/DBT/Digital%20Business%20Transformation%20Framework.pdf
10. Bygstad B, Øvrelid E, Ludvigsen S, Dæhlen M (2022) From dual digitalization to digital learning space: exploring the digital transformation of higher education. Comput Educ 182:104463. https://doi.org/10.1016/j.compedu.2022.104463
11. McCarthy AM, Maor D, McConney A, Cavanaugh C (2023) Digital transformation in education: critical components for leaders of system change. Social Sci Humanities Open 8(1). https://doi.org/10.1016/j.ssaho.2023.100479
12. OECD (2023) Develop a supportive institutional framework for the digital uptake of firms. In: Digital skills for private sector competitiveness in Uzbekistan. OECD Publishing, Paris. https://www.oecd-ilibrary.org/sites/34990246-en/index.html?itemId=/content/component/34990246-en#chapter-d1e2458-75d48d65d3
13. Digital Regulation Platform (2023) National digital transformation strategy—mapping the digital journey. https://digitalregulation.org/national-digital-transformation-strategy-mapping-the-digital-journey/
14. Ernst & Young (n.d.) How digital transformation is changing the fabric of nation. https://www.ey.com/en_kw/digital/how-digital-transformation-is-changing_the-fabric-of-a-nation
15. Patalong F (2016) Vision 2030 and the transformation of education in Saudi Arabia. Al Tamimi & Co. https://www.tamimi.com/law-update-articles/vision-2030-and-the-transformation-of-education-in-saudi-arabia/
16. Ministry of Digital Economy and Entrepreneurship. www.modee.gov.jo. Accessed June 2023

17. State Secretariat for Education, Research and Innovation (n.d.) Digitalization in the ERI Sector action plan 2019–2020 SERI. Swiss Federal Council. https://www.sbfi.admin.ch/sbfi/en/home/eri-policy/eri-21-24/cross-cutting-themes/digitalisation-eri/Action%20plan%20for%20digitalisation%20in%20the%20ERI%20sector.html
18. Smart Nation Singapore (n.d.) Transforming Singapore through technology. https://www.smartnation.gov.sg/about-smart-nation/transforming-singapore/
19. Guillén VIN, Deckert C (2021) Cultural influence on innovativeness—links between "The Culture Map" and the "Global Innovation Index". Internat J Corporate Social Responsib (1). https://doi.org/10.1186/s40991-021-00061-x
20. Naranjo-Valencia JC, Jimenez-Jimenez D, Sanz-Valle R (2016) Studying the links between organizational culture, innovation, and performance in Spanish companies. Revista Latinoamericana Psicología 48(1):30–41. https://doi.org/10.1016/J.RLP.2015.09.009
21. Buvat J, Crummenerl C, Kar K et al (2017) The digital culture challenge: closing the employee-leadership gap. Capgemini Digital Transform Inst. https://www.capgemini.com/wp-content/uploads/2017/06/dti-digitalculture_report_v2.pdf
22. Georgia Tech (n.d.) Virtual teaching assistant: Jill Watson. https://gvu.gatech.edu/research/projects/virtual-teaching-assistant-jill-watson
23. Hauser C, Amann W (2023) The future of responsible management education: university leadership and the digital transformation challenge. Humanism in Business Series, Palgrave Macmillan Cham. https://doi.org/10.1007/978-3-031-15632-8
24. Hess T (2022) Challenge of digital transformation. In: Managing the digital transformation. Springer Gabler, Wiesbaden. https://doi.org/10.1007/978-3-658-38424-1_1
25. Katuna B (2019) Effective academic leadership. In: Degendering leadership in higher education (Great Debates in Higher Education). Emerald Publishing Limited, Bingley. https://doi.org/10.1108/978-1-83867-130-320191003
26. Hashim A, Tlemsani I, Matthews RB (2022) Higher education strategy in digital transformation. Educ Inform Technol 27:3171–3319. https://doi.org/10.1007/s10639-021-10739-1
27. Timotheou S, Miliou O, Dimitriadis Y et al (2022) Impacts of digital technologies on education and factors influencing schools' digital capacity and transformation: a literature review. Educ Inform Technol 28:6695–6726. https://doi.org/10.1007/s10639-022-11431-8
28. Gui L, Lei H, Le Ba P (2022) Fostering product and process innovation through transformational leadership and knowledge management capability: the moderating role of innovation culture. Europe J Innovat Manage 27(1):214–232. https://doi.org/10.1108/EJIM-02-2022-0063
29. Klien M (2020) Leadership characteristics in the era of digital transformation. Business Manage Studies Int J 8(1):883–902. https://doi.org/10.15295/bmij.v8i1.1441
30. Gerhardt T, Karsan S (2022) Talent management in private universities: the case of a private university in the United Kingdom. Int J Educ Manage 36(4):552–575. https://doi.org/10.1108/IJEM-05-2020-0222
31. Munna AS (2021) Instructional leadership and role of module leaders. Int J Educ Reform 32(1):38–54. https://doi.org/10.1177/10567879211042321
32. Scaliza JA, Jugend D, Chiappetta Jabbour CJ et al (2021) Relationships among organizational culture, open innovation, innovative ecosystems, and performance of firms: evidence from an emerging economy context. J Business Res 140(3):264–279. https://doi.org/10.1016/j.jbusres.2021.10.065

Digital Transformation in Higher Education: Challenges and Opportunities for Developing Countries

Wael Mualla and Karim J. Mualla

Abstract Technology has become an unavoidable pillar for sustaining the progression of students and delivering a high-quality teaching and learning experience across universities worldwide, regardless of ranking, size, or domain. Various patterns of digital transformation have been studied in higher education since the digital era began to expand rapidly following the fourth industrial revolution. These patterns represent the use of technology for current practices to support strategic responses and implement structural changes to improve teaching, learning, and administrative processes. Developing countries have struggled to investigate how emerging digital services can change university-wide processes and managerial practices to sustain future success and compete with rival institutions. Adopting digital transformation in higher education in developing countries has faced several challenges regarding infrastructure, cost, digital literacy, content, language, legal issues, and equity and access. This chapter provides a review of digital transformation for higher education in developing countries with particular emphasis on the Syrian system of higher education. The chapter also presents a capability model to support universities to identify optimal services that could be implemented to achieve the desired teaching, learning and managerial objectives through a seamless and effective digital transformation process. This is particularly addressed for processes that directly interact with students, academics, and administrative teams.

Keywords Digital transformation · Higher education · Developing countries · Syria

W. Mualla (✉)
Damascus University, Damascus, Syria
e-mail: wmualla@gmail.com

K.J. Mualla
School of Computing and Mathematical Sciences, University of Leicester, Leicester, UK

1 Introduction

Technology has become an unavoidable pillar for sustaining a student's progression and delivering a high-quality teaching and learning experience across universities worldwide, regardless of ranking, size, or domain. Various patterns of digital transformation have been studied in higher education since the digital era began to expand rapidly following the fourth industrial revolution. These patterns represent the use of technology for current practices to support strategic responses and implement structural changes to improve teaching, learning, and administrative processes. Developing countries have struggled to investigate how emerging digital services can change university-wide processes and managerial practices to sustain future success and compete with rival institutions.

Developing countries can face several challenges in adopting digital transformation in higher education. The challenges are mainly regarding infrastructure, cost, digital literacy, content and language, regulatory and legal issues, and equity and access. Developing countries may lack the necessary infrastructure, such as reliable and affordable internet connectivity, electricity, and access to computers and mobile devices, to support digital transformation. This can limit the ability of institutions to deliver online education and for students to participate in digital learning. Moreover, digital transformation can be expensive, and many institutions in developing countries may not have the financial resources to invest in the necessary technology and infrastructure. The cost of digital devices, software, and training can also be a barrier to adoption. Furthermore, many students and faculty in developing countries may not have the digital skills necessary to fully participate in digital learning. This can limit the effectiveness of digital transformation efforts and create inequities in access to education.

Content and language may also pose a significant challenge, as do cultural barriers, which can affect the adoption of digital transformation. Regulatory and legal issues can have significant impact on the adoption of digital transformation in developing countries, for some countries may have regulatory and legal frameworks that are not conducive to digital transformation, including restrictions on internet access or limitations on academic freedom. These issues can create barriers to the adoption and implementation of digital technologies in higher education.

Finally, digital transformation can create or exacerbate inequalities in access to education. Students from disadvantaged backgrounds may not have access to the necessary technology or internet connectivity to participate in digital learning, while those with greater resources may benefit disproportionately from digital transformation efforts. This can create inequities in access to education and exacerbate existing inequalities in society.

This chapter provides a digital-transformation review for higher education in developing countries with particular emphasis on the Syrian system. The chapter presents a capability model to support universities to identify optimal services that could be implemented to achieve the desired teaching, learning and managerial objectives through a seamless and effective digital transformation process. This is particularly addressed for processes that directly interact with students, academics, and administrative teams.

2 Digital Transformation in Higher Education in Developing Countries

The relentless march of technological advancement has transformed every facet of human life, and the realm of higher education is no exception. In developing countries, the adoption of digital technologies has emerged as a critical driver of progress, offering the potential to democratize access to education, enhance the quality of teaching and learning, and foster collaboration among institutions and individuals. However, the path to digital transformation in higher education in developing countries is fraught with challenges, demanding a nuanced understanding of the obstacles and the opportunities that lie ahead.

3 Progress in Digital Transformation in Developing Countries

Developing countries have made significant strides in embracing digital transformation in recent years. This progress can be attributed to several factors, including:

- **Increased Access to Affordable Mobile Devices and Internet Connectivity** The widespread availability of smartphones and affordable data plans has enabled millions of people in developing countries to access the digital world for the first time. According to the International Telecommunication Union (ITU), the number of mobile phone subscriptions in developing countries grew by over 700% between 2000 and 2020, and internet penetration reached 46% in 2022 [1].
- **Growth of Digital Platforms and Services** A plethora of digital platforms and services has emerged, catering to a wide range of needs, from e-commerce and mobile banking to education and healthcare. These platforms have provided new opportunities for businesses to reach consumers, for individuals to access essential services, and for governments to deliver services more effectively [2].
- **Government Initiatives and Policies** Many developing countries have implemented policies and initiatives to promote digital transformation, such as investing in infrastructure, fostering digital literacy, and encouraging the growth of the digital economy. These initiatives have helped to create an enabling environment for digital transformation to flourish [3–5].

4 Impact of Digital Transformation in Developing Countries

Digital transformation has had a positive impact on developing countries in several ways:

- **Economic Growth** Digital technologies have created new industries, jobs, and opportunities for entrepreneurship, boosting economic growth and reducing poverty. The World Bank estimates that the digital economy could contribute up to 15% of GDP growth in developing countries by 2030 [6, 7].
- **Social Development** Access to digital tools and services has empowered individuals, improved access to education and healthcare, and promoted financial inclusion. For example, mobile banking has provided access to financial services to millions of people who were previously unbanked, and online education platforms have expanded access to quality education, particularly in remote areas [2].
- **Improved Quality of Life** Digital technologies have made everyday tasks more efficient and convenient, enhancing the overall quality of life for people in developing countries. For example, mobile applications have made it easier to access transportation, pay bills, and order goods and services, freeing up time for other activities [8, 9].

5 Challenges in Formulating and Implementing a Digital Transformation Strategy in Developing Countries

Despite the transformative potential of digital technologies, developing countries face a unique set of challenges in formulating and implementing effective digital transformation strategies in higher education. These challenges stem from a complex interplay of factors, including:

- **Infrastructure Gaps** The lack of reliable and affordable internet connectivity, particularly in rural and remote areas, poses a significant barrier to the adoption of digital technologies in higher education. Without adequate infrastructure, institutions struggle to provide access to online resources, conduct virtual classes, and harness the full potential of digital learning tools [10].
- **Digital Literacy and Faculty Development** The digital literacy skills of both educators and students in developing countries often lag behind global standards. This skill gap hinders the effective integration of digital technologies into the teaching and learning process, limiting the ability of institutions to fully leverage the benefits of digital transformation [11].
- **Funding and Resource Allocation** Financial constraints often hamper the ability of higher education institutions in developing countries to invest in the necessary infrastructure, software, and training required for digital transformation.

Limited funding restricts the acquisition of digital resources, the development of digital learning platforms, and the implementation of effective faculty training programs [12].
- **Cultural and Social Factors** Cultural norms and social perceptions can influence the acceptance and adoption of digital technologies in higher education. Resistance to change, concerns about privacy and security, and traditional pedagogical approaches may hinder the integration of digital tools into the learning environment [13].

6 The Higher-Education Sector in Syria

The higher-education sector in Syria consists of public universities, public higher institutes, private universities, and technical and vocational training institutes (Fig. 1). The Higher Education Council (HEC) is the highest policy-making body for higher education in Syria. It is headed by the minister of higher education and includes representatives from public universities (presidents and vice-presidents), private universities, student unions, the instructors syndicate, and other ministries.

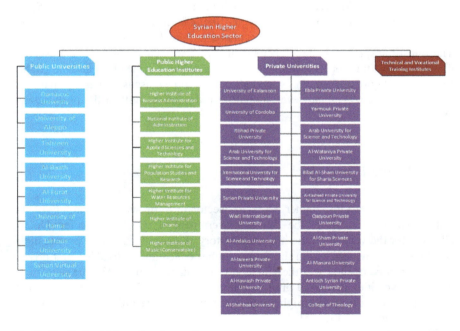

Fig. 1 The Syrian higher education sector

6.1 Public Universities

In Syria, eight public universities exist (Fig. 1). They are all regulated by the University Regulation Law of 2006, and its executive text, except the Syrian Virtual University (SVU) [14, 15]. The SVU was established in 2002 by special law and offers distance-learning courses entirely delivered online [16]. The SVU initially provided two-year and four-year undergraduate programmes, but now, it additionally offers a number of postgraduate programmes. All other public universities offer undergraduate and postgraduate programmes [15, 16].

6.2 Higher Institutes

Several types of higher institute exist in the Syrian higher education sector. Most higher institutes belong to the Ministry of Higher Education [17], such as the Higher Institute of Business Administration (HIBA); however, some higher institutes belong to other ministries, such as the Higher Institute of Music (Conservatoire) which, in turn, belongs to the Ministry of Culture. These institutes had their own special laws when established, and are not regulated by the University Regulation Law of 2006 which regulates public universities in Syria. A third type of higher institute exists and includes institutes that are established within public universities and are regulated by the University Regulation Law. These institutes, such as the Higher Institute of Earthquake Studies and Research, the Higher Institute for Research into Lasers and their Applications and the Higher Institute of Regional Planning, which all belong to Damascus University, have the same status as colleges; however, they offer programmes only at the postgraduate level [18].

6.3 Private Universities

In the pre-2001 era, the higher education sector in Syria was a monopoly of the state. However, in 2001, the Syrian government (Legislative Decree No.36) allowed, for the very first time in Syrian history, the establishment of private higher-education providers within the Syrian higher education sector. The first private university to be opened was the University of Kalamoon in 2003. The number of private universities increased gradually until it reached 22 in 2021 (Fig. 1) [17]. At the present time, private higher-education providers are only permitted to offer undergraduate programs [15].

It is worth mentioning here that two additional higher education institutions exist in the higher education sector in Syria, namely the Arab Academy for Science, Technology and Maritime Transport [19] and the Arab Academy for

E-Business [20]. Both institutions were established by special laws and are affiliated with the Arab League.

6.4 Technical and Vocational Training Institutes

Two types of technical and vocational training institute exist; technical institutes that belong to the Ministry of Higher Education (57 institutes) and technical institutes that belong to other ministries (141 institutes) [17]. They are regulated by the Supreme Council for Technical Education. The technical and vocational training institutes offer assistant bachelor degrees in applied and vocational subjects, and aim to prepare students for employment.

7 Impact of the War on Higher Education Institutions

The war in Syria has had a devastating impact on all national sectors, including higher education institutions. The damage can be described as huge and can be summarized as: losses of infrastructure, especially in areas that went out of government control; loss of intellectual capital (academics and researchers); and limited funding available for these institutions, as funds were diverted to support other urgent priorities [14, 21].

Although there is no official assessment to date on the material and non-material damages inflicted on higher education institutions in Syria as a result of the ongoing crisis, it is worth mentioning here a project conducted recently by UK NARIC and the UNESCO Beirut Office describing the impact of the conflict on Syrian higher education provision and the key challenges the country needs to address on the road to recovery [15].

8 The Status of the Information Technology (IT) Sector in the Pre-war Era and the Impact of the War

It is deemed appropriate to review the status of the IT Sector in Syria in the pre-war era, and the impact of the war on this sector as it constitutes an important factor in the formulation and implementation of a successful digital transformation strategy.

8.1 Pre-war Status of the IT Sector

Before the war, Syria was emerging as a regional leader in the IT sector, attracting international investments and partnerships. However, the ongoing conflict has severely damaged the country's reputation as a viable IT hub. The international community is hesitant to invest in a war-torn nation with shaky infrastructure and security concerns. This loss of international recognition and partnership opportunities further stifles growth and innovation within the Syrian IT sector.

In the pre-war era, and specifically, during the period 2000–2010, the Syrian IT sector witnessed the implementation of a large part of the ambitious government strategies and policies established for the sector [22]. These strategies and policies revolved around providing high-quality telecommunications services at reasonable prices, developing the information industries and digital content, and simplifying government procedures, transactions and services using information and communications technology (within the framework of the e-government program).

The delivery of communications services and access to information and knowledge to rural and remote areas has also been expanded through a range of initiatives, while working, at the same time, to build capacities in information and communications technology. The digital signature project was launched to build the basic electronic signature system, the electronic payment project, and the smart cards project. All necessary legislative frameworks for the above have also been developed, such as the Communications Law; the Network Services Law; Law 17/2012, regulating communication on the internet and combatting information crime; and others [22].

8.2 Crisis Impact

The crisis has had a devastating impact on the country's entire infrastructure, with the IT sector experiencing a particularly severe blow. In addition to the direct consequences of war, Syria's IT sector also grapples with the challenge of unilateral coercive measures, imposed by some countries, that further restricted its growth and stifled its potential.

The physical destruction wrought by the war has crippled the IT infrastructure. Telecom networks lie in ruins, data centers are destroyed, and power outages are frequent. The sanctions imposed on Syria have restricted the export of certain technologies to Syria, including hardware, software, and telecommunications equipment. This has created a critical bottleneck, limiting the access of Syrian IT professionals to the tools they need for development and innovation. Companies struggled to import essential hardware components, rendering them unable to build or upgrade their infrastructure. Furthermore, the imposed sanctions on financial transactions and trade with Syria has made it difficult for Syrian IT companies to secure international contracts and access potential markets. Foreign clients and investors become hesitant to do business with Syrian entities due to fear of legal repercussions or reputational damage. This has shrunk the available market for Syrian IT services, impacting revenue generation and stunting the sector's growth. The inability to participate in global value chains and access international funding sources has limited the competitiveness of Syrian IT companies and hindered their ability to scale-up and reach their full potential.

Perhaps one of the most negative impacts of the war on the IT sector has been the loss of human capital, or the "Brain Drain", for the long conflict has triggered a mass exodus of skilled professionals, including highly qualified IT specialists, who have migrated to other countries seeking security and better job opportunities [23].

The reduction in revenues resulting from decreased traffic due to interruption in communications services, or non-collection of revenues, especially in tense areas, have further negatively impacted the sector.

The lack of reliable internet connectivity and access to cutting-edge technology has hindered innovation and restricted the sector's potential. Companies struggled to operate efficiently, and technological advancement has come to a near standstill. In short, the once-vibrant tech scene, filled with start-ups and established companies, has been reduced to a shadow of its former self.

9 The National Development Program for Post-war Syria

In 2020, a National Development Program for Post-War Syria, "Syria Strategic Plan 2030" was developed by the Syrian government [22, 24]. The plan is a 10-year nationwide multisectoral document aiming at (i) ensuring sustainable growth for the post-war period; (ii) showing the government's intentions and plans aimed at drawing the Syrian landscape in the next stage. The National Development Program adopted five guiding policies that interact with each other and are consistent with each of its stages: (1) national dialogue and political pluralism; (2) institutional and administrative reform and integrity promotion; (3) growth and development; (4) development and modernization of infrastructure and services; (5) social and human development [25]. Twelve framework programs, which were developed on the basis of their compatibility with the strategic objectives, emerged from the National Development Program for Syria. Each framework program branches out into a group of 90 basic executive programs, from which in turn branch a group of sub-programmes, projects, and executive procedures.

Framework Program (2), which is titled: "Reconstruction and development of infrastructure and services", includes a program for developing and expanding communication and information networks and systems [22].

Framework Program (10), which is titled: "Education, innovation and scientific research system", aims to provide the appropriate environment for education, innovation, and scientific research, and to benefit from the system's outputs in meeting the requirements of economic and social development. One of the main executive programs of "Framework Program (10)" is: "The University Education and Scientific Research Development Program" which aims to develop the infrastructure and technology for university education and scientific research, and provide a suitable environment, in terms of services and technological equipment, that encourages and promotes creativity and innovation [22].

10 National Plan for Digital Transformation in Higher Education in Syria

Within the context of the National Development Program for Post-War Syria, a high-level national committee was formed by the Minister of Higher Education to propose a draft strategy for digital transformation of the higher education system in Syria [26]. The committee's task also involves building a Digital Transformation Plan for the services provided by the Ministry of Higher Education in a manner consistent with the proposed Digital Transformation Strategy for Higher Education and the Digital Transformation Strategy for Government Services approved by the Ministry of Communications and Technology.

The strategy aims to establish a general structure that helps in formulating an integrated vision of the nature of digital transformation projects in higher education and their needs (legislative environment, enabling environment, capacity building, etc.) in order to avoid any useless investment in projects that do not have the ingredients for success.

A draft strategy was prepared by the national committee that involves working in the following domains [27]:

1. **Enabling Environment** This is the basis on which the Digital Transformation Strategy for Higher Education is put into practice. The enabling environment includes not only the legislative and regulatory environment associated with the higher education system, but also the infrastructure and technical tools that must be provided, with the aim of promoting the transition to an integrated digital model of higher education and scientific research.
2. **Digital Education** The primary goal of the Digital Transformation Strategy for Higher Education lies in employing digital technologies in the service of the educational process in order to advance this process, make it closer to learning, and secure all requirements for its development. Students graduating from universities would then be capable of continuous learning, possess high technical skills whatever the nature of their specialty, and would be able to activate a knowledge-economy environment by generating initiatives, and projects, that allow supporting economic and social development. Therefore, it is necessary to begin reviewing the mechanisms for adopting digital technologies in the traditional education system and the scientific research system, as well as studying the prospects for networking between "Open" and "Virtual" education systems in Syria to activate continuous learning and lifelong learning in the Syrian higher education system.

3. **Awareness and Capacity Building** The modern education model, known as the fourth generation of education, is considered to be one of the emerging models based on developing capabilities that allow the acquisition of the skills necessary to localize and consolidate this model. Capacity building usually has two parts: the first relates to the development of human resources for those working in educational institutions (administrative or academic) and qualifying and training them to invest modern technologies in the service of academic work. The second relates to building institutional capabilities, that is, everything related to developing the administrative and academic structure, consolidating the academic independence of institutions, consolidating decentralization, and developing decision-making mechanisms and work plans and mechanisms.

11 Major Points of Weakness

As stated earlier, Syria has been experiencing a severe conflict since 2011, which has affected all economic and social sectors in the country, including the higher education sector. The impact of the war on the higher education and IT sectors was huge. Most of the points of weakness that these sectors suffer from currently relate to the impact of the war; however, many other points relate to existing legislation and institutional structure. The following are the major points of weakness which may impede the implementation of digital transformation strategy in the higher education sector [27].

Infrastructure and Readiness

- The weak infrastructure necessary to operate basic projects such as the Automated University Admission System, the Unified Student Register, the Hospital Information System, and others.

Automation and Information Systems

- The absence of an agreed-upon general strategy and the resistance to establishing any organized and transparent digital system.
- Digital services need a continuous operation and maintenance system that the current public sector' administrative systems cannot provide.

Integrating Technology into Education

- The high price of broadband in Syria in relation to income, which hinders the integration of stakeholders into any digital transformation process in education.

Educational Digital Content

- The weakness and lack of regulation regarding educational digital content in Syria, the spread of the phenomenon of "plagiarism", and the absence of any reference to educational digital content and university digital textbooks in the laws, legislation, and decrees regulating universities operations.

Human Resources

- Extreme weakness or "unwillingness" to appreciate the importance of digital transformation in educational institutions, which causes a lack of will to transform.
- The need for "attractiveness" in the labor market. Professions based on science, technology, and engineering require an appropriate economic environment dominated by innovation and led by entrepreneurial institutions. This is something that is not available in the Syrian work environment.

Legislative Environment

- The "University Regulation Law" which regulates Syrian public universities is outdated and unable to keep pace with the development that may occur in the field of digital transformation.
- Administrative-type laws regulating institutions, particularly "Contract Law No. 51 of 2004" do not suit the needs of implementing digital transformation projects.
- The absence of a partnership between the public and private sectors as a means to overcome the weak ability of public institutions to attract cadres.

12 Suggested Courses of Action

The suggested courses of action for each domain of the proposed strategy are the following [27, 28]:

Enabling Environment

- Action 1: Building information systems (the Unified Student Record and associated Student Information Systems in Higher Education Institutions).
- Action 2: Developing electronic transactions to transform them into integrated digital services (within higher education institutions in the first stage).
- Action 3: Developing the technical environment (The Syrian Higher Education Research Network infrastructure [SHERN], providing secure and efficient hosting services).

- Action 4: Developing the academic legislative environment (amending the "Universities Regulation Law" to include, formulate and legislate the concepts of digital transformation in it).
- Action 5: Developing legislation relating to intellectual property rights, open science, and Creative Commons in all matters relating to university publications.

Digital Education

- Action 1: Developing traditional education into blended education that uses e-learning logic and tools in addition to its tools.
- Action 2: Developing open and virtual education systems and establishing a link and partnership relationship between them.
- Action 3: Automating educational hospitals and utilizing the unified medical record project to build hospital information systems in standard formats.
- Action 4: Establishing peer-reviewed electronic scientific journals, providing environments for virtual conferences, and securing their operating mechanisms.
- Action 5: Developing scientific research databases and plagiarism-detection systems in the Arabic language.

Content Production and Formulation

- Action 1: Establishing regulations and standards for the production and dissemination of educational digital content, and launching initiatives to encourage educational institutions to produce educational digital content.
- Action 2: Scanning, categorizing and digitizing available content in partnership with all stakeholders to identify publishable and usable content within implemented standards and controls.
- Action 3: Ensuring the quality of educational digital content by setting quality standards for content digitization, production, availability and use. In addition, developing a project to measure and evaluate quality in the field of educational digital content and its production, and setting quality standards for digital educational and training programs.

Capacity Building

- Action 1: Developing human resources by creating training centres and developing the necessary training programs for members of the educational and administrative staff, to increase their knowledge and skills in all areas of digital transformation and the areas of academic and administrative work related to it.
- Action 2: Developing organizational structures and institutional processes in higher education institutions, and attracting trained human resources.
- Action 3: Creating technology incubators and business incubators in universities to support emerging projects in areas relating to digital transformation in the educational sector, with the aim of helping small investors, university graduates, entrepreneurs, and innovators to launch their activities, and also providing consultations and assistance in developing the necessary studies for this.

13 The Next Phase

It is envisaged by the draft Digital Transformation Strategy for Higher Education in Syria that the next phase would be to disseminate and discuss the structure of the strategy with all stakeholders with the aim of enriching its content, determining implementation priorities and responsibilities, estimating the financial and technical needs associated with projects and expected time frames, and developing and approving an integrated implementation plan.

14 A Modernised Capability Model for Digital Transformation in Higher Education

The following model illustrates a segmentation of services and processes to support higher education institutions in identifying optimal pillars to implement and achieve the desired teaching, learning and managerial objectives through an effective and logical digital-transformation plan (Fig. 2). The model specifically focuses on interactive processes that correspond with students, academics, and administrative staff.

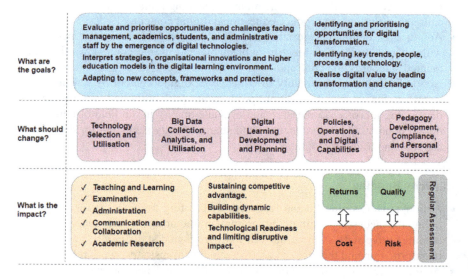

Fig. 2 A modernised capability model for digital transformation in higher education

14.1 Technology Selection and Utilization to Influence Future Education

Digital transformation in higher education is a process of using digital technologies to improve the quality of education and learning experience [29]. The effective use of digital and online technologies to support teaching can enhance the student experience, widen participation, and improve accessibility and inclusion, create opportunities to expand the university beyond the campus, and develop staff skills, knowledge and understanding of digital processes across learning, teaching and assessment. In this capability pillar, technologies are divided into the following:

- Learning management systems (LMS)
- Synchronous technologies
- Multimedia applications
- Collaborative applications
- Cloud-based technologies
- Emerging technologies

The importance of technology selection and utilization for digital transformation in higher education cannot be overemphasized. Digital technology provides a more outward system of research where results are easily accessible and knowledge can be used quickly. Higher education institutions may also use digital technology to collaborate more closely with the labour market and society on education, research, and innovation. Another aspect is utilizing technology to streamline business processes. In the field of education, digital transformation can enrich the learning experience of students and improve the overall experience for alumni, mentors, and faculty. It also assists in the process of institution management [30].

For example, the University of Leicester's senior council has recently approved the University's new Digital Strategy and Masterplan for 2023 to 2028. The strategy and masterplan set out the University's aims and priorities over the next five years, delivering [31]:

- a modern system for finance and human resources,
- a data strategy and a modern data platform,
- a curriculum management and planning system,
- a digital coach and assistant for students and staff,
- a customer relationship management (CRM) solution across the applicant and student journey,
- and trusted research environments.

Technology selection and utilization are essential for digital transformation in higher education. The use of digital technologies can enhance the student experience; widen participation; improve accessibility and inclusion; create opportunities to expand the university beyond the campus; and develop staff skills, knowledge and understanding of the implementation of digital processes across learning, teaching, and assessment. It also assists in the process of institution management.

14.2 Big Data Collection, Analytics, and Utilization

Big data is an important tool for universities and higher education institutions. It can help transform internal core competencies and business models, the academic outcomes of students, and the effectiveness of staff [32]. Insights derived from big data can also help educational institutions improve their technology systems. Big data provides an opportunity for educational institutions to use internal IT resources strategically to improve educational quality and guide students to higher rates of completion, and to improve student persistence and outcomes.

Institutions of higher education can leverage big data and analytics to thoroughly examine newly emerging challenges, explore and identify new ways to address them, and predict future outcomes for growth.

Recent studies covered various research themes under big data in education. This has mainly covered the learner's behaviour and performance, modelling and educational data warehouse, improvement in the educational system, and integration of big data into the curriculum [33].

14.3 Digital Learning Modality, Development, and Planning

This digital learning capability pillar is divided into the following modes of learning processes [34]:

- **On-campus and Technology-Enhanced Learning** On-campus learning refers to the traditional method of learning where students attend classes in person on the university campus. Technology-enhanced learning (TEL) is concerned with using technologies to support learning whether the learning is local (i.e., on campus) or remote (at home or in the workplace). Also, TEL can include elements of assessment, tutoring, and instruction. While TEL is often used as a synonym for e-learning it can also be used to refer to technology-enhanced lectures and learning with technology, rather than just through technology.
- **Hybrid and Blended Learning** Hybrid and blended learning are both educational approaches that mix in-person and online learning. In hybrid learning, some individuals participate in person, and some participate online at the same time, using video conferencing to replace or supplement the in-class experience. In blended learning, the same individuals learn both in person and online, using online resources to complement or enhance the traditional classroom teaching

[35]. Hybrid learning is a specific type of blended learning that involves synchronous lessons that are taught live and remotely. Blended learning is a broader term that encompasses all education that integrates digital technologies, especially web-based learning tools.

- **Asynchronous Online Learning** Asynchronous learning means that the instructor and the students in the course all engage with the course content at different times (and from different locations). The instructor provides students with a sequence of units which the students move through as their schedules permit. There is no live video lecture component for this type of learning. Students may view instructional materials during the week when they choose. There are still due dates, however, but students can finish coursework when it fits best for them [36].
- **Synchronous online learning** Synchronous online learning is a type of online learning that takes place in real-time. It is similar to traditional classroom instruction; however, it is conducted online using video conferencing software. Students and instructors interact with each other in real-time, and students are expected to attend classes at specific times. Synchronous online learning is often used for lectures, discussions, and other types of interactive activity. It allows students to ask questions and receive immediate feedback from their instructors and peers [37]. Synchronous online learning can be an effective way to deliver instruction to students who are unable to attend traditional classes.
- **HyFlex Learning** HyFlex learning is a course design model that presents the components of hybrid learning in a flexible course structure that gives students the option of attending sessions in the classroom, participating online, or doing both. The term "hyflex" stands for "hybrid flexible". Each class session and learning activity is offered in-person, synchronously online, and asynchronously online. Students can decide how to participate. This approach provides students with the flexibility to choose how they want to learn and engage with course content. It also allows instructors to provide a more personalised learning experience for each student.

14.4 Institutional Policies, Operational Efficacy and Digital Capabilities

This capability pillar portrays the importance and correlation between both crisis management, and technology investments in universities. Crisis management and technology investments are essential for universities' digital transformation [38]. Digital transformation is a long-term project that requires time and financial commitments from universities. For instance, frequent training around data breaches and effective approaches to respond to digital threats is essential, as is investing in the core technology and infrastructure needed to secure a university's systems.

The successful transformation of higher education requires faculty development and specific policies to improve crisis management readiness and increase institutional resilience to address unforeseen challenges in the future. As an example, the UK's higher education sector is entering a new age—an age in which the effective implementation and use of digital technologies across universities is essential to attracting talent, promoting growth and, ultimately, surviving. It has been observed that current universities not equipping themselves to adapt to the challenges ahead are most likely to struggle to compete in the near future.

14.5 Pedagogy Development, Compliance, and Personal Support

This capability is weaved into the key higher education components as follows:
- Teaching and learning
- Assessment
- Administration
- Communication and collaboration
- Academic research

In essence, pedagogy development helps universities ensure that the learning experience is effective and engaging for students [39]. Pedagogy development involves the creation of new teaching methods and strategies that are designed to take advantage of digital technologies. This can include the use of online learning platforms, interactive multimedia content, and other digital tools that can help to enhance the learning experience. By focusing on pedagogy development, universities can ensure that students are provided with the best possible education and are equipped with the required arsenal for success in the digital age.

Furthermore, students' personal support is an essential factor for digital transformation in universities, as students become more able to take full advantage of the digital tools and resources that are available to them. This can include providing students with access to training and support services that can assist them to develop the skills needed to succeed in a digital environment. By providing students with the support they need, universities can help to ensure more engagement with the digital transformation process and take advantage of all the benefits it has to offer [40].

In addition, staff compliance is essential for digital transformation in universities as it helps to ensure that everyone is working towards the same goals. This can manifest through providing staff with access to training and support services that can help develop essential skills to succeed in a digital environment. By providing both academic and administrative staff with the support they need, universities can move a step closer to ensure engagement and achievement with the digital transformation strategy.

15 Conclusions

This chapter has argued and articulated an informative review on digital transformation for higher education in developing countries. The text has placed a particular emphasis on the Syrian higher education system and has presented a capability model to support universities to identify optimal services that could be implemented to achieve the desired teaching, learning and managerial objectives through an agile digital transformation process. The model specifically highlighted strategies and future decision-making recommendations for the benefit of students, academics, administrative staff, and standard operating procedures involved in higher education institutions. The analysis illustrates the importance of integrating the organisation's short and long-term digital goals, necessary changes, and the impact of these on pedagogy, research, technology, sustainability, which directly shapes an institution's readiness and robustness to adapt and modify procedures in response to disruptive circumstances.

References

1. ITU (2023) World telecommunication/ICT indicators database 2023 (27th edition/July 2023). https://www.itu.int/en/ITU-D/Statistics/Pages/publications/wtid.aspx
2. Muhleisen M (2018) The long and short of the digital revolution. International Monetary Fund. https://www.imf.org/en/Publications/fandd/issues/2018/06/impact-of-digital-technology-on-economic-growth-muhleisen
3. Hanna N (2017) How can developing countries make the most of the digital revolution? World Bank Blogs. https://blogs.worldbank.org/digital-development/how-can-developing-countries-make-most-digital-revolution
4. ITU Publications (2018) Measuring the information society report. http://handle.itu.int/11.1002/pub/8114a552-en
5. Zakhozhyi V, Ma YJ (2023) Three ways digital transformation accelerates sustainable and inclusive development. UNDP. https://www.undp.org/blog/three-ways-digital-transformation-accelerates-sustainable-and-inclusive-development
6. World Bank Press Release (2023) Accelerating the use of digital technologies is key to creating productive jobs and boosting economic growth in Africa. https://www.worldbank.org/en/news/press-release/2023/03/13/accelerating-the-use-of-digital-technologies-is-key-to-creating-productive-jobs-and-boosting-economic-growth-in-africa
7. World Bank (2023) Digital development overview https://www.worldbank.org/en/topic/digitaldevelopment/overview
8. Siuhi S, Mwakalonge J (2016) Opportunities and challenges of smart mobile applications in transportation. J Traffic Transport Engineer 3(6). https://doi.org/10.1016/j.jtte.2016.11.001
9. Statista (2023) Share of bank account holders processing banking matters via mobile banking (smartphone or tablet) in the United States from 1st half of 2019 to 2nd quarter 2023. https://www.statista.com/statistics/1394885/mobile-banking-penetration-in-us/
10. Sepúlveda A (2018) The digital transformation of education: connecting schools, empowering learners. UNESCO. https://unesdoc.unesco.org/ark:/48223/pf0000374309
11. World Bank (2016) World development report 2016: digital dividends. https://www.worldbank.org/en/publication/wdr2016

12. World Bank (2019) World development report 2019: the changing nature of work. https://www.worldbank.org/en/publication/wdr2019
13. Meleisea E (2019) The UNESCO ICT in education programme. UNESCO. https://unesdoc.unesco.org/ark:/48223/pf0000156769
14. Mualla W (2020) The Governance of higher education in post-war Syria. In: Badran A, Baydoun E, Hillman J (eds) Higher education in the Arab world: government and governance. Springer Cham. https://doi.org/10.1007/978-3-030-58153-4
15. The State of Play in Syrian Higher Education Post 2011: a Joint Research of UNESCO Beirut and UK NARIC. https://www.unesco.org/en/articles/state-play-syrian-higher-education-post-2011-joint-research-unesco-beirut-uk-naric
16. The Syrian Virtual University. https://www.svuonline.org/
17. Ministry of Higher Education and Scientific Research. http://www.mohe.gov.sy/mohe/
18. Damascus University. Higher Institute of Regional Planning. http://damascusuniversity.edu.sy/hiorp/
19. Arab Academy for Science. Technology and maritime transport. https://aast.edu/en/
20. Arab Academy for E-Business. http://araeb.org.sy/
21. Mualla W (2022) Academic research in support of post-conflict recovery in Syria. In: Badran A, Baydoun E, Hillman JR (eds) Higher education in the Arab world: research and development. Springer, Cham. https://doi.org/10.1007/978-3-030-80122-9_17
22. Higher Commission for Scientific Research (2020) National development program for post-war Syria: Syria strategic plan 2030. https://www.hcsr.gov.sy/report/البرنامج-الوطني-التنموي-السورية-في-ما-ب/
23. UNESCO (2016) UNESCO's education response to the Syria crisis: towards bridging the humanitarian-development divide. https://unesdoc.unesco.org/ark:/48223/pf0000246279
24. Arab National Development Planning Portal, ESCWA. https://andp.unescwa.org/plans/1379
25. Food and Agriculture Organization of the United Nation (FAO), FAOLEX database. https://www.fao.org/faolex/results/details/en/c/LEX-FAOC212702/
26. Minister of Higher Education and Scientific Research (2023) Decree No 438, dated 18 July 2023 (private correspondence)
27. Ministerial Committee formed by Resolution No. 438 (2023) Draft strategy for digital transformation in higher education in Syria (private correspondence)
28. Ministerial Committee formed by Resolution No. 438 (2023) Timetable and implementation program of the digital transformation plan in the Syrian higher education sector (private correspondence)
29. Elliott, KA (2006) Delivering on Doha: opportunities and challenges for developing countries. Inst Internat Economics. https://www.piie.com/publications/chapters_preview/3926/01iie3926.pdf
30. Zitter L (2022) Digital transformation of higher education in 2024. Whatfix. https://whatfix.com/blog/digital-transformation-in-higher-education/
31. University of Leicester's Internal Strategy Document (2023) Cascade letter by SLT: Senior Learning and Teaching Council, University of Leicester
32. Weerawardane D (2021) Digital transformation of higher education: what's next? New Vistas 7(2):3–7. https://doi.org/10.36828/newvistas.147
33. Nicolaou N (2023) The role of COVID-19 in driving digital transformation in higher education. FE News. https://www.fenews.co.uk/exclusive/the-role-of-covid-19-in-driving-digital-transformation-in-higher-education/
34. Martin F, Xie K (2022) Digital transformation in higher education: 7 areas for enhancing digital learning. Educause. https://er.educause.edu/articles/2022/9/digital-transformation-in-higher-education-7-areas-for-enhancing-digital-learning
35. Marks A, Al-Ali M, Atassi R et al (2020) Digital transformation in higher education: a framework for maturity assessment. Internat J Adv Comput Sci Applic 11(12). https://orca.cardiff.ac.uk/id/eprint/139830/1/Paper_61-Digital_Transformation_in_Higher_Education.pdf

36. Bygstad B, Øvrelid E, Ludvigsen S, Dæhlen M (2022) From dual digitalization to digital learning space: exploring the digital transformation of higher education. Comput Educ 182.https://doi.org/10.1016/j.compedu.2022.104463
37. Green D, Rowland M (2023) The digital transformation of higher education: CIO perspectives on education's digital future. UCISA. https://www.ucisa.ac.uk/resources/digital
38. Jensen T (2022) Digital transformation of higher education. Internat Assoc Univ. https://www.iau-aiu.net/technology
39. Akour M, Alenezi M (2022) Higher education future in the era of digital transformation. Educ Sci 12(11):784. https://doi.org/10.3390/educsci12110784
40. Díaz-García V, Montero-Navarro A, Rodríguez-Sánchez J-L, Gallego-Losada R (2022). Digitalization and digital transformation in higher education: a bibliometric analysis. https://doi.org/10.3389/fpsyg.2022.1081595

Artificial Intelligence in Arab Universities and Economies

Wail Benjelloun

Abstract Artificial intelligence (AI) involves the augmentation, acceleration and amplification of human intelligence and capacities through the use of novel technologies, enabling more rapid processing and analysis of information. For example, AI enables computers to perform tasks requiring human intelligence and to learn while doing so (machine learning). As AI develops, it will be able to selectively extract information that may be useful to, or manipulated by, specialists. The potential impact of AI on data mining, cognitive assistance/augmentation, health sciences, engineering industries, economic strategies and even social sciences is staggering. Thus, AI promises a significant social transition with great opportunities. In the Arab region, these opportunities have a direct impact on development and may directly lead to sorely needed improvements in health and education. Artificial intelligence can also advance the transformation of industries, decreasing the region's dependence on the export of raw materials. More interestingly, AI and the consequent digital transformation can serve as a pivot between education and health services, and education and industry, facilitating their interaction and leading to results such as better employability. In fact, as AI and the consequent automation eliminate jobs held by humans, new, and different, job opportunities will be created. It is predicted that government, health care, education and hospitality services, for example, will continue to be major employers. Artificial intelligence has yet to penetrate Arab universities on a large scale. Indeed, of all the Arab countries, the Emirates seem to have made the greatest AI advances through a national strategy which has effectively encouraged the launch of AI Schools and programs in public universities. The present paper will assess AI progress in Arab universities and economies, with an overview of future prospects. The situation in the Arab region will be compared, when warranted, with other world regions.

W. Benjelloun (✉)
Mohammed V University, Avenue Des Nations Unies, Rabat, Morocco
e-mail: wbenjelloun@gmail.com

Keywords Artificial intelligence · Digital transformation · Machine learning · Augmented cognition · Arab universities · Economy · Employability

1 Introduction

The Arab States region has a population of 423 million. The region is diverse, including not only six States in the category of LDC (least developed countries), who present the weakest ICT (information and communication technology) profiles, but also some Gulf and North African countries that have made some headway with digital development. These differences may be related to economy, socio-economic development, degree of urbanization, conflicts and environmental variables including desertification and climate change. Internet usage rates across the region thus range from 100 per cent to less than 10 per cent in the region's least developed economies [1].

The OECD has defined artificial intelligence as "a machine-based system that, for explicit or implicit objectives, infers, from the input it receives, how to generate outputs such as predictions, content, recommendations, or decisions that can influence physical or virtual environments. Different AI systems vary in their levels of autonomy and adaptiveness after deployment" [2]. This revised OECD definition of AI systems responds to the complexity and the variability that have come to characterize these systems by adopting a general, non-specific approach.

Furthermore, the use of AI poses ethical questions, which UNESCO has attempted to address through the development of the "Recommendation on the Ethics of Artificial Intelligence", adopted on 23 November 2021. These recommendations address a number of Policy Action Areas, ranging from data governance to health and social well-being [3]. The UNESCO Secretary General, Azoulay [4], has stated that AI represents a new frontier for humanity, which will lead to a new form of human civilization, offering opportunities for sustainable development. Yet we must ensure that fundamental human rights and privacy are not violated in the process.

Global investment in AI has increased in recent years, rising from US$0.8 billion in 2010 to US $78 billion in 2021—an increase of over 9000% [5]. The field of AI has made major progress in almost all its standard sub-areas, with major advances in generative AI, vision and video, translation, health, and interactive robotics [6].

Compared to other geographical areas, the approach of Arab countries to AI has been rather timid. Only a limited number of Arab countries have taken steps to encourage the adoption of AI in government services or in the private sector. As the importance of the field becomes increasingly apparent, many Arab countries are starting to invest in AI education for their youth, in an effort to bolster national socio-economic development and employability opportunities. This paper gives a brief overview of the situation in the region.

The Economist identifies five Arab countries where AI policies and investments are relatively advanced, and where AI-supported economic growth may be expected by 2030: Saudi Arabia, UAE, Qatar, Kuwait and Egypt. Indeed, the potential economic impact of AI on economic growth in these countries may attain US $320 billion by 2030, due to value added by AI, and the savings related to automation, expected to improve competitivity. The highest rates of AI-related economic growth will occur in the UAE and Saudi Arabia. The Economist Intelligence Unit (EIU) estimated US $200 billion for UAE, followed by US $120 billion for Saudi Arabia, the latter largely due to investment in education [7]. Gulf investment in artificial intelligence is exemplified by the Expo 2020 site in the United Arab Emirates (UAE) and the US $7 billion devoted to the creation of a state-of-the art facility with interactive robots and automated services.

2 The Gulf and Eastern Mediterranean

2.1 Saudi Arabia

In Saudi Arabia, US$500 billion is projected for the gigantic project NEOM [8], a futuristic megapolis on the Red Sea coast. For these countries, dependent for decades on fossil fuel revenues, AI may be the answer to the challenges of the future.

The majority of Saudi Vision 2030 goals involve data and AI, and the Kingdom plans to train 20,000 data and AI specialists by the end of the decade, and create 40,000 AI-related jobs [9]. With this perspective in mind, Aramco signed an agreement with King Abdullah University of Science and Technology to fund a new research center dedicated to AI development in the country. The Kingdom had previously established the Saudi Data and Artificial Intelligence Authority (SDAIA) [10], whose platform Estishraf uses AI to provide Saudi decision makers with appropriate data. This platform is credited with the generation of 43 billion Saudi Riyals in 2019. Saudi strategy aims at setting a favorable environment for competitive development, including dependable AI, free circulation of data, intelligent cities, and the security and measurement of digital economies. Special emphasis is placed on empowering students and saving the planet.

2.2 United Arab Emirates

Perhaps the most important UAE investment in AI education is the Mohamed bin Zayed University of Artificial Intelligence (MBZUAI), launched in 2019. The University is located in the smart-innovation cluster, Masdar City, and is already highly ranked among AI research institutions. Its activities are centered on AI, computer vision, machine learning and natural language processing. In nearby Dubai, the objective is to automate 25% of all transportation by 2030 [11].

As the first country to establish a Ministry of Artificial Intelligence in 2017, the UAE recognized early on that facing the challenges of generative AI, such as ChatGPT, would require the introduction of AI in sectors such as education, health, transportation, space exploration, renewable energy, and environment. The country's economy is being prepared to include AI, and estimates of the contribution of AI to the country's GDP range from 14 to 20% by the mid 2030s, with the claim that data will be the petroleum of the future [12].

In response to ethical concerns expressed concerning this rapid adoption of AI, the Emirati government proposed that AI should be fair, transparent, responsible, and understandable. It should be used to serve protect and benefit humanity, respecting human values. It should benefit all, respecting the dignity of all [13].

This concerted national effort in the area of AI in the Emirates has already started yielding interesting results. One important advance is the development of Jais, a powerful AI language model for Arabic, resulting from an international public–private cooperative venture coordinated by Mohammad ben Zayed AI University in Abu Dhabi (MBZUAI). Jais will be available to the 400 million Arabic speakers under open-source licenses, with the possibility for users to contribute to its development. Jais is meant to offer more precise comprehension and generation of Arabic text, taking into account regional cultural contexts. Close monitoring of content is however raising the question of eventual possibilities for censorship. Jais will be widely used in Emirate government administrations and the Emirati government has already integrated ChatGPT to assist citizens in administrative procedures.

The Jais project however faces some major hurdles, resulting from the worldwide AI competition. To prepare for AI, both Saudi Arabia and the United Arab Emirates have recently purchased thousands of highly sophisticated Nvidia chips, necessary for IA programs, but the recent US limitation on export of Advanced Micro Devices and Nvidia chips to some Middle East countries may present supply problems in the future [14].

2.3 Qatar

Qatar has several branch campuses of renowned universities such as the Carnegie Mellon University, where students can pursue AI-related degrees and research. The Qatar Center for Artificial Intelligence is establishing a research and policy center, staffed by internationally recruited AI faculty. Perhaps the most important AI work in Qatar is being done through the Qatar Foundation, with its Qatar Computing Research Institute, the Qatar Environment and Energy Research Institute and the Qatar Biomedical Research Institute. In their quest to improve societal conditions, these centers undertake research in such fields as Arabic language technologies, AI policy and education, digital health, and cyber security [15].

2.4 Bahrain

Bahrain has been developing a strategic plan for using AI for economic growth, driven by the Bahrain Economic Development Board, the Information and eGovernment Authority, the higher education sector, as well as the telecom, and energy industries [16]. This strategy involves developing the national capacity for utilizing AI through the association of existing resources, in combination with the key elements that need to be introduced.

The Artificial Intelligence Society of Bahrain was founded in 2018 to support this plan [17], and to facilitate collaboration among the different stakeholders in attaining the objectives of the Bahrain Economic Plan 2030, meant to ensure the transition from reliance on oil wealth to entrepreneurship and AI [18].

2.5 Kuwait

In Kuwait, the business sector is leading the digitization and AI shift towards online platforms, with strong public support. Increasing internet usage has driven the demand for e-commerce services. E-commerce in turn has necessitated the development of efficient and secure digital payment systems. The government's accelerated digital transformation projects have also simplified access to information, to official documents, and electronic payments. Government policies have included support for start-ups and for innovation. Technologies such as artificial intelligence, augmented reality, and virtual reality are strengthening the e-commerce landscape, enhancing the online commerce experience and providing innovative ways for businesses to engage with customers [19]. An interesting phenomenon has been the appearance of an AI-generated news presenter on Kuwaiti TV [20].

2.6 Jordan

The Jordanian digital transformation plan, launched in 2016, was aimed at supporting six sectors that drive the digital economy, namely health, education, energy, clean technology, transportation, financial/fintech, telecommunications, and security. The AI plan was formulated in 2023 by the Ministry of Digital Economy and Entrepreneurship. Jordan's strategic roadmap outlines primary goals which encompass positioning the country as a forefront competitor in AI within the region. The plan also aims to establish a distinctive and appealing technological and entrepreneurial ecosystem, where AI assumes a pivotal and supportive role, seamlessly integrating into the national economy.

An initial effort to evaluate the effectiveness of Jordan's digital transformation [21] suggests that the challenges faced by the country as it shifts towards a dynamic digitized economy are mainly related to developing technologies to access big data, learning analytics, and AI to maintain education and e-learning. In the health sector, hospital and pharmaceutical industry data also need to be marshalled.

3 North Africa

3.1 Egypt

As the MENA countries turn to AI, they find that they must create systems in line with their specific socio-economic environments. Recognizing that AI is not an optional strategy, Egypt has committed to harnessing AI for economic growth. It invested heavily in vocational training programs in order to train sufficient cadres for the future. In addition, the possibilities offered by AI for international cooperation and for improving economic competitivity set the stage for developing a national AI strategy [22]. The Egyptian AI effort is designed to reach the widest possible segment of society and a clear objective is to have AI benefit all social sectors.

In this strategy, it is clearly stated that AI capacity building should enhance rather than replace human production; efforts should thus improve processes rather than eliminate jobs, thus expanding the labor market and including in the expansion those who cannot be up-skilled or re-skilled. To benefit from the gains made possible through AI, Egypt has committed to educating the general public to create a base of educated users, but also to training the technical professionals and highly skilled specialists that are needed to implement its ambitious AI plans. At the same time, Egypt intends to work towards responsible AI, through a national Charter based on the OECD AI Principles.

In what may be considered a "populist" approach, the Egyptian plan foresees programs and content that are designed for every level of society, even to those with limited or no formal education, with training opportunities for all, meant to help recipients ramp up their capacities. At the secondary school level, AI competencies will be offered initially through pilot programs. Eight AI faculties have also been launched at university level, with AI taught throughout the system as a core subject or as a support course. A large choice of graduate and post-graduate programs has additionally been created either nationally or in collaboration with European or North American universities to support technical (professional) mastery of the subject or non-technical sectorial academic competence in AI.

The economic potential of AI is not neglected in the Egyptian strategy. The interconnection between innovation and entrepreneurship is nurtured through the organization of competitions that encourage the use of AI to solve specific social and economic challenges. Through such competitions, bridges are built between young entrepreneurs and start-ups with donors and government decision makers. These competitions, part of the National AI Strategy, are critical for the attainment of Egypt's sustainable development goals and involve rethinking business models to create new areas of growth.

In its wider objectives, the Egyptian AI strategy aims to embed AI technologies into government processes to increase efficiency and transparency, to foster the use of AI in vital developmental sectors, to prepare Egyptian citizens for the AI era through training and awareness, and to encourage regional and international cooperation [23]. The priority sectors for the strategy are: agriculture/environment and water management; healthcare; natural language processing (NLP); economic planning; and manufacturing and infrastructure management.

3.2 Tunisia

In spite of the advances made by Tunisian researchers and innovations noted in the business sector, Tunisian AI suffers from a lack of coordination at the national level and a perceived lack of government support by stakeholders in the field. Ministerial initiatives aimed at organizing the sector are by and large ineffective, and different ministries seem to have different agendas. A distrust of AI is manifest at the highest levels of government, and currency-exchange regulations discourage new start-up initiatives [24]. Several years into the process, the national AI strategy has yet to be rolled out and there are complaints that its development is being done behind closed doors. Tunisian AI seems by and large to be left to its own devices and the country's AI rankings are falling.

And yet, as mentioned above, the Tunisian young-talent potential is promising, and has shown itself capable of creativity and competitivity. The turnover of AI start-ups grew from about $22 million in 2018 to about $233 million in 2020. The number of start-ups in Tunisia reached 904 in June 2023, compared to only 10 companies in 2018 [25]. These past performances point to probable future successes, if the current legal and investment obstacles can be attenuated, and the start-up exodus reversed.

3.3 Algeria

The Algerian strategy for research and innovation in AI was announced in 2021 [26]. It was designed to improve Algerian skills in AI through education, training and research, thus guaranteeing the conditions for national development. The exercise was also expected to facilitate the current digital transition by identifying potential obstacles. The strategy aims at reinforcing support for research and innovation in bioinformatics, big data, machine learning, autonomous systems, computer vision and intelligent decision-assistance systems.

The strategy also includes support to AI start-ups and the launching of two new institutions for data and AI.

Some have considered the strategy too ambitious given the poor quality of the current computer park, the delay in the introduction of digital technology in society and the total absence of the AI culture, particularly in the university. Algeria ranked 118th out of 172 countries in the 2020 Artificial Intelligence Readiness Index, placing it fourth among its North African neighbors Egypt (56), Tunisia (69) and Morocco (99).

The role of the university in the implementation of this plan is critical since it is expected to contribute not only to AI awareness in students and society at large, but also to act as a bridge between the research community and industry.

3.4 Morocco

In spite of an early interest in AI at university level and the fact that the country has made significant strides in digitization of government services and commerce, the national AI strategy has not as yet been announced. In May 2021, UNESCO published a paper on its web site entitled « Evaluation of AI needs in Africa». This was also the title of a Forum on AI organized by UNESCO and the Mohammed VI Polytechnic University (UMP6) in Benguerir, Morocco, in December 2018 [27]. In 2022 UMP6 launched the "AI Research Dome", an International Center for AI at its Rabat campus.

The Al-Khawarizmi program, and the House of Artificial Intelligence concept first launched in Oujda, are clear signals of the country's commitment to developing AI in higher education and business. Al-Khawarizmi, is a competitive national program launched in 2019 to support AI research projects. Program objectives include identifying appropriate AI actions in different national sectors, creating favorable conditions for collaboration between researchers and business, and accompanying financed projects through the processes of patenting and protection of industrial intellectual property. It also provides assistance to selected projects in commercializing their products. These objectives are meant to provide trained human capital in AI, as well as a better understanding of the socio-economic possibilities offered by AI, thus reinforcing the country's economic competitivity. Nearly $50 million were budgeted in 2020 to fund 45 AI projects in the areas of tourism, justice, computer vision, intelligent cities, big data and logistics [28].

The first AI House was inaugurated at Mohammed I University in 2022 in collaboration with EuropAI and has rapidly become a leading AI research facility in the region [29]. Its principal objective is to propagate knowledge concerning AI professions and AI applications in diverse fields including the social sciences and augmented reality in medicine, bringing together faculty, students, commercial enterprise as well as national and international institutions.

In order to face the challenges of development, Morocco has developed an inclusive National Development Model (NDM), designed to capitalize on the country's assets, transforming it into a nation of opportunity, entrepreneurship, and innovation [30]. In line with the NDM, which considers digital technology as a real lever of change and development, it is essential for Morocco to capitalize on its digital heritage and leverage the power of AI. By embracing the transformative potential of AI, Morocco can effectively implement the NDM, to accelerate progress and achieve its ambitious development goals. The 2023 Report of MoroccoAI [31], an active non-governmental AI association, has identified areas where AI can drive the implementation of the NDM and has recommended aligning the national AI strategy with the NDM objectives, with emphasis on skills and education, research and innovation, data and infrastructure, and ethics and regulation. In addition, the report identifies five priority areas for the national AI strategy: public services, healthcare, education, energy, and agriculture.

4 Conclusions

Data on digitization and the use of AI in the Arab States is sporadic at best, and frequently unreliable. This is in part due to the uneven progress made in the different countries and to "stated intentions" (plans, strategies) that are not realized. Political will is thus a necessary factor in the development of Arab AI. Access to technology also remains a major obstacle to the adoption of advanced AI in many Arab states. It is important to increase access to high-performance computing and software to ensure advances in Arab AI. National laboratories with advanced computing infrastructures, coupled with the potential created in industry and academia, could create shared pools and be a strong support for higher education institutions.

Arab governments should take steps to increase the availability of open research data and to harness the power of AI across different fields, from health to climate. European initiatives in this framework, such as the Health Data Space [32], and GAIA-X [33], which aim to build a federated data infrastructure, can serve as models for the Arab nations. Additionally, Arab research centers should be encouraged to adopt systems such as federated learning that can apply AI to sensitive data held by multiple parties without compromising privacy. An additional challenge is to work for interoperability in laboratory instruments and processes by creating common interfaces. Arab governments could bring laboratory users, instrument suppliers and technology developers together and incentivize them to achieve this goal. The acceleration of research productivity through the use of AI will thus lead to more-rapid economic and social development.

References

1. ITU (2021) Digital trends in the Arab States region 2021: information and communication technology trends and developments in the Arab States region, 2017–2020. https://handle.itu.int/11.1002/pub/8184d626-en
2. OECD (2023) Updates to the OECD's definition of an AI system explained. https://oecd.ai/en/wonk/ai-system-definition-update
3. UNESCO (2021) Recommendation on the ethics of artificial intelligence. https://unesdoc.unesco.org/ark:/48223/pf0000381137
4. Azoulay A (2021) Vers une éthique de l'intelligence artificielle. UN. https://www.un.org/fr/chronicle/article/vers-une-ethique-de-lintelligence-artificielle
5. Pasquarelli W (2022) Pushing forward: the future of AI in the Middle East and North Africa. The Economist. https://impact.economist.com/perspectives/technology-innovation/pushing-forward-future-ai-middle-east-and-north-africa
6. Littman ML, Ajunwa I, Berger G et al (2021) Gathering strength, gathering storms: the one hundred year study on artificial intelligence (AI100) 2021 study panel report. Stanford University. https://ai100.stanford.edu/2021-report https://ai100.stanford.edu/gathering-strength-gathering-storms-one-hundred-year-study-artificial-intelligence-ai100-2021-1/sq2
7. Al-Kinani M (2020) L'Arabie saoudite entrevoit un avenir centré sur l'intelligence artificielle à la veille du sommet du G20. Arab News. https://www.arabnews.fr/node/33496/monde-arabe
8. NEOM: Made to change. https://www.neom.com/en-us. Accessed Nov 2023
9. Government of Saudi Arabia, National Strategy for Data and AI. https://ai.sa/Brochure_NSDAI_Summit%20version_EN.pdf. Accessed Dec 2023
10. Saudi Data and Artificial Intelligence Authority. https://sdaia.gov.sa/en/SDAIA/AboutPortal/Pages/Sitemap.aspx
11. Oxford Business Group (2022) The competitive outlook for artificial intelligence in MENA. https://oxfordbusinessgroup.com/articles-interviews/the-competitive-outlook-for-artificial-intelligence-in-mena
12. PwC. https://www.pwc.com/m1/en/publications/potential-impact-artificial-intelligence-middle-east.html. Accessed Dec 2023
13. Minister of State for Artificial Intelligence, Digital Economy & Remote Work Applications Office (2022) AI ethics: principles and guidelines. United Arab Emirates Government. https://ai.gov.ae/wp-content/uploads/2023/03/MOCAI-AI-Ethics-EN-1.pdf
14. Lavoisard C (2023) Les Emirats lancent un langage d'intelligence artificielle en arabe. L'Orient Le Jour. https://www.lorientlejour.com/article/1347956/les-emirats-lancent-un-langage-dintelligence-artificielle-en-arabe.html
15. Qatar Foundation. Qatar foundation artificial intelligence programs in Qatar. https://www.qf.org.qa/research/artificial-intelligence. Accessed Dec 2023
16. Al-Ammal H, Aljawder M (2021) Strategy for artificial intelligence in Bahrain: challenges and opportunities. In: Azar E, Haddad AN (eds) Artificial intelligence in the Gulf. Palgrave Macmillan, Singapore. https://doi.org/10.1007/978-981-16-0771-4_4
17. Khaifa KM, Hamdan A, Alareeni B (2021) Artificial intelligence and entrepreneurship in Bahrain. In: Alareeni B, Hamdan A, Elgedawy I (eds) The importance of new technologies and entrepreneurship in business development: in the context of economic diversity in developing countries. ICBT 2020. Lecture notes in networks and systems, vol 194. Springer, Cham. https://doi.org/10.1007/978-3-030-69221-6_60
18. Bricker A (2021) Q&A: how Bahrain plans to be a regional AI leader. CIO. https://www.cio.com/article/191083/qanda-how-bahrain-plans-to-be-a-regional-ai-leader.html
19. Go-Globe, E commerce and digitization in Kuwait: trends and future opportunities https://www.go-globe.com/e-commerce-and-digitization-in-kuwait/. Accessed Jan 2024
20. Aljazeera (2023) AI-generated news presenter appears in Kuwait. https://www.aljazeera.com/news/2023/4/10/ai-generated-news-presenter-appears-in-kuwait

21. Adaileh M, Alshawawreh AR (2021) Measuring digital transformation impact in Jordan: a proposed framework. J Innovat Digital Market 2(1):19–36. https://doi.org/10.51300/jidm-2021-32
22. Radwan S, Sobeih S (2021) Egypt's AI strategy is more about development than AI. OECD AI Policy Observatory. https://oecd.ai/en/wonk/egypt-ai-strategy
23. Ministry of Communications and Information Technology, Artificial Intelligence. Egytpian Government. https://mcit.gov.eg/en/Artificial_Intelligence#:~:text=The%20National%20AI%20Strategy%E2%80%94to,technologies%20and%20transform%20the%20economy. Accessed Dec 2023
24. Zantour K (2023) Restrictive AI laws and "false hope" hinder technological innovation in Tunisia. Al Majalla. https://en.majalla.com/node/300116/business-economy/restrictive-ai-laws-and-false-hope-hinder-technological-innovation
25. Leaders (2019) Intelligence artificielle: une priorité tunisienne. https://www.leaders.com.tn/article/26676-intelligence-artificielle-une-priorite-tunisienne
26. Sawahel W (2021) Strategy for research in artificial intelligence launched. University World News Africa Edition. https://www.universityworldnews.com/post.php?story=20210131063348120
27. AfriqueITNews.com (2024) L'UNESCO présente les initiatives en intelligence artificielle au Maghreb. https://afriqueitnews.com/tech-media/unesco-presente-initiatives-intelligence-artificielle-maghreb/
28. Agence de Développement du Digital. https://www.add.gov.ma/programme-al-khawarizmi-publication-des-resultats-de-lappel-a-projet-cnrstadd. Accessed March 2023
29. Maison de l'Intelligence artificielle, Mohammed I University. https://mia.ump.ma. Accessed Oct 2023
30. La Commission Spéciale sur le Modèle de Développement (2021) The new development model. Kingdom of Morocco. https://www.csmd.ma/rapport-fr
31. MoroccoAI (2023) Recommendations towards a national AI Strategy for Morocco. https://morocco.ai/wp-content/uploads/2020/03/MoroccoAI-Recommendations-Towards-a-National-AI-Strategy-For-Morocco.pdf
32. European Commission. European health data space. https://health.ec.europa.eu/ehealth-digital-health-and-care/european-health-data-space_en. Accessed Jan 2024
33. Ministère de l'Économie des Finances et de la Souveraineté Industrielle et Numérique (2020) Concrétisation du projet "GAIA-X", une infrastructure européenne de données. Gouvernement de la République Française. https://www.economie.gouv.fr/concretisation-projet-gaia-x-infrastructure-europeenne-donnees

HTU^x: An Online Learning-Platform Model Targeting the Arab Youth

Rami AlKarmi, Tarek A. Tutunji, and Mai Hijazi

Abstract Digital transformation (DX) in higher education is an organizational, social, and technological change that is rapidly modifying teaching methodologies, expected learning outcomes, and educational platforms. With the exponential growth in volatility, uncertainty, and ambiguity facing graduates, the current education system is ripe for disruption. Universities are facing existential threats with the growth of global online learning platforms. To develop and implement a sustainable education management strategy, Arab universities must build a competitive advantage by exploring synergies to achieve a massive transformational purpose targeting the Arab region to empower a significant percentage of the 100 million Arab youth with the required skills and knowledge needed in the fast-changing global market. Al Hussein Technical University (HTU) is a young university that continues to adapt itself to the ever-changing regional and global environments. Therefore, HTU is launching its digital twin, HTU^x, an online learning platform with unique six-month-long pathways built on a stackable-course methodology. From a university perspective, the aim of HTU^x is to develop a brand reputation with an innovative and student-centered approach. This chapter will explore available online learning platforms with Arabic content for Engineering and Information Technology programs and will describe the strategic, operations, market, and technology dimensions for launching HTU^x as a case study.

R. AlKarmi · M. Hijazi
Digital Learning Center, Al-Hussein Technical University, King Hussein Business Park, Amman 11831, Jordan
e-mail: rami.alkarmi@htu.edu.jo

M. Hijazi
e-mail: mai.hijazi@htu.edu.jo

T.A. Tutunji (✉)
School of Engineering Technology, Al-Hussein Technical University, King Hussein Business Park, Amman 11831, Jordan
e-mail: tarek.tutunji@htu.edu.jo

© The Author(s), under exclusive license to Springer Nature Switzerland AG 2024
A. Badran et al. (eds.), *Higher Education in the Arab World*,
https://doi.org/10.1007/978-3-031-70779-7_11

Keywords Digital transformation · Online learning platform · Teaching and learning methodology · MOOC · Stackable-courses-based pedagogy · Educational pathways

1 Introduction

The United Nations Educational, Scientific and Cultural Organization (UNESCO) defined Sustainability Education (SE), as education that intends to empower students to make informed decisions and take responsible actions to ensure economic feasibility, environmental integrity, and a just society while respecting cultural diversity for present and future generations [1].

The United Nations recognises the importance of open education in expanding access to quality education, boosting literacy and providing high-level skills that the knowledge economy requires. The term "open" not only addresses access, it also empowers an individual to have the ability to create, modify and use information and knowledge in such a way that it is personalized to an individual [2].

Higher education (HE) institutions are expected to lead positive changes in their countries by advancing economic and social development. This will involve developing the HE structures to become more open, digitized, personalized, and collaborative [2].

Universities of the future will not have physical or geographical boundaries as students will have various options to learn multiple courses from different universities. The one-size, one-stop university philosophy will become obsolete. Universities will go through much-needed transformation and will provide multiple entry and exit options to the students [3].

The COVID-19 pandemic highlighted the importance of connecting the educational system with technology as an integral part of the teaching and learning methodology. In turn, the educational system dived into the digital ecosystems. Nowadays, technology is used to enlarge access to knowledge and information, enrich educational processes, and improve learning outcomes [4].

Digital transformation in HE encompasses a wide range of areas, including teaching and learning, administration, student services, research, and communication. Digital transformation can be divided into three categories: technological, organizational, and social. From a technological perspective, DX causes the use of new technologies. As for organization, DX allows institutions to adopt new business models and modify its processes. From a social point of view, DX makes a direct impact on human life [5].

Digital transformation is not limited to pure information technology (IT) and platforms as it involves other themes that include leadership (vision and strategic planning), people (skills and performance), and experience (customer understanding) [6]. From a university's perspective, DX strategies aim to: (a) increase the total revenue, (b) improve productivity, (c) generate value through innovative practices, and (e) develop brand recognition and novelty [7].

The main DX component is integrating and implementing digital technologies to enhance and revolutionize the way educational institutions operate, provide content, and engage with students and stakeholders. It involves the strategic use of technology to improve various aspects of the educational experience, administrative processes, and overall organizational efficiency [6].

One key component of DX is *e-learning and online education*, which is incorporating digital tools and platforms to deliver courses and educational content online. This includes learning management systems (LMS), virtual classrooms, online assessments, and interactive multimedia.

Al Hussein Technical University (HTU) is on a mission and is exploring synergies around establishing partnerships to achieve a massive transformational impetus targeting the Arab region to empower a significant percentage of the Arab youth/students with the skills and knowledge they need to excel in the Fourth Industrial Revolution by 2030 through the integration of online and hybrid learning models, a focus on skills development, partnerships with industry, and an emphasis on entrepreneurship.

HTU^x is an online education platform and micro-credential course designed, developed, and produced by OLC@HTU (the Online Learning Center at HTU) and hosted on the platform in a unique six-month-long "Accelerated Pathways" format that is designed to build towards employment.

This chapter will describe the HTU experience in launching its online learning platform and developing the e-learning courses. The chapter will provide a literature review of the present HTU background, highlight HTU strategy and HTU^x design methodology, discuss HTU^x implementation and results, and provide conclusions and implementation.

2 Literature Review

The fast technological development in computer performance, internet connections, virtual reality, animation, and artificial intelligence will play an immense role in education. The future learner will be a lifelong learner and will not be limited to a specific university as they will explore all available learning resources; this will of course include online learning. In order to grow and be successful, the digital classroom must become more flexible, accessible, interactive, innovative, affordable, and collaborative [7].

Ashmel et al. [8] developed a qualitative model that advocates how digital transformation as a propelling force could be used to build competitive advantages for universities. They concluded that DX strategies must build capabilities to influence both student centricity and discipline centricity. When universities develop the right combinations of the key components (Artificial Intelligence [AI], Cloud Computing [CC] and Big Data [BD]) of DX needed to compete in the global competition, the entire university must be concerned about the ultimate goal/s of digitalization and how it is going to build superior values to the students/stakeholders.

However, this is not enough as universities must develop an agile/evolutionary learning process/system in order to capture the impactful educational changes. It is the evolutionary learning process that must identify and determine the scope for adopting digitalization.

Other researchers [9] proposed the application of an integrated DX model to assess the maturity level that educational institutions have in their DX processes and compared them to other industries. They concluded not only that the educational sector is falling behind others, but also that its main problem may be inadequate leadership practices and a culture against change.

Alenezi [10], a researcher from Saudi Arabia, summarized the challenges of DX as: prioritization, decentralized decision making, resistance to change, gaps in digital talent, and a short-term view of return on investment (ROI). He compared three DX frameworks: KPMG, Microsoft, and Google and concluded that HE institutes are lagging behind other industries and business organizations.

Marks et al. [11], explored DX maturity in the UAE, specifically in HE. The UAE is one of the leading developing nations in terms of IT infrastructure, and the adoption of new technologies. The UAE government has made significant leaps in e-government, e-commerce, e-business, and e-services in general. They concluded that DX was more evident in enabling processes such as student administration services, library services, finance, and accounting, but less evident in learning and teaching, research processes, and planning and governance processes. Leading challenges reported included challenges with holistic vision; personnel competency and IT skills; data structure, data processing, and data reporting; redundant systems; third-party reporting systems; manual entries; and potential use by customers.

Massive Open Online Courses (MOOCs) have gained much interest and popularity in the past five years. And the idea of getting an online degree has gained much acceptance since the COVID-19 pandemic. There are several popular MOOCs, such as Coursera, edX, and Udacity, that offer courses in English.

Ruipérez-Valiente et al. [12] report data gathered from 15 MOOC providers from nine countries. They concluded that regional MOOC providers are doing a better job catering to their local learners than the global, elite providers.

There are very few professional and well-developed online courses that communicate in the Arabic language. Three popular online learning platforms, Edraak, Rwaq, and Nafham, provide good material. However, none of these provide focused and specialized courses in engineering and IT.

With the increasing young Arab population, there is a massive market demand for engineering and IT online courses. These courses should be recorded and produced to speak to the young Arab population in their own language. Furthermore, it has been shown that regional providers are better positioned to meet the goals of expanding access to HE in their regions. Culture factors and language can have positive influence when designing online learning material [12].

3 Background

Al Hussein Technical University is a Crown Prince Foundation (CPF) initiative that focuses on higher education and is established to be a disruptive technical university with unique teaching methodology. It is located in the heart of Amman's business hub and therefore provides a perfect atmosphere for industry cooperation. Moreover, HTU has added two newly constructed buildings that are certified as energy efficient, shown in Fig. 1. The university offers focused technical and bachelor's degree programs in the fields of applied engineering and IT. In addition, HTU's education is built around the following pillars: industry-based learning, BTEC-based curricula and assessment, state-of-the-art laboratories, STEM, apprenticeships, immersive English programs, soft skills, innovation, and entrepreneurship.

Al Hussein Technical University realized early on that DX in the global HE industry is a key component in determining the university's competitive edge and establishing a sustainable education strategy. Building competitive advantage is a relative, evolving, and important concept in strategy formulation. In recent years, specifically in the education industry, the notion of building a competitive advantage is challenged by global phenomena such as DX, globalization, information exchange, digitization, and social media. These phenomena have collectively made the process of building competitive advantage rapidly changing, short-term and contextual.

Fig. 1 Main Buildings at the Al Hussein Technical University in Jordan

This work provides first-hand insight into the impactful changes affecting universities' vision and how they can turn these changes to their advantages and set a road map to design–develop models to integrate and regulate these essential changes in their strategies, using an evolving learning mechanism and a DX strategy.

4 HTU^x Strategy and Objectives

Al Hussein Technical University is on a mission and is exploring synergies around establishing partnerships to achieve a massive transformational purpose, targeting the Arab region to empower, by 2033, a significant percentage of the 100 million Arab youth/students with the skills and knowledge they need to excel in the Fourth Industrial Revolution through the integration of online and hybrid learning models, a focus on skills development, partnerships with industry, and an emphasis on entrepreneurship.

4.1 Opportunity and Arab Youth

There are 22 Arab nations, spreading across North Africa, the Middle East, and Southwest Asia. This region has a total area of around 13 million km^2, and a population of 464 million, of which 32% are youth aged between 15 and 24. This young population is eager to take opportunities and equip itself with the knowledge and skills required to build a better future.

Education is about more than just what happens in the classroom. It is about preparing people for life, equipping them to handle a world where change is the only constant. The aim is to nurture a generation of learners who are flexible and able to respond to the ever-changing demands of the global job market.

By realizing this aim, the benefits stretch beyond just the individuals. Transforming education and tapping into the potential of youth can energize economies, stabilize societies, and open up new paths to innovation and growth. It is a win–win situation—for the young people, for the region, and for the global community.

4.2 The Future of Education is Ready for Disruption

Education is at a stage where it needs more than just a few tweaks. It is time for a full-scale revolution in how we teach and learn. The following are important issues to consider.

Rethinking Learning for Today's World
The basic idea behind this educational upheaval is straightforward yet profound: learning must keep pace with the fast-evolving world. The old model of confining education within classroom walls and textbook pages is outdated. Now, it is about engaging with real-world challenges, applying knowledge practically, and getting ready for a world that's always in motion. This new age of education aims to make learning an exciting, relevant journey that's deeply connected with the rhythm of today's world.

Adapting Education to the Times
In an era where both technology and social norms are constantly evolving, education cannot afford to stand still. This new wave of learning is about adapting and staying relevant. It embraces the latest tech advancements to create more interactive and captivating learning experiences. More crucially, it ensures that the skills and knowledge taught are aligned with the future workforce's needs.

The Key Features of Modern Education
What sets this new approach apart is its incredible flexibility. It is an adaptable form of education that changes as the world does, making sure learners are equipped with up-to-date and future-proof knowledge and skills. This method focuses on deep understanding, critical thinking, creativity, and building the confidence to navigate and influence the future.

Preparing for Life Beyond the Classroom
This fresh take on education goes beyond traditional academic boundaries. It is a comprehensive preparation for real-life challenges. It encourages learners to be active participants in their education, not just passive receivers of information. The emphasis is on essential life skills like problem-solving, adaptability, and continuous learning, which are crucial for success in today's dynamic world.

Welcoming a New Educational Era
This shift marks a significant move towards redefining education. It is about creating learning experiences that are suitable for today and tomorrow's challenges and opportunities, not just those of the past. As this new approach to education takes root, it promises a rejuvenating, exhilarating, and future-ready way of learning. It is more than just an educational shift; it is a step into a new era of education, promising to unlock the full potential of learners and ready them for a world full of surprises and constant change.

4.3 *HTUx Massive Transformation Purpose*

Before diving into HTU^x's specific Massive Transformation Purpose (MTP), it is crucial to understand what MTP is. An MTP is not just a goal or a mission statement; it is a visionary and aspirational drive that defines an organization's very essence. It is about creating significant, widespread impact and driving transformative change. An MTP reflects an organization's ambition to address major challenges or opportunities in a way that reshapes the world. It's about thinking big, aiming high, and having a profound, far-reaching impact.

The MTP of HTU^x: "Work with HTU^x partners to accelerate empowering an influential significant percentage of 100 million Arab students with the skills, knowledge, and attitude they need to excel in the Fourth Industrial Revolution by 2033 through the integration of online and hybrid learning models, a focus on skills development, partnerships with industry, and an emphasis on entrepreneurship." Next, we break down HTU^x's MTP.

1. *Targeting a Significant Influence on Arab Youth* The ambitious MTP of HTU^x is set to make a substantial impact on a significant segment of the 100 million Arab youth. This focus goes beyond just reaching large numbers; it's about making a meaningful and influential change in their educational and professional lives.
2. *Excelling in the Fourth Industrial Revolution* The Fourth Industrial Revolution is characterized by rapid technological change and digitalization. The focus of HTU^x is to prepare students for this new era, ensuring they are not only ready but are also leading the charge in this technological and digital frontier.
3. *Integration of Online and Hybrid Learning Models* Recognizing the changing landscape of education, HTU^x commits to innovative learning models. This includes a blend of online and traditional learning, offering flexibility and accessibility while maintaining the quality and engagement of in-person experiences.
4. *Focus on Skills Development* The cornerstone of HTU^x's approach is to develop practical, applicable skills. This is in line with the demands of modern industries and the evolving job market, ensuring that students are job-ready and have the competencies to thrive.
5. *Partnerships with Industry* Collaboration with industry partners is a key strategy. It ensures that the education provided is relevant and aligned with real-world requirements. These partnerships also open pathways for internships, job placements, and real-world project experiences for students.
6. *Emphasis on Entrepreneurship* In fostering an entrepreneurial spirit, HTU^x encourages innovation and self-starting attitudes. This is crucial in a world where traditional career paths are changing, and new opportunities are constantly emerging.

It should be emphasized that HTU^x's MTP is not just a statement but a guiding force behind its operations and strategies. This purpose drives the instructional design, teaching methodologies, curriculum production, and partnerships. It influences the creation of courses, focusing on areas like AI, robotics, and digital skills that are pivotal in the Fourth Industrial Revolution. It also shapes the community and network-building efforts of HTU^x, fostering a collaborative ecosystem where students, educators, and industry leaders come together.

4.4 HTUx Learning Model and Stackable-Courses-Based Pedagogy

The HTU^x learning model stands out with its unique approach: HTU is not just following the old sit-down-and-listen model, nor is it just creating lengthy lecture videos. At HTU^x, we believe in interactive, engaged learning where everyone contributes to each other's educational journey.

Therefore, HTU^x differs from MOOCs, which often feel like large, impersonal online classrooms. Here, learning is more personal, hands-on, and, we believe, much more enjoyable. The heart of HTU^x's model is collaboration—students working together, learning from each other, and growing as a community.

'Learning by doing' is a big part of our philosophy. This means students do not just memorize facts; they actively engage with real-world projects, tackle practical problems, and acquire skills they will use in their daily lives and future careers. It is akin to learning to swim—you don't truly learn by reading about it; you learn by getting into the water.

Group activities form a crucial part of our learning model. We bring students together to collaborate on projects, exchange ideas, and learn from each other. This is not just teacher-led, it is two-way.

Thus, HTU^x is pioneering a new approach to education with our stackable-courses-based pedagogy. This innovative model is transforming the way students learn, educators teach, and how course content is maintained and updated. It is not just about changing the structure of courses; it is about revolutionizing the entire learning experience.

It is a forward-thinking approach to learning, teaching, and course management. It provides an efficient, adaptable, and personalized education experience, keeping pace with the rapid changes in technology and industry. This model is setting a new standard in higher education, one that is responsive to the needs of students, educators, and employers alike. It is a system designed not just for the present but for the future of education. The HTU^x learning model is based on the following:

Stackable Courses: Building Blocks of Learning
Our courses are like individual building blocks. Each one is a self-contained unit, complete with its own learning objectives, outcomes, and assessments. What makes these courses special is their ability to be stacked together to form a comprehensive learning pathway. It is a bit like assembling a puzzle; each piece is unique but fits perfectly with the others to create a complete picture.

A Personalized and Adaptable Learning Experience
The beauty of this model lies in its personalization and adaptability. Students can tailor their education to their interests and career goals by selecting specific stacks of courses. This personalization goes beyond just choosing a major; it allows students to delve into specialized areas within a field, making their education as unique as their aspirations.

For Employers: Clear Skill Assessment
From an employer's perspective, this model provides clarity on a candidate's skills and knowledge. The completion of specific course stacks gives employers a precise understanding of what a potential employee has learned and can offer. It is a more efficient way to assess a candidate's fit for a particular role or project.

For Educators: A Canvas for Creativity
This model also empowers educators to be more innovative and responsive. They have the flexibility to quickly adapt course content to reflect new developments in their fields. This keeps the learning material dynamic and ensures that students are learning skills that are relevant and in-demand.

Efficient Learning Paths: No Redundancies
A significant advantage of this system is its efficiency. If a student completes a course as part of one learning pathway, and that course is also part of another pathway they are interested in, they will not need to retake it. This not only saves time but also ensures that students can build upon what they've already learned without unnecessary repetition.

Seamless Course Updates: Keeping Content Fresh
Updating course content is a unique and integral part of our design model. Instead of overhauling an entire semester-long course, we only need to update the specific stackable course or even just a set of short, three- to five-minute videos within it. This makes keeping our courses current with the latest industry trends and knowledge much more manageable and less time-consuming. In a world where information and technology are constantly evolving, this flexibility is crucial in providing our students with the most up-to-date and relevant learning material.

4.5 Unique Value Proposition

When it comes to online learning and MOOC platforms, HTU^x stands out with its unique approach and offerings, especially when compared to giants like Coursera and edX or regional MOOCs. Here is a breakdown of what sets HTU^x apart and how it fares against the competition.

Study Alone, Play Together Model
The HTU^x platform is built on a community activation model that goes beyond just learning. For instance, the Arab Sumo Robotics Competition, tied to our *Mobile RobotiX* accelerated pathway, makes STEM education both fun and socially engaging. It is not just about acquiring knowledge in isolation; it is about applying it in a community setting, turning education into an exciting, collective experience.

Emphasis on Arabic Language
While most platforms offer specialized engineering and technical content primarily in English, HTU^x breaks the barrier by delivering these courses in Arabic (white dialect). This strategic choice opens doors for over 100 million Arab youth, offering them high-quality technical education in their native language, making learning more accessible and relatable.

Backed by HTU's Reputable Brand
The certificates issued by HTU^x carry the weight of HTU's reputable brand and standard of quality. This endorsement adds significant value to the learner's achievements and is a strong testament to the quality of education and skills acquired.

Exclusive Focus on Engineering and Tech Employability
Unlike other platforms that cover a wide range of subjects, HTU^x specializes exclusively in engineering and technology, with a sharp focus on employability in these sectors. This specialization allows for a deeper and more comprehensive curriculum that is closely aligned with industry needs.

Unique Value Proposition for Each Pathway
Each accelerated pathway at HTU^x is carefully designed with its own unique value proposition, tailored to meet the specific demands and competitive landscape of the field. This means that every course pathway is crafted to provide the most relevant and practical skills, ensuring that learners are job-ready upon completion.

4.6 Competitive Analysis

In this section, we will show the competitive edge of HTU^x, globally and in the region.

Global Competitive Analysis (Coursera and edX)
When compared to platforms like Coursera and edX, HTU^x holds its ground with its unique offerings. While Coursera and edX provide a vast array of courses across various disciplines and collaborate with multiple universities globally, HTU^x offers a more focused and localized approach. The use of Arabic, emphasis on community engagement, and tailored pathways provide HTU^x with a competitive edge in reaching and resonating with the Arab youth.

Regional Competitive Analysis
When we compare HTU^x to other MOOCs and online learning platforms targeting Arabic learners, several points of contrast emerge. Here, we will compare HTU^x with three popular online Arabic platforms: Edraak, Rwaq, and Nafham.

1. **Edraak** is a well-established online learning platform in the Arab world. It offers a diverse array of courses ranging from personal development to academic subjects. https://www.edraak.org/en/

    - **Audience and Course Focus** While Edraak serves a broad audience with a variety of interests, HTU^x zeroes in on a more niche market. The HTU^x curriculum is specifically tailored to engineering and technology, offering depth and specialization that is particularly beneficial for students looking to enter these industries.

    - **Course Design** Edraak's courses are designed to cater to general learning requirements, which is excellent for learners seeking a wide range of knowledge. However, HTU^x offers courses that are deeply integrated with industry needs, providing practical and application-focused learning, essential for those aiming for careers in engineering and tech sectors.

2. **Rwaq** is another significant online platform in the Arabic-speaking world, offering courses on a multitude of subjects. https://www.rwaq.org/

    - **Specialization** Rwaq and HTU^x share the advantage of providing content in Arabic, making education accessible to the Arab-speaking community. However, HTU^x distinguishes itself with its emphasis on specialized, industry-aligned courses in engineering and technology, as opposed to Rwaq's broader academic approach.

    - **Career-Oriented Learning** Rwaq offers a wide educational spectrum but lacks the focused, career-oriented pathways that HTU^x emphasizes, whereas HTU^x's courses are meticulously crafted to align with specific career paths in the tech and engineering sectors, offering a more-direct route to employment in these fields.

3. **Nafham** stands out for its extensive collection of educational videos, primarily targeting school-level education. https://www.nafham.com/

    - **Target Audience** The fundamental difference lies in the target audience. Nafham is more focused on school-level education, providing a valuable resource for school students. In contrast, HTU^x is tailored for higher education and professional development, targeting university students and professionals looking to advance their careers.

    - **Content Depth and Professional Development** Nafham is an excellent platform for foundational learning and academic support at the school level. On the other hand, HTU^x delves deeper into subject matter, focusing on advanced concepts, latest technologies, and skills in engineering and technology, thereby catering to a more-mature audience seeking professional growth and job readiness.

5 HTU^x Design Methodology

The transformation at HTU started with a core group of HTU leaders who gathered to refine the envisioned HTU^x model. This stage was pivotal for gathering insights and fine-tuning our approach towards higher engagement and buy-in. However, a significant challenge emerged: shifting the faculty's mindset to address their concerns. We needed to convey that, in an era of rapid educational and industrial changes, traditional multi-year degree programs were no longer the sole path to employability; moreover, as a faculty member with a digital version of your course available, that does not make you redundant or replaceable. It actually might represent a lucrative financial opportunity for you that can be much more rewarding than your current income. Next, we will highlight the main steps that HTU worked on to design HTU^x.

5.1 The HTU Townhall Meeting: Setting the Stage

To address this, HTU leadership held an all-hands townhall meeting and highlighted major trends, such as global labor shortages, the great resignation, and the rise of remote work and automation, that were reshaping education and employment during this age of extreme uncertainty. We showcased the growing demand for new-collar jobs and the surge in non-degree job opportunities, exemplified by a LinkedIn search revealing a demand of over 18,000 non-degree jobs at Google in the US.

5.2 Launching the Faculty and Staff Hackathon

The townhall meeting paved the way for our first faculty and staff hackathon, announced by the HTU President and structured into three strategic rounds (Fig. 2):

1. **ROUND1: Formation and Pitching** Teams, comprising five members, some including an industry professional, were formed to ideate and pitch their course concepts.
2. **ROUND2: Design and Production** The selected teams then moved on to design and produce a complete set of stackable courses, forming accelerated, employment-focused learning pathways no longer than six months. Courses developed should be based on current HTU study plans. Cross-academic program pathways were encouraged to foster interdisciplinary learning.
3. **ROUND3: Launch and Marketing** The final phase involved launching and effectively marketing these pathways.

Fig. 2 The three launching rounds for the online learning platform HTU[x]

5.3 Incentives and Revenue Sharing

A critical component of this hackathon was the introduction of incentives and a unique revenue-sharing model:

- **Fixed Incentive** Teams that successfully completed the design and production phase were awarded a fixed incentive. This was a key motivator for participants, ensuring commitment and high-quality output.
- **Revenue Sharing** For the go-to-market phase, an innovative legal framework governing revenue sharing was implemented. This was designed to incentivize teams not just for creating the courses but also for successfully marketing them and attracting learners.

5.4 Participation, Development, and Outcomes

- **Participation** Seventy HTU staff members formed 23 teams to participate in the hackathon.
- **Selection Process** These teams pitched their ideas over four days to a panel comprising the HTU President and the Digital Learning Center team, from which 17 teams were shortlisted as semi-finalists.
- **Development Process** The semi-finalists underwent 10 bi-weekly development sprints, subject to three stage gates, focusing on designing and developing the courses.
- **Final Outcome** Nine teams with one pathway each successfully reached the go-live stage, marking their readiness for enrollment by students. These results are shown in Table 1.

The HTU Faculty and Staff Hackathon was a groundbreaking initiative, fostering innovation and practical application in course design. The hackathon not only led to the creation of new, industry-relevant learning pathways but also played an

Table 1 Number of participating teams in the faculty and staff hackathon used to develop the courses on the HTU^x platform

	Numbers	Percentage from original (%)
Pitching teams	23	100
Selected teams	17	74
Production teams	9	39

instrumental role in shifting the faculty's perspective towards modern educational needs. The incentives and revenue-sharing model further underscored the practical and sustainable approach of HTU^x, aligning faculty interests with the institution's strategic goals. This event marked HTU^x's commitment to stay ahead of the curve in higher-education disruption, ensuring our programs are closely aligned with the evolving dynamics of the job market and the needs of our students.

5.5 Legal Framework and Intellectual Property Management

As explained in our description of the hackathon, we recognized the need for an innovative and robust legal framework to facilitate our ambitious educational model. Our objective was to create a win–win, exponential-growth-based business and operating model that engages HTU faculty, staff, and third-party content creators, including individuals, organizations, and fellow higher education institutions. This framework was inspired by models used in venture-capital investments and the Hollywood studio system, where investments in creative projects are recouped through revenue sharing and royalties. The core elements of the legal framework are listed next:

1. **Content Creation** The framework provides clear guidelines for content creation, ensuring that the educational material produced is of high quality and aligns with HTU^x's objectives.
2. **The Services** Detailed descriptions of the services provided by HTU^x, including instructional design, content design, production, and outreach, are outlined. This clarity ensures that all parties involved understand the scope and nature of the services offered.
3. **Fees and Payment** The framework details the financial arrangements, including payment terms for services rendered, ensuring transparency and fairness in financial dealings.
4. **Intellectual Property (IP)** A critical component of the framework is the management of IP rights. It grants HTU an exclusive, irrevocable, royalty-free, and perpetual license to use the educational content created. This arrangement ensures that HTU^x retains the rights to use and distribute the content while recognizing the creators' contributions.

5. **Confidentiality** The agreement includes strict confidentiality clauses, protecting the proprietary information and materials shared during the content creation process.
6. **Term, Default, and Termination** This section outlines the duration of agreements, conditions for default, and termination clauses, providing a clear roadmap for the lifecycle of the partnership.
7. **Warranty, Governing Law, and Jurisdiction** The framework includes warranties and specifies the governing law and jurisdiction, ensuring legal compliance and addressing dispute resolution.

At HTU^x, we have redefined the management of IP in educational content creation, turning it into a commercially viable asset. This innovative approach involves:

- **Exclusive and Perpetual Licensing** The IP created under HTU^x grants the university an exclusive, irrevocable, royalty-free, and perpetual license. This means that while creators retain their rights to recognition and certain uses, HTU^x can freely use, adapt, and distribute the content, turning it into a continuous asset for the institution.
- **Commercial Viability** By securing the rights to educational content, HTU^x can explore various commercial avenues. This could include partnerships with other educational institutions, private-sector collaborations, or even offering the content on various public and private platforms, generating revenue that can be reinvested in the university and its programs.

5.6 Cost-Effectiveness and Service Rate Card

The ability of HTU^x to offer competitive rates for its services is rooted in its highly efficient operational model:

- **In-House Team of Specialists** By insourcing a team of instructional designers, building our in-house studios and film production crew, and employing edtech specialists, HTU^x maintains a high level of quality control while keeping costs manageable.
- **HTU^x Platform and EdTech Tools** The development and maintenance of the HTUx platform, along with proprietary edtech tools and plugins, are handled internally. This not only ensures seamless integration and customization of learning experiences but also contributes to overall cost efficiency.
- **Operational Scalability** Since HTU^x boasts a large pool of creative resources, we are able to expand our operations on demand. This scalability is crucial for meeting varying project sizes and timelines without compromising quality or incurring excessive costs.
- **Rate-Card Transparency** The clarity in the rate card for our services—including instructional design, content design, production, and outreach—provides

potential collaborators and content creators with transparent and predictable pricing models. This transparency is key in establishing trust and long-term partnerships.

5.7 Leveraging Operational Efficiency for Innovation

The synergy between HTU^x's innovative IP management and its operational efficiency creates a dynamic ecosystem for educational content creation:

- **Enhanced Creativity and Quality** The in-house team's expertise and the advanced technological infrastructure foster an environment where creativity and quality are paramount. This results in educational content that is not only effective and engaging but also commercially appealing.
- **Rapid Response to Market Needs** The HTU^x operational model allows for quick adaptation to changing market demands and educational trends. This agility ensures that the content remains relevant, up-to-date, and in line with industry and academic standards.
- **Sustainable Business Model** The combination of IP commercialization and operational efficiency underpins a sustainable business model. This model supports the ongoing creation of high-quality educational content, ensuring that HTU^x continues to be a leader in innovative online education.

The innovative legal framework and IP management strategy of HTU^x are foundational to its operational model. This comprehensive legal structure not only facilitates smooth collaboration and content creation but also ensures that all parties are fairly compensated and that their contributions are recognized. It sets the stage for sustainable growth, allowing HTU^x to thrive in the competitive landscape of online education while fostering a creative and collaborative environment for educational content development.

5.8 Pathway Development Steps

The pathways were developed using five concrete design stages (see Fig. 3): preparation, design, development and production, implementation, and evaluation.

The *Preparation Stage* consists of gathering all the information needed and analyzing the learners' needs and learning content, and finding the appropriate mix of learning activities and technical solutions to create effective and engaging courses. The *Design Stage* is essential to ensure course effectiveness and learners' motivation and participation. The design stage consists of the following steps:

- Determine the course objectives and learning outcomes.
- Define the order (sequence) in which the objectives should be achieved.
- Select instructional, media, evaluation, and delivery strategy.

Fig. 3 Steps for development of HTU^x pathways

In the *Development & Production Stage*, the subject-matter expert works with the technical team to write the content, collect the required knowledge and information of the course, develop media and interactive components, produce the course content in the digital format, then conduct the course content review. They will then digitize, produce, and advertise for it. The *Implementation Stage* entails the implementation of the content developed on the platform, a review of the course design by experts, and starting the marketing campaign.

Finally in the *Evaluation Stage*, some research is conducted to collect the required information and feedback from all relevant parties to identify the enhancement, improvement, and finalization of the content, courses design, and the learning experience.

6 HTU^x: Implementation and Results

The platform, HTU^x, was devised to host the online courses produced by the Digital Learning Center at HTU (DLC@HTU) in the form of Accelerated Pathways which are customized programs built on a stackable-course methodology, each pathway consisting of a number of Minimal Viable Stackable Courses (MVSC). Each MVSC is a self-standing course containing the learning content and its own assessment, which allows the learners to choose multiple stackable courses from different pathways or register in the pre-designed pathways. The main page of HTU^x https://htux.org/ is shown in Fig. 4.

The HTU^x platform is a fully customizable online learning management system developed to provide a user-friendly environment for learners to get access to educational and practical material with the ability to create a professional community of practice with the other learners and experts in the offered pathways (Fig. 5).

Accelerated learning pathways are offered on HTU^x under different areas of practice, namely, engineering, computing, and business technology fields aiming to equip the learners with the knowledge and skills to master and practice a specific technical field and promote their opportunities to find jobs. These identified areas will enhance the development of pathways to include more specialized content for each topic, initiating technical tracks that further promote the learner's experience in multiple employability fields, whereby the learners will undertake the courses on instructor-led modality.

In a span of two years, HTU was able to record, produce, and upload ten pathways, as shown in Fig. 6 and listed in Table 2. These recorded pathways include 396 stackable courses and 2,189 uploaded videos, as shown in Fig. 7.

Fig. 4 Main page of the HTU^x platform

Fig. 5 Features of the HTU^x platform

To better understand the pathways model, the structure of three pathways (Mobile RobotiX, Programming from Zero to Hero, and Data Analytics and Business Intelligence Technology) are shown in Table 3. The listed stackable courses are integrated to form a pathway.

The student can register for the Pathway or register for a single course, thus creating their own pathway by selecting several courses from different pathways.

To further describe the Pathway structure, Table 4 shows the breakdown elements for the *Mobile RobotiX Pathway*, which comprises five courses, each composed of its own blocks. *Dynamics System Modeling* is composed of five blocks; *Sensors and Actuators* is composed of four blocks; *Control Systems* is composed of six blocks; *Unmanned Ground Vehicles* is composed of three blocks; and *Unmanned Aerial Vehicles* is composed of three blocks.

The learners can register for the courses, view a variety of learning resources and activities, and interact with the learners and the courses' instructors through a virtual learning environment. Each online course will consist of three main elements:

Fig. 6 Icons for the areas of practice of the HTU^x platform

Table 2 Ten Accelerated Learning Pathways of the HTU^x platform

Engineering	IT	Business
Mobile RobotiX	Programming from zero to hero	Data analytics and business intelligence technology
Electrical circuits	Full stack web development	A step in the world of freelancing
Clinical engineering professional	Python power-up: mastering coding with replit's magic	
Handy Matlab		
Rapid prototyping and adv. manufacturing technology		

Table 3 Selected pathways and their stackable courses

Mobile RobotiX	Programming from zero to hero	Data analytics and business intelligence technology
Dynamic system modeling	Setup development environment	Essential principles
Sensors and actuators	Basic coding procedural paradigm	Management
Control systems	Object oriented programming paradigm	Business analysis
Unmanned ground vehicles (UGV)	Event driven paradigm	Data science
Unmanned aerial vehicles (UAV)	Road to oracle	Artificial intelligence
		Leadership

 396 Stackable Courses 10 Pathways 2189 Videos 12,672 Minutes

Fig. 7 Pathways and courses of the HTU^x platform

Table 4 Mobile RobotiX pathway showing its five stackable courses and associated blocks for each course

Dynamics system modelling	Sensors and actuators	Control systems	Unmanned ground vehicles (UGV)	Unmanned aerial vehicles (UAV)
Math review	Transducers	Control basics	Vehicle block dynamics	Quadcopter modelling and simulation I
Basic dynamics	Signal conditioning	PID controller	Solid works	Quadcopter modelling and simulation II
Vehicle dynamics	DC motors	Control simulation	Build UGV	Build UAV
Transfer functions and state-space	Drive circuits	Embedded systems		
Simulation modelling		Arduino board		
		PID implementation		

- **Learning** The course provides alternative means of access to multimedia content in formats that meet the needs of diverse learners (instructional videos, interactive videos, reading materials, Interactive images, learning cards, summary presentations, audio files, and infographics…)
- **Collaboration and Engagement** To maintain the communication channel between learners and learners and instructors the course will cover different levels of engagement through multiple tasks and activities: Learner–Learner, Learner–Instructor, and Learner–Content.
- **Application** The application component will provide the learners with an opportunity to apply and experiment with what they learned during the learning weeks. Examples: assignment submission, capstone project, portfolio, quiz, check for understanding activities.

6.1 *Strategic Partnerships and Expansions, Collaborating for Wider Impact*

- HTU's partnership with the Al Ghurair Foundation (AGF) and their NOMU regional program marked a significant milestone. As an anchor partner, AGF joined forces for a pivotal role aiming to enhance career outcomes for 2000 Jordanian learners to be enrolled in HTU^x's pathways during the next couple of years.

- Another proud collaboration was with Injaz Al-Arab, the JA regional office (Junior Achievement organization). As their Edtech partner, HTU tailored a custom version of the HTU^x platform to their needs, and white-labeled it to create the "Injaz Academy". This platform now efficiently operates for 1 million students across their 18 member nations in the Arab world, with ambitions to reach 1.25 million students next year.
- HTU's unrivaled proven track record and expertise in instructional design and educational content design and creation led to partnerships with several institutions, including HELP Logistics. We provided them with customized courses, embodying the HTU^x stackable course ethos and pedagogy.

6.2 The Evolution of HTUx Premium Edtech Services and Customizing Edtech Solutions

- The success of the content and platform paved the way for HTU^x Premium Edtech Services. These bespoke services catered to the nuanced needs of our partners, offering them a slice of HTU^x's innovative educational approach.
- From designing tailor-made courses to adapting our platform for different institutional requirements, the premium services covered a broad spectrum. This included white-labeling our platform, showcasing its adaptability and user-friendly nature.

7 Conclusions

The HE system worldwide is on the verge of disruption because online learning has become a strong competitor to the traditional brick-and-mortar universities. As in other industries, DX is taking a hold of the educational system. Higher education is arguably the last system to resist disruptions to its comfortable structure, but there is no denying that change is happening and will accelerate fast. In this work, we have shown the importance of launching educational online platforms, specialized in engineering and IT, with Arabic content. Our target audience is the 100 million Arab youth.

We have highlighted the vision and traced the stages and steps that gave birth to the online learning platform, HTU^x. We have shown the uniqueness of this platform model, as it focuses on engineering and IT themes, talks to the Arab youth, builds pathways based on stackable courses, personalizes the learning experience, and provides required market and industry skills.

Although HTU^x is a newly born learning platform, it is already up-and-running with ten pathways with 396 stackable courses and 2189 uploaded videos totaling 12,672 recorded minutes. The stackable courses have become more than just educational content; they are keys to unlocking potential and paving new career paths for students across the Arab world.

Not only has HTU^x grown in terms of content and partnerships but it has also evolved into a leader of innovation in digital learning and education. Our partnerships, particularly with the Al Ghurair Foundation and Injaz Al-Arab, are not just collaborations but alliances in transforming education and empowering the youth. The reach of the Injaz Academy and its potential to expand further is a testament to the scalability and impact of our platform.

References

1. UNESCO (2017) Education for sustainable development goals: learning objectives. United Nations Educational, Scientific and Cultural Organization, France. https://unesdoc.unesco.org/ark:/48223/pf0000247444
2. Makoe M (2021) Future of higher education 2050, Concept Note. UNESCO publication. https://www.iesalc.unesco.org/eng/wp-content/uploads/2021/03/Makoe-EN.pdf
3. Mittal P (n.d.) Future of higher education. UNESCO. https://www.iesalc.unesco.org/eng/wp-content/uploads/2021/03/Mittal-EN.pdf
4. Digital learning futures (n.d.) Futures of education, UNESCO. https://www.unesco.org/en/futures-education/digital-learning-futures
5. Zitter L (2022) Digital transformation of higher education in 2024 (+Examples). Whatfix. https://whatfix.com/blog/digital-transformation-in-higher-education/. Accessed 25 Jan 2024
6. McCarthy AM, Maor D, McConney A, Cavanaugh C (2023) Digital transformation in education: critical components for leaders of system change. Social Sci Humanities 8(1):100479. https://doi.org/10.1016/j.ssaho.2023.100479
7. OECD (2016) Innovating education and educating for innovation: the power of digital technologies and skills. Center Educ Res Innov. https://doi.org/10.1787/9789264265097-en
8. Ashmel M, Hashim M, Tlemsani I, Matthews R (2022) Higher education strategy in digital transformation. Educ Inform Technol 27:3171–3195. https://doi.org/10.1007/s10639-021-10739-1
9. Rodríguez-Abitia G, Bribiesca-Correa G (2021) Assessing digital transformation in universities. Future Internet 13(2). https://doi.org/10.3390/fi13020052
10. Alenezi M (2021) Deep dive into digital transformation in higher education institutions. Edu Sci 11(12). https://doi.org/10.3390/educsci11120770
11. Marks A, AL-Ali M, Atassi R et al (2020) Digital transformation in higher education: a framework for maturity assessment. Internat J Adv Comput Sci Applic 11(12):504–513. https://www.researchgate.net/publication/348364436
12. Ruipérez-Valiente JA, Staubitz T, Jenner M et al (2022) Large scale analytics of global and regional MOOC providers: differences in learners' demographics, preferences, and perceptions. Comput Educ 180:104426. https://doi.org/10.1016/j.compedu.2021.104426

Digitalization, Communication, and Identity Formation: Directions for Research in Higher Education

Doha Saleh Almutawaa

Abstract Nowadays, digitalization is evident in various aspects of our daily lives, ranging from individual activities to business operations. The subject of digitalization has gained particular prominence in the marketing discipline, whereby digital marketing plays a central role in creating brand awareness, communicating brand image, and connecting with the target audience, as well as acquiring and retaining customers. The aim of this chapter is to address the importance of social media marketing in facilitating communication and identity formation for both business institutions and their relevant stakeholders. It particularly explores this phenomenon in the context of higher education institutions. With the prominence of active social media users, higher education institutions worldwide are heavily reliant on social media platforms to connect and communicate with various stakeholders, such as alumni, employees, collaborators, policymakers, and current and prospective students. Akin to any other business, the main objective of higher education institutions within the private sector is to increase revenue and maximize profit. As such, while higher education institutions seek to deliver value to their stakeholders, in return, stakeholders serve as both consumers and co-creators of value. In particular, students, both prospective and current, represent the core stakeholder group of higher education institutions, and therefore, are the focus of this chapter. This chapter highlights the moderating role of social media marketing in facilitating brand–consumer communication and identity formation within higher education institutions. Relatedly, the chapter also emphasizes the importance of exploring differences in cross-cultural adaptation of social media marketing in higher education institutions, with emphasis on Middle Eastern Arab countries. The chapter also offers directions relating to social media marketing for higher education institutions for Middle Eastern Arab countries.

D.S. Almutawaa (✉)
Australian University, West Mishref, Kuwait City, Kuwait
e-mail: d.almutawaa@au.edu.kw

Keywords Digitalization · Communication · Identity · Higher education · Social media · Marketing · Consumer behavior · Middle East

1 Introduction

Digital. What crossed your mind when you first read the word 'Digital'? Is it technology? Connectivity? The internet? Automated processes? Robotics? Social media platforms? Or something else? While the word 'Digital' has different associations for different people, one thing in common is that digital is the opposite of traditional; the former relies on online processes conducted through the use of electronic technology and the latter involves processes that employ offline efforts. Taking interpersonal communication as an example, individuals can rely on digital forms of communication, which involve e-mails, instant messages, video chats, social media etc. or traditional forms of communication, including posted letters, telephone calls, face-to-face interaction etc.

Technological advancements have led businesses to shift from traditional to technological methods of operation, and higher education institutions (HEIs) have equally been influenced by this revolution [1]. From the marketing-discipline perspective, the methods of consumer marketing are evolving due to the increased popularity and usage of social media platforms [2]. According to recent statistics, 59% of the global population were active social media users in January 2023 [3]. Some of the popular social media platforms include Facebook, Twitter, Snapchat, TikTok, and LinkedIn. The increasing numbers of active social media users resulted in changes relating to how HEIs communicate with their relevant stakeholders [2], such as alumni, employees, collaborators, policymakers, and current and prospective students. In fact, universities' social media has become more important than their official website [1]. Additionally, "with social media rising in popularity and frequency across university campuses and among college students in particular, it is becoming more pertinent to understand the kinds of impacts universities are having with their social media efforts" [2] (p. 2) in relation to the attraction, retention, and engagement of students.

This chapter addresses the importance of social media marketing in facilitating brand (university)–consumer (student) communication and identity formation within the context of HEIs. "Before social media technologies, the communication between companies and their stakeholders was mostly a one-way communication, where the company had total control over brand communication" [4] (p. 308). In other words, communication in companies used to be centralized. Nowadays, however, while HEIs seek to deliver value to their stakeholders, in return, stakeholders serve as both consumers and co-creators of value. Strong relationships with stakeholders enable HEIs to manage market-place challenges and utilize them as opportunities to create change [5]. Within the private sector, the main objective of HEIs is to increase revenue in the short-term, thereby leading to maximized profit in the long-term. As indirect and direct consumers, students (both prospective and current) represent the core stakeholder group, and main source of revenue, for HEIs. It is therefore important for HEIs to employ a student-centric approach and ensure fulfillment of student satisfaction to achieve success and development.

The proceeding sections of this chapter are structured as follows. Initially, the role of social media marketing in moderating brand (university)–consumer (student) communication and identity formation within HEIs is discussed. Then, the importance of cross-cultural adaptation of social media marketing (SMM) in HEIs, with emphasis on Middle Eastern Arab countries, is outlined. Thereafter, research directions related to SMM of HEIs for Middle Eastern Arab countries are presented. Finally, concluding thoughts are offered.

2 Social Media Marketing, Communication, and Identity Formation Within Higher Education Institutions

What does the term "identity" mean? In simple terms, identity refers to one's self-perception or view of oneself. Individuals convey their public identities through self-presentations and impression management [6], which involve highlighting certain aspects of themselves and hiding others. Identities are dynamic and multiple; for example, the same individual identifies as an employee, a student, a spouse, and a parent, with these identities shifting depending on the context and changing circumstances. It is argued that two main aspects constitute our identity formation, namely, the tangible (i.e., objects) and the intangible (i.e., other people, experiences, places etc.) [7]. We already know that tangible objects are the most visible aspects of our identities. This includes everything we possess and wear on our bodies. However, although intangible experiences also constitute our identity formation, there is limited research conducted in this area. All types of services are examples of intangible experiences, such as leisure activities, traveling and tourism, and education. "Literature exploring the social media use by higher education institutions is very scarce despite the fact that its use has become an integral part of the strategy for promotion and recruitment of new students of nearly all colleges and universities" [4] (p. 310). This section focuses on the intangible experiences offered by HEIs, and the role of SMM in facilitating university–student communication and identity formation.

Traditionally, communication between a business and its stakeholders occurred in a unidirectional manner, whereby the business fully controls what and how messages are communicated [4]. Examples include newspaper advertisements, flyers, billboard campaigns, outdoor banners etc. Stakeholders were passive recipients of marketing communications. Nowadays, however, digitalization enables stakeholders to play an active role in engaging with a company and contribute to its identity formation. Examples of digital marketing include SMM, mobile advertisements, e-mail advertisements etc. With the increased popularity of social media, shared content can easily go viral. Social media platforms, and particularly SMM, create a connection between the brand and consumer. Social media marketing can be defined as "introducing a brand's products, services, and a brand itself in a sincere manner and providing a variety of services to consumers who engage in social media activities as means of marketing communications" [8] (p. 31). Marketing techniques through social media occur over various social media platforms, such as Facebook, Twitter, Snapchat, TikTok, and LinkedIn. Each platform is intended to help businesses reach a certain target audience.

On the other hand, social media engagement (SME) refers to the consumer side in participating in a business's marketing communication process. It "involves the process from consuming the content through interacting with the interface to cognitively immersed in the content and then participation behaviour such as discussion and sharing of content" [9] (p. 2). Examples of SME include, liking, commenting, reposting, sharing, and content creating. The ultimate goal of businesses is to establish mutual benefits with stakeholders via their social media platforms; businesses aim to deliver value via SMM and expect stakeholders to serve as co-creators of value via SME.

Globalization has led to the rapid growth of businesses and increased worldwide competition [1]. Like other sectors, the education sector is effected by this growth [1]. When it comes to HEIs, it is worth mentioning that universities represent business institutions that offer various products (tangible) and services (intangible) to diverse stakeholders under their brand (university) name [10]. Apart from the transfer of knowledge, other intangible offerings within student life include student activities, clubs, associations, athletics, and employment. Akin to any other business, HEIs, particularly within the private sector, seek to generate revenues to enable their long-term survival and development. This requires the adoption of a customer-centric approach by focusing on addressing the needs and wants of their core stakeholder group, namely, the students (both prospective and current) [5].

There is evidence that HEIs are increasingly relying on social media platforms to communicate with their target audience [11]. Some of the leading management institutions worldwide, such as Harvard Business School and MIT-Sloan, utilize social media to ccommunicate with their various stakeholders (i.e., potential and current students, employees, collaborators etc.) [11]. Moreover, although the main objective of HEIs is to educate and develop students, other crucial activities include engaging internal (i.e., students, faculty, staff) and external (i.e., alumni, collaborators) stakeholders [2]. As students are the core stakeholder group, their SME with educational institutions (e.g., positive or negative electronic word of mouth) contributes to the formation of institutional identity.

The following question arises, how do students contribute to the formation of the institutional identity of HEIs? Students serve as both consumers and co-creators of a university's identity [12–14]. That is, while students' association with a certain university contributes to their individual identity formations, in return, students' SME with a university also supports the development of its identity. For instance, not all university students are perceived in the same way, but rather, the university's ranking, reputation and associated brand image plays a crucial role in differentiating one student from another. A positive or negative university identity is transferable to, and has a direct impact on, the identities of its associated students. Similarly, students have the power to shape a university's identity through SME. This includes engaging through a university's social media platforms or acting as a brand ambassador by generating content relating to a university via their own social media accounts. Figure 1 summarizes the moderating effect of SMM on brand–consumer communication and identity formation from a university–student perspective.

Figure 1 demonstrates how SMM moderates the relationship between the brand (university) and the consumer (student). It shows that SMM facilitates a reciprocal (or two-way) relationship between the university and the student. More specifically, SMM enables value creation on behalf of the university and value co-creation from the student side. Mutual benefits are reaped in this reciprocal relationship; students benefit from receiving value (i.e., information about a university's academic ranking, student life, faculty expertise), and in return, satisfied students engage with a university's social media accounts (i.e., by liking, commenting on, reposting, sharing content) and become active creators of value by generating content for the university on their own accounts (e.g., testimonials such as YouTube vlogs and Instagram posts/podcasts). The university can use student social-media-generated content and engagement to keep up to date with students'

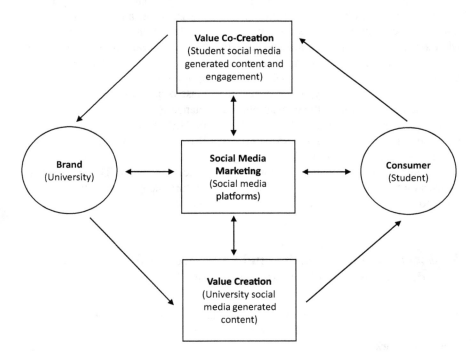

Fig. 1 The moderating effect of SMM on brand–consumer communication and identity formation: university–student perspective

changing desires, and accordingly, further develop value. Therefore, the communication and identity formation between a university and students represents a cyclical process.

In light of the above, it is clear that there is an interdependent relationship between institutional and individual identity constructions, and a crucial role is played by social media in enabling this reciprocal relationship. Yet, there is limited research that addresses the impact of social media on students' university choice [15] and "the process through which consumers increase the connection between the brand and the self through SMM activities has yet to be examined" [8] (p. 2). Students perceive university choice as a fundamental decision that requires months/years of preparation and an extensive information search to minimize any financial, social, and psychological risks [15]. Furthermore, "we often hear students and alumni report how their educations have profoundly impacted their lives and their identities" [10].

Accordingly, marketing managers must understand the decision-making process of students to be able to deploy effective marketing strategies at different stages [10]. Figure 2 applies a student perspective to the consumer decision-making process.

Figure 2 shows the different stages that students pass through in their university decision-making process. Three distinct phases are elaborated, namely, (1) pre-purchase phase, (2) purchase phase, and (3) post-purchase phase. The pre-purchase phase occurs before a consumption choice is made, and it includes problem/need recognition (i.e., what is my need as a student?), information search (i.e., what sources of information are available for me?), and evaluation of alternatives (i.e., what factors matter the most in my consumption choice?). This is followed by the purchase phase, which is when a consumption choice is made based on the pre-purchase phase. Finally, the post-purchase phase occurs after consumption and results in an evaluation of the consumption experience.

This section demonstrates the importance for HEIs to understand how to (1) attract prospective students via SMM efforts, (2) retain current students via SMM efforts, and (3) encourage students' engagement with their social media accounts and content creation on their personal social media accounts. The next section focuses on the need for HEIs to consider cross-cultural adaptation in the SMM, in order to effectively achieve the aforementioned points.

3 Social Media Marketing and Cross-Cultural Adaptation in Higher Education Institutions

The success of HEIs happens by market research not by luck. Globally, it is evident that the majority of HEIs have one or more social media accounts; however, the marketing strategies deployed should not be generalized. Merely having a social media presence does not guarantee the success of HEIs or students'

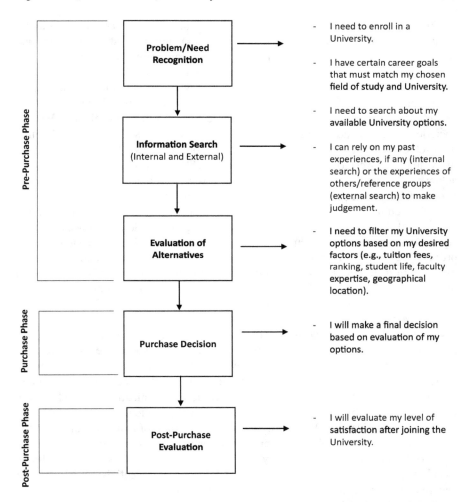

Fig. 2 The consumer decision-making process: student perspective. *Source* based on John Dewey's five-stage consumer decision-making process and author's own appropriation

engagement and content generation. The key to long-term survival is to establish a strong university–student relationship through social media [2]. If not utilized efficiently and effectively, SMM can have a negative effect on HEIs. Although social media operates on low cost, it nonetheless costs institutions money to employ people who operate their platforms [15]. Also, if not managed correctly, institutions' social media accounts can be detrimental to their reputation [15]. To help minimize any potential challenges, it is essential that HEIs familiarize themselves with the local culture in which they reside. Otherwise, how can HEIs communicate with their students without understanding their mentalities and rationale behind their behavior? Relatedly, how can HEIs influence student behavior?

From a consumer behavior perspective, culture factors, including "images, ideas (including beliefs, values, and stereotypes), norms, tasks, practices, and social interactions" [16] (p. 421) largely dictate how individuals perceive themselves, perceive others, and construct their identities [17]. The independent self is more socially dominant in Western societies, whereby individuals tend to prefer a separateness self-concept and define themselves in terms of "who am I?" as an individual [18, 19]. Conversely, the interdependent self is prevalent in Eastern societies, whereby individuals emphasize a connectedness self-concept and define themselves in terms of "who are we?" as a group [18, 19]. For example, while individuals in Western societies tend to define themselves in terms of personal achievements and assets, those situated in Eastern societies rely on others (i.e. friends, family members, co-workers etc.) in forming parts of their identities.

Often, cultural adaptation is widely discussed in terms of selling tangible objects [20, 21]; however, its importance in selling intangible experiences requires equal attention. Culture ought to have an impact on a student's decision-making process [22], including how they perceive and react to SMM strategies deployed by HEIs in different countries. Culture also impacts an individual's social media preferences. For example, Greek students and teachers have a preference towards using Facebook, YouTube, and Skype [23], while Instagram and Twitter are preferred in Kuwait [24, 25].

Accordingly, it is crucial for HEIs to consider the most-effective social media platform to utilize for marketing purposes (i.e., 'which' social media platform is most suitable?) in a given cultural context. In addition, HEIs must also carefully decide the content to be communicated (i.e. 'what' will be communicated?) and the method of communication (i.e. 'how' will the communication be conducted?). In other words, what type of information/content do students seek to encourage them to join a university? What is their preferred method of communication? What influences their choice of one university over another? It is important to note that answers to these questions not only vary across cultures but also within cultures based on each country [1]. For example, individuals in collectivist cultures might generally prefer advertisements that portray other people's opinions and perceive them to be more-credible sources of information. However, even within collectivist cultures, there ought to be contextual preferences in terms of both content and method of communication.

Furthermore, as students are globally dispersed, HEI's that seek to attract international students need to understand their culture. Although cross-cultural research has rapidly increased, Middle Eastern countries are significantly underrepresented [26]. Numerous studies have explored the impact of SMM in HEIs on students in non-Arab contexts [2, 4, 5, 9, 27]. On the other hand, only a few studies have been conducted in Middle Eastern Arab countries [28–30]. Islam is the dominant religion in Middle Eastern countries. Their socio-cultural environment can be classified as conservative in terms of traditional and social norms and expectations, religious practices, and gender constructions. Taking this into consideration, for example, global apparel brands such as H&M, Zara, Tommy Hilfiger, and Dolce and Gabbana are changing their fashion designs to conform with female-modesty expectations in Islamic countries [21]. Similarly, social media marketing communications within HEIs in such countries must be carefully crafted.

Three critical cultural considerations related to managing social media accounts of HEIs in Middle Eastern countries are: textual, visual, and informative content. Textual and visual content are interrelated and concern sensitive issues. Textual content relates to the written text while visual content relates to the graphics used in SMM of HEIs. Textual content that is positively perceived in one culture might have a negative impact on a university's reputation in another culture. Similarly, visual content must be created with the consideration of cultural factors, such as social values, gender, and religion. How students are portrayed varies across cultures. For example, even if a university follows a British or American system of education, it is illegal to disseminate campaigns that promote or feature the LGBT community in Middle Eastern Islamic countries. For example, female students wearing traditional and religious attire (e.g., long and loose clothing, sometimes accompanied with a hijab/head cover) are often represented in universities located in Middle Eastern countries. Also, physical proximity between males and females is avoided in campaigns for religious reasons. Similarly, what interests males versus females varies in terms of student life. Conversely, informative content relates to the dissemination of information. In collectivist Middle Eastern countries, it is common that group identities are emphasized in SMM of HEIs. For example, student achievements often include the opinions of family members and the role of classmates/group members. The sense of community and belonging is often promoted by HEIs.

This section addresses the importance of cross-cultural adaptation in the SMM of HEIs in Middle Eastern countries. The next section outlines several research directions to guide future researchers.

4 Social Media Marketing and Research Directions for Higher Education Institution

As discussed in the previous sections, although research relating to SMM in HEIs is a timely topic, it still appears to be in its infancy stage, particularly in relation to Middle Eastern Arab countries. Below are various research avenues that could potentially offer a fruitful contribution to existing literature that bridges between higher education and SMM in the Middle East.

First, while students are a core stakeholder group for universities, it is important to recognize the impact of other stakeholders that play a significant role in establishing a university's identity. For example, faculty and their related academic backgrounds and fields of expertise dictate the quality of education offered by a university. Alumni also have a powerful voice in influencing prospective students' decision-making process. Accordingly, future research can explore the experiences of internal and external stakeholder groups in relation to their preferred social media platforms and desired content marketing. This includes who is deemed the most credible source of information to communicate with each stakeholder group. For example, prospective students might trust alumni experiences while their family members appreciate a message from the president addressing the university's academic ranking and global reputation. Understanding the social media interests of various stakeholders enables HEIs to effectively target each stakeholder group, thereby leading to lowering costs of trial-and-error marketing. It also enables universities to establish a competitive advantage.

Second, although SMM is a widely employed marketing method across cultures and HEIs, it is imperative to conduct cross-cultural studies to examine the role of culture in influencing social media usage, including the specific platforms used for different purposes, desired types of social media content, and related responsiveness by stakeholders from different countries. This would enable HEI's to reach a wider and more diverse stakeholder group. Attracting stakeholders from different cultures will enable HEI's to gain international recognition.

Third, merely having social media accounts does not guarantee students' access to and engagement with HEIs. Instead, it is imperative to explore the motive behind students' engagement (i.e., what encourages students to positively engage with a university's social media platforms? What encourages students to generate content for a university?) in order to facilitate action. For example, providing incentives for students' engagement and content generation might encourage positive electronic word of mouth. Students can be a more credible and reliable source of information when they share their experiences. This allows marketing managers to boost a university's awareness among other students.

Fourth, social media enables HEIs to view metrics related to engagement, which, in return, serve as key performance indicators. However, metrics alone are quantitative data that simply provide statistics in terms of number of followers, likes, comments, shares etc. Therefore, it would be beneficial to conduct research that analyzes what each type of engagement means to students. In other words, what is the difference between a like, share, and/or comment? Also, what triggers the different types of reactions?

Fifth, given the increased competition between HEIs and the changing needs of students, it would be erroneous to assume that the most popular or preferred social media platforms in any given culture/country are fixed. A long-term study will provide insight into the changing social media trends over time and across generations within a specific context.

Sixth, in addition to conducting primary research relating to stakeholders' experiences with social media platforms, observing and comparing the social media marketing strategies deployed by HEIs on a national and international level can provide significant secondary data to leverage.

Seventh, rather than assuming generalizations, it is intriguing to explore the expectations and experiences of students who identify with different educational levels and demographics. For example, there ought to be differences between the interests of undergraduate versus postgraduate students, employed versus unemployed students, married versus unmarried students, male versus female students, disabled students etc. Each subgroup needs to be targeted with unique marketing strategies.

This section proposes several research avenues to develop knowledge in the area of SMM within HEIs in Middle Eastern Arab countries. Notably, however, the same can be applied to other cultural contexts to provide more in-depth research about SMM within HEIs worldwide.

5 Conclusions

This chapter addresses the role of digital marketing, particularly SMM, as being one of the most effective brand–consumer communication methods. It further emphasizes that SMM facilitates the interrelationship between institutional and individual identity formations. The chapter focuses on the fact that HEIs represent businesses and, within the private sector, such institutions operate with the aim of achieving profit. Students are the core stakeholder group for HEIs, and a university's profitability is highly contingent upon student satisfaction.

Due to the popularity and accessibility of social media platforms, especially among university students, various universities are creating social media accounts and relying on SMM to communicate with students. In fact, universities' social media has become more popular than their websites. A university's social media platforms can be the first point of contact which determines if students are willing to explore further by visiting the website. Social media platforms have the capability of offering a comprehensive overview of a university's environment via different communication methods (e.g., text, videos, live sessions, testimonials etc.). This can play a major role in students' decision-making process of either joining or remaining enrolled in a university.

Drawing onto the above, it is imperative for HEIs to understand (1) how to reach and attract prospective students, (2) how to retain current students, and (3) how to engage prospective and current students. To successfully achieve this, universities must deploy SMM strategies that are student centric, with cross-cultural adaptation being an important factor to consider. The chapter highlights the dearth in literature related to higher education SMM strategies in Middle Eastern Arab countries. Several research avenues are proposed to develop knowledge in the aforementioned area of study. In addition, future researchers can explore the impact of SMM on stakeholders' experiences and responsiveness in other institutional contexts (e.g., banks, hospitals etc.).

Acknowledgments I dedicate this chapter to my beloved grandfather, Hussain Makki Al-Juma. A noble man who led by example, by showing the pervasive impact of giving without return. Baba Hussain, your philanthropic life and selflessness taught me that it takes one person to transform the lives of many. I aspire to be that person for generations of students. Baba Hussain, you left us but remain eternally alive within and through us.

References

1. Salem O (2020) Social media marketing in higher education institutions. SEA–Practical Applic Sci 8(23):191–196. https://www.researchgate.net/publication/342633146_Social_Media_Marketing_in_Higher_Education_Institutions
2. Clark M, Fine MB, Scheuer CL (2017) Relationship quality in higher education marketing: the role of social media engagement. J Market Higher Educ 27(1):40–58. https://doi.org/10.1080/08841241.2016.1269036
3. Dixon SJ (2023) Number of social media users worldwide from 2017 to 2027. Statista. https://www.statista.com/statistics/278414/number-of-worldwide-social-network-users/
4. Vukić M, Vukić M (2019) The impact of social media on the recruitment of students by higher education institution. In: Tourism international scientific conference Vrnjačka Banja-TISC 4(1):307–326. https://www.tisc.rs/proceedings/index.php/hitmc/article/view/258
5. John SP, De Villiers R (2022) Factors affecting the success of marketing in higher education: a relationship marketing perspective. J Market Higher Educ 1–20. https://doi.org/10.1080/08841241.2022.2116741
6. Markus H, Wurf E (1987) The dynamic self-concept: a social psychological perspective. Ann Rev Psychol 38(1):299–337. https://doi.org/10.1146/annurev.ps.38.020187.001503
7. Belk RW (1988) Possessions and the extended self. J Consum Res 15(2):139–168. https://www.jstor.org/stable/2489522
8. Panigyrakis G, Panopoulos A, Koronaki E (2020) All we have is words: applying rhetoric to examine how social media marketing activities strengthen the connection between the brand and the self. Internat J Advert 39(5):699–718. https://doi.org/10.1080/02650487.2019.1663029
9. Song BL, Lee KL, Liew CY, Subramaniam M (2023) The role of social media engagement in building relationship quality and brand performance in higher education marketing. Int J Educ Manage 37(2):417–430. https://doi.org/10.1108/IJEM-08-2022-0315
10. McAlexander JH, Koenig HF, Schouten JW (2006) Building relationships of brand community in higher education: a strategic framework for university advancement. Int J Educ Adv 6:107–118. https://doi.org/10.1057/palgrave.ijea.2150015
11. Chauhan K, Pillai A (2013) Role of content strategy in social media brand communities: a case of higher education institutes in India. J Product Brand Manage 22(1):40–51. https://doi.org/10.1108/10610421311298687
12. Dollinger M, Lodge J, Coates H (2018) Co-creation in higher education: towards a conceptual model. J Market Higher Educ 28(2):210–231. https://doi.org/10.1080/08841241.2018.1466756
13. Fiaz M, Ikram A, Basma A et al (2019) Role of social media marketing activities in creating university brand image and reputation: the mediating role of customer value co-creation behavior. In: 8th International conference on information and communication technologies (ICICT), Karachi, Pakistan. https://doi.org/10.1109/ICICT47744.2019.9001927
14. Smørvik KK, Vespestad MK (2020) Bridging marketing and higher education: resource integration, co-creation and student learning. J Market Higher Educ 30(2):256–270. https://doi.org/10.1080/08841241.2020.1728465
15. Fishbein A (2022) The influence of institutional social media and college students' choice, Masters theses. Eastern Illinois University, 4922. https://thekeep.eiu.edu/theses/4922
16. Markus HR, Kitayama S (2010) Cultures and selves: a cycle of mutual constitution. Perspect Psychol Sci 5(4):420–430. https://doi.org/10.1177/1745691610375557
17. Gjersoe NL, Newman GE, Chituc V, Hood B (2014) Individualism and the extended-self: cross-cultural differences in the valuation of authentic objects. PLoS ONE 9(3):e90787. https://doi.org/10.1371/journal.pone.0090787
18. Wang R, Hempton B, Dugan JP, Komives SR (2008) Cultural differences: why do Asians avoid extreme responses? Surv Pract 1(3). https://doi.org/10.29115/SP-2008-0011

19. Almutawaa DS, Nuttall P, Mamali E, Al-Mutawa FS, AlJuma DHM (2023) Paradoxes of (un) veiling and the extended self: the experiences of Arab-Muslim women in Kuwait. J Islamic Market 15(1). https://doi.org/10.1108/JIMA-07-2022-0196
20. Saeed M, Azmi IAG (2018) A cross-cultural comparison of Muslim religious commitment on US brand switching behaviour. Int J Islamic Market Brand 3(2):144–161. https://doi.org/10.1504/IJIMB.2018.094086
21. Sandıkcı Ö (2020) Religion and the marketplace: constructing the 'new' Muslim consumer. Religion 48(3):453–473. https://doi.org/10.1080/0048721X.2018.1482612
22. Shavitt S, Barnes AJ (2019) Cross-cultural consumer psychology. Consum Psychol Rev 2(1):70–84. https://doi.org/10.1002/arcp.1047
23. Lampropoulos G, Siakas K, Makkonen P, Siakas E (2021) A 10-year longitudinal study of social media use in education. Int J Technol Educ 4(3):373–398. https://doi.org/10.46328/ijte.123
24. Alsalem F (2021) Kuwait: from "Hollywood of the Gulf" to social media diwaniyas. In: Richter C, Kozman C (eds) Arab media systems. Global Communications. https://doi.org/10.11647/OBP.0238.10
25. AlAli AM, Nazar H (2023) Preferences, perception and impact of using dental social media in Kuwait. Kuwait Medic J 55(2):151–158. https://www.researchgate.net/publication/350107993
26. O'Connell C (2020) How FOMO (Fear of Missing Out), the smartphone, and social media may be affecting university students in the Middle East. North Am J Psychol 22(1). https://www.researchgate.net/publication/339721452
27. Zhu Y (2019) Social media engagement and Chinese international student recruitment: understanding how UK HEIs use Weibo and WeChat. J Market Higher Educ 29(2):173–190. https://doi.org/10.1080/08841241.2019.1633003
28. Ahmad SZ, Hussain M (2017) An investigation of the factors determining student destination choice for higher education in the United Arab Emirates. Stud Higher Educ 42(7):1324–1343. https://doi.org/10.1080/03075079.2015.1099622
29. Mahboub RM (2018) The impact of social media usage on performance of the banking sector in Middle East and North Africa countries. Int J Econ Bus Admin 6(3):3–20. https://doi.org/10.35808/ijeba/162
30. Al Husseiny F, Youness H (2023) Exploring the role of social media marketing in students' decision to select universities in Lebanon: a proposed emerging framework. QScience Connect 2023(1). https://doi.org/10.5339/connect.2023.spt.4

Digital Transformation of Higher Education in Jordan: Does Production of Academic Material in Electronic Form Optimize Learning Outcomes?

Nathir M. Obeidat, Mohammed A. Khasawneh, Nael H. Thaher, and Rida A. Shibli

Abstract Towards the end of the twentieth century, academic systems around the world were witnessing significant transformations, in various forms, all of which were primarily aimed at the betterment of academic outcomes as the world, in the twenty-first century, was inherently delving into the 4th industrial revolution. Many academic establishments had already determined that their outcomes were anything but sufficiently market worthy due to the outdated educational routines that had been in place throughout the preceding couple of centuries. The industrial sector found itself having to retool college graduates so that their skills were more suitable for the various industrial establishments that were accepting them for jobs and careers. In the meantime, and as part of the underlying professional development objectives, various industrial organizations were already hosting entities of their own which they often referred to as "universities". However, none of these entities had the infrastructures or the type of organized course offerings that were characteristic of proper academic institutions. These "industrial university entities" endeavored to promote professional development to suit the underlying needs of the organization. Some of these endeavors were accomplished by means of technically relevant short courses and training workshops. Such activities often involved specialist lecturers in addition to materials circulated to the audiences in

---

N.M. Obeidat · M.A. Khasawneh · N.H. Thaher · R.A. Shibli (✉)
The University of Jordan, Amman 11942, Jordan
e-mail: r.shibli@ju.edu.jo

N.M. Obeidat
e-mail: nobeidat@ju.edu.jo

N.M. Obeidat
e-mail: president@ju.edu.jo

M.A. Khasawneh
e-mail: m.khasawneh@ju.edu.jo

N.H. Thaher
e-mail: n.thaher@ju.edu.jo

© The Author(s), under exclusive license to Springer Nature Switzerland AG 2024
A. Badran et al. (eds.), *Higher Education in the Arab World*,
https://doi.org/10.1007/978-3-031-70779-7_13

paper and/or electronic formats. Other industrial organizations that were involved in employee preparedness and professional development efforts often produced their training programs solely in electronic digital formats which were delivered to the constituents in person or by mail at the request of the seekers. A few other organizations had in place digital material that was rendered in interactive formats, which often also involved automated smart-assessment activities of the participants. In the aftermath of the COVID-19 pandemic, most of the academic institutions the world over found themselves having to prepare to counter similar situations in the future and were compelled to re-orient their offered academic courses to handle similar emergency circumstances. In the process, academic institutions had to leverage ongoing forms of technology to deliver their academic courses by adapting one or more of the prevailing known forms of course delivery paradigm, which included online learning, hybrid and in-person modes of learning, or any viable mix thereof. As educational systems throughout the world had been witnessing transformations of various forms, all of which were aimed towards the amelioration and betterment of the academic delivery systems, there was inherently an imminent need for automation of the different processes and protocols involved. Commensurate with that, processes were already in place to reorient the various academic outcomes to better suit the needs of the industrial sector to cope with the fourth industrial revolution. Going hand in hand with the COVID-19 transformations that impacted, in one way or another, academic systems in the Arab world, there is now a stark need for these systems to move one step further and put together an academic process that can be delivered entirely and reliably in an automated digital format. Hoping that we can leverage what has been achieved thus far in Jordan, and possibly other places around the Arab world, there is now the need to study how best academic systems in Arab countries can transform in such a way that all evolving technology-based, artificial intelligence (AI)-leveraging industries will be better served by steering the academic processes into more student-centric outcome-based endeavors, where the remaining question will always be: "How far can digitization/automation of academic courses carry a successful academic transformation into the smart digital age?" This chapter will attempt to answer the question by recommending ways and approaches that can help the academic sectors in Jordan, and those around the Arab world, implement the most appropriate digital transformations that would serve to enhance the fourth industrial revolution.

Keywords E-learning · Educational technology · Learning management systems · Online learning · Hybrid learning · Digital academic production · Digital transformation in higher education · Adaptive e-learning

1 Introduction

Academic institutions of higher learning have existed for well over a millennium. Since their inception, they have always been destinations for knowledge seekers throughout the world. These institutions delivered knowledge by means of the standard classroom setting wherein students would be seated in a regular pattern and would face a blackboard upon which a lecturer would write the lecture material [1]. Some considerable time has passed with this paradigm of knowledge delivery in place. It was not until the latter part of the twentieth century that the classroom setting started to take on more adaptable forms than just the standard seating arrangements and the podia lecturers used to address their students. From the late 1970s to the early 1980s, there was a revolution in the way in which classrooms within institutions of higher education were arranged and equipped for administering the educational material [2]. A tendency evolved whereby a lecturer in the classroom started to see a gradual increase in educational equipment that was meant to assist teachers to deliver the teaching material to the students. To that end, the educational system that evolved at academic institutions of higher learning the world over was one that grew into what later became known as a lecture-based setting wherein a learner would come to the classroom to attend a lecture and obtain the teaching material from the classroom blackboard [3]. A lecturer would deliver the material to be taught in a one-way approach, meaning that the students involved would have little, if any, or no input during the process. Such a paradigm of education dragged on for decades and was about the only existing regime for delivering new knowledge in the classroom.

In the mid to late 1990s, a new way of teaching had started to emerge—one that put students center stage in the process and required student involvement in the educational lifecycle. From there on, a trend evolved whereby the student became a primary player in the academic delivery process of higher education regimes. In this, the student was expected to play an active role in putting together a new educational regime in the higher education system. Hence, it became evident that the students had, to a great extent, to rely on their ability to self-learn, in conjunction with what an educator was doing on his/her part. The new academic teaching paradigm was classified as *outcome-based* learning, or an *outcome-based academic system* [4].

Under *outcome-based* learning, a student's learning experience was expected to fulfil certain measurable outcomes. Hence, academic institutions operating under such regimes had to tally some key performance indicators relating to the course to ensure that appropriate standards were being reached by both instructors and learners [4]. Therefore, it was not totally unfamiliar to find various academic institutions defining sets of learning outcomes of their own, some addressing university and college requirements, others addressing the learning outcomes set by the students' college majors. In so doing, a student was not allowed to graduate solely based on the underlying lecture-based conventional grading system. Instead, in the final graduation months, students were required to build portfolios showing evidence that they had, indeed, achieved the targeted learning outcomes of the academic cycle. This evidence would include activities in which the constituents participated, reports, assignments, projects, exam outcomes, etc. and would, necessarily, require each graduating student to be interviewed by an especially qualified committee that could make its own assessments of student achievements. Figure 1 reflects the various paradigms that academic institutions worldwide would primarily have subscribed to in the process of administrating their educational lifecycles.

As the outcome-based model began to diverge from the classical norm of learning in higher education and evolve into an identity of its own, academic institutions started to be classified in yet another way! This time classification focused on the primary functions of these academic institutions, resulting in institutions that were classified as *research institutions, teaching-only institutions, and academic institutions in general (or conventional academic institutions exhibiting a well-rounded academic functionality)* [5]. In research institutions, the primary focus was on research with a less-pronounced focus on teaching. Teaching-only institutions, on the other hand, had teaching and delivery of taught material at center stage with little or no obvious focus on research. Conventional academic institutions, meanwhile, kept a balance of focus across the worlds of research, teaching, and community service. Such classifications, though, did not preclude research institutions from being involved in teaching and delivering material in the classroom. By the same token, teaching-only institutions were not precluded from any involvement in research. The large bulk of the remaining institutions fell under the classification of conventional academic institutions [5].

Under the realm of research institutions, the primary focus of institutional operations happens to be research. Although institutions classified as such are usually those institutions that rank highly amongst other global institutions, it is notable that such institutions were often historically classified as traditional or conventional academic institutions that had to digress from their primary status into one that would put them front and center on the world stage by leveraging the

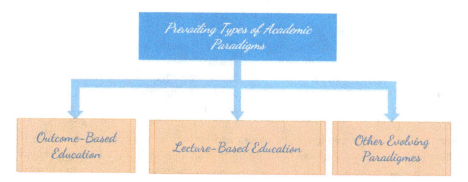

Fig. 1 Various academic paradigms adopted by academic institutions

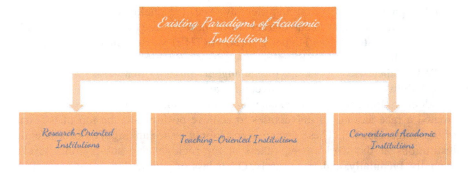

Fig. 2 Existing classifications of academic institutions

outstanding capabilities and commitments of their research cadres. While the primary focus here happens to be research, other academic activities, such as teaching and extension services, would still be in place but outside the primary focus of operation. Institutions defined by these criteria often receive the lion's share from funding opportunities made available by governments, military establishments, and the underlying industrial sectors.

However, institutions that are classified as teaching-only institutions often base the bulk of their operations on academic instruction, and have fewer chances of acquiring funding resources; any successful funding, once it happens, depends in large part on the individual efforts of the faculty members involved. In this case, the institutions involved have to leverage other means and mechanisms to satisfy the professional development and promotion requirements of the faculty body. Even so, in such institutions one would still tend to see a limited number of faculty members involved in research activities in a manner that would ultimately fulfill their professional ambitions.

Nonetheless, the bulk of academic education across the world takes place in universities that are best classified under the category of (conventional) academic institutions. Most of these conventional institutions still, as the academic traditions dictate, maintain a balance between teaching and involvement in research and community service [6]. Universities classified as such usually receive accreditation and ranking opportunities that fall below or well below those of institutions that are classified as research institutions. Figure 2 is intended to reflect the various classifications of academic institutions in existence today.

2 Development of Global Rankings

From the middle to the latter part of the 8th decade of the nineteenth century, organizations that gave ranking levels to academic institutions started to emerge. This was driven by a need to classify academic institutions pursuant to their social impact across the communities involved, the quality of the outcomes of their constituents, and their market worthiness. These organizations include entities such as the Times Higher Education (THE) World University Rankings, Quacquarelli Symond (QS), and the Academic Ranking of World Institutions (ARWU; otherwise known as the Shanghai ranking) that have assumed the responsibility of ranking world universities against one another in well-structured and defined approaches. The existence of these ranking entities has inherently created a race among all universities to achieve positions at the top of the lists of these agencies [7]. These agencies commonly issue ranking lists of academic institutions at the world level, others at the regional and sub-regional levels, annually, biennially, and/or quarterly. Other less-official ranking entities, including the US News and World Report in the United States of America, rank academic institutions worldwide monthly. These various ranking agencies usually leverage data solicited from Thompson Reuters and QS to compile the rankings of academic institutions.

The ranking agencies commonly leverage data such as faculty-to-student ratios, employers' satisfaction surveys, international visibility, research collaborations with other academic institutions, citation indices of the institution, international recruitments of faculty, percentage of international students in the student body of an institution, etc. The impact of each of these criteria varies from one ranking agency to another according to the amount of weight allocated to each criterion by the agency, but the final rankings tend to be similar. Ongoing ranking activities by these agencies have inherently driven academic institutions to bolster academic and research efforts in their pursuits to achieve top-of-the-list ranking statuses [8]. This has affected institutional efforts to improve student outcomes and their market worthiness and has had the effect of stimulating the research endeavors by faculty. Together with activities that would ensure quality of the delivered product, published rankings have prompted most academic institutions to enter a race towards acquiring international accreditation of their individual colleges and faculties.

The race to acquire engineering accreditation, for instance, has produced accreditation bodies like ABET in the United States, the Canadian Engineering Accreditation Board (CEAB), the Japan Accreditation Board for Engineering Education (JABEE), the Accreditation Board for Engineering Education of Korea (ABEEK), the European Network for Accreditation of Engineering Education (ENAEE), and the Chinese Engineering Education Accreditation Association (CEEAA), amongst others. Accreditations for other disciplines also exist around the world. These include URAC, ACBSP, ACPE, ACCM, SAF and NRPA/COA, amongst others, which accredit educational programs in Pharmacy, Business, Medicine, and Agriculture and Bio-Resources. Such accreditation bodies have, as their focus, a means of identifying key learning outcomes and ways to gauge achievement levels under the various degree programs being assessed.

3 Outcome-Based Systems

Outcome-based degree programs, and academic programs in general, have adapted and made themselves amenable to learning-outcome measurements and assessments. Moreover, outcome-based systems have, associated with the learning outcomes, certain other requirements as well. These involve building and bolstering the soft skills of the recipients (Fig. 3), such as global awareness, leadership training, presentation and writing skills, effective communication, critical thinking and problem solving, and team and group work spirits, among other possible skill sets. Furthermore, outcome-based routines of education have commonly placed the student at the center of the learning process, meaning that students are expected to be primary stakeholders in fulfilling the requirements of an educational lifecycle [9]. To do that, during the educational lifecycle, additional learning material should be made available and accessible to the recipients, on top of the effort/s that the constituents themselves are expected to expend in the process. This would readily require storage of huge amounts of the learning materials in various forms (papers, books, handouts, audio, video, interactive components, etc.) across the diversity of curricular programs an academic entity usually has to offer. This would inherently require spacious repository facilities together with the associated implementation and maintenance costs, i.e., storage capabilities that can be accessed with swiftness, effectiveness, high reliability, and ease.

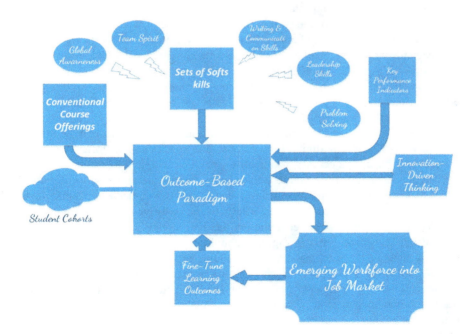

Fig. 3 Illustrative diagram of the functionality of an outcome-based system with the associated learning outcomes impacting its operation

Under an outcome-based paradigm, certain skill sets are coupled to the educational regime in addition to key performance indicators, which are commensurate with the stated learning outcomes of the program offered. The list of soft skills that constitute a primary component of an outcome-based program commonly includes global awareness, team spirit, leadership traits, and essential communication skills, in addition to critical thinking and problem solving, as outlined earlier—elements that are integral to a successful outcome-based system. Furthermore, innovation-driven thinking under such a paradigm becomes of paramount importance to the success of the program/s involved. Once the workforce is about ready to delve into the job market, the success of the program can readily be gauged against the degree of fulfilment of the underlying program outcomes, as judged by various assessment means including, but not confined to, an exit interview committee; this readily leaves room for fine-tuning of the existing learning outcomes to align them more closely with current job-market needs. Figure 3 illustrates how an outcome-based academic regime functions under evolving academic models.

4 Evolution into the Digital Academic Paradigm; *Digital Transformation of a Higher Education System*

The enormous progress in computer technologies together with the rapid evolution of communication and internet technologies in the latter part of the twentieth century to the early part of the twenty-first century have provided opportunities for institutions to store unlimited amounts of data in various forms relatively cheaply. The versatility of these technologies has made the data amenable to quick and reliable access by diverse beneficiaries from anywhere, everywhere and around the clock. In this, the industrial and private sectors were pioneers in exploiting the emerging technological progress. Various industrial-sector entities began to leverage these capabilities to enhance the professional development of their constituents, making the required technical materials available in digital format, be they on CDs, DVDs or simply in digital formats hosted in spacious repositories, and made them accessible across network protocols to specified recipients.

The increasing use of digital technologies by the private sector for professional development and continuing education endeavors has enticed academic institutions to follow suit. From the late 1980s to the early years of the twenty-first century, some professors at academic entities had already been reaping the benefits of the known progress in digital technologies. In fact, they were exploiting them by making the teaching material available to students following classroom lectures, allowing those students who may have missed a class or needed a recap of the material to gain a better grasp of the subject matter, each at their own pace. Several universities were also exploiting the availability of such material and using it in training courses, with the consent of the professors involved, or for purposes of continuing education [10].

COVID-19 was a turning point for both the academic and the industrial sectors to leverage the strength of digital and information and communication technologies (ICTs) to enable people to work from home during periods of lockdown. Almost every institution around the world had to retool their digital infrastructures to accommodate the increasing utilization of the internet to allow workers/students to access their workplaces (academic institutions) via their tablets, desktops and/ or laptops. The ever-rising needs of academic institutions and their constituents to achieve and improve the learning outcomes of the recipients came hand in hand with COVID-19 lockdown requirements to shore up existing digital infrastructures with more capabilities and support [11]. It turns out that ongoing enhancements to the educational infrastructure leveraging ICT and computer gear greatly benefitted those students and industrial workers (under training and/or professional development exercises) who were innately slow learners, as they were able to access the relevant learning/training materials as many times as they needed to reach the required levels of understanding and comprehension of the subject matter.

This was a turning point for institutions that were seeking a digital transformation of their operations, be they educational or otherwise. Digital transformation of operations that academic institutions were undertaking went hand in hand with the inherent requirements of accreditation bodies that were seeking the fulfilment of learning objectives as precursors for granting institutions the accreditation types/levels they were pursuing. Thus, the leverage of the digital era had already been ongoing at many industrial establishments in delivering training courses and in fulfilling the professional development goals of their employees [10]. Indeed, many industrial organizations including, but not limited to, CISCO, Oracle, Microsoft, Intel, to mention just a few, had already been exploiting digital transformation in developing and presenting, to trainees, course materials with some embedded level of intelligence in the fully digital assessment exercises that were taking place.

5 Digital Transformation for Holistic Development

In the academic paradigms that exist today, one would tend to find institutions that leverage what may be dubbed "adaptive e-learning" or "iterative e-learning" to bring about versatility in the learning processes of students who exhibit varying degrees of ability to achieve an adequate level of understanding of a particular subject. Under this paradigm of learning, a poorly performing student, in terms of their level of comprehension, has the means to access relevant educational repositories as many times as it takes to achieve the required level of knowledge, because the system adapts to the learning style of the recipient by presenting additional modules in the learning process to bridge existing deficiencies exhibited by the student. Mainstream students, under this regime, are expected to satisfy the course requirements within a preset amount of time, as determined by the designers of the educational lifecycle. Meanwhile, highly accomplished, fast learners are allowed to jump to more advanced modules earlier than all others, thereby rewarding their high achievements. Such a regime of learning is readily capable of tackling learners who come with diverse learning backgrounds and learning capabilities.

With the growing needs for versatility and adaptability of learning regimes, digital systems that lend themselves well to the learning process have evolved around new developments in the fields of ICT, upscale digital systems, recognition of learners' needs, modularity, and the ongoing updates in the curricular lifecycles and course syllabi [10]. Such developments have found themselves quite fitting within the realms of fields like AI and machine learning. While ongoing developments in the areas of medicine, robotics, space exploration, industrial assemblies, and aeronautics, amongst others, are all benefitting from the rapid evolution in AI and the Internet of Things (IoT), much is still to be done in the areas of education and learning. It is projected that many of the limitations that faced the fields of education, learning and teaching can now easily be overcome when AI and machine learning are deployed to improve these processes [12]. Many leading institutions have indeed started exploiting these technologies to improve their academic course offerings and the relevant learning outcomes. This is because academic regimes can be built around AI-exploiting foundations that can be designed to create the much-needed coupling between what an academic module can provide and the types of outcomes that need to be fulfilled in the process. Customization of the educational regime can therefore be achieved with much ease and higher efficiency.

Academic institutions that seek an innovative work ethos find themselves more motivated to invest heavily towards improving the overall academic processes they must deliver. As the world delves deeper into the 4th industrial revolution, academic institutions that aspire to be more involved in producing a suitably trained workforce find themselves more enticed to leverage the latest technological developments to improve on their academic offerings and make the outputs of the academic process, the graduates, better geared for job-market needs [13]. This would create just about the right coupling between market needs and the academic institutions that deliver well-trained workforces. In the process, close collaborations and partnerships across the various sectors involved are in order.

In the aftermath of COVID-19, various academic institutions, globally, geared up to accommodate in-person education as well as courses that must be delivered on-line or a mix thereof. These institutions established the governance needed to cater for such changes. Infrastructural upgrades were inherently at the center of the processes involved. Putting the curricular offerings in digital formats had been the center of focus for many academic institutions that were seeking much needed (twenty-first century) suitable transformations of their operations. These institutions readily realized that putting a functional digital infrastructure in place would make available the necessary foundations that every other process could leverage for the much-sought high levels of performance [10]. Moreover, these institutions also came to realize that a well-tuned digital infrastructure would also cater for greater adaptation and scalability, as needed. It turns out that with the implementation of AI-leveraging technologies various course offerings can readily be tuned to achieve the pre-set learning outcomes and, by the same token, learning outcomes on a particular course offering can also suggest which subject matters in a particular knowledge domain must be available to the constituents.

6 Leveraging Digital Transformation for Development

Just about three decades ago, a great many countries around the world sustained a huge digital divide, which was a big obstacle to these countries' developmental efforts. As a result, the educational systems (K-12) and the academic systems of higher education were at a big disadvantage. However, over the years, many countries have managed to retool themselves and steer themselves in ways that ultimately helped them to be on the paths of faster development. The models of India, Ireland and China serve as recent examples of success in the ways of bridging the digital rift for some of these countries. Countries in the Arab world, to varying degrees of achievement, were no different in such pursuits. Certain countries like Egypt, Jordan, United Arab Emirates and Lebanon led efforts towards entering the club of countries that had benefitted from the ongoing progress in the digital age. In these countries the private sectors took the lead in this direction with many firms successfully transcending the boundaries and becoming prosperous multinational firms. Apart from these examples, countries in the Arab world had a long history of not achieving much success in industrializing their economies in ways that would contribute significantly to the gross domestic products (GDPs) of those countries. Real industrial breakthroughs have not materialized with most industries that exist today oriented towards lightweight and remodeled industries that have little bearing on the economic lifecycles and, consequently, the GDPs of the nations involved [14].

Over the years, the industrial and academic sectors in the Arab world have sat at a big disconnect; the essential ingredient that inherently lies at the core of success for any real industrial evolution has been missing. The academic sector has been busy developing curricular offerings that, for the most part, mimic those in the Western world and bear little relevance to any local industrial evolution. Furthermore, research endeavors have had little bearing on the local and regional industrial sectors, as much of the ongoing research efforts by faculty either follow global mainstream research that is often not geared towards solving local industrial problems or, in some cases, serves the menial narrow objectives of the researchers towards fulfilling their immediate requirements for academic promotion. Evidently, the Arab world has never been successful in tying loose ends together and capturing the main aspect of what was taking place on the industrial world stage. The lack of real industrial progress, with industries that can have a measurable impact on the economic lifecycle/s, and the lack of the necessary competencies industry-wise have all contributed to an industrial stalemate which has separated the Arab world from the rest of the industrial world.

To achieve a successful industrial evolution in the Arab world, academic institutions ought to lead the way and be able to present success stories of their own creation to convince the industrial community and inspire confidence around what an academic sector can offer. Academic institutions are at a point where they must invest in terms of recruiting faculty who have had significant industrial experience and, in addition, must encourage the research community to get involved in industrial training abroad where they can leverage their years of sabbaticals at global industrial establishments. Furthermore, academic institutions must give more focus to the recruitment of faculty who possess industrial expertise or those that have served as post-doctoral fellows and were involved in solving problems at industrial firms around the world.

Since the Arab world has already foregone a myriad of invaluable chances to capture windows of opportunity to develop and progress, this part of the world must now not miss out on the possibility of harnessing existing capabilities of renovating and reinventing its higher education regimes. Higher education in the Arab world has lagged for decades and requires drastic measures to benefit from the astronomical progress that has taken place in recent decades in the areas of ICT and computer technologies [11]. In fact, by drawing on the revamping of digital infrastructures that took place in the wake of COVID-19, many of the Arab universities are already in positions that would allow them to successfully lead major transitions from the classical ways of higher-education delivery to one that can serve the new paradigm of student-centric outcome-based learning. Digital transformation in higher education around the Arab world should now be looked upon as a necessity if higher education is to see light at the end of the tunnel. With a higher education sector that is decoupled, to a large degree, from local, regional, and international industrial developments, digital transformation should only be about bridging the rifts between the two sectors: *industrial and academic* [11]. This can be done by employing digital links across the two sectors in ways that would identify the current industrial needs and connect them to relevant academic processes while at the same time leveraging the enablers the AI world has provided for use by the various interested communities.

7 Key Elements for Successful Transformation

Digital transformation of higher education is a process that implies delivering the classically presented classroom educational materials at institutions of higher learning in digitally recorded formats, which include typed materials, video-recorded lectures, learning-aid materials, and simulation and animation software packages, together with the necessary digital interactivity that would support an effective presentation of the course to the intended recipients [14]. To get started along a path leading to such a transformation, academic institutions need to benefit from what was developed by faculty members during the era of COVID-19 while also working with the faculty to optimize their achievements in the delivery of the academic courses, as it would be anticipated that these institutions would be willing to shore up their digital infrastructure beyond what was made available during the pandemic era. Figure 4 illustrates the various components critical for the successful transformation of an academic paradigm into a fully operational digital academic model. Any digital transformation of the academic delivery system would require these key elements for it to succeed and, thereby, be functional:

1. Professional presentation of the academic material involved.
2. Securely administered state-of-the-art assessment methodologies.
3. Educational aid material in addition to well-equipped classrooms.
4. Professionally capable digital hardware.
5. Professionally capable networking infrastructure.
6. Possession of medium- to high-end personal computers/tablets by students and faculty.
7. A repository of learning material for each course offering, with automated links to access the types of materials sought.
8. Intelligent search capabilities to access the learning material in question, likely leveraging the capabilities of artificial intelligence and machine learning.

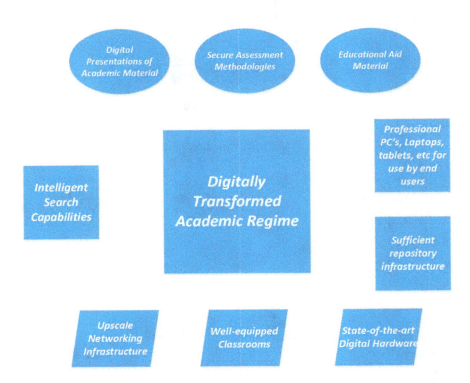

Fig. 4 The key elements for the successful digital transformation of an academic system

Although the capabilities/enablers 6–8 (above) are available to a large extent at a good number of Arab universities, there are varying deficiencies in the provision of enabler 2, and many universities still suffer dire shortages of these technological enablers, which are critical for digital transformation. It is assumed that surrounding local and regional industries would also be benefitting from the digital transformation of universities, particularly from those implementing outcome-based education, as industries would become direct stakeholders in the process by identifying which learning outcomes are more appropriate for their immediate operations, thereby enabling academic institutions to tune their program offerings to fulfill industrial needs. This would occur to a greater extent with universities that heavily leverage AI in designing the academic course offerings (enablers 7, 8). Once a good running order is established, the successful delivery of a digitally transformed academic system hinges upon various components, as illustrated in Fig. 5.

To achieve industrial–academic collaboration in the manner prescribed here, the process would require appropriate governance to be put in place by both players. Attaining the necessary level of governance is expected to facilitate any forms of collaboration and would ensure that any proprietary information is protected and safeguarded in accordance with the traditions of such collaboration [15]. This would also pave the way for mutual collaboration to take place when continuing education is part of the process. Academic institutions, as such, would be kept in

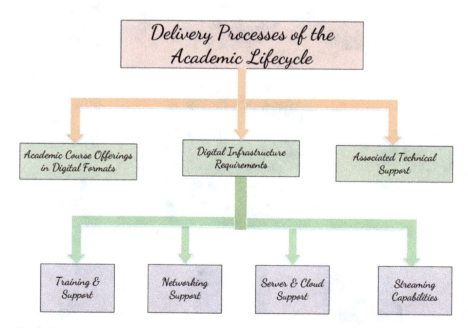

Fig. 5 The various components for the successful delivery of a digitally transformed academic system

the loop regarding any changes in industrial requirements dealing with the academic outcomes for the workplace. Furthermore, as academic institutions cater for such outcomes, they would also have prepared the grounds that fulfill the accreditation requirements of various global accreditation bodies. This is inherently fulfilled because the means of measurement and assessment of many of the outcomes and activities rendered by the constituents are readily available to the accrediting bodies/agencies.

8 Implications of the Present

Digital transformation of the academic process would lend itself fairly well to ensuring quality of delivery and administration of that process because it would have all the necessary embedded capabilities to gauge the quality of delivery and would inherently meter the amount of usage by any individual/establishment benefiting from the process [16]. Many academic institutions would, thereby, rest assured that any administered academic process can be measured and monitored as needed, and where needed. Such a feature would also be of great importance to academic institutions, particularly to those that aspire to commercialize suitable parts of the academic process by producing learning/training-aid materials that can be used by other academic institutions, independent learners, and for online/offline industrial training of participating industrial establishments. Digital transformation of the academic process is, in essence, a process that would offer flexibility and adaptability in preparing and packaging the learning materials in question in different formats, as needed, in the subject matters of interest to the recipients.

The ability of academic institutions to commit to a process of digital transformation would readily reflect the keenness of these institutions to deliver the educational materials to their recipients in an effective and lasting manner, while at the same time warranting that the educational material is of with high quality and impact. The required effort of leading such a transformation is worth the costs shouldered as it would put in place a mechanism that can contribute to the amelioration of the outputs in the various systems of higher education. Digital transformation in higher education, indeed, hinges upon the nucleus to all of this: the academic entities involved in the process. It all starts out with the cumulative efforts of the specific faculty body to deliver much of the academic material in a professionally most-effective manner. This must, however, rest upon the institutions fostering an appropriate infrastructure that would offer the accessibility levels required by the intended public. Such an infrastructure, together with the digital material, must continuously undergo upgrades and updates commensurate with the prevailing technological evolutions.

Various enablers exist and are direly needed to bolster the efforts involved in the process of digital transformation. Firstly, the upgrades and updates to the digital infrastructural technologies, both hardware and software, that took place during the pandemic can readily serve as a common platform upon which everything else can fit. Secondly, the efforts fostered by the faculty body at the academic entities involved constitute a solid lever upon which many things can hinge. Thirdly, all technical support staff and the associated training programs to get everyone onboard are features that are deemed indispensable. Fourthly, good server technologies and server farms, together with networking gear that makes everything bottleneck-free, all shored up by the capacity of the client/s to access and derive the fullest benefit from what is provided, are a cornerstone in the success of any evolving digital transformation process. Finally, the upkeep of all these components in good running order is something that needs to be in place for all other components to run in unison.

9 Conclusions

An acceleration of the process of digital transformation can be fostered in various ways. For one, academic institutions that are well off financially can equip lecture rooms, or subsets thereof, with technological gear that can help educators to record their lecture efforts in real time and then make digitally recorded material, in video and typed text, available to the constituents on-demand, a process that would serve digital transformation but would take little effort on the part of the faculty. This would require baseline technological equipment that can leverage varying degrees of automation and the deployment of artificial intelligence in storing recorded data and rendering it when needed. This, in essence, would resemble to a certain extent the types of technology fostered by YouTube services, which are made readily available to the public, on-demand or in real-time, and would inherently build the data repositories much needed by the academic institutions. Acceleration of a digital transformation regime would also hinge upon the readiness and commitment of the faculty body to make their teaching material available to the constituents in typed texts and in PowerPoint-like digital presentation formats. The typed and/or handwritten texts of the material to be taught would, in essence, constitute a centerpiece in the success of the overall system, as shown by the illustrative schematics in Figs. 6 and 7.

A successful digitally transformed system of higher education would require incorporating other support corners into the overall paradigm. For instance, in many cases a successful digitally transformed system would also cater for some form of automation and provide an effective account of recent trends in artificial intelligence. This would set a solid foundation for faculty members to serve their constituents better by offering automated tutoring sessions, with little administrative and/or financial burdens on the serving institutions. It would also cater for elements like adaptive e-learning, as well as automated and secure student-assessment links to be accessed reliably, effectively, and securely. However, the way in which an institution approaches digital transformation is highly dependent on its culture, values, and strategic priorities [10].

Digital Transformation of Higher Education in Jordan ...

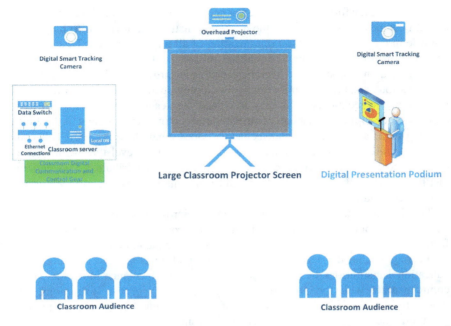

Fig. 6 One possible manifestation of a classroom environment as it contributes to the success of the overall system after digital transformation

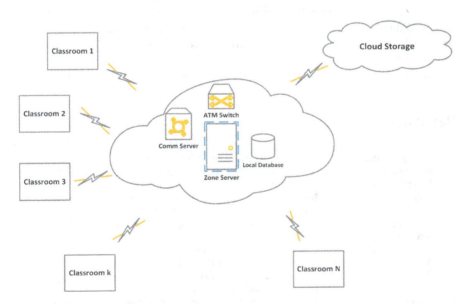

Fig. 7 A diagram illustrating the connectivity of several well-equipped classrooms in ways that would contribute to the success of the overall system after digital transformation

As digital transformation of higher education reaches certain degrees of maturity, it becomes incumbent upon the academic institutions involved to play a central role in the amelioration and optimization of all ongoing efforts. This may lead academic institutions to adopt continuous professional training of faculty and all supporting administrative and technical cadres in order to build the capabilities of the various constituents and effectively employ such transformation to the full benefits of the recipients. This may also lead the academic institutions to foster higher-degree diplomas that can contribute to accepting newer trends in the educational systems at the primary and secondary educational phases (K-12). This could also, inherently, lead to programs at the master's degree level that would end up creating professional workforces that can effectively contribute to systemizing, instilling and localizing the overall digital transformation process into various educational communities.

The instatement of digital transformation across academic systems in the Arab world would lend itself well to rigorous processes of monitoring and performance assessment; assessment, that is, of both educators and recipients. This would require that the academic functionality, both teaching and learning, of the educational institutions be closely coupled to key performance indicators (KPIs) commensurate with the prevailing strategic planning of the institutions. This inherently could affect the fine details of the educational processes in question, including course syllabi, the achievement percentage/s, the associated assessment processes, the fulfilment of the course requirements, fulfilment of the major and university learning outcomes, in addition to measuring the degree/s of proficiency levied under each course offering. Towards the end, each program offering, departmental performance, and college compliance with the institutional strategic planning would lend itself fairly well to a process that can award grades that reflect the degree of adherence to institutional overall strategic fulfilment. This, in essence, would offer an indigenous capability of measuring the level and efficiency of performance for each individual operating under the umbrella of the institution.

References

1. Jeremy N, Bailenson NY et al (2008) The use of immersive virtual reality in the learning sciences: digital transformations of teachers, students, and social context. J Learn Sci 17(1):102–141. https://doi.org/10.1080/10508400701793141
2. Cohen AM, Kisker CB (2009) The shaping of American higher education: emergence and growth of the contemporary system, 2nd edn. Wiley (ISBN: 978-0-470-48006-9). https://www.academia.edu/80144400/The_shaping_of_american_higher_education_Emergence_and_growth_of_the_contemporary_system
3. Rogers PL (2001) Traditions to transformations: the forced evolution of higher education. Assoc Advance Comput Educ 9(1):47–60. https://www.learntechlib.org/primary/p/17775/
4. Ross V (2012) From transformative outcome based education to blended learning. Futures 44(2):148–157. https://doi.org/10.1016/j.futures.2011.09.007
5. Taylor J (2007) The teaching:research nexus: a model for institutional management. Higher Educ 54:867–884. https://doi.org/10.1007/s10734-006-9029-1

6. Jongbloed B, Enders J, Salerno C (2008) Higher education and its communities: interconnections, interdependencies and a research agenda. Higher Educ 56:303–324. https://doi.org/10.1007/s10734-008-9128-2
7. Brankovic J, Ringel L, Werron T (2018) How rankings produce competition: the case of global university rankings. Z Soziol 47(4):270–288. https://doi.org/10.1515/zfsoz-2018-0118
8. Benner M (2020) Becoming world class: what it means and what it does. In: Rider S et al (eds) World class universities. Evaluating education: normative systems and institutional practices. Springer, Singapore. https://doi.org/10.1007/978-981-15-7598-3_3
9. Bremner N, Sakata N, Cameron L (2022) The outcomes of learner-centred pedagogy: a systematic review. Int J Educ Devel 94:102649. https://doi.org/10.1016/j.ijedudev.2022.102649
10. Obeidat NM, Shibli RA, Khasawne MA, Thaher NH (2023) Distance education: is it any longer a paradigm of choice? The University of Jordan; a case study. In: Badran A et al (eds) Higher education in the Arab world: e-learning and distance education. Springer, Cham. https://doi.org/10.1007/978-3-031-33568-6_5
11. Thaher NH, Shibli RA, Khasawneh MA et al (2022) Leveraging research and innovation for the post COVID-19 era: lessons learned and future plans towards economic resilience. In: Badran A et al (eds) Higher education in the Arab world: new priorities in the post COVID-19 era. Springer, Cham. https://doi.org/10.1007/978-3-031-07539-1_8
12. Kamalov F, Santandreu CD, Gurrib I (2023) New era of artificial intelligence in education: towards a sustainable multifaceted revolution. Sustainability 15(16):12451. https://doi.org/10.3390/su151612451
13. Khasawneh MA, Thaher NH, Shibli RA et al AM (2022) Bolstering economic growth in the Arab region through commercialization of research outcomes. In: Badran A et al (eds) Higher education in the Arab World: research and development. Springer, Cham. https://doi.org/10.1007/978-3-030-80122-9_8
14. Gkrimpizi T, Peristeras V, Magnisalis I (2023) Classification of barriers to digital transformation in higher education institutions: systematic literature review. Educ Sci 13(7):746. https://doi.org/10.3390/educsci13070746
15. Shibli RA, Khasawneh MA, Thaher NH (2020) Innovation as a principle in university governance: a holistic approach for Arab universities. In: Badran A et al (eds) Higher education in the Arab world: government and governance. Springer International Publishing AG. https://doi.org/10.1007/978-3-030-58153-4_5
16. Røe Y, Wojniusz S, Bjerke AH (2022) The digital transformation of higher education teaching: four pedagogical prescriptions to move active learning pedagogy forward. Frontiers Educ 6:784701. https://doi.org/10.3389/feduc.2021.784701

The Growth of Knowledge and Its Link to Digital Transformation in Arab Institutes of Higher Education

Hamdan Al Fazari

Abstract The growth of knowledge, and the consequential need to record and store ever-increasing amounts of data, plays a fundamental role in the promotion of digital transformation, and this is particularly true of its use in Arab higher education institutions (HEIs). Moreover, as a result of the increasing role played by technology in everyday life and, in particular, in shaping the way HEIs across the world adapt to new opportunities and challenges, the growth of knowledge drives the innovations that enable large-scale digital transformation. This, of course, leads to changing expectations of education in a knowledge-based society. Universities and other providers of education must now expect to undergo substantial digital transformation if they are to fulfill the demands of today's generation of students and the fully digitized world in which they will be living (Jassim and Rahman in Turkish J Comput Math Educ 12(13):5152–516, 2021, [1]). In the twenty-first century, a knowledge-based workforce, and economic and technological competition between countries, will become increasingly important. This will require the preparation of generations of learners who can master the skills of the modern technologies that are obligatory for development, and for the dissemination of culture between the generations. In this regard, today, digital transformation based on the growth of knowledge has become a cornerstone of higher education; for example, without digital transformation education could not have continued during the COVID-19 pandemic. Furthermore, digitalization and technology have made online learning, distance education and blended learning accessible to people of different backgrounds from all over the world. The accelerated pace of the growth of knowledge in society, and developments in information technology and the digital economy, have created a digital environment which provides the essential skills and competencies for achieving professional success. In the case of HEIs, this success is related to: teaching and learning, research and

H. Al Fazari (✉)
Sohar University, Sohar, Oman
e-mail: HFazari@su.edu.om

innovation, industry and community engagement, HEIs' global profiles and their institutional effectiveness.

Keywords Knowledge growth · Digital transformation · Innovation · Knowledge-based society · Digital journey

1 Introduction

I would like to highlight the importance of the growth of knowledge and its link to digital transformation in Arab HEIs which is, in turn, linked to the globalized and digitalized era. It is beyond dispute that the growth of knowledge, or knowledge evolution, and digital transformation have become significant parts of the higher education landscape and are worth extensive investigation and discussion. Growth of knowledge and the following digital transformation will, in the twenty-first century, inevitably continue to greatly affect all aspects of human life, in terms of knowledge, technology and education, as well as life skills and their daily applications. This is a direct result of the tremendous expansion of scientific knowledge and the rapid technological progress that the world is currently witnessing. The twenty-first century has already been marked by the expansion of knowledge and by economic and technological competition between countries. These developments require the preparation of generations of learners who can master the skills that modern digital transformation demands. Many digitally transformed processes are now essential in the teaching and learning environment and to daily life, and their use, development, and dissemination can bridge the gap between generations. Even so, continued progress in this area can only be achieved through the efforts of educational institutions, researchers and those interested in this field. In addition, digital transformation and related sources of technology have become the most important pillar of change in the field of higher education. We now work within a system governed by small screens and interactive platforms. We draw on, and we learn about, the components of their virtual world which is, for example, based on artificial intelligence (AI) and platforms such as ChatGPT. It is therefore necessary to focus on students obtaining the requisite knowledge that will lead to the creativity and innovation that will, in turn, lead to digital transformation. All this will all depend on enhancing applied research at universities and promoting applications that are commensurate with the cognitive acceleration we are witnessing today, and this focus undoubtedly requires those in charge of the education sector to review their policies and plans of teaching and learning, so that courses, evaluation methods and the characteristics of our learners keep pace with these developments. This is particularly important for the higher education sector in the Arab states if those states are to move from consumers of knowledge to creators of knowledge.

It is imperative that programs that include courses on AI, cyber security, big data and the Internet of Things (IoT) are now taught at higher education institutions. These new programs are needed to replace some of the programs that are still being taught in university but no longer meet the aspirations and needs of our time, as scientific facts and reality data indicate that there are many professions that will disappear during the next ten years, and new jobs will appear. Therefore, these new programs will be required in order to pursue the growth of knowledge and digital transformation agendas. This calls for the updating of the mindset of learners and lecturers, and the updating of plans and the formulation of policies to prepare future generations for such change in the Arab states.

Finally, as confirmation that digital transformation will play a fundamental role in shaping the future of HEIs in Arab states, the *"National Transformation in the Middle East: A Digital Journey"*, identifies six high-impact themes relevant to the public sector in the UAE, KSA, Qatar and Kuwait: *smart cities, smart tourism, next-generation care, classrooms of the future, smart government,* and *the future of mobility* [2].

2 Sources of Growth of Knowledge (Knowledge Evolution)

Growth of knowledge can be obtained from many sources, some of which are listed below:

- Scholars
- Books
- Computers, internet and digital libraries
- Artificial intelligence, IoT and three-dimensional (3D) streaming
- Open source (Metaverse).

Digitalization has helped in acquiring new knowledge and therefore, leads to lifestyle transformation. The future of digital transformation is to connect with free access as there is no need for authentication. This leads to a change to the way we should construct higher-education facilities, in terms of (a) program delivery, (b) lecture halls, classrooms and laboratories (c) landscape and campus infrastructure.

3 Digital Transformation in Teaching and Learning

To understand the benefits of digital transformation to teaching and learning; it is necessary to investigate by performing comparative studies and analysis of the strategic approach [3]. Digital transformation in teaching and learning consists of, but is not limited to:

- Artificial intelligence
- Cloud computing

- Big data
- Internet of things
- Three-dimensional streaming.

Accordingly, and linked with the above technologies, innovation, entrepreneurship, applied and industrial research, knowledge transfer, education, and training, are major tools in universities that should be rooted in digital transformation. In addition, universities with the correct strategic agenda will generate increased research productivity, more indexed papers, and increased patents, intellectual property (IP) and research outcomes, leading to an innovation ecosystem that produces a massive digital transformation in universities.

Thus, in the era of globalization and digitization, AI, cloud computing, big data, IoT and 3D streaming are rooted in all the layers of education and in the delivery of educational programs, so their benefits are common in universities. The world is moving beyond the conventional metaverse.

4 Digital Transformation Initiatives at Sohar University

Sohar University believes in this continuous change in science and knowledge and in application of this change, and we anticipate that the future reality will be full of cognitive changes and accelerations. We are currently witnessing remarkable developments in all fields, in the quality of our programs and the development of new ones. These include the opening of new programs on AI and cyber security commensurate with scientific and technological development, promoting scientific research and innovation, encouraging the development and patenting of IP, promoting entrepreneurship, and providing an appropriate scientific and learning environment. We provide multiple, and advanced, laboratories, together with distinguished academic and research staff, while linking all of this to modern technology and techniques as part of digital transformation. In addition, we are in the process of establishing many partnerships with other HEIs and with industry to enhance innovation that is delivered from knowledge. We have moved from on-line and blended learning during COVID-19 to digital transformation through the adoption of technology [4]. As a result of the creation of a knowledge-based society, technology now plays a major role in everyday life and that, in turn, produces a rapid growth in knowledge, leading to the changing expectations of education.

There is wide spectrum of reasons why digital transformation should be implemented by HEIs: it offers more flexibility; it offers multi-channel delivery and customized learning resources; it enables learning to take place through social interaction; it is cost-effective as there is less need for large premises; it provides access to multiple programs with wider choices and different learning resources; learners can revisit the classes they miss at any time, or rewind to ensure full understanding; it saves time and travel, and permits working from home. Therefore, digital content is generally preferred by learners [5].

5   Why Growth of Knowledge and Digital Transformation is the Future in the Arab States

Prosperity in the twenty-first century depends on the growth of knowledge and digital transformation, which are based on innovation, in order to have a knowledge-based economy. Future generations of learners will need to master the skills of the modern technologies that have become obligatory for development and the dissemination of culture; this will help to foster the digital transformation era.

It is most important for the HEIs in the Arab states to shed light on: education and educational content, conducting research with impact, internalization, globalization, student-exchange programs relating to technology, and partnerships, at the same time linking all these different facets to achieve the digital transformation that countries seek.

Digital transformation is the future, but it depends on a better digital infrastructure, the availability of high-speed internet connections, and lows costs in obtaining an internet connection. Most important, however, is the availability of the modern sources of digital transformation that are linked with advances in AI, IoT, cyber security, and ChatGPT. In some Arab countries, especially the states of the Arab Gulf, these technologies are already available, and this will help those countries to lead the digital transformation era and the knowledge evolution. Other Arab countries, however, do not have such advantages due to political, economic, and social reasons and, therefore, these countries will lag behind in this regard and will need many years to catch up. These disadvantages will seriously affect the HEIs in those countries.

6   Conclusions

The modern world, including the advanced Arab states, will live in a three-dimensional era surrounded by options, advantages, facilities, and renewed innovations on every side, and all of this will be due to the knowledge revolution and digital transformation. Even so, in order for the HEIs in Arab states to succeed in a digital society, there is a need to invest in students (people), especially the talented ones who have the creativity and innovative ideas (knowledge) that are required to lead to a successful digital transformation. Therefore, it is of the utmost importance that HEIs in the Arab states develop the education systems necessary to produce students who possess the knowledge and skills to engage with technology. The next generation is likely to be marked by enormous changes, given the rapid pace in evolving knowledge and digital transformation. This all has to be supported by the digital transformation tools in the content of AI, IoT, cloud computing and 3D streaming and other AI-related technologies.

Today, digital transformation has become the cornerstone of education, and this will doubtless enhance and develop the higher education sector, not only in the transmission of knowledge, but also in research and innovation that will create impactful IP and patents. This has the possibility of benefitting some of the advanced Arab states by raising their status in the Global Innovation Index (GII) and by creating strong economies that are based on knowledge and led by digitalization. In summary, some of the wealthier Arab societies have made significant and positive steps in digital transformation in higher education while others have not, due to the reasons stated above. This calls for an updating of the current educational approaches to prepare future generations for changing circumstances. It is therefore suggested that the growth of knowledge and its evolution should be utilized to blend with the digital transformation technologies that are fundamental to the future of education in the Arab states.

Finally, the preceding arguments strongly indicate that the Arab states need to forge collaborations and support one another towards improving higher education in the globalized and digitalized era in order to be able to sustain digital transformation in their HEIs.

References

1. Jassim AN, Rahman AK (2021) Digital transformation at higher education institutions for the academic year (2020– 2021): Departments of College of Administration and Economics, University of Basrah as a model. Turkish J Comput Math Educ 12(13):5152–5161. https://doi.org/10.17762/turcomat.v12i13.9702
2. Deloitte (2017) National transformation in the Middle East, a digital journey. https://www2.deloitte.com/xe/en/pages/technology-media-and-telecommunications/articles/dtme_tmt_national-transformation-in-the-middleeast-a-digital-journey.html
3. Asewaidi AY, Zaidan AM (2022) The world beyond conventional Metaverse. Publisher: Asalet Eğitim Danışmanlık Yayın Hizmetleri İç ve Dış Ticaret Sertifika No: 40687 (ISBN: 978-625-8336-18-4) (ISBN: 9781471614866) (PDF) The world beyond the traditional "Metaverse" (researchgate.net)
4. Sohar University. https://www.su.edu.om/index.php/en/
5. Al-Fazari (2023) Delivery of online and blended-learning higher education programs in the Arab world—a case study from Sohar University in Oman. In: Badran A et al (eds) Higher education in the Arab world: e-learning and distance education. Springer Nature (ISBN: 978-3-031-33567-9)

The Perspectives of Deans of Medical Schools on Introducing Artificial Intelligence and Computer Literacy to Medical Curricula in Arab Countries

Nabil Mansour, Fatima Msheik El-Khoury, Ghazi Zaatari, and Mahmoud Harb

Abstract Digital transformation in higher education has revolutionized the delivery and exchange of knowledge and information between the educator and the students, and has thus led to a major shift in the paradigm of education where the responsibilities and roles have dramatically changed. This transformation has necessitated revisions to the design, implementation, and evaluation of medical curricula by incorporating into them the new scientific discoveries utilizing emerging and novel technologies. In view of this global changing trend in medical education, a survey was conducted to address the pressing challenges facing medical educational institutions in the region. The objectives of this study were twofold: (1) to investigate the perspectives of Arab medical school deans regarding the integration of Artificial Intelligence (AI) and Computer Literacy (CL) topics into medical education curricula, and (2) to assess the readiness of Arab medical schools and colleges in implementing AI and CL education within their undergraduate medical curricula. Between June and September 2023, the authors conducted a cross-sectional study among 104 deans of medical schools and colleges in Arab countries, employing a 30-item self-developed questionnaire. Thematic analysis was used to examine the survey responses, and inductive coding of these responses allowed the identification of emerging themes. Two meta-themes surfaced: the benefits of integrating AI and CL into medical education, and the challenges of including AI and CL in medical education. Each meta-theme spanned multiple

---

N. Mansour (✉) · F. Msheik El-Khoury · G. Zaatari · M. Harb
Faculty of Medicine, American University of Beirut, Beirut, Lebanon
e-mail: nm08@aub.edu.lb

F. Msheik El-Khoury
e-mail: fm50@aub.edu.lb

G. Zaatari
e-mail: zaatari@aub.edu.lb

M. Harb
e-mail: mh05@aub.edu.lb

© The Author(s), under exclusive license to Springer Nature Switzerland AG 2024
A. Badran et al. (eds.), *Higher Education in the Arab World*,
https://doi.org/10.1007/978-3-031-70779-7_15

themes, subthemes, and categories. Three benefits of integrating AI and CL into medical education reflect the tripartite mission of academic medicine: advancements in medical research, breakthroughs in clinical practice, and innovations in medical curricula or medical education. Seven main challenges to integrating AI and CL emerged from this study, categorized as: resource challenges; educational preparedness; dynamic nature of AI; curriculum and coverage constraints; patient care quality and safety; ethical and legal complexities; and governance structure and hierarchical frameworks, and hierarchical challenges. This study highlighted the growing belief among the leadership of medical schools in the Arab countries that integrating AI into medical curricula is inevitable. The perspectives of academic deans vary due to differences in education systems, governance structures, and learning objectives. While recognizing the transformative benefits in medical education, clinical practice, and research, the study emphasizes the need for modifications in medical curricula to accommodate AI and CL topics, without compromising the focus on the medical ones. The potential of AI to revolutionize healthcare is evident, but challenges include limited resources, institutional readiness, ethical dilemmas, and the absence of legal frameworks. Overcoming these challenges requires strategic decision-making, multidisciplinary collaboration, and steps to enhance educational preparedness and awareness among students and faculty. Embracing AI is crucial for the future of medical education and healthcare advancement in this rapidly evolving technological landscape.

Keywords Digital transformation · Artificial intelligence · Medical education · Medical curriculum · Master adaptive learner · Digital health · Computer literacy

1 Introduction

Digital transformation has revolutionized higher education and altered dramatically the exchange of knowledge and information between the educator and students; one outcome has been the empowerment of students to have greater control of the entire learning experience. This transformation created a paradigm shift in designing, implementing, and evaluating the medical curriculum as it embraces the novel insights and breakthroughs in medicine [1]. Among these medical discoveries are genome analysis, predictive analytics, a personalized clinical approach to identify and stratify medical risks, and medical imaging recognition [2]. This paper explores the impact of digital transformation on medical education systems and curricula and identifies the challenges that can be potentially faced by the overseers of the educational programs in enhancing and strengthening the technological literacy of the future generation of medical doctors in order to sustain a good quality of education.

The incorporation of digital technologies into medical education has brought several benefits [3] including enhanced student engagement, personalized learning, and improved student outcomes [2]. The use of virtual and augmented reality and simulation technologies provides improved surgical skills training outcomes and robotic simulators benefit medical students the most [4]. The use of digital platforms has also facilitated collaborative learning, enabling students to interact and learn from their peers and instructors [5]. Digital technologies have made medical education more accessible to learners from diverse backgrounds, reducing barriers to entry [6], and increasing diversity in the medical workforce. Research results have emphasized the need to train medical students in metacognition, data science, informatics, and artificial intelligence, and medical curricula are to be restructured to emphasize the use of the Master Adaptive Learner approach rather than simply content delivery [1].

Despite widespread availability of technology in healthcare institutes, digital health topics are rarely found in any medical curriculum [2] as a core learning module. Even if present, they are not mandatory and only interested students sign up for them [7]. Conversely, research outcomes emphasized the deliberate need to restructure the medical curricula to include AI-related materials that would help medical doctors assume their future roles [8–10]. The learning strategies, however, should focus on critical thinking, and analytical skills while approaching digital health, due to the rapid evolution of these technologies [1]. Thus, introducing computer literacy, data analytics, and AI concepts into medical curricula should be integrated and interwoven into the learning objectives and outcomes of any program. Keeping in mind the spirit of integration, as described by Atwa et al. [11], obstacles that exist between different academic fields, such as mathematics, computer science, artificial intelligence, and engineering, should be removed, and effective learning opportunities should be facilitated; moreover, students should be helped to acquire practical and significant knowledge for clinical practice that can be easily retrieved, modified, updated, and developed continuously as a part of their lifelong learning process.

This approach can be achieved through introducing courses or modules such as programming, data science, deep learning, wearables, and medical devices at an earlier stage in any medical education program. This approach might also be integrated spirally and in a scaffolded manner, by introducing more advanced modules in AI and data literacy as the students advance in the medical curriculum. Implementing this integration will lead the path towards ensuring a seamless process of digital transformation and lead to better outcomes in medical education.

In summary, there is a growing belief among those involved in curriculum development that integrating artificial intelligence into medical curricula is essential. The introduction of these modules could be taken at the level of pure technical understanding of computer programing and knowledge, and at the level of applied computer literacy for clinical medical sciences. The goal of digital transformation of medical curricula is to develop a deeper understanding by future physicians of the field of AI, big data analysis, and electronic health-record systems, thereby increasing the need for skilled physician–machine interaction [12] to create a better synergy between physicians and machines. While significant benefits of the favorable impact of digital transformation on medical curricula are acknowledged, there are several remaining limitations and challenges that could hinder complete adaptation. Some of these limitations are: *a* the lack of AI and Machine Learning (ML) skill-mastering by physicians [13]; *b* the high cost of integration; *c* the inaccessibility of these technologies to some medical programs that are operating with limited resources; and *d* the absence of skilled and competent medical educators who can inculcate these cutting-edge technological skills to medical students.

Therefore, the integration of AI and CL into medical education is a transformative global trend that holds immense potential for enhancing the capabilities of future healthcare professionals. However, in the Arab region, a critical gap exists in our understanding of the perspectives of deans of medical schools regarding the incorporation of AI and CL topics into medical education curricula. Furthermore, there is a notable lack of evidence on the readiness of medical schools in the Arab world to embrace and implement these essential advancements in education. The study reported here is of paramount significance as it delves into the perspectives of Arab medical school deans, providing crucial insights into their attitudes and concerns regarding the integration of AI and CL into medical education. This exploration is vital for informing decision-making among education leaders in the Arab world and aligning educational strategies with evolving healthcare demands. Additionally, the assessment of readiness among Arab medical schools to implement AI and CL education is pivotal, offering a comprehensive overview and guiding the formulation of targeted interventions.

2 Methods

This study is based on a survey of the medical schools and colleges in the Arab countries. Ethical approval for this study was secured from the American University of Beirut (AUB) Institutional Review Board (IRB) (SBS-2023-0091, dated May 6, 2023). Targeted participants were the academic deans of medical schools and colleges in Arab countries. The list of these medical schools was retrieved from SCIMAGO Institutions Ranking [14]. In total, 104 deans were invited to participate in this study through an online survey administered via the LimeSurvery portal. The invitation provided the details and objectives of the study (Appendix 1), along with an informed consent to be signed electronically, if they agreed to participate (Appendix 2). The informed consent stated that participation was voluntary, responses were anonymous, and participants were free to withdraw at any time. Non-responders received up to three follow-up reminders to encourage survey completion. The survey was designed to be completed within 30–40 min and was prepared in the English language.

The contact information, specifically emails of the respective deans, was secured from the public information available on the website of each school, or by requesting emails directly from the administrators of these schools. To mitigate selection bias and acknowledging that the economic status of a country and the global ranking of medical schools significantly influence the medical education system, the survey was distributed to medical schools across a spectrum of high, middle, and low-income Arab countries, encompassing a range of international rankings.

We evaluated the perspectives of deans of medical schools toward the integration of AI and CL and assessed the readiness of medical schools for AI and CL by employing a 30-item questionnaire grouped into three sections: Importance and Benefits of AI/CL (14 questions), Curriculum Structure (8 questions), and Challenges and Readiness (8 questions) (Appendix 3). These questions particularly dwelled on exploring the perspectives of deans on introducing AI and CL into medical curricula in their medical schools, their curriculum structures, and the challenges they might face if they have plans to integrate AI and CL into their curriculum.

The survey items were formulated by reviewing existing literature to identify evidence-based metrics relating to the integration and implementation of AI and CL into medical education curricula. Content validity was developed by two experienced research team members in medical education at the American University of Beirut Medical Center. All questions received a rating of 3 or 4 for relevance, resulting in a perfect content validity index (CVI) of 1. Another two research team members from the same institution assessed the clarity and comprehensibility of each question. The survey demonstrated positive face validity, indicating unanimous agreement on its appropriateness for assessing the perspectives of deans and the readiness of medical schools regarding the integration of AI and CL.

The collected data were retrieved from LimeSurvey in Microsoft Excel format. Data were analyzed using content analysis [15]. Two investigators (MH & NM) independently conducted a line-by-line open coding on the transcripts, recording initial codes. Thematic analysis was used to examine the content of the survey responses, and inductive coding of these responses allowed the identification of emerging themes. Recurring concepts and patterns were identified, and themes were categorized through constant comparison, refining categories in the process. Discrepancies were resolved through in-depth conversations. Through consensus, the coding scheme was established and then applied to all transcripts. The codes were discussed and further refined with co-authors in two follow-up meetings. All data coding and analyses were performed manually.

3 Results

Surveys were sent to 104 deans of medical schools and colleges, in 18 Arab countries. A total of 45 deans (43.2%) responded with various degrees of completeness. Two meta-themes surfaced, namely, the benefits of integrating AI and CL into medical education and the challenges of including AI and CL in medical education. Each meta-theme spanned multiple themes, subthemes, and categories. The themes are discussed below, with quotes from the deans to evidence our findings. Out of all the respondents, 86% expressed support for integrating AI into medical curricula, and suggested dedicating between 2–10% of overall credit hours/weeks to AI theoretical and practical topics. Also, 83% endorsed the idea of revising the medical curriculum's learning objectives to encompass elements related to AI and CL and accommodating other technological advances. Despite the high percentage of respondents supporting AI integration (86%), however, only 14% mentioned having qualified faculty members to teach AI and CL related topics.

3.1 Benefits of Integrating AI and CL

The ten benefits of integrating AI and CL into medical education fell under three overarching themes, as indicated below (Fig. 1).

3.1.1 Advancements in Medical Research: "Drug Discovery and Treatment Optimization"; "Data Management: Collection, Analysis, and Interpretation"; and "Literature Review and Evidence Synthesis"

The theme "advancements in medical research" encompasses three key subthemes identified by participants. Firstly, participants highlighted the potential impact of equipping students with AI and CL on "drug discovery and treatment optimization". Both AI and CL were seen as powerful tools in enhancing the efficiency of identifying novel drugs and optimizing treatment strategies. Secondly, the theme included "data management: collection, analysis, and interpretation", emphasizing that introducing AI and Cl into the medical education curriculum has the potential to equip learners with skills in handling and making sense of vast amounts of medical data, through data analysis, pattern recognition, predictive modeling, risk assessment and discovery of new insights. Thirdly, participants underscored the benefits of AI and CL on the learners' medical research output in "literature review and evidence synthesis", underscoring the value of AI and CL in streamlining the research process. These benefits are articulated in the following verbatim statements:

> AI has the potential to revolutionize medical research and innovation. By equipping medical students with AI skills, they can actively contribute to advancements in areas such as medical imaging, genomics, drug discovery, and clinical decision support systems. AI literacy enables them to navigate the research landscape and collaborate effectively with data scientists and AI experts [Verbatim #1].

> Data Analysis and Pattern Recognition: AI algorithms can analyze large and complex datasets, including medical records, genomic data, imaging data, and research studies. By utilizing machine learning techniques, AI systems can identify patterns, correlations, and biomarkers that may not be readily apparent to human researchers. This can lead to more accurate and comprehensive insights into disease processes and potential risk factors. Predictive Modeling and Risk Assessment: AI can develop predictive models based on patient data, genetic profiles, lifestyle factors, and other variables. These models can

The Perspectives of Deans of Medical Schools ... 315

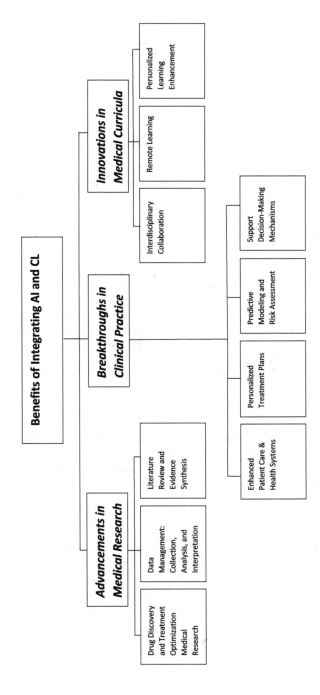

Fig. 1 Benefits of integrating AI and CL into medical education in Arab countries

be used to assess an individual's risk of developing certain diseases, helping researchers identify early warning signs and high-risk populations. This enables proactive interventions, preventive measures, and targeted monitoring for disease prevention and early detection. Drug Discovery and Treatment Optimization: AI algorithms can analyze vast amounts of biomedical literature, drug databases, and molecular structures to identify potential drug candidates or optimize treatment plans. By leveraging AI, researchers can discover new therapeutic targets, repurpose existing drugs, and tailor treatments based on patient-specific factors, leading to more effective and personalized medicine. Image Analysis and Medical Imaging: AI-based image analysis techniques can assist researchers in analyzing medical images such as X-rays, MRIs, and pathology slides. AI can help identify subtle abnormalities, assist in early detection, and provide quantitative measurements for more accurate diagnosis and monitoring of diseases. Literature Review and Evidence Synthesis: AI can aid researchers in conducting systematic reviews and meta-analyses by automatically scanning and extracting relevant information from a vast array of scientific literature. This helps researchers save time, improve the accuracy of evidence synthesis, and identify gaps in current knowledge. Clinical Trial Design and Patient Recruitment: AI can support the design and optimization of clinical trials by analyzing patient data, identifying suitable participants, and stratifying patient cohorts based on specific criteria. This can enhance the efficiency of trial recruitment, increase the likelihood of successful trial outcomes, and enable more targeted and personalized therapies. Real-Time Monitoring and Surveillance: AI-powered systems can continuously monitor and analyze health data from various sources, such as wearable devices, electronic health records, and population health databases. By leveraging AI, researchers can detect disease outbreaks, monitor public health trends, and identify early warning signs or patterns that may indicate the emergence of new diseases or health risks [Verbatim #2].

Revolutionizing medical research, enabling the analysis of large datasets, identifying patterns, and discovering new insights. By incorporating AI education, medical students can contribute to research advancements, leverage AI techniques for data analysis, and collaborate effectively with data scientists and AI experts in driving medical breakthroughs [Verbatim #3].

3.1.2 Breakthroughs in Clinical Practice: Includes "Enhanced Patient Care and Health Systems", "Personalized Treatment Plans", "Predictive Modeling and Risk Assessment", and "Support Decision-Making Mechanisms"

Respondents discussed various aspects of integrating AI into medical education, emphasizing potential benefits such as equipping physicians with enhanced clinical decision-making abilities through the available AI tools, leading to more accurate diagnoses and personalized treatment plans. They also underscored the potential for improved patient outcomes by leveraging AI for early detection and predictive modeling. Additionally, the advanced diagnostic capabilities of AI algorithms in analyzing medical images and pathology slides were highlighted, contributing to enhanced diagnostic accuracy and efficiency, and it was considered highly crucial to equip physicians with the needed skills to optimize these features and utilize them in clinical practice. The benefits are conveyed in the following statement:

The future of medicine is in personalized care, interpreting the patient's data on the background of a huge database and tailoring the treatment based on AI algorithms. This applies to the diagnosis of disease, for example, the kind of tumor that somebody has, once they define the genetic markup of that tumor, then it can be looked at against all these thousands of similar cases that the literature, and people can decide what is the best treatment. Then the genetic background of the patient is also required to combine both and develop specific therapeutics, individualized therapeutics for that patient. So, in every aspect of the medical profession, from the interview with the patient, all the way to the treatment will be greatly enhanced by providing data from artificial intelligence bases or databases, Enhanced Clinical Decision-Making: AI can provide data-driven insights and decision support, augmenting the clinical reasoning skills of medical students. By incorporating AI education, students can learn how to effectively integrate AI tools and algorithms into their decision-making processes, leading to more accurate diagnoses and personalized treatment plans. Improved Patient Outcomes: AI can contribute to improved patient outcomes by aiding in early detection, predictive modeling, and personalized medicine. By teaching AI in the medical curriculum, students can learn how to leverage AI technologies to optimize patient care, leading to better treatment outcomes and patient satisfaction. Advanced Diagnostic Capabilities: AI algorithms can assist in the analysis of medical images, pathology slides, and other diagnostic tests. Integrating AI education into the curriculum equips students with the skills to effectively use AI tools for image interpretation, pattern recognition, and early disease detection, thereby enhancing diagnostic accuracy and efficiency [Verbatim #4].

3.1.3 Innovations in Medical Curricula Represented by: "Interdisciplinary Collaboration", "Remote Learning", and "Personalized Learning Enhancement"

Participants highlighted the transformative impact of AI and CL on medical education, emphasizing "interdisciplinary collaboration", "remote learning", and "personalized learning enhancement." This includes empowering medical students to make informed decisions, address ethical concerns, and contribute to research, preparing them for the digital age. This has been articulated in the following verbatim statements:

> We have been successful so far in implementing AI education at the School of Medicine, but some challenges still exist despite the partnership with the school of engineering, computer science program, etc. These challenges include the lack of expert workforce (we need more experts dedicated to healthcare), and the lack of dedicated time for that [Verbatim #5 reflecting the interdisciplinary collaboration].
>
> Teaching AI and computer literacy to medical students empowers them to harness the potential of AI in healthcare, make informed decisions, address ethical concerns, contribute to research, and stay ahead in an increasingly technology-driven field. It prepares them to be well-rounded healthcare professionals equipped to deliver high-quality, patient-centered care in the digital age [Verbatim #6 reflecting the empowerment of medical students to make informed decisions].

Other participants commented on this area from a different perspective, emphasizing the transformative impact of AI on healthcare delivery, envisioning improved efficiency through streamlined workflows, automated administrative tasks, and optimized resource allocation:

> Efficient Healthcare Delivery: AI has the potential to streamline healthcare workflows, automate administrative tasks, and optimize resource allocation. By integrating AI education, medical students can learn how to leverage AI solutions to improve healthcare delivery, reduce administrative burdens, and enhance efficiency in patient management. [Verbatim #7].

When considering advances in medical sciences and technology, respondents also highlighted the imperative for medical graduates to be well-versed in these technologies, especially as they play a crucial role in the emerging trend of managing chronic-disease patients at home, as articulated in the following statement:

> With the advances in medical sciences, clinical management, and technology medical devices, it is imperative that medical graduates are savvy with AI and CL. Besides, interaction and follow up of chronic disease patients at home is becoming a new trend where AI and CL are essential tools to be utilized by modern physicians and healthcare systems [Verbatim #8].

Other participants noted ongoing integration of AI and CL in pre-medical years and hoped this integration would be extended to the medical school curriculum. This has been articulated in the following statement:

> Quality is part of who and where and how things are delivered to students. But the content of medical education will change dramatically with that. And starting with the pre-med curriculum, which is what we're doing now, hopefully we'll be able to complete this all the way through medical school and further on in life [Verbatim #9].

Other participants emphasized the profound potential of AI in reshaping medical education and the healthcare profession, as evident in the following:

> "The inclusion of AI in the medical curriculum has the potential to significantly impact the overall quality of medical education and shape the future of the healthcare profession.", be it in "Enhanced Clinical Decision-Making…Improved Patient Outcomes… Advanced Diagnostic Capabilities…Efficient Healthcare Delivery…Advancements in Medical Research" [Verbatim #10].

3.2 Challenges of Including AI and CL in Medical Education

The seven main challenges of including AI and CL in medical education are (Fig. 2).

The Perspectives of Deans of Medical Schools ...

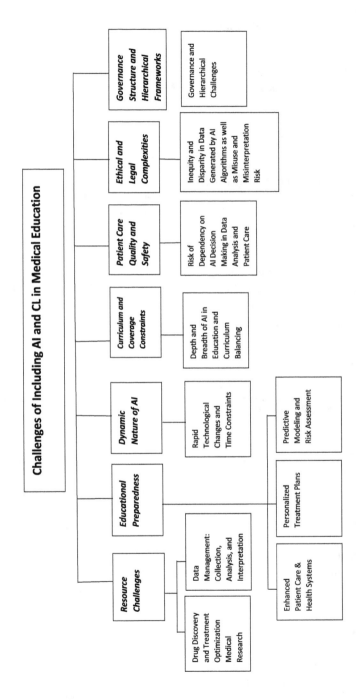

Fig. 2 Challenges of integrating AI and CL into medical education in Arab countries

3.2.1 Resource Challenges Represented by: "Financial Constraints" and "Entrepreneurial Support and Technical Challenges"

In addressing the challenges of integrating AI into medical curricula, participants highlighted the key hurdles encapsulated in "financial constraints" and "entrepreneurial support and technical challenges." These challenges encompass the need for diverse expertise, where medical professionals proficient in AI applications may lack curriculum development skills, and vice versa. Technical collaboration is identified as crucial, requiring a blend of medical and technological expertise.

3.2.2 Educational Preparedness Represented by: "Faculty Development/Capacity Building", "Buy-in of Education Stakeholders", and "Medical Students' Awareness of AI and its Added Value"

One of the main challenges reported was the buy-in from stakeholders of medical schools, whether the leadership or faculty members. Respondents reported having various types of challenges, from financial, technical, and lack of qualified teaching staff, labelling them as critical impediments against the integration of AI and CL:

> "Serious reasons to incorporate AI in the curriculum" and they believe as well that "it is too early to introduce AI and we would rather wait for further improvement in this technology", and that "even the most enthusiastic teachers still feel challenged in that area (integrating AI & CL) they might not be ready to work" [Verbatim #11].

> "Deficient qualified staff" [Verbatim #12], "Suffering primarily from financial limitations", "Inability to free time for these (AI & CL) topics not to compromise core curriculum deliverability" [Verbatim #13].

> Some challenges still exist despite the partnership with the school of engineering, computer science program, etc. These challenges include the lack of expert workforce (we need more experts dedicated to healthcare), and the lack of dedicated time for that [Verbatim #14].

Along the same lines, respondents expressed their fears not only about a lack of qualified teaching staff, but also about having academic disruption as a result of senior physicians deciding to quit practicing medicine, creating a knowledge gap, because they will *"not be able to adapt"* [Verbatim #15]. Respondents were also concerned about the need to recruit younger people, who have the new set of skills and are in high demand in the market, which would require that healthcare institutions and medical schools pay premium salaries and incur more expenses, let alone that they have to *"Pay the price on the experience side and on the humanistic side"* [Verbatim #16].

Besides the above-mentioned challenges, medical schools will probably face a paradigm shift in their methods of curriculum development, implementation, and student assessment, especially when it comes to assessing students on their *"Creative projects, essays, presentations, and in the terms of personal assessment of students*" [Verbatim #17] as referred to by one of the respondents. On another note, respondents elaborated on this topic, stating that:

> The method of assessment should change to accommodate the changes in curriculum... as currently we are talking about the advocate, and the healer doctors, and both are not related to medicine per se, but to personality [Verbatim #18].

> How to approach medicine? It's not the science of medicine, it is how physicians deal with patients, and the family of patients, and thus, the assessment methodology should be adapted to incorporate new methods to cover the personality, characteristics, and competences, while embracing AI [Verbatim #19].

3.2.3 Dynamic Nature of AI: "Rapid Technological Changes and Time Constraints"

The primary challenges of AI and CL lie in their volatility, continuous improvements, and disruptive changes that they go through. What proves to be valid and practical today, might undergo disruptive change tomorrow without any prior notice, be it medical equipment, an AI algorithm, or a computer language, which require *"Continuous adaptation to technological advances"* [Verbatim #20], as reported by one of the participants. Maintaining proficiency in this field demands substantial financial, technical, and human-resources investments. However, the primary goal of medical schools is to graduate doctors capable of effectively integrating and utilizing AI within their medical practice, rather than producing engineers specializing solely in AI. This matter was expressed by respondents who mentioned that these technological changes may easily lead to physicians *"Falling behind in medical and technological advancements"* [Verbatim #21], or *"Result in missed opportunities to leverage AI tools for improved patient care, diagnostics, and research"* [Verbatim #22]. Moreover, physicians *"May be limited in their ability to contribute to research advancements, ...or explore new avenues for patient care improvement"* [Verbatim #23]. Since *"AI is rapidly advancing and transforming healthcare"* [Verbatim #24], these rapid technologies and advancements *"May lead to a technology gap and potential inefficiencies in healthcare delivery"* [Verbatim #25].

3.2.4 Curriculum and Coverage Constraints: "Depth and Breadth of AI in Education and Curriculum Balancing"

This challenge of balancing the depth and breadth of AI in education and the curriculum poses a significant obstacle for Arab medical schools to the successful integration of AI and CL into medical curricula. Respondents raised concerns about the potential strain of adding additional material to an already comprehensive curriculum, as evidenced in the following:

> The medical curriculum is already packed with essential foundational knowledge and clinical skills. Integrating AI education requires careful consideration of the curriculum's structure and balance to ensure that students receive adequate training in both AI and core medical disciplines [Verbatim #26].

Respondents also underscored the challenge of achieving a balance in integrating AI and CL into the medical curriculum, ensuring that it should complement rather than overwhelm the core content of medical education:

> The medical curriculum is already packed with essential foundational knowledge and clinical skills. Integrating AI education requires careful consideration of the curriculum's structure and balance to ensure that students receive adequate training in both AI and core medical disciplines [Verbatim #27].

3.2.5 Patient Care Quality and Safety: 'Risk of Dependency on AI Decision Making in Data Analysis and Patient Care"

When it comes to patient care and safety, respondents shared their concerns about relying too heavily on AI decision-making in data analysis. They pointed out that AI is still in its early stages, especially in the medical field where decisions about human health are critical. Respondents emphasized the need to handle the introduction of AI carefully, suggesting we should *"Avoid dependency on AI"* [Verbatim #28] when making medical decisions affecting patient care and safety.

Some respondents expressed worries about students becoming overly dependent on AI, fearing that it might hinder their understanding and memorization of important medical concepts. As one respondent put it, relying too much on AI might lead to neglecting essential parts of medicine: *"Relying on it too much... to the point of not trying to understand and memorize some important parts in Medicine"* [Verbatim #29]. Others highlighted concerns about potential negative effects on students' medical reasoning: *"At some point students might count completely on AI which will affect their medical reasoning"* [Verbatim #30]. Furthermore, there were worries that an excessive reliance on AI could impact students' ability to conduct independent research and analysis, with one respondent mentioning that the *"Overuse might reduce the student ability for research and analysis"* [Verbatim #31].

3.2.6 Ethical and Legal Complexities: "Inequity and Disparity in Data Generated by AI Algorithms as Well as Misuse and Misinterpretation Risk"

The ethical and legal aspects surrounding AI and CL were a notable concern among respondents, particularly regarding issues of inequity and disparity in data generated by AI algorithms, as well as the risks of misuse and misinterpretation. Respondents highlighted the need to address these complexities, emphasizing the importance of explaining the limitations of AI and CL. They also pointed out that while the limitations are expected to change over time, it is crucial to consider the potential for abuse. Respondents expressed concerns about potential misuse for purposes that are not morally correct, such as blackmail or insurance fraud. As stated:

> Their (AI & CL) limitations should be explained, and these limitations are going to change with time. Our limitations now will not be limitations in five years, but the potential for abuse should also be considered, particularly by these databases from malignant sources or from non-physicians or for purposes that are not morally correct such as blackmail or insurance fraud or whatever [Verbatim #32].

Respondents pointed to the imperative for medical schools to integrate the *"Ethical considerations of AI and CL"* [Verbatim #33] within their curricula. However, the challenge lies in developing dedicated courses and modules that effectively cover complex topics such as data privacy, bias, transparency, accountability, informed consent, and the responsible use of AI in clinical practice and research:

> Dedicated courses and modules that cover topics such as data privacy, bias, transparency, accountability, informed consent, and the responsible use of AI in clinical practice and research. [Verbatim #34].

Moreover, respondents underscored another challenge about integrating AI ethics subjects into the medical education curriculum, namely, the difficulty in finding bioethicists who are well-versed in the intricacies of AI and can teach ethics amidst all the changes occurring and its implications on human subjects.

3.2.7 Governance Structure and Hierarchical Frameworks: "Governance and Hierarchical Challenges"

Respondents brought attention to challenges related to governance and hierarchical structures. They noted that the integration of AI and CL into the medical curricula might face obstacles from leadership teams and hierarchical frameworks in certain medical schools that remain unconvinced about the efficiency of AI in medical education and its ultimate impact on patient care. A few respondents expressed reservations about introducing AI to medical education, stating, *"It is too early to introduce AI and we'd rather wait for further improvement in this technology"* [Verbatim #35].

4 Discussion

Our study delved into the crucial challenges confronting medical educational institutions in Arab countries amidst the global transformation in medical education and the swift progress of AI domains impacting the healthcare industry, including all the AI types such as machine learning, natural language processing, virtual realities, augmented Realities, open AI, etc. With the primary aim of exploring the perspectives of Arab medical school deans on integrating AI and CL into medical education curricula and evaluating their readiness for such a mandate, we identified a spectrum of viewpoints regarding the potential benefits and challenges associated with this integration. The varied perspectives observed may indicate differences in viewpoints and in the readiness of institutions to embrace such a mandate and the resources available to each of them.

4.1 Varied Perspectives and Readiness: AI and CL Integration into Arab Medical Curricula

The perspectives of the academic deans of medical schools and colleges in the Arab countries towards integrating AI and CL into medical curricula varied widely among respondents. These differences may be attributed to three main reasons: (1) the diverse medical education systems that are implemented in these medical schools and colleges; (2) the governance of these medical schools and colleges; and (3) the governments or the administrative relationships between the governments in these countries and the medical schools and colleges in these same countries. These differences might also exist within the same country in addition to intercountry differences.

Based on the published vision and mission statements of the medical schools, the medical education system in the Arab world exhibits substantial diversity both within individual institutions and across countries. A thorough comparative analysis of the vision and mission statements of these institutions reveals significant disparities in the envisioned goals for graduating physicians, encompassing a range of competencies. For instance, the variations reflect various, not often common, expected learning outcomes, curriculum structures, teaching methodologies, and methods of assessing learners. Among the factors that led to these distinctions are the political systems, epidemiological trends, demographic shifts, microeconomic plans, technological advancements, and healthcare systems, that pressure these medical schools to adapt to these transformations by making their curricula more meaningful and responding to contemporary needs, including AI etc. Variations in the expected learning outcomes, curriculum structures, teaching methodologies, and methods of assessing learners are the tools that medical schools use to respond to various disruptive technologies. These distinctions directly contribute to the differing perspectives and readiness levels observed among medical schools, underscoring the influential role of each institution's unique vision and mission.

Delving further into the medical education systems, it is important to highlight, that three main systems exist in the Arab countries, shaped by historical and political factors: the British medical education system with a six-year medical curriculum, the seven-year French medical curriculum, and the American system which comprises a three-year undergraduate premedical education leading to a bachelor's degree, followed by a four-year medical program. These three different medical educational systems each have a unique governance model.

Governance ranges from a fully government-controlled educational institution, mostly overseen by the Ministries of Higher Education in each country, to a hybrid system where medical schools enjoy decision-making while being subject to supervisory roles by the government. There is also the model of total autonomy, where the medical schools and colleges have full control over curriculum development and implementation while maintaining a dotted line with the government for quality assurance purposes.

The roles and relationships between governments and medical schools and colleges vary significantly between countries, and even among universities. Some universities are entirely government-owned and funded, labeled as public universities. In contrast, others may be privately owned by non-profit, non-governmental bodies, religious organizations, or business sectors. Joint ventures between various governments and business entrepreneurs also contribute to the diversity in the governance structures.

4.2 Benefits of Integrating AI and CL

Three benefits of integrating AI and CL into medical education reflect the tripartite mission of academic medicine: advancements in medical research (Sect. 3.1.1), breakthroughs in clinical practice (Sect. 3.1.2), and innovations in medical curricula or medical education (Sect. 3.1.3). Under these main themes, certain subthemes emerged under medical research, which includes topics like drug discovery, treatment optimization, data management (collection, analysis, and interpretation), along with the literature review and evidence synthesis. Within the clinical practice subtheme, topics include enhanced patient care and health systems, personalized treatment plans, predictive modeling and risk assessment, and support decision-making mechanisms. For innovations in medical education, the emerging topics encompass interdisciplinary collaboration, remote learning, and personalized learning enhancement.

4.2.1 Benefits of Integrating AI and CL: Advancements in Medical Research

Despite the varying levels of readiness and perspectives among Arab medical schools regarding the integration of AI and CL into their medical education programs, the positive impact of AI on clinical and medical research emerges as a significant advantage when medical students are equipped with AI and CL skills. Respondents in the study highlighted the diverse ways AI literacy can empower medical students in the realm of clinical research. Artificial-intelligence-literate physicians, through their acquired AI knowledge, skills, and abilities, can actively participate in identifying potential drug candidates, predicting drug interactions, and optimizing treatment regimens. This involvement addresses challenges in the development of new and effective pharmaceutical interventions. The capabilities of AI algorithms play a pivotal role in this process by analyzing extensive biomedical literature, drug databases, and molecular structures. This analytical power aids in the identification of potential drug candidates, fostering a more efficient and personalized approach to medicine. The integration of AI processes enhances the overall efficiency of medical research that allows for tailoring treatments based on individual patient-specific factors.

The rapid growth of AI and machine learning (ML) within clinical research suggests a new age where data-driven algorithms are the driving force for medical innovation. Continuous developments and evaluations of the current regulations relating to AI in clinical research contribute to reshaping the landscape of medical education and transforming how healthcare is provided to patients. The body of the literature provides ample evidence of the crucial role that AI can play in revolutionizing drug-discovery processes, underscoring the necessity to train and equip medical professionals with AI skills in this domain.

As noted by Mak et al. [16], traditional drug development programs face challenges of increased costs and reduced efficiency. However, AI processes and tools have proven to be capable of addressing these challenges by substantially improving the cost-effectiveness and speed of drug screening. For instance, a virtual compound library of several billion molecules can be screened within a few days with the assistance of AI, while traditionally this process would take several months and requires millions of US dollars. Thus, AI methods help us navigate past challenges in analyzing large datasets and laborious screening of compounds. Moreover, AI has the power to transform drug discovery by massively reducing the research and development cost and time, which traditionally exceeded US\$2.5 billion or more as well as a decade [17]; AI has, therefore, become a transformative force in drug discovery. An abundance of evidence further underscores the significant potential utility of AI in various aspects of drug discovery, including drug screening assays, predicting physical properties and toxicity, structure predictions, and even automating certain aspects of the drug discovery cycle [18].

The revolutionary influence of AI goes beyond reshaping the notion of clinical trial design—a gold standard in clinical research. When AI-guided biomarkers or genomics are integrated into advanced adaptive trials, they have the potential to greatly impact every aspect of the clinical trial process, spanning through study design, recruitment, conduct, intervention, and interpretation [19]. Through this transformational approach, several benefits can be observed such as rapid formulation of hypotheses, improved perspectives on disease understanding as well as refinement of drug discovery and monitoring processes [20]. This can increase the precision of patient-outcome prediction and trial-success estimation. In predicting patient outcomes, AI algorithms simulate data for efficient statistical measures, and potentially reduce the duration of trials. Through the analysis of electronic medical records, AI can predict the likelihood of trial dropouts, allowing targeted interventions and reducing overall sample sizes [19, 21]. Therefore, ML algorithms play a critical role in predicting trial success, offering early detection and prognosis capabilities [21].

Participants also emphasized the importance of imparting AI skills to medical graduates so that they could help in systematic reviews and meta-analyses. This can be illustrated by the transformative function of AI integration in systematic reviews and meta-analyses, particularly in the synthesis of evidence. The search process, involving both creative and mechanical tasks, provides an ideal opportunity for the incorporation of advanced AI-based tools. Automated scanning and extraction of relevant information from extensive scientific literature by AI not only saves researchers valuable time but also enhances the precision and accuracy of evidence synthesis. It furthermore allows researchers to save time and concentrate on more creative aspects that require human interpretation and expertise. This streamlined AI-facilitated process is crucial for identifying gaps in existing knowledge and aiding researchers navigate through the complexities of literature more effectively [22].

For instance, van Dijk et al. [23] highlights that AI tools can serve as valuable innovation in current systematic reviewing practices, provided they are used appropriately and ensure methodological quality. An open-source AI tool named 'ASReview' was introduced in 2021 [24] to streamline the title and abstract screening process in systematic reviews. This tool's application has shown its capacity to enhance systematic review efficiency, as evidenced by simulations showing its time-saving benefits [25]. In the realm of medical scientific research, it would be advantageous for major systematic review institutions, such as Cochrane and PRISMA, to officially integrate AI into their systematic reviewing practices [23]. The establishment of guidelines for the use of AI in systematic reviews, once widely recognized, would contribute to the uniform conduct and transparent reporting of AI-supported systematic reviews. Only through the adoption of such guidelines can we fully leverage the time-saving potential of AI and mitigate unnecessary research-time expenditure [23]. There have been also several suggestions from several articles on how AI can assist non-native English speakers to enhance their writing proficiency and skills as well as provide a more comprehensive translation of foreign language content [26].

Furthermore, respondents highlighted the evident impact of AI on revolutionizing medical research through big data analytics, pattern recognition, and discovery of novel insights. The integration of AI education into medical training equips medical students with AI techniques for data analysis and provides them with avenues to collaborate with data scientists and AI experts in their research. This collaborative approach to research, where medical professionals collaborate seamlessly with AI experts, holds the potential to accelerate the pace of medical discoveries and improve patient outcomes.

4.2.2 Benefits of Integrating AI and CL: Breakthroughs in Clinical Practice

Deans of Arab medical schools highlighted the transformative impact of integrating AI into medical education. They described how the impacts of AI have been observed as breakthroughs in clinical practice through advanced diagnostic capabilities, enhanced clinical decision-making, better treatment outcomes, increased patient satisfaction, and overall advancements in the practice of medicine. Artificial intelligence, particularly ML, emerges as a transformative tool in healthcare, offering potential solutions to diagnostic challenges [27]. The efficacy of ML relies on the quality and quantity of input data, making it crucial for overcoming diagnostic complexities. Deep learning, employing Convolutional Neural Networks (CNN) and data mining, aids in identifying key disease patterns within extensive datasets [27]. Studies, like one in the UK focusing on breast cancer diagnosis, highlight AI's ability to significantly reduce false positives and negatives [28], whereas ML has great potential to provide accurate diagnosis and prognosis of neurodegenerative diseases through analyzing medical history, molecular profiles, and imaging data [29]. Additionally, these technologies may contribute to the identification of more-targeted diagnostic biomarkers. Artificial-intelligence tools promise improved accuracy, cost reduction, and timesaving in diagnostics, paving the way for real-time clinical support. Krittanawong [30] concluded that AI will effectively transform the way data are being analyzed and used in decision-making and clinical care with better diagnosis and outcome. The integration of AI in medical imaging analysis, X-rays, CT scans, and MRIs, facilitates quicker and more accurate diagnoses [31]. Moreover, AI's role extends to clinical laboratory testing, enhancing accuracy and efficiency through automated techniques, offering benefits like faster antibiotic selection for positive blood cultures [32–34]. Overall, AI's potential in medical diagnosis is expansive, with ongoing research exploring diverse applications and benefits.

4.2.3 Benefits of Integrating AI and CL: Innovations in Medical Curricula

In addition to envisioning the positive impacts of AI on clinical decision-making, patient outcomes, diagnostic capabilities, healthcare delivery, and medical research, deans of Arab medical schools underscored the significant potential of AI and CL to induce innovations in medical curricula. They provided supporting perspectives for integrating AI into the various stages of medical education, from pre-medical years to medical school, which reflects their commitment to update curricula as technology continues evolving.

A recent systematic review showed the current uses of AI in medical education were mainly for learning and knowledge development, assessment, program evaluation, curriculum analysis, and development. The primary utility of AI lies in its ability to provide immediate and customized feedback, which is essential for identifying learning goals and knowledge gaps, as traditional methods struggle to offer timely and structured feedback in clinical contexts [35]. In the realm of surgical skills training, the primary rationale for implementing AI lies in its capacity to deliver feedback. This facilitates users in obtaining real-time, objective feedback and tailored training, enabling prompt adjustments and correction of inaccuracies during operations. Research has shown the importance of learning from mistakes in the training process [36]. The emphasis on AI in undergraduate education is attributed to its potential for shaping students' learning earlier in their medical careers while sharing common advantages with problem-based learning that provides step-by-step guidance [37]. Nevertheless, it is important to note that AI-based teaching platforms cannot establish social connections with medical students and stimulate their thoughts and feelings like real medical teachers, as they are automated to provide feedback based on knowledge level rather than based on the context of the learning experience [38]. Therefore, AI might face certain limitations in providing feedback that aids students in recognizing conceptual misunderstandings. Crafting an AI system necessitates expert domain knowledge to feed the system with the requisite curriculum knowledge essential for contextually informed education [8].

Other sources pointed out the application of AI, particularly artificial neural networks (ANN) and support vector machines (SVM), for the development and evaluation of students' curricula [39]. This approach offers a valuable means of evaluating the curriculum's effectiveness and eliciting feedback on students' satisfaction with the program. Such a model is crucial for the training of future medical professionals, aiding in their development of skills in medical diagnosis and treatment.

Additionally, other sources highlighted the utilization of advanced analytics and AI models for curriculum mapping [40]. One of the biggest challenges in a curriculum's design is to ensure it is up-to-date and uses the same vocabulary as the learning setting. Higher education institutions have traditionally created new curricula using their own personnel, professors, and lecturers as domain-specific experts. However, curriculum mapping is crucial and represents the relationships between different components of a curriculum's learning objectives, content, instructional methods, and assessment techniques. It provides reassurance that what is taught, how it is taught, and how learning outcomes are measured are interconnected and aligned with academic standards and institutional goals. Indeed, AI has shown a proven potential to revolutionize curriculum mapping and the way educators approach instructional design. This is achieved through automating and simplifying the process, reducing the time and effort required in traditional methods, eliminating manual errors, ensuring precision and accuracy, and providing flexible templates that can be adapted to suit various educational contexts and needs. Furthermore, AI facilitates seamless collaboration among teachers, enabling real-time updates and shared access to curriculum maps, and enabling educators to quickly identify and address gaps or redundancies in the curriculum, promoting ongoing enhancement [40, 41]. Hence, by utilizing AI for curriculum mapping, we are not just adopting a tool but rather fostering a culture of continuous improvement and collaborative planning in education; AI provides a streamlined process to analyze, revise, and improve curricular elements, paving the way for enhanced teaching and learning experiences.

4.3 Challenges of Integrating AI and CL

Seven main challenges emerged from this study, categorized as: resource challenges (financial constraints, entrepreneurial support and technical challenges; Sect. 3.2.1); educational preparedness (faculty development/capacity building, buy-in of education stakeholders, medical student's awareness of AI and its added value; Sect. 3.2.2); dynamic nature of AI (rapid technological changes and time constraints; Sect. 3.2.3); curriculum and coverage constraints (depth and breadth of AI in education, curriculum balancing; Sect. 3.2.4); patient care quality and safety (risk of dependency on AI decision making in data analysis and patient care; Sect. 3.2.5); ethical and legal complexities (inequity and disparity in data generated by AI algorithms as well as misuse and misinterpretation risk; Sect. 3.2.6); governance structure and hierarchical frameworks, and hierarchical challenges (Sect. 3.2.7).

4.3.1 Challenges of Integrating AI and CL: Resource Challenges

While delving into the obstacles of integrating AI within medical education, our study participants highlighted several resource challenges as a significant roadblock to smoothly incorporating AI into medical curricula. It is not just about financial resources—participants stressed the intricate relationship between financial limitations and the urgent need for leadership support. Therefore, education and healthcare leaders should be provided with enlightening evidence that incorporating AI into healthcare introduces novel avenues for innovation and advancements in patient care across diverse domains. Through the utilization of AI-driven tools, health care professionals can create tailored solutions, enhance diagnostic capabilities, streamline workflows, and facilitate accessible health care via telemedicine, remote monitoring, mental health support, and population health management [3]. The continuous evolution of AI positions it as a crucial player in shaping the future of healthcare and revolutionizing approaches to patient care. With the potential to generate annual savings of US $150 billion for the healthcare industry by 2026, AI is anticipated to transform various facets of healthcare services and administration. Embracing the AI revolution presents healthcare entrepreneurs with many opportunities to develop innovative solutions that address significant challenges in the field [3]. This transformative approach enriches the quality of care and enhances patient outcomes globally.

Participants also highlighted technical challenges and underscored the necessity for collaboration, emphasizing the importance of combining medical and technological expertise to tackle these challenges. The best approach to these technical challenges can be overcome by using a multidisciplinary approach that combines expertise in computer technology, medicine, education, and ethics [9]. This emphasizes the intricate nature of integrating AI into medical education and underscores the crucial need for collaborative strategies to navigate these complex resource and technical challenges effectively.

4.3.2 Challenges of Integrating AI and CL: Educational Preparedness

Participants also highlighted the shortage of a specialized workforce dedicated to medical education as well as healthcare within the scope of artificial intelligence integration. To tackle the identified challenge of a shortage in a specialized workforce for medical education and healthcare within the context of artificial intelligence integration, rigorous faculty development and training programs are inevitable. These programs should place a strong emphasis on developing proficiency in data analytics, AI algorithms, and ethical considerations related to AI use. Equipping educators and healthcare professionals with these essential skills is crucial for the seamless integration of AI technology into various aspects of medical education, including curriculum development, instructional delivery, and assessment procedures. Enhancing faculty preparedness can be achieved through focused faculty development programs conducted by medical schools. Furthermore, it is essential to acknowledge that the dynamic landscape of AI in medical education necessitates continuous learning and collaboration between academia, industry, and regulatory agencies. This collaborative approach is indispensable for staying abreast of the rapidly evolving field of AI and ensuring that the workforce is adept at navigating its complexities.

Participants also underscored the significance of medical students' and educators' perceptions in influencing their acceptance of AI. A recent study that utilized the Unified Theory of Acceptance and Use of Technology (UTAUT2) model [42] to delve into these perceptions identified performance expectancy, motivation, habit, and trust as crucial drivers influencing AI acceptance among medical students. Moreover, medical educators' positive reception of information technologies is closely linked to performance expectancy. In this sense, hedonic motivation, representing the pleasure derived from using a system, was firmly established to influence behavioral intention positively [42].

Notably, almost half of medical students reported unfamiliarity with medical AI, highlighting the need for targeted interventions. In response to the research findings, comprehensive recommendations were proposed to promote the acceptance of AI among medical students, increase their familiarity, and advance medical AI education. Firstly, there is a pressing need to increase awareness, given the significant proportion of students unfamiliar with medical AI; thus, educational initiatives should be intensified. Secondly, collaborative efforts between academia and industry should actively work towards enriching the curriculum by integrating medical AI topics. Lastly, addressing students' needs is crucial, focusing on performance expectancy, hedonic motivation, habit formation, and trust, all identified as pivotal factors influencing medical AI adoption. This involves prioritizing instruction on leveraging medical AI for enhanced training outcomes, ensuring enjoyable experiences to address habit and hedonic motivation, and guiding students in assessing the reliability of medical AI systems to bolster trust. Collectively, these recommendations aim to foster a more informed and adept generation of medical professionals in artificial intelligence [42].

4.3.3 Dynamic Nature of AI: Rapid Technological Changes and Time Constraints

Navigating the dynamic landscape of AI poses substantial challenges, primarily stemming from the rapid technological changes and time constraints inherent in this field. The volatility, continuous improvements, and disruptive changes in AI demand constant adaptation to technological advances, as highlighted by participants. The ever-evolving nature of AI presents a significant hurdle, making it challenging for medical schools to keep pace with the latest advancements.

The primary concern voiced by respondents is the risk of physicians falling behind in both medical and technological advancements. The fear is that the dynamic nature of AI might lead to missed opportunities for leveraging AI tools in patient care, diagnostics, research, and medical education. As expressed by respondents, the rapid transformation in healthcare driven by AI could result in a technology gap, potentially leading to inefficiencies in healthcare delivery. In this context Kumar [2] cited that the main hurdle in integrating technological tools is the ever-evolving nature of these technologies, mainly the scarcity of qualified faculty, struggling to keep up with new advancements, and requiring continuous and substantial investment in professional development, financial, technical, and human resources to maintain required proficiency. However, the overarching goal of medical schools is not to produce engineers specialized solely in AI but to graduate doctors capable of effectively integrating and utilizing AI within their medical practice. Striking the right balance between staying current with AI advancements and delivering a comprehensive medical education becomes a critical challenge for medical schools.

4.3.4 Curriculum and Coverage Constraints: Depth and Breadth of AI in Education Curriculum Balancing

The integration of AI and CL into medical curricula faces the challenge of balancing the depth and breadth of these technologies. Respondents emphasized concerns about the strain of adding additional material to an already comprehensive medical curriculum. Integrating AI education necessitates careful consideration of the curriculum's structure and balance to ensure that students receive adequate training in both AI and core medical disciplines. The challenge lies in achieving integration that complements, rather than overwhelms, the core content of medical education. Striking this balance becomes crucial to avoid potential gaps in foundational knowledge and clinical skills. The need to graduate doctors well-versed in both AI and core medical disciplines is paramount for effective integration into medical practice. Hu et al. [43], considering the congested nature of the medical curricula, recommended: (a) "identifying the core AI competencies" required by healthcare professionals that can be integrated into existing competency-based medical curricula; (b) creating "AI case studies: Similar to clinical vignettes, case-based instruction may consolidate abstract concepts by identifying relevance to clinical problems"; (c) using "experiential learning" and repeated application to master clinical skills; (d) expanding "to multi-disciplinary participants", an exercise that involves interaction from various disciplines in the process of curriculum development and implementation.

4.3.5 Patient Care Quality and Safety: Risk of Dependency on AI Decision Making in Data Analysis and Patient Care

Concerns regarding patient care quality and safety center around the perceived risk of excessive dependency on AI decision-making in data analysis. Respondents highlighted the early stage of AI development, especially in the critical field of medicine where decisions impact human health. There is a shared sentiment that careful handling is essential to avoid unwarranted reliance on AI, particularly in making decisions that affect patient care and safety. Lynn [44] stated that the main issue involved in a clinical care setting is the intellectual reliance on AI, particularly AI with limited communication abilities, which may lead to diminishing the perceived necessity for healthcare professionals to comprehend intricate pathophysiology or engage with complex care. Concerns also arise about the safety and efficacy misalignment with current care models in AI medical software. Regulatory standards for assessing AI algorithmic safety are not formalized in many countries, posing barriers, and enabling unsafe practices in healthcare [45].

Respondents expressed worries about students becoming overly dependent on AI, potentially hindering their understanding and memorization of essential medical concepts. The fear is that overreliance on AI could lead to neglecting critical aspects of medicine and impact students' medical reasoning, independent research, and analysis abilities. Balancing the incorporation of AI into education while maintaining the traditional foundations of medical practice emerges as a significant challenge. Similarly, Lynn [44] indicated that the future AI-dominated scenario might alleviate concerns about oversight quality, the present focus should be on the transitional state, akin to the current phase in automated driving where AI performance necessitates real-time human evaluation and supervision.

4.3.6 Ethical and Legal Complexities: Inequity and Disparity in Data Generated by AI Algorithms as Well as Misuse and Misinterpretation Risk

Ethical and legal concerns surrounding AI and CL represent a critical challenge, particularly in addressing issues of inequity and disparity in data generated by AI algorithms. Respondents stressed the importance of explaining the limitations of AI and CL, recognizing that these limitations may change over time. However, the potential for misuse and misinterpretation, including nefarious activities such as blackmail or insurance fraud, poses a serious ethical dilemma. Likewise, Tsamados et al. [46] reported that the ethics of algorithms is a prominent topic among scholars, tech providers, and policymakers, especially in the context of the widespread use of machine learning algorithms, requiring thorough consideration of associated risks despite the potential for positive outcomes. The imperative for medical schools to integrate ethical considerations of AI and CL into their curricula is clear. However, the complexity lies in developing dedicated courses and modules covering intricate topics such as data privacy, bias, transparency, accountability, informed consent, and responsible AI use. Additionally, the shortage of bioethicists well-versed in AI intricacies adds another layer of difficulty to this challenge. Implementing AI in healthcare effectively encounters ethical hurdles, notably in addressing potential biases, safeguarding patient privacy, and earning trust from clinicians and the public [45].

4.3.7 Governance Structure and Hierarchical Frameworks: Governance and Hierarchical Challenges

Challenges relating to governance and hierarchical structures in medical schools add a layer of complexity to the integration of AI and CL. Respondents highlighted potential obstacles from leadership teams and hierarchical frameworks that may be unconvinced about the efficiency of AI in medical education and its ultimate impact on patient care. The reluctance to embrace AI in medical education, with some suggesting it is too early to introduce AI, creates governance challenges. Overcoming these challenges requires addressing the reservations through evidence-based arguments that showcase the benefits of AI integration. Effective communication and collaboration between proponents of AI integration and hierarchical decision-makers become essential to navigate these governance hurdles. Besides these limitations, Reddy et al. [45] highlighted the different perspective of unexplained algorithmic decision-making, continuous changes, and auto-updating, which may necessitate continuing policy updates through multiple interference from institutional leadership.

5 Conclusions

In conclusion, this comprehensive study sheds light on the intricate landscape of opportunities and challenges facing medical educational institutions in Arab countries in integrating AI and CL into their curricula. The perspectives of academic deans on this subject vary significantly, reflecting differences in medical education systems in the Arab countries and administrative governance structures, be it for private institutions or state-funded and national colleges. These differences are also related to the diversity in expected learning objectives and outcomes, curricular structures, teaching, and students' assessment methodologies.

This study highlights the growing realization of the benefits of integrating AI and CL into medical education, particularly in transforming medical curricula, improving clinical practice, and advancing medical research. The transformative impact of AI is also evident in many areas beyond education, such as drug discovery, clinical trial design, systematic reviews, and big data analysis, that will potentially result in enhancing efficiency, cost-effectiveness, and better outcomes. The breakthroughs in clinical practice, personalized medicine, better diagnostic capabilities and treatment outcomes, underscore AI's potential to revolutionize healthcare delivery, and open doors for partnerships in between healthcare institutions and entrepreneurial initiatives.

However, the challenges for integrating AI and CL in medical education are numerous and substantial, ranging from limited human and financial resources, institutional preparedness, lack of vision, and most importantly the existing medical curricula which are already congested with knowledge-based medical topics. The latter must be modified to incorporate the dynamic but complex nature of AI. Generally speaking, the focus of medical curricula is to graduate physicians; however, integrating AI requires a multi-disciplinary approach and collaborations that go beyond the traditional medical sciences to include computer sciences, engineering disciplines, physics, and mathematics. Added to this are the multiple AI-associated ethical dilemmas and the lack thus far of agreed-upon legal frameworks. Furthermore, there are financial limitations, scarce entrepreneurial support, and several technical challenges that stand as key obstacles to achieving this objective effectively and efficiently.

Addressing these complex challenges requires institutional strategic decision-making that incorporates a staged and multidisciplinary approach that recognizes the intricate and dynamic interplay between medical education, the rapidly evolving technology, a supportive legal framework, and appropriate ethical practices. Strategies to enhance educational preparedness, raise awareness among medical students and faculty, and foster positive perceptions of AI are crucial steps in ensuring successful integration of AI into medical education. As Arab medical schools struggle with these complexities, embracing the potential of AI is a crucial first step in this educational transformation that, in this rapidly and technologically advancing world, carries an obvious impact on medical curricula and consequently on shaping the future healthcare workforce, clinical practices, and advancement in medical sciences.

Appendix 1

AUB Social and Behavioral Sciences
INVITATION SCRIPT.
Invitation to Participate in a Research Study

This notice is for an AUB-IRB Approved Research Study for Dr. Ghazi Zaatari at AUB
Professor and Chairperson, Department of Pathology and Laboratory Medicine,
Former I/Dean for the Faculty of Medicine
American University of Beirut Medical Center

It is not an Official Message from AUB

I am inviting you to participate in a research study about: "The Perspective of Deans of Medical Schools on Introducing Artificial Intelligence and Computer Literacy to the Medical Curricula in the Arab Countries".

You will be asked to complete a short survey/questionnaire with demographic information.

You are invited because we are targeting "Deans of Medical Schools and Colleges in Arab countries" as an eligibility criterion for inclusion in this study.

The estimated time to complete the questionnaire is 30–40 min. The research is conducted online and is hosted on AUB server.

Please read the consent form and consider whether you want to be involved in this study. If you have any questions about this study, please contact the following research team members:

- Nabil Mansour, Director of Operations—Faculty of Medicine, AUB. email: nm08@aub.edu.lb, AUB ext. +961 1350000 ext 4716, or mobile/WhatsApp: +961 70918525-Mahmoud Harb, Medical Education Unit Coordinator—Faculty of Medicine, AUB. email: mh05@aub.edu.lb, AUB ext. +961 1350000 ext 4702, or mobile/WhatsApp: +961 70116713

Version Date March 21, 2016
Version Number 1.1

American University of Beirut
Institutional Review Board
04 May 2023
APPROVED

Appendix 2

Consent to Participate in an Online Research Study

This notice is for an AUB-IRB Approved Research Study for Dr. Ghazi Zaatari at AUB.
It is not an Official Message from AUB

You are invited to participate in a research study entitled "The Perspective of Deans of Medical Schools on Introducing Artificial Intelligence and Computer Literacy to the Medical Curricula in the Arab Countries" conducted by Dr. Ghazi Zaatari, Faculty of Medicine at the American University of Beirut. The conduct of this study will adhere to the IRB approved protocol.

The IRB approved method for approaching subjects is using LimeSurvey. The purpose of the study is to try answering the following questions:

Are the Medical Schools and Colleges, and their respective faculty members, in Arab countries prepared for introducing Artificial Intelligence and Computer Literacy education competencies into undergraduate medical education?

What is the perspective of the leadership of Medical Schools and Colleges in Arab countries toward the inclusion of Artificial Intelligence and Computer Literacy topics into the medical education curricula, and to what extent are they ready to give these subjects space from the Medical Curricula without compromising the medical critical contents?

Procedures

This message invites you to: Read the consent document and consider whether you want to be involved in the study.

And to note:

Participation is completely voluntary.

Completing the questionnaire will take around 30–40 min.

Only the data you provide in the questionnaire will be collected and analyzed. The research team will not have access to your name or contact details.

The results of the survey will be published in a research article

The study includes specifically the Deans of Medical Schools and Colleges in Arab Countries as listed by "Scimago" institutions ranking.

Potential Benefits to Subjects and/or to Society

You will not receive payment for participation in this study.

The results of the study will have a direct impact on opening the eyes of the leadership teams in medical schools and colleges in Arab countries on Artificial Intelligence and Computer Literacy topics and their importance in preparing future generations of medical doctors and invite them to start thinking about how to integrate these topics into their medical curricula. It will also provide an opportunity for these leaders to learn how other medical schools are approaching such topics and learn from others' experiences.

Potential Risks to Subjects and/or Society

The risks of the study are minimal.

Confidentiality

The collected data will remain confidential and anonymous.

The data collection process may be audited by the IRB while assuring confidentiality.

Participation and Withdrawal

If you voluntarily consent to take part in this study, you can change your mind and withdraw at any time without consequences of any kind.

Refusal to participate or withdrawal from the study will involve no penalty or loss of benefits to which the subject is otherwise entitled, and neither will it affect their relationship with their organization and AUB/AUBMC.

Questions About the Study

If you have any questions about the study, can contact the research team at:

- Nabil Mansour, Director of Operations—Faculty of Medicine, AUB. email: nm08@aub.edu.lb, AUB ext. +961 1350000 ext 4716, or mobile/WhatsApp: +96,170918525
- Mahmoud Harb, Medical Education Unit Coordinator—Faculty of Medicine, AUB. email: mh05@aub.edu.lb, AUB ext. +961 1350000 ext 4702, or mobile/WhatsApp: +961 70116113

Access to the Survey

If after reading the consent document and having your questions answered, you voluntarily agree to take part in the study; you can access the survey by clicking on the following link.

Concerns or Questions About Your Rights

If you have concerns about the study or questions about your rights as a participant, you can contact the AUB IRB Office: irb@aub.edu.lb AUB ext: +961 1350000 ext 5454.

Appendix 3

LimeSurvey Questionnaire

Dear Dr. xxxxx

Dean of yyyyy Medical School

Invitation to Participate in a Research Study

This notice is for an AUB-IRB Approved Research Study for **Dr. Ghazi Zaatari,** Professor and Chairperson, Department of Pathology and Laboratory Medicine, Faculty of Medicine and Medical Center, American University of Beirut

It is not an Official Message from AUB

I am inviting you to participate in a research study about: "**The Perspective of Deans of Medical Schools on Introducing Artificial Intelligence and Computer Literacy to the Medical Curricula in Arab Countries**".

You will be asked to complete a short survey/questionnaire with demographic information. You are invited because we are targeting "Deans of Medical Schools and Colleges in Arab countries" as an eligibility criterion for inclusion in this study. The estimated time to complete the questionnaire is 30–40 min. The research is conducted online and is hosted on AUB server.

Please read the consent form and consider whether you want to be involved in this study.

If you have any questions about this study, please contact the following research team members:

- Nabil Mansour, Director of Operations—Faculty of Medicine, AUB. email: nm08@aub.edu.lb, AUB ext. +961 1350000 ext 4716, or mobile/WhatsApp: +961 70918525.
- -Mahmoud Harb, Medical Education Unit Coordinator—Faculty of Medicine, AUB. email: mh05@aub.edu.lb, AUB ext.+961 1350000 ext 4702, or mobile/WhatsApp: +961 70116713.

Questions:

Importance and Benefits of AI/CL

1. In your opinion, how important it is to include the subjects of AI & CL in the medical curricula? Please rate on a scale of 1–10, with 1 being not important at all and 10 being extremely important:
2. What are your reasons for believing that AI & LC should be included in the medical curriculum?
3. What are your reasons for believing that AI & LC should NOT be included in the medical curriculum?
4. In your opinion, what are the potential benefits of including AI & CL in the medical curriculum (benefits to graduates themselves, their patients, healthcare institutions, the whole society, etc…)?
5. What are some potential consequences of not including AI & CL in the medical curriculum?
6. What are the potential drawbacks of including AI in the medical curriculum?
7. Do you think the inclusion of AI & CL in the medical curriculum could lead to greater collaboration between medical professionals and computer scientists?
8. In your opinion, which areas of medicine do you believe would benefit the most from the inclusion of AI & CL in the medical curriculum?
9. How do you think the inclusion of AI in the medical curriculum could impact the overall quality of medical education and the future of the healthcare profession as a whole?
10. What are your thoughts and opinion on using AI to augment the decision-making process in medicine and clinical practice, whether for diagnosis or for treatment planning?
11. How important is it for medical schools to prioritize teaching students about the limitations, potential biases, and ethical dilemmas of AI algorithms?
12. How important do you think it is for medical students to be proficient in data analysis and programming in the context of AI in medicine?
13. What role do you think AI & CL could play in training future generations of medical professionals?
14. How do you think AI & CL could be used to improve the accuracy and efficiency of medical research, as well as to identify early warning or detection signs of diseases?

Curriculum Structure

1. Does your current curriculum include AI and/or CL courses? If yes, please provide the number of hours and their percentage out of the whole curriculum.
2. How many hours does your curriculum dedicate to elective/selective modules? What is their percentage out of the whole curriculum?
3. What percentage of overall credit hours/weeks of the medical curriculum do you believe should be dedicated to the subject(s) of AI & CL?
4. What do you think should be the primary focus of teaching AI & CL in the medical curriculum: theoretical concepts, practical applications, or both?
5. Do you believe that medical schools should offer separate courses on AI & CL, or should it be integrated into existing courses?
6. Do you think the inclusion of AI & CL in the curriculum will enhance the assessment techniques and methods of medical students?
7. Do you think the inclusion of AI & CL will affect the learning objectives of the curriculum?
8. How do you think the inclusion of AI in the medical curriculum could impact the overall quality of medical education and the future of the healthcare profession as a whole?

Challenges and Readiness

1. What are the potential challenges in implementing AI & CL in the medical curriculum at your medical school or college (financial, technical, unavailability of qualified staff to teach these topics, inability to free time for these topics not to compromise core curriculum deliverability, etc...)?
2. Do you think that the present faculty members are prepared and have the competency required to include and teach subjects like AI & CL?
3. What steps do you think medical schools should take to prepare faculty for teaching a modified curriculum that embraces subjects of AI & CL?
4. What resources do you believe would be necessary to effectively implement AI & CL in the medical curriculum (financial, technical, capacity building, decision making, etc...)?
5. Do you think your current medical students are willing to accept the introduction of AI & CL topics to their medical curriculum, and what will be their overall impression about this matter?
6. In your opinion, what are some of the key skills that medical students should develop when learning about AI & CL in medicine?
7. What role should medical schools play in preparing students for the ethical implications of AI & CL in medicine, and how do you anticipate playing such a role?
8. What role should medical schools play in developing AI technology to advance healthcare innovations, in partnership with technology start-ups?

References

1. Cutrer WB, Spickard WA III, Triola MM et al (2021) Exploiting the power of information in medical education. Med Teach 43(suppl 2):S17–S24. https://doi.org/10.1080/0142159X.2021.1925234
2. Kumar D (2023) How emerging technologies are transforming education and research: trends, opportunities, and challenges. In: Choudhary D, Palakurthy S, Yadav D (eds) Infinite horizons: exploring the unknown. CIRS Publication. https://www.researchgate.net/publication/375526157_INFINITE_HORIZONS_EXPLORING_THE_UNKNOWN
3. Brann DW, Sloop S (2006) Curriculum development and technology incorporation in teaching neuroscience to graduate students in a medical school environment. Adv Physiol Educ 30(1):38–45. https://doi.org/10.1152/advan.00068.2005
4. Pantelidis P, Chorti A, Papagiouvanni I et al (2018) Virtual and augmented reality in medical education. In: Tsoulfas G (ed) Medical and surgical education—past, present and future. Intechopen. https://doi.org/10.5772/intechopen.71963
5. Fakomogbon MA, Bolaji HO (2017) Effects of collaborative learning styles on performance of students in a ubiquitous collaborative mobile learning environment. Contemp Educ Technol 8(3):268–279. https://doi.org/10.30935/cedtech/6200
6. O'Doherty D, Dromey M, Lougheed J et al (2018) Barriers and solutions to online learning in medical education—an integrative review. BMC Med Educ 18(130). https://doi.org/10.1186/s12909-018-1240-0
7. Tsopra R, Peiffer-Smadja N, Charlier C et al (2023) Putting undergraduate medical students in AI-CDSS designers' shoes: an innovative teaching method to develop digital health critical thinking. Int J Med Inform 171(104980). https://doi.org/10.1016/j.ijmedinf.2022.104980
8. Chan KS, Zary N (2019) Applications and challenges of implementing artificial intelligence in medical education: integrative review. JMIR Med Educ 5(1). https://doi.org/10.2196/13930
9. Masters K (2019) Artificial intelligence in medical education. Med Teach 41(9):976–980. https://doi.org/10.1080/0142159X.2019.1595557
10. Sapci AH, Sapci HA (2020) Artificial intelligence education and tools for medical and health informatics students: systematic review. JMIR Med Educ 6(1). https://doi.org/10.2196/19285
11. Atwa HS, Gouda EM (2014) Curriculum integration in medical education: a theoretical review. Intel Prop Rights 2(2):113. https://doi.org/10.4172/2375-4516.1000113
12. Sitthipon T, Kaewpuang P, Jaipong P et al (2022) Artificial intelligence (AI) adoption in the medical education during the digital era: a review article. Rev Advan Multidisiplin Sci Engineer Innovat (Ramsey) 1(2):1–7. https://www.researchgate.net/publication/362154238
13. Celi LA, Davidzon G, Johnson AE et al (2016) Bridging the health data divide. J Med Internet Res 18(12):e325. https://doi.org/10.2196/jmir.6400
14. SCIMAGO Institutions Ranking. https://www.scimagoir.com/rankings.php?area=2700&ranking=Overall&country=ARAB%20COUNTRIES. Accessed 3 May 2023
15. Stemler S (2001) An introduction to content analysis. ERIC Digest. ERIC Clearinghouse on Assessment and Evaluation, College Park, MD, USA. https://files.eric.ed.gov/fulltext/ED458218.pdf
16. Mak KK, Pichika MR (2019) Artificial intelligence in drug development: present status and future prospects. Drug Discov Today 24(3):773–780. https://doi.org/10.1016/j.drudis.2018.11.014
17. Mohs RC, Greig NH (2017) Drug discovery and development: role of basic biological research. Alzheimer's Dementia Translat Res Clin Intervent 3(4):651–657. https://doi.org/10.1016/j.trci.2017.10.005

18. Hofmarcher M, Rumetshofer E, Clevert DA et al (2019) Accurate prediction of biological assays with high-throughput microscopy images and convolutional networks. J Chem Inform Model 59(3):1163–1171. https://doi.org/10.1021/acs.jcim.8b00670
19. Lee CS, Lee AY (2020) How artificial intelligence can transform randomized controlled trials. Translat Vision Sci Technol 9(2):9–9. https://doi.org/10.1167/tvst.9.2.9
20. Delso G, Cirillo D, Kaggie JD et al (2021) How to design AI-driven clinical trials in nuclear medicine. Seminars Nuclear Med 51(2):112–119. https://doi.org/10.1053/J.SEMNUCLMED.2020.09.003
21. Sangari N, Qu Y (2020) A comparative study on machine learning algorithms for predicting breast cancer prognosis in improving clinical trials. 2020 International conference on computational science and computational intelligence, IEEE.https://doi.org/10.1109/CSCI51800.2020.00152
22. Wagner G, Lukyanenko R, Paré G (2022) Artificial intelligence and the conduct of literature reviews. J Inform Technol 37(2):209–226. https://doi.org/10.1177/02683962211048201
23. van Dijk SH, Brusse-Keizer MG, Bucsán CC et al (2023) Artificial intelligence in systematic reviews: promising when appropriately used. BMJ Open 13(7):e072254. https://doi.org/10.1136/bmjopen-2023-072254
24. van de Schoot R, De Bruin J, Schram R et al (2021) An open source machine learning framework for efficient and transparent systematic reviews. Nat Machine Intell 3(2):125–133. https://doi.org/10.1038/s42256-020-00287-7
25. Ferdinands G (2021) AI-assisted systematic reviewing: selecting studies to compare Bayesian versus Frequentist SEM for small sample sizes. Multivar Behav Res 56(1):153–154. https://doi.org/10.1080/00273171.2020.1853501
26. Abd-Alrazaq A, AlSaad R, Alhuwail D et al (2023) Large language models in medical education: opportunities, challenges, and future directions. JMIR Med Educ 9(1):e48291. https://doi.org/10.2196/48291
27. Manjurul Ahsan M, Siddique Z (2021) Machine learning based disease diagnosis: a comprehensive review. Cornell Univ arXiv:2112.15538. https://doi.org/10.48550/arXiv.2112.15538
28. McKinney SM, Sieniek M, Godbole V et al (2020) International evaluation of an AI system for breast cancer screening. Nature 577(7788):89–94. https://doi.org/10.1038/s41586-019-1799-6
29. Myszczynska MA, Ojamies PN, Lacoste AM et al (2020) Applications of machine learning to diagnosis and treatment of neurodegenerative diseases. Nature Rev Neurol 16(8):440–456. https://doi.org/10.1038/s41582-020-0377-8
30. Krittanawong C (2018) The rise of artificial intelligence and the uncertain future for physicians. Euro J Internal Med 48:e13–e14. https://doi.org/10.1016/j.ejim.2017.06.017
31. Alowais SA, Alghamdi SS, Alsuhebany N et al (2023) Revolutionizing healthcare: the role of artificial intelligence in clinical practice. BMC Med Educ 23(1):689. https://doi.org/10.1186/s12909-023-04698-z
32. Peiffer-Smadja N, Dellière S, Rodriguez C et al (2020) Machine learning in the clinical microbiology laboratory: has the time come for routine practice? Clin Microbiol Infect 26(10):1300–1309. https://doi.org/10.1016/j.cmi.2020.02.006
33. Smith KP, Kirby JE (2020) Image analysis and artificial intelligence in infectious disease diagnostics. Clin Microbiol Infect 26(10):1318–1323. https://doi.org/10.1016/j.cmi.2020.03.012
34. Vandenberg O, Durand G, Hallin M et al (2020) Consolidation of clinical microbiology laboratories and introduction of transformative technologies. Clin Microbiol Rev 33(2):10–1128. https://doi.org/10.1128/CMR.00057-19
35. Hattie J, Timperley H (2007) The power of feedback. Rev Educ Res 77(1):81–112. https://doi.org/10.3102/003465430298487
36. Foss CL (1987) Learning from errors in ALGEBRALAND. Institute for Research on Learning, IRL87-0003

37. Hewson MG, Little ML (1998) Giving feedback in medical education: verification of recommended techniques. J Gen Internal Med 13(2):111–116. https://doi.org/10.1046/j.1525-1497.1998.00027.x
38. Zhang W, Cai M, Lee HJ et al (2023) AI in medical education: global situation, effects and challenges. Educ Informat Technol. https://doi.org/10.1007/s10639-023-12009-8
39. Chen CK (2010) Curriculum assessment using artificial neural network and support vector machine modeling approaches: a case study. IR Applications 29. https://eric.ed.gov/?id=ED524832
40. Ketamo H, Moisio A, Passi-Rauste A, Alamäki A (2019) Mapping the future curriculum: adopting artificial intelligence and analytics in forecasting competence needs. In: Proceedings of the 10th European conference on intangibles and intellectual capital ECIIC 2019. Academic Conference Publishing International. https://urn.fi/URN:NBN:fi-fe2019053117966
41. Alshanqiti A, Alam T, Benaida M et al (2020) A rule-based approach toward automating the assessments of academic curriculum mapping. Int J Adv Comput Sci Appl 11(12). https://doi.org/10.14569/IJACSA.2020.0111285
42. Li Q, Qin Y (2023) AI in medical education: medical student perception, curriculum recommendations and design suggestions. BMC Med Educ 23(1):852. https://doi.org/10.1186/s12909-023-04700-8
43. Hu R, Fan KY, Pandey P et al (2022) Insights from teaching artificial intelligence to medical students in Canada. Commun Med 2(1):63. https://doi.org/10.1038/s43856-022-00125-4
44. Lynn LA (2019) Artificial intelligence systems for complex decision-making in acute care medicine: a review. Patient Safety Surgery 13(6). https://doi.org/10.1186/s13037-019-0188-2
45. Reddy S, Allan S, Coghlan S, Cooper P (2020) A governance model for the application of AI in health care. J Am Med Inform Assoc 27(3):491–497. https://doi.org/10.1093/jamia/ocz192
46. Tsamados A, Aggarwal N, Cowls J et al (2022) The ethics of algorithms: key problems and solutions. AI & Soc 37:215–230. https://doi.org/10.1007/s00146-021-01154-8

Printed in the USA
CPSIA information can be obtained
at www.ICGtesting.com
CBHW070943021024
15245CB00003B/120